Astronomy Education, Volume 1
Evidence-based instruction for introductory courses

AAS Editor in Chief

Ethan Vishniac, John Hopkins University, Maryland, US

About the program:

AAS-IOP Astronomy ebooks is the official book program of the American Astronomical Society (AAS), and aims to share in depth the most fascinating areas of astronomy, astrophysics, solar physics and planetary science. The program includes publications in the following topics:

GALAXIES AND COSMOLOGY

INTERSTELLAR MATTER AND THE LOCAL UNIVERSE

STARS AND STELLAR PHYSICS

EDUCATION, OUTREACH AND HERITAGE

HIGH-ENERGY PHENOMENA AND FUNDAMENTAL PHYSICS

THE SUN AND THE HELIOSPHERE

THE SOLAR SYSTEM, EXOPLANETS, AND ASTROBIOLOGY

INSTRUMENTATION, SOFTWARE, LABORATORY ASTROPHYSICS AND DATA

Books in the program range in level from short introductory texts on fast-moving areas, graduate and upper-level undergraduate textbooks, research monographs, and practical handbooks.

For a complete list of published and forthcoming titles, please visit iopscience.org/books/aas.

About the American Astronomical Society

The American Astronomical Society (aas.org), established 1899, is the major organization of professional astronomers in North America. The membership (~7,000) also includes physicists, mathematicians, geologists, engineers and others whose research interests lie within the broad spectrum of subjects now comprising the contemporary astronomical sciences. The mission of the Society is to enhance and share humanity's scientific understanding of the universe.

Astronomy Education, Volume 1
Evidence-based instruction for introductory courses

Chris Impey and Sanlyn Buxner
University of Arizona, Tucson, AZ 85721, USA

IOP Publishing, Bristol, UK

© IOP Publishing Ltd 2020

All rights reserved. No part of this publication may be reproduced, stored in a retrieval system or transmitted in any form or by any means, electronic, mechanical, photocopying, recording or otherwise, without the prior permission of the publisher, or as expressly permitted by law or under terms agreed with the appropriate rights organization. Multiple copying is permitted in accordance with the terms of licences issued by the Copyright Licensing Agency, the Copyright Clearance Centre and other reproduction rights organizations.

Permission to make use of IOP Publishing content other than as set out above may be sought at permissions@ioppublishing.org.

Chris Impey and Sanlyn Buxner have asserted their right to be identified as the authors of this work in accordance with sections 77 and 78 of the Copyright, Designs and Patents Act 1988.

ISBN 978-0-7503-1723-8 (ebook)
ISBN 978-0-7503-1721-4 (print)
ISBN 978-0-7503-1722-1 (mobi)

DOI 10.1088/2514-3433/ab2b42

Version: 20191101

AAS–IOP Astronomy
ISSN 2514-3433 (online)
ISSN 2515-141X (print)

British Library Cataloguing-in-Publication Data: A catalogue record for this book is available from the British Library.

Published by IOP Publishing, wholly owned by The Institute of Physics, London

IOP Publishing, Temple Circus, Temple Way, Bristol, BS1 6HG, UK

US Office: IOP Publishing, Inc., 190 North Independence Mall West, Suite 601, Philadelphia, PA 19106, USA

Contents

Preface	xi
Editor biographies	xii
Contributors	xiii

1   Learner-centered Teaching in Astronomy — 1-1

- 1.1 Introduction — 1-1
- 1.2 What Is Learner-centered Teaching? — 1-2
- 1.3 How Humans Learn: The Rationale for LCT — 1-3
- 1.4 Knowing, Engaging, and Assessing Students — 1-7
- 1.5 Learner-centered Teaching, Universal Design for Learning, and Inclusive Excellence — 1-8
    - 1.5.1 Universal Design for Learning — 1-8
    - 1.5.2 Inclusive Excellence — 1-9
- 1.6 Learner-centered Teaching as a Motivational Tool — 1-10
- 1.7 Learner-centered Teaching as a Means to an End: The Importance of Learning Objectives and Backward Design — 1-12
- 1.8 Setting up Learner-centered Teaching in Your Class — 1-12
    - 1.8.1 Trying to Do Too Much at Once — 1-13
    - 1.8.2 Not Getting Student Buy-in — 1-13
    - 1.8.3 Not Getting Teaching Team Buy-in — 1-14
- 1.9 Promoting the Use of Backward Design and Learner-centered Teaching at the Department Level — 1-15
    - 1.9.1 Advantage of Backward Design across a Program of Study — 1-15
    - 1.9.2 Advantages of Backward Design at the Course Level — 1-16
    - 1.9.3 Advantages of Promoting Learner-centered Teaching Techniques across a Program of Study and in Individual Courses — 1-16
    - 1.9.4 The Head of Department as Role Model and Resource Provider — 1-16
- 1.10 Evaluating Learner-centered Teaching — 1-17
- 1.11 Frequently Asked Questions about Learner-centered Teaching and Its Implementation — 1-18
- References — 1-20

2   Effective Course Design — 2-1

- 2.1 Introduction — 2-2

2.2	What is Your Teaching and Learning Philosophy?	2-3
2.3	Course Design Overview	2-4
	2.3.1 Course Design Methods	2-5
	2.3.2 Course Design Prep	2-7
2.4	Step 1: Developing Learning Objectives	2-8
	2.4.1 Big Ideas, Goals, and Questions	2-8
	2.4.2 Significant Learning	2-10
	2.4.3 Tutorial: Writing Learning Objectives	2-11
2.5	Step 2: Assessing Student Learning	2-17
	2.5.1 Types of Assessment	2-17
	2.5.2 Feedback Loops	2-19
	2.5.3 Assessment Strategies	2-20
	2.5.4 Designing Assessments that Align	2-21
2.6	Step 3: Creating Learning Experiences	2-24
	2.6.1 Active Learning Primer	2-24
	2.6.2 Choosing and Aligning Learning Activities	2-26
	2.6.3 Resources	2-27
2.7	Step 4: Putting It All Together	2-29
	2.7.1 Checking for Alignment	2-29
	2.7.2 Finding the Flow	2-30
	2.7.3 Communicating Your Course Plan	2-31
2.8	Conclusion	2-32
	Acknowledgments	2-33
	References	2-33
3	**Lecture-tutorials in Introductory Astronomy**	**3-1**
3.1	Introduction	3-1
3.2	Preparing to Implement Lecture-Tutorials	3-3
3.3	Best Practices when Facilitating Collaborative Groups Working though Lecture-Tutorials	3-11
3.4	Case Study: The Astro 101 Megacourse	3-13
3.5	Summary	3-19
	Acknowledgments	3-20
	References	3-20
4	**Technology and Engagement in the University Classroom**	**4-1**
4.1	Introduction: Why Engagement is Important, and How Technology May Increase or Reduce It	4-2

4.2	Backward Design Makes Technology Use More Successful	4-5
4.3	A Range of Technologies	4-6
4.4	Technology that Reduces Student Engagement and Learning—Smartphones and Laptop Computers	4-11
4.5	The Same Technology, Highly Different Outcomes: Why? Differences in Implementation	4-19
4.6	Do Not Assume that Students Will Use It Like You Designed It	4-21
4.7	The Importance of Metacognition	4-21
4.8	Assessment: How Do You Know If You Reached Your Goal?	4-22
	References	4-22

5	**Using Simulations Interactively in the Introductory Astronomy Classroom**	**5-1**
5.1	Characteristics of Computer Simulations	5-1
5.2	The College Astronomy Education Landscape	5-3
5.3	A Framework for Interactive Simulation Usage in the Classroom	5-5
5.4	Implementing the Framework: Example 1—The NAAP Lunar Phase Simulator	5-9
5.5	Implementing the Framework: Example 2—The PhET Gravity and Orbits Simulator	5-13
5.6	Conclusions	5-15
	References	5-16

6	**Practical Considerations for Using a Planetarium for Astronomy Instruction**	**6-1**
6.1	Introduction	6-1
6.2	Instruction in a Planetarium	6-3
6.3	"Classic" (Optomechanical) Planetarium	6-4
6.4	Digital Planetariums	6-5
6.5	Portable Planetariums	6-7
	6.5.1 About Portable Planetariums	6-7
	6.5.2 Advantages and Disadvantages	6-8
	6.5.3 Sources and Resources for Portable Planetariums	6-10
6.6	Ancillary Planetarium Resources	6-10
6.7	How to Get Started	6-16
	References	6-18

7	**Authentic Research Experiences in Astronomy to Teach the Process of Science**	7-1
7.1	Introduction	7-2
7.2	The RBSE Curriculum	7-3
7.3	The Projects	7-4
7.4	Student Discoveries	7-8
7.5	Student Gains	7-9
7.6	Other Resources and Programs for Authentic Research Experiences in Astronomy Classes	7-9
7.7	Conclusions	7-9
	Acknowledgments	7-10
	References	7-10

8	**Citizen Science in Astronomy Education**	8-1
8.1	Overview	8-2
8.2	Astro 101: Zooniverse-based Citizen Science Opportunities	8-4
	8.2.1 Zooniverse	8-5
	8.2.2 Improving Student Attitudes toward Science with a Citizen Science Assignment	8-7
	8.2.3 Engaging Students in Authentic Research through Citizen Science	8-10
	8.2.4 Mixing Hands-on Activities with Online Citizen Science	8-16
8.3	Astronomical Citizen Science Data Collection Projects	8-17
	8.3.1 Description of the RECON Citizen Science Project	8-17
	8.3.2 Citizen Science Insights from the RECON Project	8-20
8.4	Summary	8-21
	References	8-22

9	**WorldWide Telescope in Education**	9-1
9.1	Introduction	9-1
	9.1.1 WorldWide Telescope and Its History	9-2
9.2	Samples of WWT in Astronomy Education	9-4
	9.2.1 WWT in College Introductory Astronomy Courses	9-4
	9.2.2 WWT in K–12 Education	9-11
	9.2.3 Technology Requirements for Running the WWT K–12 Labs	9-19
9.3	Discussion and Future Developments	9-20
	Acknowledgments	9-21
	References	9-22

10	**Measuring Students' Understanding in Astronomy with Research-based Assessment Tools**	**10-1**
10.1	Introduction	10-1
10.2	Diagnostic Tests and Concept Inventories	10-2
	10.2.1 Some Definitions	10-2
	10.2.2 Diagnostic Tests	10-2
	10.2.3 Concept Inventories	10-9
10.3	Instrument Development and Quality	10-14
10.4	Using Diagnostic Instruments in Astronomy Courses	10-16
10.5	Conclusions	10-18
	References	10-18
11	**Everyone's Universe: Teaching Astronomy in Community Colleges**	**11-1**
11.1	Introduction	11-2
11.2	Why It Matters: Get to Know the Players	11-2
	11.2.1 Enrollments	11-3
	11.2.2 Who Takes Astro 101?	11-4
	11.2.3 Special Considerations	11-7
	11.2.4 Who Teaches Astro 101?	11-9
11.3	You Matter: The Job of Community College Faculty (in Astronomy)	11-13
	11.3.1 Environment, Workload, and Resources	11-13
	11.3.2 Compensation and Benefits	11-17
	11.3.3 Other Part-time Challenges	11-18
	11.3.4 Rays of Hope	11-18
	11.3.5 Some Advice	11-20
11.4	Conclusions	11-25
	Acknowledgments	11-25
	References	11-26
12	**Making Your Astronomy Class More Inclusive**	**12-1**
12.1	Introduction	12-1
	12.1.1 Making Your Instruction Inclusive	12-2
12.2	Dimensions of Diversity	12-2
	12.2.1 Gender	12-3
	12.2.2 Ethnicity	12-4

	12.2.3	Race	12-5
	12.2.4	LGBTQIA*	12-5
	12.2.5	Socioeconomic	12-6
	12.2.6	Disability	12-6
	12.2.7	Neurodiversity	12-8
	12.2.8	Religion	12-9
	12.2.9	Age	12-10
	12.2.10	Family Obligations	12-10
	12.2.11	Intersectionality	12-10
12.3	Barriers to Inclusion	12-11
	12.3.1	Implicit Bias	12-11
	12.3.2	Stereotype Threat	12-11
	12.3.3	Micro/Macro Aggressions/Affirmations	12-12
	12.3.4	Imposter Syndrome	12-12
12.4	Strategies to Mitigate Bias and Increase Inclusion	12-12
	12.4.1	Before the Course	12-13
	12.4.2	During the Course	12-14
	12.4.3	After the Course	12-17
12.5	Making Astronomy Inclusive	12-17
	12.5.1	Examples	12-17
	12.5.2	Metaphors	12-18
	12.5.3	Connections	12-18
	12.5.4	Demonstrations	12-19
	12.5.5	Stories	12-19
12.6	Resources	12-20
	References	12-22

Preface

This book is intended to be a practical resource for introductory astronomy instructors, many of whom have received no formal training in teaching and learning. Astronomy is one of the most popular subjects for non-science majors, and it often represents their last formal exposure to science. Introductory astronomy classes therefore play a critical role in science literacy, as well as informing a broad audience about the dramatic recent progress in our understanding of the universe. Our intention is to provide information and resources for instructors who will be teaching for the first time or those who want to add to their toolkits and improve their students' learning. The book's authors are all experienced astronomy education researchers, instructors, curriculum designers, instructional designers, and professional development specialists who work in the field and share their insights with the reader.

Many books exist on implementing better teaching and learning practices in education and science in general; this one is intended for a specific audience of undergraduate astronomy instructors. It provides examples, resources, and advice for astronomy specifically. The goal is to acquaint instructors with teaching methods that are validated by research, and to include tools that go far beyond the traditional, passive model of an instructor delivering a lecture. Topics include learner-centered practices, designing effective courses by thinking about goals, using different astronomy curricula, online resources and visualizations, ideas for utilizing the planetarium, engaging students in astronomical research and citizen science projects, advice for teaching at community colleges, and making your courses more inclusive to all students. Thanks to the ebook format, each chapter has links to online instructional resources as well as references to the education research literature.

Editor biographies

Chris Impey

Chris Impey is a University Distinguished Professor of Astronomy and Associate Dean of the College of Science at the University of Arizona. He has over 180 refereed publications on observational cosmology, galaxies, and quasars, and his research has been supported by $20 million in NASA and NSF grants. He has won eleven teaching awards and has taught two online classes with over 180,000 enrolled and 2 million minutes of video lectures watched. Chris Impey is a past Vice President of the American Astronomical Society and he has been an NSF Distinguished Teaching Scholar, the Carnegie Council's Arizona Professor of the Year, and most recently, a Howard Hughes Medical Institute Professor. He's written over 50 popular articles on cosmology and astrobiology, two introductory textbooks, a novel called Shadow World, and eight popular science books: The Living Cosmos, How It Ends, Talking About Life, How It Began, Dreams of Other Worlds, Humble Before the Void, Beyond: The Future of Space Travel, and Einstein's Monsters: The Life and Times of Black Holes.

Sanlyn Buxner

Sanlyn Buxner is an Assistant Research Professor in the Department of Teaching, Learning, and Sociocultural Studies at the University of Arizona where she also serves as the Director of Graduate Studies. In addition, she is a Research Scientist and Education and Communication Specialist at the Planetary Science Institute. She is the current Education and Public Outreach Officer for the Division for Planetary Sciences of the American Astronomical Society and serves on the Executive Committee for the Education Section of the American Geophysical Union. Her research focuses on studying innovations in higher education STEM settings and assessing scientific and quantitative literacy of students and lifelong learners. She also studies the impact of research experiences on middle and high school teachers' classroom practices and student outcomes.

Contributors

Janelle M. Bailey is a faculty member in the Department of Teaching and Learning at Temple University, where her research focuses on astronomy and Earth science teaching and learning as well as science teacher education. She is a past president of the American Association of Physics Teachers (AAPT) and serves as a reviewer for several research and practitioner journals. Janelle earned her PhD in Teaching & Teacher Education (minor in Astronomy) with a focus on Astronomy Education from the University of Arizona; an MEd in Science Education from the University of Georgia; and a BA in Astrophysics from Agnes Scott College. She previously worked on the faculty of the University of Nevada, Las Vegas, and as a physics and chemistry teacher in Wyoming.

Kelly Borden is a career informal science educator. She is currently the Director of Teen Programs at the Adler Planetarium where she leads a team of educators, program facilitators, and curriculum developers within the Department of Citizen Science. Previously, she led Zooniverse educational efforts by designing and implementing curricula to bring citizen science into formal and informal learning environments.

Erik Brogt is a Reader in Academic Development at the University of Canterbury in Christchurch, New Zealand. He received his MSc in Astronomy from the University of Groningen (the Netherlands), and his PhD in Teaching and Teacher education from the University of Arizona. As an academic developer, Erik supports faculty in all matters related to teaching, learning, pedagogy, and curriculum and assessment design to help them shape their classes to optimize student learning. Erik's research interests are in Discipline-Based Education Research, working with faculty to investigate their teaching, academic development, and the educational psychology of university teaching and learning environments. He is a Fellow of the Higher Education Research and Development Society of Australasia, a Fellow of the Staff and Educational Development Association, and a Senior Fellow of the Higher Education Academy.

Marc Buie is an Institute Scientist at the Southwest Research Institute office in Boulder, Colorado. He is a member of the science team for the *New Horizons* and *Lucy* missions. He is an observational planetary scientist and works with telescopes around and above Earth, both big and small, and works primarily on studies of bodies in the outer solar system. Along the way, he has been heavily involved in both automated observatory operation and founded the Research and Education Collaborative Occultation Network (RECON), which is a new kind of citizen science project.

Carie Cardamone brings her passion for making science education inclusive and exciting to her work as the Associate Director for STEM and Professional Schools at the Tufts University's Center for the Enhancement of Learning & Teaching, and as a Program Presenter at Boston's Museum of Science Planetarium & Observatory. As a member of Galaxy Zoo's science team, her research program encompasses the evolution of galaxies and attitudinal changes of introductory science students participating in Citizen Science projects.

Kim Coble is a Professor of Physics and Astronomy at San Francisco State University (SFSU), with expertise in physics and astronomy education research and extensive experience teaching reformed introductory physics and astronomy classes. Her research centers on understanding students' ideas about modern topics in science (such as cosmology), recognizing the strengths that diverse learners bring to the classroom and to STEM professions, and creating innovative, active-learning environments that engage students in realistic scientific practices. She is currently the chair of the Education Committee of the American Astronomical Society (AAS) and serves on the Committee for the Status of Minorities in Astronomy. She was a member of the AAS Task Force on Diversity and Inclusion in Graduate Astronomy Education, served on the Committee on Diversity of the American Association of Physics Teachers (AAPT), and was an organizer of the Inclusive Astronomy 2015 conference. At SFSU, she is the director for the Learning Assistant program, a member of the Faculty Agents of Change, and a faculty collaborator for the Center for Science and Math Education. She was formerly an NSF Astronomy and Astrophysics Fellow and obtained her PhD from the University of Chicago.

Douglas Duncan is an astronomer at the University of Colorado. He earned degrees at Caltech and UC Santa Cruz and was part of the project that first found sunspot cycles on other stars; he then joined the staff of the *Hubble Space Telescope*. In 1992, Duncan accepted a joint appointment at the University of Chicago and the Adler Planetarium, beginning a trend of modernization of planetariums which has spread throughout the U.S. At Colorado, he oversaw the modernization of the Fiske Planetarium into the most technically advanced planetarium in the U.S. Duncan is the author of "Clickers in the Classroom," a guide to the powerful technology that enables teachers to know what all of their students are thinking, not just the ones that raise their hands. He has served as the National Education Coordinator for the American Astronomical Society, and in 2011, received the prestigious Richard Emmons award presented to the "Outstanding University Astronomy Teacher in the U.S."

Patrick Durrell is a Distinguished Professor of Physics & Astronomy at Youngstown State University and is the Director of the Ward Beecher Planetarium. He has been teaching introductory astronomy classes for over 20 years and has long been interested in integrating his teaching and the latest advances in planetarium technology.

Julie Feldt was the Citizen Science Education Specialist within the Zooniverse team at the Adler Planetarium from 2013 to 2017. She wrote the Planet Hunters educators guide and assisted in the development of the classroom.zooniverse.org Galaxy Zoo curriculum. Julie currently works as the Membership Coordinator and part of the guest services team at the Mid-Hudson Children's Museum in Poughkeepsie, NY.

Rica Sirbaugh French is a Professor of Astronomy and Physics and directs the Astronomy Program at MiraCosta College. She spent years researching star clusters and planetary nebulae before realizing she preferred other targets: non-science majors and their instructors. With collaborators at the Center for Astronomy Education (CAE) she is part of the nation's largest college-level astronomy education research initiative and facilitates professional development experiences for educators nationwide. She has served on the AAS Education Committee, the board of the North County Higher Education Alliance, managed a professional development program for the California Community Colleges Chancellor's Office, and maintains resources for faculty at https://tiny.cc/rfrenchfacultyshare.

Erin Galyen is an Associate Professor of Practice in the Office of Instruction and Assessment at the University of Arizona in Tucson. She earned an MS in Astronomy from San Diego State University and a PhD in Teaching and Teacher Education from the University of Arizona. She has taught introductory astronomy lecture and laboratory-style classes at various two- and four-year colleges. Erin currently supports graduate students and faculty in learning about and implementing evidence-based teaching approaches and coordinates a Certificate in College Teaching program. Erin's academic interests focus on learner-centered education, the scholarship of teaching and learning, academic development, and future faculty preparation.

Adrienne Gauthier is a learning designer at Dartmouth College. She collaborates with STEM faculty through course design projects that focus heavily on learner-centered strategies. Other projects include managing the undergraduate Learning Fellows Program, designing MOOCs, and investigating new educational technologies. Previously, she worked as an instructional technologist and astronomy educator in the Department of Astronomy at the University of Arizona, working with faculty and other astronomy community professionals to innovate with technology-enhanced learning. These included student creative projects and IYA 2009 in Second Life, co-designing online and hybrid astronomy courses, collaborating on the Astronomy Visualization Metadata standard, and managing open online astronomy resources like Astropedia, now known as TeachAstronomy.com.

Alyssa Goodman is the Robert Wheeler Willson Professor of Applied Astronomy at Harvard University, co-Director for Science at the Radcliffe Institute for Advanced Study, and a Research Associate of the Smithsonian Institution. Goodman's research focuses on new ways to visualize and analyze the tremendous data volumes created by large and/or diverse astronomical surveys, and on improving our understanding of the structure of the Milky Way Galaxy. She works closely with colleagues at the American Astronomical Society, helping to expand the use of the

WorldWide Telescope program, in both research and in education. Goodman was awarded the Newton Lacy Pierce Prize from the American Astronomical Society in 1997, was named a Fellow of the American Association for the Advancement of Science in 2009, and chosen as Scientist of the Year by the Harvard Foundation in 2015.

Harry Houghton is an education researcher and technology specialist with the WorldWide Telescope Ambassadors program and with the Science Education Department at the Center for Astrophysics | Harvard & Smithsonian. His specialization is in the proper implementation of technology resources in K–12 curricula. He began using WWT as part of the ThinkSpace research project, for which he created media resources, based on the WWT platform, for the Seasons and Moon Phases curricula.

Erin Johnson was previously Program Facilitator for the WorldWide Telescope Ambassadors Program, where she helped cultivate relationships with partner teachers and schools, and participated in development of WWT-based curricula. Erin's experience in special education provides a lens for critically engaging students with various learning styles. She is now Program Manager for Harvard University's Public School Partnerships team.

Edwin Ladd is a Professor of Physics and Astronomy at Bucknell University in Lewisburg, PA. The recipient of the Bogar Award for Excellence in Teaching in the Natural Sciences, Ladd has over 20 years experience teaching experiential lab-based Astro101-type courses to undergraduate students. He led the development of WWT activities designed for introductory astronomy labs, with support from the National Science Foundation.

Kevin Lee is a Research Associate Professor at the University of Nebraska–Lincoln (UNL). His appointment is shared by an academic department where his duties focus on instruction and an educational center where he works on curriculum development, outreach, teacher training, and technology support. He oversees the Astronomy Education at the University of Nebraska website at http://astro.unl.edu, which houses computer simulations, a library of dynamic peer instruction questions, a suite of interactive ranking and sorting tasks, and a growing library of astronomy demonstration videos available on YouTube. The simulations have been used globally by astronomy faculty for more than 10 years. He has recently returned to UNL after a three-year stint as a rotating program officer in the National Science Foundation's Division of Undergraduate Education.

John Keller is a PI for RECON along with Marc Buie. Keller is the Director of the Fiske Planetarium and a planetary scientist with research interests in astronomy education and teacher preparation. Previously, he was co-Director for the Center for Engineering, Science, and Mathematics Education (CESAME) at California Polytechnic State University in San Luis Obispo, and Executive Director for the

STEM Teacher and Researcher (STAR) Program, which provides paid summer research experiences at national labs for aspiring science and math teachers.

Steve Kortenkamp is an astronomer at the University of Arizona and teaches astronomy courses in the Flandrau Planetarium. He develops custom computer animations allowing teachers and students to more easily visualize science concepts. Currently, he is working to adapt his techniques to include 3D-printed resources for students who are blind or visually impaired. Kortenkamp is also an accomplished children's author. His most recent book, *Exploring Mars*, was written in an interactive Choose Your Own Adventure style and is available as an audio book.

Bethany Cobb Kung is an Associate Professor of Honors and Physics at the George Washington University (GW). She graduated from Williams College in 2002 and received her PhD in astronomy at Yale University in 2008 for research on massive stellar explosions called gamma-ray bursts. From 2008 to 2010, she did research at the University of California, Berkeley as a National Science Foundation Astronomy & Astrophysics Postdoctoral Fellow. As a dedicated educator at GW, she specializes in teaching astronomy and physics to non-science-majoring students and was awarded the 2016 Morton A. Bender Teaching Award. More broadly, she works across many fronts to support great teaching at GW.

Karen Masters is a professor at Haverford College and astronomer/astrophysicist researching galaxies in the universe. She is the Sloan Digital Sky Survey (SDSS)-IV Spokesperson and the Project Scientist of the Galaxy Zoo citizen science/Zooniverse project. She obtained her PhD in Astronomy from Cornell University, and after a postdoc at Harvard spent ten years working at Portsmouth University (as a postdoc, then faculty), before moving to Haverford as an Associate Professor in 2018 January. As well as her research in extragalactic astronomy, she has previously published research on informal science learning via citizen science projects.

Bryan Méndez is an astronomer and education specialist at UC Berkeley's Space Science Laboratory. Dr. Méndez works to educate and inspire others about the wonder and beauty of the universe. He develops programs for the public through the web and museums; develops educational resources for students, teachers, and the public; conducts professional development for science educators; and teaches courses in astronomy and physics at UC Berkeley and local community colleges.

Kate Meredith has more than 25 years of teaching and curriculum development experience in both formal and informal education. She has engaged in curriculum development and project management for the Zooniverse, the Sloan Digital Sky Survey, the Lawrence Hall of Science, the Adler Planetarium Space and Science Museum, and the University of Chicago Yerkes Observatory.

Thomas Nelson is the Director of External Relations at City of Asylum, a literary nonprofit in Pittsburgh, PA, that gives sanctuary to endangered writers from around the world. Before leaving academia, he worked most recently as a Research Assistant Professor at the University of Pittsburgh, where his research focused on observational studies of nova explosions and the development of teaching materials for introductory astronomy classes.

Michelle Nichols is Director of Public Observing at the Adler Planetarium in Chicago, IL. She earned a Bachelor of Science degree in Physics and Astronomy from the University of Illinois at Urbana-Champaign in 1995, and a Master's of Education degree in Curriculum and Instruction from National-Louis University in 2002. Ms. Nichols directs the Adler's Doane Observatory and leads the Adler's various telescope and sky observing efforts, both via on-site programs and outreach to the community.

Stella S. R. Offner is an assistant professor at the University of Texas at Austin. Previously, she was faculty at the University of Massachusetts, Amherst. She first began using WWT for education and outreach as an NSF Astronomy & Astrophysics postdoctoral fellow at the Center for Astrophysics | Harvard & Smithsonian. Dr. Offner's research focuses on understanding how stars like the Sun form. She is the recipient of a Hubble Postdoctoral fellowship, an NSF CAREER Award, and a Cottrell Scholar Award.

Catherine Pilachowski holds the Daniel Kirkwood Chair in Astronomy at Indiana University Bloomington. She incorporates aspects of the RBSE curriculum into her courses for non-science majors to engage students in the excitement of astronomy and to improve student learning.

Julia Plummer, an Associate Professor at Pennsylvania State University, has a combined PhD in Astronomy and Education from the University of Michigan. She has spent more than a decade teaching children and adults in the planetarium and other informal settings. Her research focuses on how embodied cognition and embodied design support spatial thinking in astronomy, as well as the role of informal settings in engaging young children in science practices through astronomy.

Edward E. Prather is a Professor in the Department of Astronomy, at the University of Arizona (UA). Ed is the Executive Director of the Center for Astronomy Education (CAE) at UA. His research focuses on investigating the teaching and learning of topics in STEM. Ed and his collaborators have conducted numerous research studies to uncover students' conceptual, reasoning, and problem-solving difficulties over a wide array of physical science topics taught in astronomy, astrobiology, physics, geoscience, and planetary science. The results from these studies have informed the development of innovative active-learning instructional strategies shown to intellectually engage learners and significantly improve their understandings, problem-solving abilities and self-efficacy related to learning about science. Additional efforts have focused on the development of classroom assessment tools, educational technologies, and public outreach activities. Ed has also led the development of a variety of education materials in support of several NASA- and NSF-funded science missions. Dissemination of this work has been provided through industry-leading active-learning professional development workshops that have reached thousands of science educators around the world.

Andrew W. Puckett is an Associate Professor of Physics and Astronomy at Columbus State University. He is co-discoverer of more than 40 minor planets in our solar system. Since 2005, he has been designing observing projects in asteroid orbit refinement for students from high school to undergraduate level. Andy also develops software to support such projects, including the Polaris and OrbitMaster programs described in this book.

Travis A. Rector is a Professor of Physics and Astronomy at the University of Alaska Anchorage. For the last 20 years, he has been developing curriculum designed to engage students in authentic research experiences in astronomy. He was a co-developer of the RBSE program at the National Optical Astronomy Observatory.

Philip Rosenfield was a recent director of the WorldWide Telescope program for the American Astronomical Society. Previously, he was an NSF Astronomy and Astrophysics Postdoctoral Fellow at the Center for Astrophysics | Harvard & Smithsonian where he used data from the *Hubble Space Telescope* to constrain, in a fully probabilistic framework, uncertain physics in stellar evolution models. He earned a PhD in Astronomy from the University of Washington. He has taught astronomy, science communication, science teaching pedagogy, and software engineering skills to scientists, and has been deeply involved in inclusion and equity programming.

Philip Sadler is the Director of the Science Education Department at the Center for Astrophysics | Harvard & Smithsonian, and he is Harvard's F.W. Wright Senior Lecturer in Astronomy. In 1977, he invented Starlab, the first practical portable planetarium, now used throughout the world. His current research interests include assessment of students' misconceptions and how they change with instruction, the transition to college of students who wish to pursue STEM careers, and the professional development of science teachers. Dr. Sadler has won the *Journal of Research in Science* Teaching Award, the AIP's Computers in Physics Prize, the American Astronomical Society Education Prize, and the American Association of Physics Teachers' Millikan Medal.

Wayne Schlingman is the director of the Arne Slettebak Planetarium at The Ohio State University. He completed his graduate work at the University of Arizona and then went on to work at the University of Colorado Boulder as a Science Teaching Fellow working with the non-science-major introductory astronomy classes, creating and adapting activities for in-class recitations. While at Colorado, he also worked with the staff and students of the newly remodeled Fiske Planetarium, encouraging the use of active-engagement learner-centered instructional strategies in public talks. While at OSU, he has continued this work as well as developed partnerships between many disciplinary programs, from Earth science, chemistry, art, music, optometry, and more.

Christine Shupla manages the Lunar and Planetary Institute (LPI) Education and Public Engagement staff, assisting with all of the program efforts. She joined the LPI education team in 2005 October after many years in the planetarium field and has led a variety of its programs, including professional development and materials development for out-of-school-time programmers, librarians, teachers, and informal science educators. She leads LPI's scientist engagement efforts, providing professional development and resources to assist planetary scientists in their efforts to share their science with public audiences. She holds a Bachelor of Arts in Astronomy from the University of Texas in Austin, and a Master of Arts in Curriculum & Instruction from the University of North Carolina at Chapel Hill.

Angela Speck is an astrophysicist who recently left the University of Missouri after 17 years. She was a Professor and the Director of Astronomy, and built the MU astronomy program starting with her arrival at MU. She is now the Chair of the Physics & Astronomy Department at UT-San Antonio, where she is looking forward to combining her passions for science, communication, and social justice work. Dr. Speck's academic career exemplifies the idea that there should be a strong synergy between the research, teaching, and service components for any faculty member. She is originally from Yorkshire (England), has a doctorate in Astronomy from University College London, and was named after the iconic Angela Davis.

Mark SubbaRao, is an astronomer and Director of the Space Visualization Laboratory at the Adler Planetarium and President of the International Planetarium Society. His area of research is cosmology, particularly the large-scale structure of the Universe. He was a builder of the Sloan Digital Sky Survey, which produced a 3D map of over one million galaxies. Dr. SubbaRao utilizes the capabilities of the Adler's immersive theaters in his scientific visualization work.

Susan E. Sunbury is an Educational Researcher in the Science Education Department of the Center for Astrophysics | Harvard & Smithsonian with more than 20 years of experience in the development and facilitation of formal and informal educational programs as well as extensive experience researching and evaluating curriculum projects. Additionally, she taught for seven years in elementary- and middle-school science classrooms and has taught science education courses at three universities.

Laura Trouille is co-PI for Zooniverse and Vice President of Citizen Science at the Adler Planetarium, where she leads the Adler–Zooniverse web development and Teen Programs teams. She is also a Research Associate at Northwestern University. While earning her PhD in Astrophysics, she also earned the Center for the Integration of Research, Teaching and Learning (CIRTL) Delta certificate for

STEM education research. As a Northwestern University CIERA Postdoctoral Fellow, she continued her supermassive black hole research as well as helped lead the Computational Thinking in STEM project, bringing computational thinking and modeling curricular materials to high school science and math teachers.

Patricia Udomprasert is Project Director for the WorldWide Telescope Ambassadors Program at Harvard University. Her interests include science education research on technology in classrooms and development of innovative curricula involving the use of rich 3D visualizations to support spatial thinking and modeling of complex phenomena. She holds a PhD in Astronomy from Caltech and formerly taught high school astronomy, physics, and math.

Nicole P. Vogt is an affiliate professor of astronomy at New Mexico State University. Her General Education Astronomy Resource (GEAS) projects include an adaptive online tutor, laboratory exercises suitable for both traditional and distance learners, and short films highlighting diverse members of underrepresented groups in astronomy. She develops applications for analysis of telescope images and spectra, and leads small-group workshops to support instructor usage.

Colin S. Wallace is a Teaching Assistant Professor in the Department of Physics and Astronomy at the University of North Carolina at Chapel Hill. He earned his PhD in Astrophysical and Planetary Sciences in 2011 from the University of Colorado Boulder. Before coming to UNC-Chapel Hill, he did a three-year postdoc at the Center for Astronomy Education (CAE) at the University of Arizona. His scholarly work focuses on astronomy and physics education research.

Matthew Wenger is an education program manager at Steward Observatory at the University of Arizona. He develops and teaches online astronomy classes and conducts research on student learning in different astronomy courses. His research interests also include free-choice and informal learning contexts. He previously was an educator for informal programs at the Adler Planetarium and a graduate associate at the Flandrau Planetarium and Science Center at the University of Arizona.

Michelle M. Wooten is a postdoctoral scholar in physics education at Michigan State University. In addition to studying the impact of curricular interventions in secondary and postsecondary science learning contexts, Michelle studies methodological approaches used toward the study of science learning, including their historical formulations and effects.

Curtis Wong retired from a 35 year career at the intersection of media, arts, technology, public broadcasting, astronomy, and education to eventually build the WorldWide Telescope with Jonathan Fay at Microsoft. His collaboration with PBS produced innovative programs that redefined the nature of television and have been recognized with awards, including the British Academy Award, Emmy, and Webby nominations for innovative programs. He currently works with some of the top Leonardo da Vinci scholars around the world to build a translation device to allow everyone to understand Leonardo da Vinci's notebooks such as the Codex Leicester.

Erika Wright is an Education Specialist in the Science Education Department at the Center for Astrophysics | Harvard & Smithsonian. With a Master's Degree in Museum Education and nearly 10 years of experience in museums and informal learning institutions, including the Smithsonian's National Museum of Natural History and NASA's Goddard Visitor Center, she focuses on broadening access to the STEM community through informal learning opportunities. At the Center for Astrophysics, she contributes to NASA- and NSF-funded curricula and programming centered around the MicroObservatory Robotic Telescopes and WorldWide Telescope, as well as social media and science communication efforts for NASA's TEMPO Mission.

Astronomy Education, Volume 1
Evidence-based instruction for introductory courses
Chris Impey and Sanlyn Buxner

Chapter 1

Learner-Centered Teaching in Astronomy

Erik Brogt and Erin Galyen

In this chapter, we discuss learner-centered teaching from various perspectives. We start with some background on what learner-centered teaching is, how it is related to the educational and psychological theories on how humans learn, and how we need to take students' knowledge, attitudes, and beliefs into account to optimize student learning. Following this, we discuss how we can use learner-centered teaching as a means to promote inclusivity in the classroom and to motivate students to engage with the course. We then talk about how to implement learner-centered teaching (and avoid the most common pitfalls), using backward-design principles, at the course level, before moving to a broader discussion of implementing learner-centered teaching at the department level. We finish the chapter by discussing some of the frequently asked questions about learner-centered teaching.

Chapter Objectives
By the end of this chapter, readers will be able to
1. describe the educational approach known as learner-centered teaching,
2. describe the rationale for using learner-centered teaching in astronomy classes,
3. give examples of ways to implement learner-centered teaching in astronomy classes and programs, and
4. discuss commonly asked questions about and objections to the implementation of learner-centered teaching in astronomy.

1.1 Introduction
Learner-centered teaching (LCT; sometimes used alongside "student-centered," "evidence-based," "reformed," or "scientific" teaching) is a commonly used phrase in the educational literature and likewise in the astronomy education community. It is often compared and contrasted with the teacher-centered (sometimes called "traditional" or lecture-based) approach. As research-informed teachers wanting

to do right by our students, LCT is grounded in theories on how humans learn and has a strong foundation in research, with LCT-based instruction showing significant increases in student engagement and learning (e.g., National Research Council 2000, 2012; Kober 2015; National Academies of Sciences, Engineering, and Medicine 2018). This approach has been validated not only in college courses in general, but also in teaching astronomy specifically (National Research Council 2012; Kober 2015). Teaching is often discussed using specific methods (e.g., active learning) or strategies (e.g., think–pair–share, group work, lecture tutorials). While these are important to the conversation about astronomy education, this chapter focuses on LCT as an evidence-based approach or paradigm of teaching.

Similar to the geocentric and heliocentric paradigms of the universe, which shaped everything from conversations among scientists to practical data collection and analysis (Kuhn 2012), the LCT paradigm or approach guides thinking about teaching, as well as specific teaching practices and how they are used. This provides the framework for the active-learning and student-engagement techniques described elsewhere in this book, which are must-have tools in our teaching arsenal. Many faculty are actually already using an LCT approach, even if they may not be familiar with the education jargon. In the first part of this chapter, we will discuss LCT as an evidence-based approach to teaching, its basis in research on human learning, how it compares with other evidence-based teaching approaches prevalent in 21st century higher education, and its benefits and drawbacks. We will then focus on ways to implement LCT in classes, be that your own course, a larger program of study, or an entire department, using a complementary course design method—backward design—as a learner-centered planning framework. We finish the chapter by answering some of the most frequently asked questions about LCT.

1.2 What Is Learner-centered Teaching?

If you answered *yes* to any of the questions in Table 1.1, then you are already using a learner-centered astronomy teaching approach to some extent (National Research Council 2012; Kober 2015; Blumberg 2016). What distinguishes LCT and makes it more effective than previous teaching approaches is what lies at its center, i.e., learners and their learning. Kober (2015, p. 95) notes that "student-centered approaches place less emphasis on the instructor transmitting factual information

Table 1.1. Reflection on Teaching Practices

Have you ever...
- taken into account the needs and prior knowledge of your particular students when planning courses or lessons?
- chosen your teaching methods based on specific learning goals, objectives, or outcomes that students should learn, including both astronomy knowledge and skills (e.g., data analysis, observational skills, critical thinking)?
- had students learn through engaging activities or exercises—in person, online, or for an assignment?
- used assessments of students' learning to adjust your teaching to better help them learn?

by lecturing and more emphasis on students building their own understanding with careful structuring and guidance from the instructor." Biggs & Tang (2007) discuss three "levels" of teaching: a focus on what students are (good, bad, smart, etc.), what teachers do, and what students do. LCT sits squarely in the third category.

In this model of teaching, the instructor serves multiple roles, not only as content expert, but also as course designer and facilitator, who works to create rich learning experiences within which "students are expected to be actively and cognitively engaged" (Kober 2015, p. 95). Other aspects of this approach that distinguish it from the teacher-centered approach are changes to the focus of the course and lesson planning, the varied roles of assessments, and the distinct purposes of learning opportunities (Weimer 2013; Kober 2015). Table 1.2 compares teacher-centered and learner-centered approaches on these various dimensions.

1.3 How Humans Learn: The Rationale for LCT

We know more about how humans learn now than at any other time in human history. In this section, we offer a very short primer into human learning. This empirical research forms the foundations of LCT and informs how it can effectively be applied in teaching astronomy.

Table 1.2. Comparison of Teacher-centered and Learner-centered Approaches

Dimension	Teacher-centered approach	Learner-centered approach
The teacher is focused on:	What the teacher teaches	What and how students need to learn
The role of the teacher is:	Expert, knowledge disseminator	Facilitator, discussion leader, the person who asks the gnarly questions, tour guide
Courses/lessons are planned to:	Deliver/Cover topics and concepts	Achieve learning outcomes (e.g., what students need to be able to do)
Assessments are intended to:	Test what learners know in order to assign grades (assessment *of* learning)	Support learning in progress and demonstrate to what extent the learning objectives were met (assessment *for/as* learning)
Assessment takes place:	At the end of a chapter, section of content, or end of course (summative assessment)	Throughout the learning process (formative and summative assessment)
Learning opportunities are designed to:	Reinforce concepts, replicate methods of the discipline, verify existing knowledge	Master concepts, apply methods of the discipline, guide exploration and inquiry, develop higher-order thinking skills (e.g., scientific and quantitative reasoning, communication, critical and creative thinking, collaboration)

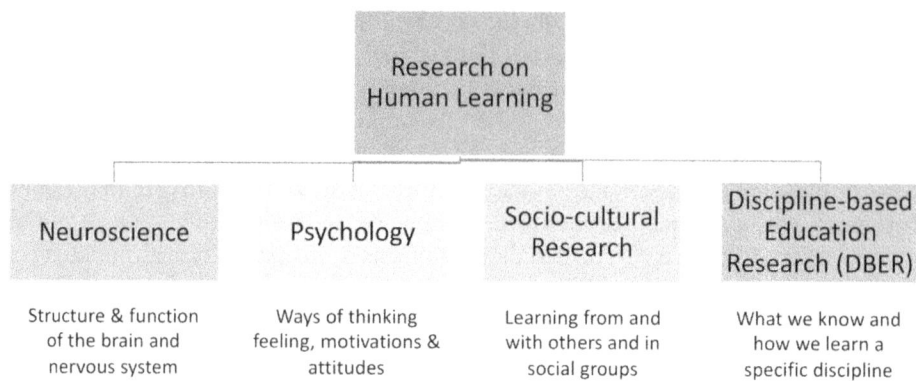

Figure 1.1. Domains informing research on human learning.

Research on human learning that informs learner-centered astronomy teaching draws from four main areas (Figure 1.1).

While highly simplified, this serves as a general overview of results from these areas of study that relate to astronomy teaching. Neuroscience research is relevant as it encompasses the physical architecture for how we detect, process, and store sensory input in and retrieve memories from neuronal networks. Psychology and cognitive science have emphasized how we think about thinking and learning, including the role our motivations, attitudes, and emotions play, which affect students' thought processes and mediate both learning and memory. Sociocultural research not only incorporates how we learn from and with other humans, including how we learn from peers, but also encompasses the role that cultural norms, social institutions, and identities play in our learning, especially among marginalized groups. Discipline-based Education Research (or DBER) offers specific results from investigations into learning concepts or skills in a discipline, such as student understandings of the cause of the seasons, stellar evolution, or quantitative reasoning (National Research Council 2000, 2012; Kober 2015; National Academies of Sciences, Engineering, and Medicine 2018). What we now know is:

> Learning is a process of actively constructing knowledge. Learning is not simply the accrual of information; rather, it involves a process of conceptual reorganization. The brain actively seeks to make sense of new knowledge by connecting it with prior knowledge and experience. Through this process, the learner "constructs" new understanding and meaning (Kober 2015, p. 57).

This learning theory is known as "constructivism." Neurologically, neurons build networks and in so doing encode and "store" everything we think, feel, and remember, such as sensory information, ideas, beliefs, attitudes, emotions, and other experiences. This means that each individual has a highly individualized set of mental models (or schemas), beliefs, and attitudes based on their prior experience and thinking that they bring into any situation. We also now understand "memory involves reconstruction rather than retrieval of exact copies" (National Academies of Sciences, Engineering, and Medicine 2018, p. 4). In other words, human memory is less like a computer that can be simply overwritten, and more like a building that is constructed and remodeled over time (National Research Council 2000).

Other key research findings from the fields of study mentioned above have informed the shift in teaching to an LCT focus on learners and learning:

1. "Each learner develops a unique array of knowledge….as they navigate through social, cognitive, and physical contexts…. A person's brain will develop differently depending on her experiences, interpretations, needs, culture, and thought patterns" (National Academies of Sciences, Engineering, and Medicine 2018, pp. 2–3, 59).
2. "Decisions about how to teach should be based in large part on goals for what students should learn. These outcomes address the specific knowledge and skills, as well as the more general habits of mind and professional conduct, that students are expected to learn" (Kober 2015, p. 90).
3. "Interactions with others can promote learning. The evidence is very strong that collaborative activities enhance the effectiveness of student-centered learning over traditional instruction and improve retention of content knowledge. When students work together on well-designed learning activities, they can help each other solve problems by building on each other's knowledge, asking each other questions, and suggesting ideas that an individual working alone might not have considered" (Kober 2015, p. 62).
4. "Educational assessment does not exist in isolation, but must be aligned with curriculum and instruction if it is to support learning" (National Research Council 2001, p. 3). "Student-centered approaches to teaching and learning call for different methods of assessment. In a student-centered undergraduate class, many of the learning activities themselves are a form of assessment that provide instructors with richer information about students' understanding than they could obtain from traditional assessments" (Kober 2015, p. 122).

You may recognize these four key findings as the same themes from the "Have you ever…" questions in Table 1.1.

Learning, especially when dealing with mental models that people have held for a long time, can be as much about deconstruction as it is about construction. Part of the difficulty is that our beliefs, attitudes, and emotions serve to protect important information we may have learned that is key to our survival or sense of identity. When a new experience challenges our current knowledge, to protect the existing structure, we often disbelieve or discount the new idea. This happens most often when the topic is tied to a belief system that defines one's sense of identity, and also includes self-confidence and self-image. When students respond confrontationally about the Big Bang Theory or Evolution by Natural Selection, that is a clear expression of feeling that their identity is threatened. Similarly, when a student cries or becomes angry over an exam or assignment grade, this is an expression that their self-confidence or self-image has been threatened (National Research Council 2001).

Even when students do not experience a psychological "threat" from what they are learning, what we learn is built on top of an imperfect mental model. Depending on how much the mental model differs from the scientific understanding, more or less "reconstruction" may be necessary. For example, students can come into classes with mistaken ideas about the cause of the seasons, moon phases, and other commonly taught topics in our courses. If that is the case, then much more work is required to re-construct a more accurate model, a process called "conceptual change" (Posner et al. 1982). This is often accomplished by creating experiences where students are able to engage with and think through believable evidence that counters their existing model (also called "cognitive conflict" or "cognitive dissonance") in a way that does not threaten their beliefs or sense of identity. Therefore, knowing, planning, teaching, and assessing learning with students' knowledge, skills, and attitudes in mind is crucial for effective learning.

While beliefs and attitudes can stymie learning, they can also have a positive influence, serving to support or accelerate the "construction" process. Motivation, interest, and excitement about a topic can help students not only focus attention for longer periods of time, but also help improve characteristics such as determination, persistence, and learning in general (e.g., Pintrich 2003; Lazowski & Hulleman 2016). Table 1.3 below has several strategies for supporting students' motivation.

Other ways of generating interest include asking students about their interests and then incorporating these topics into a course, as well as expressing your own enthusiasm for astronomy in general, as well as particular topics. Capitalizing on curiosity by encouraging and answering students' questions, or creating opportunities for students to pursue and answer their own questions through inquiry-based learning is another way to engage motivation and interest. Relating topics to real-world examples or issues that students care about, incorporating gamified learning (e.g., games, competitions, simulations, role plays), and using creative or service-based projects can also harness students' prior knowledge, skills, and attitudes to help them learn in the present (e.g., Clark et al. 2016). Another powerful boon to learning is helping students find value in what they are learning and how it might help them in their future work or life (more on how LCT can serve as a motivational tool later in this chapter).

Table 1.3. Ways to Support Students' Motivation

A few ways of supporting learners' motivation:
- Helping students to set desired learning goals and appropriately challenging goals,
- Creating learning experiences that students value,
- Supporting students' sense of autonomy,
- Helping students to recognize, monitor, and strategize about their learning progress, and
- "Creating an emotionally supportive and nonthreatening learning environment where learners feel safe and valued" (National Academies of Sciences, Engineering, and Medicine 2018, p. 6)

1.4 Knowing, Engaging, and Assessing Students

As discussed in the previous section, each individual constructs their own knowledge, beliefs, and attitudes based on their experiences. How then can LCT help students learn in astronomy courses? Fundamentally, LCT is about *knowing, engaging, and effectively assessing students*. Because engaging students' individuality is key to what they will learn, it is crucial to get to know students as individuals. However, there are general characteristics in any group of people that can be assumed. For example, there always will be disparate levels of interest, knowledge, and skill levels. Some individuals will be highly motivated, while others will be more passive and uninterested. Some may come into a course very knowledgeable about the topic or with advanced study skills, while others may struggle with learning challenges or have divided priorities that can interfere with focus or time for study (e.g., part- or full-time jobs, parenting or other caregiving responsibilities). In addition, students' own views about themselves relative to learning astronomy (or learning in general) affect their willingness to engage. Helping empower students "by providing them with opportunities to have some control over their learning" (Osborne & Jones 2011, p. 144), such as making choices about projects or assignments, can help support more learning-centered views about themselves (Weimer 2013). Similarly, asking students to reflect on or articulate how what they are learning is relevant or of value to them can also help break them out of their own negative mindset about a particular subject or topic; this is often heard when students say things like, "I'm just not a science person" or "I can't do math" (Osborne & Jones 2011).

Another common first step in getting to know students, for example, is by asking them to complete a start-of-term or start-of-topic survey, quiz, or exam. This can provide valuable information on students' knowledge, skills, attitudes, and other attributes, which can be useful "data" for tailoring your planning and instruction for specific groups or individual students. It can also serve as a pre-assessment, which could be matched with a similar survey, quiz, or exam as a post-assessment following teaching to compare what students have learned. The survey could include not only tests of astronomy knowledge, but attitudes and interests in specific topics, particular skills they bring to the class, or challenges they face. As will be discussed later in this chapter, another important attribute of LCT is the planning of clear instructional objectives or outcomes, which combined with the knowledge of the learners, forms the basis for the planning of the curriculum, teaching practices, and assessment (Angelo & Cross 1993; Weimer 2013). A number of validated astronomy content tests and concept inventories exist, which can be used to measure students' learning of astronomy in general and in key areas, such as the cause of Moon phases, light and spectroscopy, and stellar evolution (see Bailey 2011 for a review). In taking a scholarly approach to measuring learning, whether through a quiz, exam, laboratory report, research, observation project, or something else, "a fair assessment is one that yields comparably valid inferences from person to person and group to group" (National Research Council 2001, p. 176). We will expound on this idea later in the chapter.

As revealed by the scholarship on teaching and learning, humans learn better through active engagement. In a class setting, this means "learning through activities and/or discussion in class, as opposed to passively listening to an expert. It emphasizes higher-order thinking and often involves group work" (Freeman et al. 2014, pp. 8413–8414). These results have been rigorously tested across disciplines, including astronomy (e.g., Prather et al. 2009) and for science majors and non-majors alike (e.g., Springer et al. 1999; Freeman et al. 2014; Kober 2015). As specific examples of active learning in astronomy teaching are discussed throughout the rest of this book, we will not reiterate them here, but there are many astronomy-specific active-learning tools that have been developed and are ready to use, either by individual students, pairs, or small groups.

In a general sense, how might you determine if your course or specific teaching practices are learner-centered? There are a number of useful tools that, while not astronomy specific, are very useful for planning and assessing your class. On the course level, Palmer et al. (2014) have developed a rubric for assessing the extent to which a syllabus reflects a learner-centered course. As for assessing particular lessons, a number of validated observation protocols exist for examining the use of a learner-centered (or evidence-based) teaching approach in face-to-face undergraduate courses. While not exhaustive, three that were developed with science courses in mind include the Reform Teaching Observation Protocol (RTOP; Piburn & Sawada 2000), Teaching Dimensions Observation Protocol (TDOP; Hora et al. 2013), and the Classroom Observation Protocol for Undergraduate STEM (COPUS; Smith et al. 2013). For assessing online courses, the most commonly used tool in higher education is the membership-based Quality Matters Rubric, which has been adopted by over 850 colleges and universities in the U.S., the standards of which are "based on best practices that are well established in online education" (Legon 2015).

1.5 Learner-centered Teaching, Universal Design for Learning, and Inclusive Excellence

Education has seen the simultaneous rise of several models of teaching that share much of the same research foundations and similar goals, i.e., to optimize learning by accounting for students' needs, and tailoring courses and learning environments accordingly. The three most common models used in higher education are LCT, Universal Design for Learning (UDL), and Inclusive Excellence. While each of these other models could also encompass their own chapter, we will describe them briefly here and discuss how they can be used in coordination with LCT.

1.5.1 Universal Design for Learning

UDL originated in the 1990s to address the needs of students with disabilities who encountered barriers to learning in school and the possibilities that developments in technology offered to remove at least some of these barriers. Similar to the shift in focus from teachers to learners in LCT, UDL applied results of neuroscientific and education research, especially disability studies, as well as the movement toward barrier-free design in the field of architecture, to "shif[t] the focus from 'fixing' kids to fixing the curriculum" and "to design learning environments that from the outset offered options for diverse learner needs" (Meyer et al. 2014, p. 5). The term "Universal Design" in fact originated in the field of architecture (Story et al. 1998). The UDL guidelines (CAST 2018) expand on LCT's commitment to consider students' individual characteristics when planning, instructing, and assessing learning by offering a variety of means and options for *student engagement* (e.g., "provide tasks that allow for active participation, exploration and experimentation"), *representations of knowledge* (e.g., "offer ways of customizing the display of information"), and *means of expression* (e.g., "solve problems using a variety of strategies"). Many of these principles have been incorporated into the architectural design of individual institutions and into multimedia and other instructional technologies, such as built-in ramps in physical classrooms, websites that are compatible with screen readers for visually impaired students, or online videos that are closed captioned. This makes it much easier for individual instructors to reduce learning barriers for all students.

1.5.2 Inclusive Excellence

Similar to LCT and UDL, Inclusive Excellence (sometimes used alongside Diversity and Inclusion, and/or Equity) shares the goal of optimizing learning for all (e.g., Williams et al. 2005; American Association of Colleges and Universities 2015). This model originates in sociocultural research, including sociology, social psychology, anthropology, and cultural and gender studies. The aim of inclusive excellence is to advance culturally-responsive teaching (Gay 2000) in order to reduce bias, prejudice, and oppression, which serve as barriers to learning, to reduce achievement (and opportunity) gaps between student groups, and to reduce underrepresentation in specific majors and professions, especially in STEM fields (Considine et al. 2017). One of the central tenets of Inclusive Excellence or culturally responsive pedagogy is

> that teachers need to incorporate the experiences and perspectives of students...being responsive to diverse racial, ethnic, language, and social class backgrounds in designing curriculum, learning activities, classroom climate, instructional materials, teaching strategies, and assessment procedures" (Gay 2000 as cited in Considine et al. 2017, p. 173).

In astronomy classes, this can mean small gestures, such as learning and using students' names, inviting students to share and use appropriate gender pronouns and reducing or eliminating microaggressions,[1] as well as larger ones, such as deliberately including historical and current contributions of individuals of diverse genders, cultures, backgrounds, disabilities, etc., and bringing in guest speakers who represent diversity in astronomy and STEM. Another important mechanism for

---

[1] "[B]rief and commonplace daily verbal, behavioral, or environmental indignities, that communicate hostile, derogatory, or negative racial slights and insults toward people of color of which the perpetrators are often unaware" (Sue et al. 2007, p. 237).

breaking down biases and promoting inclusion is to have students work in diverse groups to achieve success together. Research has also revealed that teacher "behaviors such as eye contact, gesture, movement, smiling, and a relaxed body position" (Considine et al. 2017, p. 177) can all impact learning and motivation, as well as intentions to persist in college. Mentoring and creating opportunities to increase visibility of these issues within a course or department, as well as setting the tone for the learning environment in your course to one in which diversity is not only respected but desired, can also be effective ways to particularly encourage members of underrepresented and marginalized groups (e.g., Ong et al. 2018).

There is another element of culturally responsive pedagogy that extends beyond the classroom. As Astro 101 is so often a terminal science course for students, it is a (last) vehicle to talk about how science, society, and culture interact. We can use astronomy, with its broad popular appeal, to highlight and discuss issues of equity, inclusion, and global citizenship, and the role astronomy and science can play in that effort (e.g., IAU's Office of Astronomy for Development, http://www.astro4dev.org/). Another element of culturally responsive pedagogy deals with curriculum design, in particular around decisions on topics and concepts to include, and how to include them. Culturally responsive pedagogy also means giving voice to astronomers who are not consistently part of the traditional Western narrative, such as contributions from non-Western societies, women in astronomy, and the rich and beautiful indigenous astronomy traditions (e.g., https://www.maoriastronomy.co.nz/; http://www.aboriginalastronomy.com.au/; Cajete 1994; Holbrook et al. 2008; Antonellis 2013). Despite the brief descriptions of these other approaches here, the overlap and complementarity between LCT, UDL, and Inclusive Excellence work in tandem to achieve better learning outcomes for all students. In the next section, we look toward specific aspects of the LCT approach and how they can play out in an astronomy course.

1.6 Learner-centered Teaching as a Motivational Tool

LCT requires students to be more active in their learning. The popular appeal of astronomy, which captures the imagination, makes students on average more likely to want to engage with the materials in the course, giving us an advantage as astronomy teachers when using LCT techniques. It is important to realize that in Astro 101 courses, this higher intrinsic motivation on one hand is usually met with some trepidation on the other hand. In particular, when teaching non-science-major students, we must be aware as teachers that a good fraction of our students will have science and math anxiety (e.g., Tobias 1978; Mallow 1986; Udo et al. 2004), especially around the manipulation of (algebraic) equations. Regardless of its cause, science and math anxiety will consume a certain amount of student mental resource, meaning that there is less mental resource available for the task at hand, and inhibit engagement in certain types of activities, due to fear of (public) failure (e.g., answering direct questions from the instructor). However, while these students may lack self-confidence in their science and math abilities, this does not mean that they are not capable of engaging with mathematical concepts. For example, when comparing brightnesses of stars, one can plug the numbers in the Stefan–Boltzmann equation, or one could use proportional reasoning that shows appropriate conceptual understanding of the material without doing the detailed math (both temperature and size matter, and temperature matters more than size). The approach taken should match the target audience, and both can be considered academically rigorous (Brogt & Draeger 2015). LCT techniques, in particular peer discussions and group work, can also help engage students with math and science anxiety (as well as others) as the power distance between students is much lower than the power distance between teacher and students. In addition, representing the opinion of the group is far less daunting than representing your own individual opinion; in essence, the responsibility is divided by N, with N being the number of people in the group.

In addition, as briefly described earlier, LCT can sometimes be used to increase motivation and self-efficacy (students' beliefs about their capabilities to "produce desired effects by their actions," Bandura 2010), with students who feel less confident in their abilities (see, e.g., Brogt 2009). An example is the use of Socratic dialogue, where the instructor or activity probes students to reason their way through a problem, asking questions to guide their thinking, and asking them to justify their reasoning (see e.g., Brogt 2007a). Oftentimes, students can do quite a bit of the reasoning themselves, and as teachers, we only have to intervene at those places where their thinking goes off the rails. Once they are back on track, they can usually finish their own line of thought. For students who have low math or science self-efficacy, this is a huge motivational booster, as they just did something (solving an astronomy problem) that they were convinced they could not do. In other cases, students can justify their reasoning based on criteria different from those used in science. A classic example would be an exercise where we ask students to classify galaxies without telling them the classification criteria commonly used in the profession. While students will need to come to grips with the classification scheme used in astronomy, in particular if they wish to engage in citizen science projects like Galaxy Zoo (https://www.galaxyzoo.org), having them create, use, and defend their own system can be a powerful way to reach critical thinking and science-as-a-process learning outcomes.

It is also worth noting that LCT more closely mimics the scientific process than traditional lecture. It treats the subject as something to be explored by the students (under the guidance of a teacher), rather than as a more-or-less closed body of knowledge to be transferred. It provides us as teachers with more authentic opportunities to bring (our own) research and research processes into the teaching and the learning environment (teaching–research nexus). This is of course provided that they are discussed at a level appropriate to the course and that the discussion serves a pedagogical purpose (e.g., aimed at motivating students, building rapport by showing your own enthusiasm for the subject, aligned with a particular learning objective, etc.). Bringing in the creativity of research and the sense of wonder we feel for our research into class makes the course material more relatable than when it is presented simply as a body of knowledge. It also provides an opportunity to show how, as professionals in the field, we deal with questions we do not know the answer to, or cases where the knowledge and understanding of a (sub)field is rapidly changing (e.g., the many surprising results in the last two decades and the many questions remaining around exoplanets), and that scientific knowledge is constantly evolving.

1.7 Learner-centered Teaching as a Means to an End: The Importance of Learning Objectives and Backward Design

LCT is not a goal in and of itself. Rather, it is the means to an end: to support and promote better student engagement and student learning. LCT informs the three-step process of constructive alignment (e.g., Biggs & Tang 2007) or backward design, as it is more commonly referred to in the U.S. Constructive alignment starts with the learning objectives, works backwards to assessments, and then the teaching and learning activities. In our work with faculty, we ask three questions:
1. What do the students need to know or be able to do at the end of the course/lecture/lab? [learning objectives]
   a. Bonus question: Are your learning objectives appropriate to your target audience?
2. What question can I ask for which an answer would satisfy me that the student has met that outcome? [assessment]
3. For me to be able to ask that question, what needs to happen in the class? What do I need to do as a teacher, and what do students need to do? [teaching and learning activities]

Activities only make sense if they are linked to the learning objectives of the course. Unless they serve a clearly identified pedagogical purpose, they are likely to fall flat as students (and faculty) do not really know why they are doing them. Formulating good intended learning outcomes is not as easy as many people think it is. In our experience, a first attempt often results in something like "students should understand," followed by a laundry list of topic and concepts. It is important to look at the target audience and the course in its relation to the program of study (mandatory, elective, general education, etc.). Using SMART (Specific, Measurable, Achievable, Relevant, Time-bound) strategies and taxonomies such as Bloom's (Bloom et al. 1956; Anderson & Krathwohl 2001) can help create intended learning outcomes that are realistic, achievable, and measurable. Backward design is discussed in further detail in Chapter 2.

1.8 Setting up Learner-centered Teaching in Your Class

Setting up a learner-centered classroom, online experience, or other learning environment can be a very rewarding experience. However, there are several traps along the route that are best avoided. The most common ones are
- trying to do too much at once,
- not getting student buy-in, and
- not getting teaching team buy-in.

1.8.1 Trying to Do Too Much at Once

It can be very tempting, at least at first, to try and start with a clean slate. Throw out the old, and in with the new! This approach works well if you have a lot of time to spare, know exactly what you are doing, and/or have access to considerable teaching support resources. One of us was involved in a project in the past to support one professor who wanted to do a full, radical overhaul of his introductory astronomy course (Brogt 2007b). While it was ultimately quite successful, it required substantial teaching support resources (two teaching assistants/staff developers) during the semester. These resources are not typically available at these levels or sustainable long term. An additional risk with radical overhauls is simply that there are too many free parameters. It will be difficult, if not impossible, to pinpoint causes for success or failure, meaning you may succeed or fail in the implementation without knowing how or why. Consequently, an evolutionary approach to implementing LCT is typically preferred. This will allow you to spread the teaching design over several semesters and make small incremental changes that you can evaluate one by one. Another advantage is that you get more accustomed to the LCT approach, so it becomes part of your repertoire of routine teaching, meaning that you will be less dependent on external support for your teaching (e.g., staff developers), and that there is a higher likelihood of self-sustained teaching change.

A similar argument can be made for implementing many (highly) technological and multimedia innovations in class. For those of us who remember the introduction of PowerPoint in the 1990s and the tendency among presentation makers to use every single bell and whistle available, just because something is possible does not mean it is necessarily a good idea. As a rule of thumb, all activities in class should serve a clear pedagogical purpose. As staff developers, we often ask our colleagues to explain "why this particular activity, in this format, at this place and time in the lecture/course?" LCT can be, but does not have to be, high tech. It simply depends on the goals you are trying to achieve.

1.8.2 Not Getting Student Buy-in

Students come to our classes, in particular in their first year, with a certain set of expectations on how courses should be run that may or may not conform to the reality of how the courses are actually run. Students' expectations naturally are based on their previous experiences in education. LCT requires students to do more in class than passively sitting and absorbing information for later regurgitation (commonly referred to as the "hidden contract"; see e.g., Slater 2003). However, this is precisely the teaching mode that students (a) are most familiar with and (b) have been successful in (or they would not be at college). Students will be (understandably) reluctant to engage in teaching and learning activities that are unfamiliar to them in the sense that it may not be clear how those activities will lead to a successful outcome (e.g., passing the course, getting a high grade).

For LCT to get buy-in from students, encourage them to engage, and change their behavior, two things need to be in place:

1. A clear research-based rationale for what you are doing. It has to be clear to students that the learner-centered approach used in the class is there for a purpose, namely to help them understand the material better and help them succeed in the course.
2. A clear "path to success." When the students know what it is they need to do to succeed in the class, they will be more likely to engage, rather than spending time and energy trying to figure out the new "rules of the game".

Critical to student buy-in is alignment between teaching and the assessments (the second piece of backward design). We can use all the learner-centered techniques we want and emphasize the importance of conceptual thinking, but if we then turn around and give a declarative knowledge-based assessment, students will (a) quickly see the misalignment between the professed relevance and assessed material, (b) feel rightfully misled, and (c) will not engage in teaching and learning activities that are not clearly advantageous to their performance on the assessment.

1.8.3 Not Getting Teaching Team Buy-in

Team buy-in has two facets to it. The first is the team teaching the course (professors, teaching assistants, lab personnel, learning assistants). It is critical that (at least publicly) all members of the teaching team are on board with LCT and are actively engaged in them in class. If this is not the case, then students can drive wedges between teaching team members, which threatens the overall classroom climate and inhibits achieving the goals for the course. Of particular relevance is the training of teaching assistants and ensuring that they are on board, take it seriously, are trained in the appropriate use of the approach, and act accordingly.

The second facet of the team is the broader department out of which the course is being taught. Being the single course that uses LCT principles is not a problem when you are teaching a non-science-major, non-advancing course. It can become a problem in larger programs of study, where the same students go through a suite of courses in the department. That makes the LCT course the odd one out, with an increased likelihood of student complaints (as it is the only course that requires them to do things differently). This is not an easy situation to solve. Student buy-in can be increased somewhat by using the same two techniques listed above, but you are likely to face increased scrutiny. Ultimately though, student performance in the course should provide good data (assuming appropriate alignment between teaching and assessment, of course) on the validity of the LCT techniques used. For example, in a study replicating the Carl Wieman Science Education Initiative (see www.cwsei.ubc.ca) in the New Zealand educational system, Kennedy et al. (2013) reported about a faculty member who was not himself entirely on board with LCT, but had nonetheless agreed to participate in the study. He ultimately became convinced about the validity of LCT after he had seen the positive impacts on student performance in his class.

1.9 Promoting the Use of Backward Design and Learner-centered Teaching at the Department Level

LCT is at its most powerful when it is done system-wide (e.g., a whole department). To make the strategic shift to department-wide implementation of LCT requires leadership at all levels, from individual teaching staff to the head of department (or even dean). For people in managerial/administrative positions like the head of department, this can be a delicate balancing act between faculty members' individual academic freedom, strategic priorities of the institution (e.g., student retention), resource (time and otherwise) investment and return on investment, and staff workload management. This balancing act is not always that visible to individual teaching staff, but it is good to be aware of these "other variables in the equation" as part of a constructive conversation about LCT at the department level. In the remainder of this section, we opted to address the head of department directly as the person in the department with formal leadership responsibilities. This is not meant to suggest that LCT at the department level is a top-down affair; most successful implementations we have been involved in as faculty developers and those reported in the educational change literature had a bottom-up as well as a top-down component, and were highly collegial in nature.

If you are a head of department, what are the merits and drawbacks of promoting and supporting the use of LCT among your teaching staff and in the courses in your department? We would argue that any department-wide discussion on the use of LCT is more meaningful within a broader (and longer-term) discussion about the department's course offerings and teaching-related objectives. In that way, LCT becomes part of a broader strategic discussion and as a means to an end, rather than an end in and of itself. We think such a discussion is also best held in conjunction with a strategy to promote backward-design principles consistently in a department. Backward design can then be used as a springboard for a discussion about LCT in a department, as devising learning and teaching activities is the final stage in the backward-design process.

1.9.1 Advantage of Backward Design across a Program of Study

Using backward design at the program level can be a very interesting and revealing exercise. More often than not, teaching staff are (understandably) focused on their own courses and do not typically look at what is happening in other courses. This means that over time, curricular overlaps, gaps, and mismatches will naturally develop. From a program cohesion point of view, it is thus advantageous to go through a (verification of the) backward-design exercise for all courses. While this process will take some time to complete, in particular in a program with a high level of student choice through elective courses, tidying up the various loose ends you will typically encounter makes for a stronger program overall, increased student experience, and better student progression/retention in the program. It will also come in handy during departmental visitations, accreditations, and other formal review processes.

1.9.2 Advantages of Backward Design at the Course Level

At the individual course level, promoting backward-design principles have three other advantages for a department. The first is that by an agreed-upon set of outcomes, the student experience in different sections of the same course will be more equitable. The individual sections may still vary based on individual teaching staff member's teaching style and academic freedom, but the outcomes should be about the same when agreed upon by all colleagues teaching the course. The second advantage from a workload and sabbatical/leave management perspective is that backward design, with clear and agreed-upon outcomes, makes portability of a course from one colleague to the next easier. Most of us have been in the situation where we "inherited" a course, with all its materials, and had no clue where to start. The learning objectives for the course will be a guide in that case, making it easier to map individual lectures/tutorials to the course outcomes, and save considerable time and stress. The third advantage is that backward design, and the various aligned teaching and learning activities, makes it easier to identify resource needs and provide a clearer justification for resource expenses (e.g., field trips).

1.9.3 Advantages of Promoting Learner-centered Teaching Techniques across a Program of Study and in Individual Courses

Each department will have its cast of characters, from gung-ho early adopters to skeptics. For LCT to be successful at the department level, it is important that it becomes normalized, i.e., the "this is just the way we work in this department" attitude among the teaching staff, and with no single course being the "odd one out." A single course using LCT is almost always considered the "odd one out," with increased student complaints about the teaching as a result. Once a whole department moves into the direction of LCT, the number of student complaints should get lower (it is the "new normal"), while at the same time seeing increased student performance, student experience, and subsequent retention in the program.

The key to normalizing LCT is to have your best teachers, who are willing and able to use LCT, teach the largest classes, bringing the "new normal" to as many students as possible, creating an expectation for LCT in follow-on courses.

1.9.4 The Head of Department as Role Model and Resource Provider

As the head of department, you have a role model function for your staff, in particular junior staff. It is important to walk the talk yourself and lead by example. Your staff will see what you truly value through your actions. Proclaiming the importance of LCT rings hollow if you are not on the journey yourself. That makes generating buy-in from your staff and colleagues much more difficult. Talking about the importance of LCT and even providing support resources are not as effective as doing that, while also engaging in LCT yourself (and sharing your journey with your colleagues).

Your priorities also come through in where and how you decide to spend the (limited) teaching support resources of the department. While LCT does not have to be resource intensive in itself, the development, the alignment with learning objectives and assessments, and getting comfortable using them take time. While this time is typically (but not always) recouped later through increased efficiencies and reduced teaching preparation time, it does provide a significant up-front investment. Recognizing this and providing workload relief for teaching staff where possible at the development stages of implementing LCT will go quite a way to generating the necessary buy-in and creating (self-initiated and sustained) engagement, rather than (performance-management-driven) compliance behavior.

For staff who have limited teaching experience and/or limited training in teaching (and most academics are hired for their content expertise, rather than their teaching expertise; see, e.g., Walczyk et al. 2007), having access to pedagogical support and other resources is critical. Engaging the equivalent of a teaching and learning center at your institution (if present) would be highly advisable. There is a myriad of resources on LCT available, of varying quality. The teaching and learning center can help you locate the (research-based) resources that would be helpful for your particular context (there are no one-size-fits-all solutions), and advise you on their use.

1.10 Evaluating Learner-centered Teaching

A good implementation of LCT is not complete without a proper evaluation to determine the effects of LCT on various constituents (students, faculty, department, etc.). Depending on the type of intervention you wish to evaluate, a variety of quantitative or qualitative research methodologies can be used. This chapter is not the place to discuss this in detail, though we would caution against relying solely on quantitative and/or statistical data. The methodology and data collection that are appropriate depend on the question you are asking, the size of the constituent populations, and the type of intervention you are evaluating, among other things. In our experience working with faculty, we have seen numerous cases where faculty insisted on using surveys and statistics (because they were reasonably comfortable with those), which when used would have led to invalid or uninterpretable results. We would strongly recommend working with colleagues with a background in educational or social science research design if you have never done this type of work before (for example in the Teaching and Learning Center, if you have one on campus). For a valid evaluation, it is important to not have changed too much in one go, as it will give you too many free parameters to make meaningful causal attributions, as mentioned earlier. Should you wish to go beyond purely internal use of these data for teaching improvement purposes and publicize the results (which is a broader term than publish, and includes conferences, posters, reports, etc.), ethics approval prior to any data collection is required. In particular, when you are investigating classes/students you are responsible for as a teacher, very careful consideration needs to be given to the ethical dimensions of the research design to ensure informed and voluntary consent from the students, and to comply with legal requirements (see, e.g., Antonellis et al. 2012; Brogt et al. 2008, Section 3.3).

1.11 Frequently Asked Questions about Learner-centered Teaching and Its Implementation

In this last section, we list and answer common questions about LCT that we have fielded both as faculty developers and from colleagues teaching astronomy over the years.

1. If I use a LCT approach, do I have to stop lecturing?
2. Doesn't LCT result in the "dumbing down" of content?
3. How can I cover all my material if I use LCT?
4. Will LCT only work for non-majors, or also for majors?
5. Will LCT work with a mathematically based course?
6. My students hate group work; how do I get them to do it?
7. Will LCT work in a large enrollment class?
8. How do I find time to design learner-centered activities?
9. Is LCT academically rigorous?

1. If I use an LCT approach, do I have to stop lecturing?

LCT is about using the appropriate teaching practice in a given context, aimed at optimizing student learning. The literature is clear that students tend to learn better using interactive techniques. That does not mean, though, that there is no place for a "traditional, stand-and-deliver" lecture in courses. In terms of information delivery, the lecture is a perfectly appropriate vehicle. Given the economy of scale and the financial constraints most institutions find themselves in, the lecture is not going to disappear any time soon. The encouragement we give to faculty as faculty developers is to explore ways in which the lecture can be made more interactive, and make informed and conscious decisions on what sort of teaching is most appropriate to achieve the goals for the lecture/class session or course. In our experience, relatively small changes in the lecture format, in particular around question-asking techniques, can have a strong positive impact on the learning environment.

2. Doesn't LCT result in the "dumbing down" of content?

LCT tends to result in higher outcomes in terms of student learning than traditional teacher-centered instruction on a variety of well-validated and standardized diagnostic tests (e.g., Hake 1998). This is in part due to the fact that LCT forces students to process and apply the course material. As such, they are actively developing their own, and more expert-like, mental models of the concepts. LCT can (and should) still be intellectually challenging for students, and it does not mean or imply hand-holding of students.

3. How can I cover all my material if I use LCT?

Learner-centered techniques take more time than traditional lecture-only instruction. However, as we argued in this chapter, LCT is a means to an end within a backward-design framework. The learning objectives are the goal, and the assessments and teaching and learning activities the means by which we endeavor to help students achieve those goals. This is different from a focus on content coverage, which is how a lot of course design is still done today. Just because something is mentioned in a lecture does not imply that it is "taught," nor does it follow that it will then be "learned." As one colleague once questioned in a research talk, "are you really teaching if no one is learning?" If you are teaching the non-science-major, non-advancing courses, it is particularly instructive to review your learning objectives. Content coverage is not necessarily the main objective of such courses. For example, making students aware of how the scientific process works in general (and how that applies to astronomy) or helping students overcome math and science anxiety might be equally relevant goals for such courses (Dokter 2008; Brogt 2009).

4. Will LCT only work for non-majors, or also for majors?

LCT is a means to an end, namely to help students achieve the learning objectives for the course. Research has consistently shown LCT to lead to higher student performance. This is true for non-major students, major students, and graduate students. LCT is based on our understanding of how humans learn, and as such is not dependent on major or stage of learning.

5. Will LCT work with a mathematically based course?

LCT focuses on matching teaching with how humans learn. Consequently, the topic or concepts to be learned do not matter for the overall validity of LCT. LCT approaches have been validated not only in astronomy and science fields, but also in mathematics courses required for physics and astronomy majors (e.g., linear algebra, differential equations).

6. My students hate group work; how do I get them to do it?

Group work is one particular LCT technique. Research has shown that students learn more in (well-functioning) groups (see e.g., Johnson et al. 2014; Dohaney et al. 2012). Most of the issues around group work tend to be around group functionality and perceptions of unfairness (people not pulling their weight), or other issues where students perceive to be not fully in control over the outcomes (grades). While these can be quite serious concerns (in particular for those students who wish to enter limited-entry programs that have GPA targets), at the core those are logistical and implementation issues. There are a number of ways in which those can be addressed, including choice of group members, group collaboration as part of the grade, or peer review of effort. On a very practical level though, students will spend most of their careers working in (interdisciplinary) teams they do not necessarily get to pick, so learning how to navigate group dynamics is a fundamental employability skill.

7. Will LCT work in a large enrollment class?

LCT is not necessarily dependent on class size. Particular teaching techniques may work better or worse in classes of different sizes or may require a slightly different logistical setup, so it is a matter of picking the right techniques for the size of the class. However, the underlying idea of LCT remains. LCT approaches have been validated across a variety of course sizes, up to 250 students and beyond as discussed in other chapters. Most resources on LCT will provide you with some advice on how to implement it in your class, and what techniques might work well depending on the size and format of your class.

8. How do I find time to design learner-centered activities?

Designing your own activities takes time, expertise, and experience. The question to ask yourself is whether you have the time to invest and the necessary expertise to do it properly to the benefit of your students. There is little point trying to reinvent the wheel, and oftentimes there are perfectly serviceable wheels to be found that can be adapted to your needs.

There are numerous resources available on LCT techniques. The following chapters in this book provide samples of such techniques. Many of those are reasonably "off the shelf," and often come with suggestions on how to implement them in your class. In other cases, a consultation with a faculty developer or instructional designer (usually located in a Teaching and Learning Center) might be a good starting point. In case you do want to design your own, we strongly recommend working with experienced others the first time around. That will help you avoid some of the more common design and implementation problems.

9. Is LCT academically rigorous?

One commonly heard argument against LCT is that it is not as "rigorous" as traditional, content-focused teaching. As one colleague of ours, teaching a course for non-science majors, once mentioned (facetiously): "how can you reach salvation if you don't know about the forbidden oxygen transitions in planetary nebulae?" The question however is what exactly is meant by "rigor." Often in astronomy this appears to be a focus on content (facts and concepts), the use of mathematics, the language of science, and the mathematical relations between concepts. The question is whether such a conceptualization of rigor is appropriate in all circumstances. Brogt & Draeger (2015) used the definition of academic rigor by Draeger et al. (2013), which states that a course can be considered academically rigorous if it involves (a) active engagement, (b) higher-order thinking, (c) meaningful content, and (d) high expectations. They concluded that introductory astronomy classes can be considered rigorous in that sense, provided that expectations, goals, assessments, and curriculum are properly aligned.

References

American Association of Colleges and Universities 2015, Committing to Equity and Inclusive Excellence: A Campus Guide for Self-study and Planning (Washington, DC: Association of American Colleges and Universities)

Anderson, L. W., & Krathwohl, D. R. 2001, A Taxonomy for Learning, Teaching, and Assessing: A Revision of Bloom's Taxonomy of Educational Objectives (New York: Longman)

Angelo, T. A., & Cross, K. P. 1993, Classroom Assessment Techniques: A Handbook for College Teachers (San Francisco, CA: Jossey-Bass)

Antonellis, J. C. 2013, PhD thesis, Univ. Arizona

Antonellis, J. C., Brogt, E., Buxner, S. R., Dokter, E. F. C., & Foster, T. 2012, in Reviews in PER Volume 2: Getting Started in Physics Education Research, ed. C. Henderson, & K. A. Harper

(College Park, MD: American Association of Physics Teachers) http://www.per-central.org/items/detail.cfm?ID=11757

Bailey, J. 2011, Astronomy Education Research: Developmental History of the Field and Summary of the Literature, https://sites.nationalacademies.org/cs/groups/dbassesite/documents/webpage/dbasse_168276.pdf

Bandura, A. 2010, in The Corsini Encyclopedia of Psychology, ed. I. B. Weiner, & W. E. Craighead (4th ed.; Hoboken, NJ: Wiley)

Biggs, J. B., & Tang, C. 2007, Teaching for Quality Learning at University (3rd ed.; Maidenhead: McGraw Hill Education & Open University Press)

Bloom, B. S., Engelhart, M. D., Furst, E. J., Hill, W. H., & Krathwohl, D. R. 1956, Taxonomy of Educational Objectives: The Classification of Educational Goals. Handbook I: Cognitive Domain (New York: David McKay)

Blumberg, P. 2016, College Teaching, 64, 194

Brogt, E. 2007a, AEdRv, 6, 50

Brogt, E. 2007b, AEdRv, 6, 20

Brogt, E. 2009, PhD thesis, Univ. Arizona

Brogt, E., & Draeger, J. 2015, Journal of General Education, 64, 14

Brogt, E., Foster, T., Dokter, E., Buxner, S., & Antonellis, J. 2008, AEdRv, 7, 57

Cajete, G. 1994, Look to the Mountain: An Ecology of Indigenous Education (Durango, CO: Kivaki Press)

CAST 2018, Universal Design for Learning Guidelines version 2.2, http://udlguidelines.cast.org

Clark, D. B., Tanner-Smith, E. E., & Killingsworth, S. S. 2016, Review of Educational Research, 86, 79

Considine, J. R., Mihalick, J. E., Mogi-Hein, Y. R., Penick-Parks, M. W., & Van Auken, P. M. 2017, New Directions for Teaching and Learning, 151, 171

Dohaney, J., Brogt, E., & Kennedy, B. 2012, JGeEd, 60, 21

Dokter, E. F. C. 2008, PhD thesis, Univ. Arizona

Draeger, J., del Prado Hill, P., Hunter, L. R., & Mahler, R. 2013, Innovative Higher Education, 38, 267

Dweck, C. S. 2006, Mindset (New York: Random House)

Freeman, S., Eddy, S. L., McDonough, M., et al. 2014, PNAS, 111, 8410

Gay, G. 2000, Culturally Responsive Teaching: Theory, Research, and Practice (New York: Teachers College Press)

Hake, R. R. 1998, AmJPh, 66, 64

Holbrook, J., Medupe, R. T., & Urama, J. O. 2008, African Cultural Astronomy - Current Archeoastronomy and Ethnoastronomy in Africa (Berlin: Springer)

Hora, M. T., Oleson, A., & Ferrare, J. J. 2013, Teaching Dimensions Observation Protocol (TDOP) User's Manual (Madison, WI: Wisconsin Center for Education Research, University of Wisconsin–Madison)

Johns, M., Schmader, T., & Martens, A. 2005, Psychological Science, 16, 175

Johnson, D. W., Johnson, R. T., & Smith, K. A. 2014, Journal on Excellence in College Teaching, 25, 85

Kennedy, B., Brogt, E., Jordens, Z., et al. 2013, Transforming Tertiary Science Education: Improving Learning during Lectures (Wellington: Ako Aotearoa, National Centre for Tertiary Teaching Excellence)

Kober, N. 2015, Reaching Students: What Research Says about Effective Instruction in Undergraduate Science and Engineering (Washington, DC: National Academies Press)

Kuhn, T. S. 2012, The Structure of Scientific Revolutions: 50th Anniversary Edition (4th ed.; Chicago, IL: Univ. Chicago Press)

Lazowski, R. A., & Hulleman, C. S. 2016, Review of Educational Research, 86, 602–40

Legon, R. 2015, American Journal of Distance Education, 29, 166

Mallow, J. V. 1986, Science Anxiety: Fear of Science and How to Overcome It (Rev. ed.; Clearwater, FL: H&H Publications)

Meyer, A., Rose, D. H., & Gordon, D. 2014, Universal Design for Learning: Theory and Practice (Wakefield, MA: CAST, Inc.)

National Academies of Sciences, Engineering, and Medicine 2018, How People Learn II: Learners, Contexts, and Cultures (Washington, DC: National Academies Press)

National Research Council 2000, How People Learn: Brain, Mind, Experience, and School, Expanded Edition, ed. J. D. Bransford, A. L. Brown, & R. R. Cocking (Washington, DC: National Academies Press)

National Research Council 2001, Knowing What Students Know: The Science and Design of Educational Assessment, ed. J. Pelligrino, N. Chudowsky, & R. Glaser (Washington, DC: National Academies Press)

National Research Council 2012, Discipline-based Education Research: Understanding and Improving Learning in Undergraduate Science and Engineering, ed. S. R. Singer, N. R. Nielsen, & H. A. Schweingruber (Washington, DC: National Academies Press)

Ong, M., Smith, J. M., & Ko, L.T. 2018, JRScT, 55, 206

Osborne, J. W., & Jones, B. D. 2011, Educational Psychology Review, 23, 131

Palmer, M. S., Bach, D. J., & Streifer, A. C. 2014, To Improve the Academy, 33, 14

Piburn, M., & Sawada, D. 2000, Reformed Teaching Observation Protocol (RTOP): Reference Manual, Arizona Collaborative for Excellence in the Preparation of Teachers (ACEPT), Technical Report, IN00-3

Pintrich, P. R. 2003, Journal of Educational Psychology, 95, 667

Posner, G. J., Strike, K. A., Hewson, P. W., & Gertzog, W. A. 1982, SciEd, 66, 211

Prather, E. E., Rudolph, A. L., Brissenden, G., & Schlingman, W. M. 2009, AmJPh, 77, 320

Slater, T. F. 2003, PhTea, 41, 437

Smith, M., Jones, F., Gilbert, S., & Wieman, C. 2013, CBE-Life Sciences Education, 12, 618

Springer, L., Stanne, M. E., & Donovan, S. S. 1999, Review of Educational Research, 69, 21

Story, M. F., Mueller, J. L., & Mace, R. L. 1998, The Universal Design File: Designing for People of all Ages and Abilities (Revised ed.; Raleigh, NC: North Carolina State Univ.) https://eric.ed.gov/?id=ED460554

Sue, D., Capolidupo, C. M., Torino, G. C., et al. 2007, American Psychologist, 62, 271

Tobias, S. 1978, Overcoming Math Anxiety (New York: Norton)

Udo, M. K., Ramsey, G. P., & Mallow, J. V. 2004, JSEdT, 13, 435

Walczyk, J. J., Ramsey, L. L., & Zha, P. 2007, JRScT, 44, 85

Weimer, M. 2013, Learner-Centered Teaching: Five Key Changes to Practice (2nd ed.; San Francisco, CA: Jossey-Bass)

Williams, D. A., Berger, J. B., & McClendon, S. A. 2005, Toward a Model of Inclusive Excellence and Change in Post-secondary Institutions (Washington, DC: Association of American Colleges & Universities) https://www.aacu.org/sites/default/files/files/mei/williams_et_al.pdf

Astronomy Education, Volume 1
Evidence-based instruction for introductory courses
Chris Impey and Sanlyn Buxner

Chapter 2

Effective Course Design

Adrienne J Gauthier

This workshop-in-a-box style chapter will guide instructors and education professionals through an integrated course design method. What will students know and be able to do with that knowledge by the end of the learning experience? How will you know that they are successful and help them monitor their progress along the way? What will students be doing, practicing, and experiencing while learning? You will answer these questions and more by exploring resources, brainstorming, writing reflections, and completing worksheets. This chapter has a tangible outcome—that you walk away with the instructional framework for at least one course goal. Find a colleague to go through the adventure with you, and you will have built-in feedback every step of the way. Let's get started!

Learning Objectives

By the end of this chapter, you will be able to
- discuss the benefits and challenges of using a structured course design method,
- brainstorm and describe factors that influence the learner and the learning environment,
- describe big-picture course goals and questions that will have enduring meaning and relevance for learners,
- articulate descriptive, realistic, and measurable learning objectives for your learners,
- discover and align assessment strategies and feedback loops between you, your learners, themselves, and the content,
- discover and align learning activities and experiences that engage the learner and help them successfully meet the learning goals and objectives, and
- communicate the flow and alignment of your course with learners and colleagues.

2.1 Introduction

Welcome to a task-oriented chapter on the basics of course design, a "workshop-in-a-box" experience that you can complete at your own pace. My hope is that you will walk away with a solid start on designing a new course or taking a fresh look at a course you have taught before. You will be asked to complete reflections and worksheets that mimic an introductory course design workshop series or an individual consultation between a professor and an instructional (or learning) designer.

You will not be asked to design your entire course in this chapter; instead, you will write one course goal and drill down into a unit or set of topics. Once you can see the entirety of the process through focusing on one course goal, you can then go back and work more effectively on your whole course. You will skim the surface of setting learning goals and objectives, designing assessments, creating feedback strategies, and developing learning activities. You will be provided with additional resources that include specific activities, ways to provide content to students, how to build effective assessments, and deeper information on how people learn. Take from this chapter what you will and use the ideas however they fit best for your course, students, and teaching philosophy.

Why devote the time and energy to a structured course design process? Summarized from the voices of past workshop participants, *the course design process has helped me:*
- have a clear vision of the course from the start,
- decide what to keep or remove from an overstuffed and content-heavy course,
- figure out where active learning would work best,
- find the flow between classes and topics,
- feel like everything in the course has intention and purpose, which made the learning better and deeper,
- gain clarity in the learning objectives and course goals, which made figuring out assessments easier, and
- communicate the rigor and robustness of the course to other professors, the department, and institution.

Your students will also have some major benefits. When the course plan is explicitly shared with students on your course website or in class, they not only know what you expect of them but have a vision for how to get there. They will be able to see the relevance in what you are asking them to do and how one assignment flows into the next and helps them learn.

Types of activities to work through:
- Reflect: Strategically placed reflection prompts help prep you for a topic by revealing what you already think, feel, and know. Use whatever you like to complete these prompts—pen and paper, typing into a document, or audio recording your responses.
- Task: You will be asked to complete the steps of course design in an organized and systematic way. The tasks are intended to be done in order

as presented. Most tasks refer to a guiding worksheet, while others might include brainstorming and exploring external resources.
- Worksheets: Worksheets can help guide and organize your work. Use whatever method works best for you as you go through the steps. You can download all worksheets (.docx and .pdf) from the Course Design Workshop companion site: https://sites.google.com/view/cdw-companion.

Before you dig into this chapter, please consider the following:
- Working through the main steps in this chapter and focusing on one course goal could take you 10–15 hours, spread over a week or two. However, breezing through in more of a brainstorming and draft mode will take less time (4–6 hours) and give you a broad overview of the process.
- Find your teaching and learning center at your campus, or another group that might have instructional designers, learning designers, course designers, or faculty developers. Having someone to help guide you through the course design process or give feedback on what you are working on is invaluable.
- Recruit colleagues to join you in this adventure! They do not need to be in your department or your institution, but they should be working on a course. You can work through this chapter together and have frequent feedback from a peer.
- Timing! A structured course design method takes a lot of time, energy, and iteration. Please consider your available time before embarking on a full course design project and how far before the term you will need to start.

> *Reflect.*
>
> Please outline your own steps and process when you are creating a new course or getting ready to teach. For the reflections, use whatever you have available to you—computer, pen, and paper, etc. Be sure to save your notes as you will be asked to refer to them throughout the chapter.

2.2 What is Your Teaching and Learning Philosophy?

Please take a moment to think about your approach to teaching and learning. In this online Faculty Focus article,[1] Haave (2014) asks a few questions that will help you examine your teaching and learning philosophy. Do you know where you fall on the spectrum of teacher-centric to learner-centric environments? Later, you will be asked to answer Haave's questions.

This chapter reflects a learner-centered perspective, which means that it focuses on what you want the learners to be able to do, understand, and experience, not what you (the instructor) will be doing or teaching. You will be asked to consider what your students will need in order to meet the learning goals of the course, and

---
[1] https://www.facultyfocus.com/articles/philosophy-of-teaching/six-questions-will-bring-teaching-philosophy-focus/.

then design your course with those needs in mind. Weimer (2012) outlines how an instructor might embody learner-centered teaching strategies. Please read this Teaching Professor blog post[2] to get more in-depth examples and explanations.

Weimer (2012) describes the effective teaching strategies of learner-centered teaching as follows:
1. ... engages students in the hard, messy work of learning,
2. ... includes explicit skill instruction,
3. ... encourages students to reflect on what they are learning and how they are learning it,
4. ... motivates students by giving them some control over learning processes, and
5. ... encourages collaboration

Reflect.

What are some learner-centered things you already do in your teaching? What are you asking the students to do to help them learn? How are they interacting with the course content and each other?

Task.

Investigate your teaching philosophy by completing *Worksheet 1: Teaching Philosophy*. Download the worksheets from here: https://sites.google.com/view/cdw-companion.

2.3 Course Design Overview

The course design method in this "workshop" can be guided by these questions:
- What will the learner know and be able to do with that knowledge by the end of the learning experience?
- How will they (and I) know what they are able to do (and not yet do)?
- What will they be doing, practicing, and experiencing while learning?
- How can I communicate my course plan to learners in an approachable way?

You will aim to answer these questions while participating in the activities in this chapter. Learning design consultations with instructors can take many avenues and are full of questions and reflections to help the instructor gain clarity and think from alternate viewpoints. Obviously, this chapter cannot replicate a one-on-one consultation; however, there are multiple opportunities presented for you to stop, take a step back, and be reflective on what you are creating. If you can find a colleague to

---

[2] https://www.teachingprofessor.com/topics/teaching-strategies/active-learning/five-characteristics-of-learner-centered-teaching/.

partner with on the work in this chapter, it would be of great value to discuss each other's course design plans.

2.3.1 Course Design Methods

This chapter relies on two popular course design models: *integrated course design* (Fink 2013) and *backward design* or Understanding by Design (Wiggins & McTighe 2008). Backward design was created for the K–12 world, is somewhat prescriptive, but has a lot to offer higher education. Integrated course design is less prescriptive, but still relies on basic principles and philosophies. A common thread between them is the focus on the learner. Figure 2.1 presents the primary principles of each method and outlines the steps in this chapter.

The starting point in Figure 2.1 is "Developing Learning Objectives." Once you are able to articulate *what the learner will be able to do*, the process pivots to "Assessing Student Learning." It might not be intuitive to think about how you might assess or evaluate students before you have come up with the learning activities. Following Fink's (2013, p. 71) advice, "creating the assessment activities first, greatly clarifies and facilitates answers to the question of what the learning activities need to be". After defining learning objectives and identifying assessment and feedback strategies, you will be asked to design activities and experiences that will help the learner practice skills, connect concepts, and think deeper about the course topics. When the assessments directly evaluate if the student has met the learning objectives, and the activities are relevant to practicing the skills and knowledge they will be assessed on, then we would say the course is *aligned*. You will work on recognizing when this is happening, how to make it happen, and how to communicate it to students.

The course design process is iterative and frequently loops back to prior elements. There can be a lot of back and forth thinking about the different aspects of the learning experience for the students, which can mean revisiting learning objectives and assessments

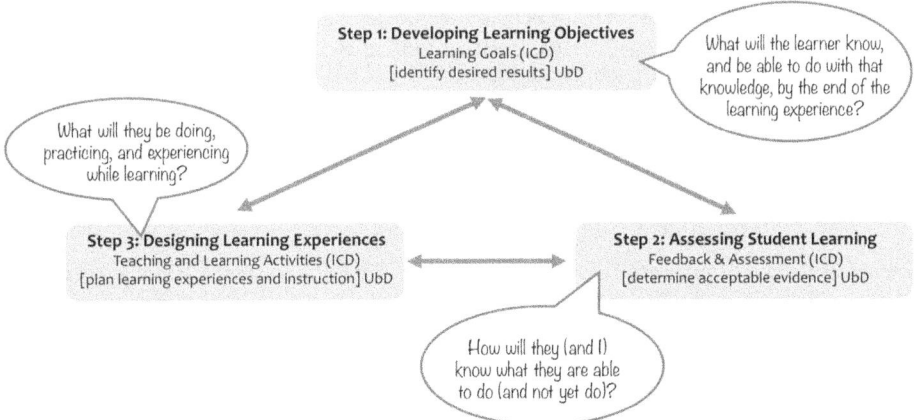

Figure 2.1. A merger of integrated course design and backward-design methods. Integrated Course Design (ICD; Fink 2013) and Understanding by Design (UdB; Wiggins & McTighe 2008) are very similar and will be the sequence followed in this chapter.

after you think they are completely designed. You might also be thinking about activities when brainstorming assessments, and as you write learning objectives, you will have ideas for both activities and assessments. When focusing on one area of the course design method, you can jot down any extraneous ideas on a sticky note for use later.

Presented below is an example from an introductory astronomy course using the course design method in this chapter. This example focuses on only one unit related to one of the course-level objectives and only shows a snippet of the learning objectives, assessments, and activities. It is not a complete unit of a course, and there are concepts and activities not shown in this brief example. There are also areas that could be improved—what catches your eye?

Example
Course: Astronomy 1 "The Universe"

Related Course-level Learning Objective: Elaborate on how astronomers "see" and study astronomical objects through multi-wavelength light, data, and theoretical models.

Unit-level Learning Objective: Create visual and text materials that will communicate information and relationships about multi-wavelength light, astronomical objects, and how we "see" the universe, suitable for a general public audience.

Topic-level Learning Objectives:
Acquiring Knowledge (low cognitive level)
- Identify the different categories of light, from low energy to high energy.
- Recall the relationships between the temperature, wavelength, energy, and frequency of electromagnetic radiation.

Assessments	Activities	Feedback
(Formative) Answer end-of-chapter questions in the online textbook website. Just in time scoring and hints.	Watch animations and videos on textbook website to learn basic concepts	Textbook website auto-graded and gives immediate feedback and hints.
(Formative) In-class polling responses	Participate in think-pair-share in-class polling activities with peers	Discussion with peers and through polling results
(Formative) Submit 'muddiest point' responses.	Reflect at the end of class.	Instructor feedback at the beginning of next class or in online video recap

Making Meaning (mid cognitive level)
- Interpret color scales in multi-wavelength imagery (Earth and astronomical).
- Compare and contrast multi-wavelength images of the Sun by relating temperature, energy, and wavelength of light in the imagery.

Assessments	Activities	Feedback
(Formative) In-class polling responses	Participate in think-pair-share in-class polling activities with peers Infrared Zoo/Everyday Objects lesson	Discussion with peers and through polling results
(Summative) Group worksheets submitted to Canvas during class	Small group work during class with multi-wavelength imagery	Discussion with peers in small groups Comments on group worksheets in Canvas

Transfer of Knowledge (high cognitive level)
- Analyze multi-wavelength images of the same astronomical object and relate detection method/telescope to the observation.

Assessments	Activities	Feedback
(Formative) Submit progress report and outline.	Team contracts/reflection points Small group work in and out of class on project	Feedback on team outline in Canvas Feedback on team dynamics
(Summative) Create a multi-media blog/news post. Graded (rubric) and final peer group feedback. Submit individual reflection.	Research objects/telescopes, work in small teams, develop narrative, create blog post	Peer feedback given back to teams. Graded via rubric with comments.

2.3.2 Course Design Prep

Before moving forward into the course design steps, please consider the Situational Factors[3] (Fink 2005a) related to your course and students. Situational factors are things like logistical details, institutional expectations, real-world relevance, nature of the content discipline, what the learners are like, and what your own teaching experiences have been (Fink 2005a). Answering these questions will be your lighthouse to guide you through designing a relevant and robust course for you, your learners, and your institution.

---

[3] https://www.ideaedu.org/Portals/0/Uploads/Documents/IDEA%20Papers/IDEA%20Papers/Idea_Paper_42.pdf.

> *Task.*
>
> Complete *Worksheet 2: Situational Factors*[4] and prep your frame of mind by thinking about qualities of the learners, learning environment, institution, and your own teaching experiences.

> *Reflect.*
>
> In the Introduction, you were asked to reflect on how you usually design a course or get ready for a term of teaching. In reviewing the course design method in Figure 2.1—in what ways is it similar to your process? What challenges do you think you might have trying out this model?

2.4 Step 1: Developing Learning Objectives

In Step 1: Developing Learning Objectives, you will brainstorm at least one overarching course goal and express the big ideas or "enduring understandings" of your course. You will write clear course-level, unit-level, and topic-level learning objectives, and sort them into categories that describe depth and rigor. This is usually the longest step in the process as this is truly the foundation of everything else in your course. It is worth the effort.

2.4.1 Big Ideas, Goals, and Questions

Have you thought about the big ideas and overarching questions of your course? You might have these written in the course description or course goals section of your syllabus. If it is a new course you are working on, take this time to brainstorm and figure out what you want the learners to ultimately take away from the experience. Wiggins & McTighe (2008) refer to these ultimate takeaways as enduring understandings. What do you want students to be able to remember a few years later? What are the broad understandings that connect pieces of course content to each other and to their lives beyond your class? It is easy to get caught up in the microtopics of a course, when the true nature of the course might have a broader context. Do you care if students remember how to classify galaxies, or do you instead want them to have a good understanding of the process of scientific discovery throughout history?

Another way to think about and phrase your course goals might be as "essential questions." Wiggins & McTighe (2013) characterize an essential question as being "open-ended…thought-provoking…intellectually engaging…higher-order thinking…important, transferable ideas…raises additional questions…requires support and justification…and recurs over time."

When creating course goals and big ideas in a learner-centered way, they are less about what you will teach students, and more about what students will be able to do, describe, answer, and understand for longer than the end of the term. Focus on what

---

[4] https://sites.google.com/view/cdw-companion/worksheets.

you want your students to understand about the content, at a deep level, and how they might connect ideas together.

If your course is part of a sequence for majors in your department, find out what the goals and objectives are for the other classes to see where your course fits into the student experience. If your course is meant to fulfill a general interest or science distributive at your institution, your long-lasting goals might not be the actual content at all. Your overarching course goal might be more about the nature of science or science and society. How does your course fit into the overall student experience at your institution?

You will be reminded throughout this chapter that course design is a highly iterative process. You might come back and change your course goals and essential questions a little (or a lot!) as you get deeper into the details of units or activities later in the chapter. You might realize that what you thought was a course goal is not really addressed. Or, you might discover other important understandings that deserve to be a course goal. Be prepared and open to discovering missed opportunities or the need to remove course content.

Example course goals and big-picture questions:
- How does the scientific understanding of our universe change over time?
- Understand different scales in the universe, from micro to macro, from DNA to large-scale structure.
- How do scientists "see" and observe the universe?
- Appreciate the different types of astronomical objects and how they show an evolving universe as astronomers look back in time.
- What does it mean when we say "telescopes are time machines"?
- How are scientists creative in their work?

Course Goals Guide.

Consider these questions as you write and review your course goals, enduring understandings, and/or essential questions. Use whichever format feels right to you.
- *Are they written in nonexpert jargon?*
    Course goals, big ideas, and central questions should be approachable to nonexperts. Survey courses might use different language from an advanced course. Take into account the background knowledge students will have coming into your course.
- *Do they describe connections between course concepts or connections to real-world (outside of class) contexts?*
    Students should clearly see how your course connects to the world around them and how it might affect their own personal worldview or life. Why should they care or be interested in your course?
- *Are they lofty or vague?*
    Sometimes, the "big picture" can come off as vague. Students should be able to read your course goals and, without too much effort, know what they will experience and get from your course.
- *Do they inspire curiosity and promote an intellectually engaging learning environment?*
    Get them curious by using active and descriptive language.

> **Task.**
>
> Use *Worksheet 3: Course Goals*[4] to think through and write out your goals and/or big-picture ideas, which will in turn focus how you work on the course design steps in this chapter.

2.4.2 Significant Learning

Now that you have some course goals in mind, take a moment to reflect on Fink's Taxonomy of Significant Learning (2013, 2005b). Fink (2013, p. 7) presents a way to think about the different types of learning that can happen in a course beyond the course content itself. Fink summarizes the teaching philosophy as "teaching should result in something others can look at and say, 'that learning experience resulted in something that is truly significant in terms of the students' lives'".

Are your course goals only about ways for students to understand and apply course content, or do your goals encourage students to make meaningful connections to the world around them? Are learners going to be highly engaged and think critically about how the content is personally relevant? Take a look at descriptions of the types of significant learning and then revisit your course goals, enduring understandings, or essential questions. Do any fall into Fink's taxonomy, or can they be modified to capture the essence of "significant learning"? If you are not ready to dive into Fink's philosophy yet, just move onto the next section on learning objectives. You might get some ideas as you move through the course design steps.

Fink's Taxonomy of Significant Learning
Fink (2005a, p. 2) states, "One important feature of this taxonomy is that each kind of learning is interactive. That is, each is able to stimulate any of the other kinds of learning. For example, "Foundational Knowledge" may stimulate "Critical Thinking," which in turn may stimulate "Connecting Ideas," encouraging one to "Learn About Oneself," etc. The intersection of these interrelated kinds of learning defines "Significant Learning," the purpose of the Integrated Design process". Fink (2005a, p. 3) describes his Taxonomy of Significant Learning as the following:

- *Foundational Knowledge.*
  What key information (facts, terms, formulae, concepts, principles, relationships, etc.) is/are important for students to understand and remember? What key ideas or perspectives are important in this course?
- *Application.*
  What kinds of thinking (critical, creative, practical) are important for students to learn? What skills are required? Should students be expected to learn how to manage complex projects?
- *Integration.*
  What connections should students recognize and make among ideas within this course? Among information, ideas, and perspectives from this course and

those in other courses or areas? Between material in this course and the students' personal, social, and/or work life?
- *Human Dimension.*
   What should students learn about themselves? What should they learn about understanding others and/or interacting with others?
- *Caring.*
   What changes/values should students adopt? Should interests be affected? Feelings? Commitments?
- *Learning How to Learn.*
   What should students learn about how to be good students in a course like this? How to learn about this specific subject? How to become a self-directed learner (developing a learning agenda and a plan for meeting it)?

2.4.3 Tutorial: Writing Learning Objectives

The language of learning objectives (LOs) inherently promotes a learner-centered philosophy. Earlier, this was described as thinking about what the learner will be able to do, which is different from what an instructor will teach. You will work on a hierarchy of LOs for your course, starting with course-level LOs. Organized below your course-level LOs will be unit-level LOs, and under those will be topic-level LOs. It might be that your course is better organized as a concept map, where multiple unit-level LOs feed into a bigger course-level LO. For courses that have a central theme, such as "the nature of science," students might visit that topic throughout the course, and various levels of LOs might look more like a tapestry.

There are a variety of tools and methods for crafting LOs so that they are clear, explicit, and easy to communicate to others. Sharing your course goals and LOs with students will make your teaching more transparent and can promote increased engagement and ownership of learning. The Eberly Center for Teaching Excellence[5] summarizes the benefits of sharing LOs with students perfectly:

> "To become self-directed learners, students must learn to (a) assess the demands of the task (in other words, the learning objectives/outcomes), (b) evaluate their own knowledge and skills, (c) plan their approach, (d) monitor their progress (which they can only do if they understand the type of knowledge they are expected to gain), and (e) adjust their strategies as needed."[6]

In this tutorial, you will use a popular cognitive learning taxonomy named Bloom's Revised Taxonomy (Anderson et al. 2001) as your main tool for articulating the levels of learning in your course. In the future, you might explore other tools or methods that are more aligned with your philosophy and course content. For

---

[5] The Educational Value of Course-level Learning Objectives/Outcomes, https://www.cmu.edu/teaching/resources/Teaching/CourseDesign/Objectives/CourseLearningObjectivesValue.pdf.
[6] See the full resource here: https://www.cmu.edu/teaching/resources/Teaching/CourseDesign/Objectives/CourseLearningObjectivesValue.pdf.

example, there is a robust taxonomy that aligns with Fink's Significant Learning (2013) in Barkley & Major (2016).

Bloom's Revised Taxonomy
What is meant by learning taxonomy? A learning taxonomy is a way of describing the complexity, depth, or level of thinking students will encounter. The categories of the taxonomy can help you gain clarity in what you are asking students to do, and if it is at the right level. Learning taxonomies are not all theory, but come with resources like action verbs to help the learning designer categorize the cognitive processes of the learner.

In Bloom's Revised Taxonomy (Anderson et al. 2001), there are six categories or levels of cognitive process. When using categorized action verbs to assist with course design, it is easy to get caught up in what cognitive level a specific verb belongs in. Though the action verb "identify" is listed in the lowest cognitive level of Bloom's in many resources, it might be that asking students to "identify" something is a higher-level task that brings together many different concepts. For example: identifying wavelengths on a typical electromagnetic spectrum chart is a "memorizing" task and fairly low level. However, identifying exoplanets in a visualization of star brightness data might require advanced understanding of variable stars, detection methods, and limitations of observations. In that case, maybe there is a better and more descriptive action verb for finding exoplanets in visualized data. How does analyze or discriminate work better in that context?

The best way to understand how Bloom's taxonomy works is to start using it, which you will do in the next section.

Level of complexity	Category	Description (Anderson et al. 2001, pp. 67–68)	Example action verbs
Lower levels of thinking and doing	Remembering	Retrieving, recognizing, and recalling relevant knowledge from long-term memory.	Identify Define List
	Understanding	Constructing meaning from oral, written, and graphic messages through interpreting...classifying, summarizing...comparing, and explaining.	Describe Explain Relate
Intermediate levels of thinking and doing	Applying	Carrying out or using a procedure through executing or implementing.	Compare Manipulate Determine
	Analyzing	Breaking material into constituent parts, determining how the parts relate to one another and to an overall structure or purpose.	Distinguish Correlate Classify

Higher levels of thinking and doing	Evaluating	Making judgements based on criteria and standards through checking and critiquing.	Predict Infer Criticize
	Creating	Putting elements together to form a coherent or functional whole; reorganizing elements into a new pattern or structure through generating, planning, or producing.	Create Hypothesize Adapt

You can find examples of Bloom's and Fink categorized verb lists in these resources:
- Vanderbilt University's Center for Teaching: https://cft.vanderbilt.edu/guides-sub-pages/blooms-taxonomy/.
- Azusa Pacific University has a posted copy of a popular verb list, original source unknown: https://www.apu.edu/live_data/files/333/blooms_taxonomy_action_verbs.pdf.
- Northeastern University's Center for Advancement in Teaching and Learning Through Research has posted an extensive verb list: http://www.northeastern.edu/nuolirc/wp-content/uploads/2018/01/Blooms-Taxonomy-Handout.pdf.
- In Barkley & Major's (2016, p. 19) *Learning Assessment Techniques* book, there is a robust verb list organized into Fink's Significant Learning Taxonomy categories.

Transform Goals into Course-level Learning Objectives
Review your course goals from *Worksheet 3: Course Goals*[4] and turn them into course-level LOs using action verbs. Course-level LOs articulate what students will be able to do at the end of your course to demonstrate what they have learned and understood. Find inspiration from your course goals and/or essential questions as you rewrite using the LO language. Course-level LOs should be the highest level of challenge where students are synthesizing, creating, and transferring application of the understandings. Also consider noncognitive domain course objectives. These are things like reflecting on worldviews or the nature of science, communicating science to different audiences, and learning how to work in teams are all wonderful noncognitive objectives and are important in creating educated global citizens.

Examples of developing course-level LOs:

Enduring understanding/essential question	Potential course-level learning objective *By the end of the course, the student will be able to*
Understand different scales in the universe, from micro to macro, from DNA to large-scale structure	Construct and communicate a mental model of various scales of the universe and how they relate to each other.

(Continued)

(Continued)

Enduring understanding/essential question	Potential course-level learning objective *By the end of the course, the student will be able to*
How do scientists "see" and observe the universe?	Elaborate on how astronomers "see" and study astronomical objects through multiwavelength light, data, and theoretical models.
What does it mean when we say, "telescopes are time machines"?	Construct a concept map of the universe, organizing astronomical objects by distance and evolutionary stages.
How are scientists creative in their work?	Discuss the importance of scientific inquiry in the context of real-world examples, what it means to be a skeptic, and how it impacts daily life.

As you write your course-level LOs, you will get ideas for how students will demonstrate their understandings to you, what they might produce or hand in, and what they might do as activities in or outside of class. Do not skip ahead; instead, use sticky notes to jot down your ideas and then set them aside for later.

You might be thinking, "so what do I do with my course goals and essential questions from Worksheet 3 now that I've rewritten them?" Keep them! Use them as your course description in your syllabus or online course site in the learning management system (Canvas, Blackboard, D2L, etc.) Your course goals are the heart of your course and will complement your newly written course-level LOs in a more narrative form.

Learning Objectives Guide.

Consider the following questions as you develop and review LOs (course level, unit level, and topic level):

1. *Do your LOs convey something about a single skill or understanding about the content?*
    Multiple skills or layers should be broken out into separate LOs. They should be able to answer *what*, *why*, and/or *how*.
2. *Do your LOs speak to an action or task?*
    LOs should use action verb language like *compare* and *contrast* or *analyze*. LOs should start with "the learner will be able to" which then implies that a verb or two will follow.
3. *Do your LOs describe specifically what the learner will be able to demonstrate?*
    The evidence of learning should be clear to anyone who reads the objective. This is what the instructor (and the learner) can assess and evaluate to know if the LO is met. Verbs like "understand," "appreciate," and "demonstrate" are vague and do not actually describe what the learner would do.
4. *Are they written in jargon-free language?*
    As novices in the subject matter, learners appreciate having approachable and understandable LOs. Introductory courses and senior-level majors' courses have different types of "novices," and so the language used would be different. Think about the audience when writing LOs. Generally, the more granular the LO (topic level versus course level), the more jargon you can use.

> *Task.*
>
> Write and review your course-level LOs using *Worksheet 4: Course-level Learning Objectives*.[4]

Unit-level Learning Objectives
The next step is to develop unit-level LOs. Unit-level LOs organize underneath the course-level LOs and are fairly high level. In some courses, topics might be broken out into themes which weave through different sections of the course over the term. If that is the case, pick a theme to work on for the rest of this chapter. As you gain clarity in the unit-level LOs, you might find yourself wanting to change the course-level LOs. Please do! This is part of the iterative course design process.

Examples:
By the end of the unit (or theme) students will be able to
- debate and defend the scientific, political, and environmental considerations for various observatories and telescopes;
- compose an explanation that will communicate what is meant by the phrase "the nature of science," that can interest, inform, and be relevant to a nonscientist/expert audience; and
- evaluate different exoplanet detection methods and relate to an online exoplanet citizen science experience.

> *Task.*
>
> Use *Worksheet 5: Unit-level Learning Objectives*[4] to outline, write, and review your unit-level LOs.

Topic-level Learning Objectives
Within each unit of your course, you might have a module or topic structure—something that lasts a few days or a week. You can even continue into more granularity by thinking about the activity or assignment level. Only go as far as you are engaged and interested to go in this "introduction to course design" experience. Even if you only write course and unit-level LOs, you are doing great and it will be a significant benefit to you and your learners.

For topic-level LOs, you will want to consider all levels of Bloom's Revised Taxonomy. There are times when learners need to first acquire the basics and be able to remember and recall content and facts. Learners will then apply those understandings to activities like solving a simple problem, where they will make meaning of what they have already learned. Sometimes, this intermediate level is as far as the complexity goes. Other times, learners will need to transfer their intermediate understanding and skill to new and complex situations in order to demonstrate mastery.

Wiggins & McTighe (2008) refer to this concept as AMT or acquiring knowledge (A), making meaning (M), and transfer (T). "A" is the lowest level, and "T" is the highest. It can be challenging to distinguish between making meaning and transfer. Think of transfer as bringing multiple ideas together in a new way or applying something in a novel context or situation.

An example of categorizing topic-level LOs as A, M, or T is a flipped course where students watch short videos prior to class in order to solve or discuss beginner- to intermediate-level problems during class. The topic-level LOs in *(A) acquiring knowledge* focus on basic knowledge that students learn from the video clips. Tasks like recalling a definition, duplicating a diagram, or matching answers to pictures fall into this category. During class, they would use the knowledge gained from the first exposure (video) to solve problems, answer conceptual questions, or discuss concepts with peers. Those would be *(M) making meaning* experiences. (M) ranges from entry-level conceptual questions through mid-level problem solving or analyzing data. *(T) Transferring* knowledge indicates the highest level of learning and usually happens near the end of a unit or after multiple concepts are learned. (T) is about synthesizing everything students have learned and directing that knowledge and understanding to a new context or project. An example of authentic transfer is to ask students in an upper-level astronomy course to design an actual observing plan for a research-grade telescope.

Examples of A, M, and T for one of our example unit-level LOs:

Unit-level LO: Evaluate different exoplanet detection methods and relate them to an online exoplanet citizen science experience.

A, M, T level	LO
(A) Acquiring knowledge	Describe different types of extrasolar planets.
(A) Acquiring knowledge	Match the type of extrasolar planet observation to a telescope facility.
(M) Making meaning	Compare and contrast the methods that scientists use to search for and observe extrasolar planets.
(M) Making meaning	Relate the habitable zone of an exoplanet system to our own solar system.
(T) Transfer	Distinguish between an observation of an extrasolar planet and various variable stars while presenting reasons for the findings.

> *Task.*
>
> Use *Worksheet 6: Topic-level Learning Objectives*[4] to outline, write, and review topic-level LOs. As you review, categorize each LO as A, M, or T.

Congratulations! You have completed Step 1!
Take a break from this chapter. Let Step 1 slosh around a bit in your brain. Review the worksheets, make any changes, or include additional ideas, and then continue on with Step 2 in a few days.

2.5 Step 2: Assessing Student Learning

In Step 2: Assessing Student Learning, you will review different types of assessment, think about the importance of feedback, research and find assessment methods, and check that the assessment strategies align with your LOs. Designing opportunities for assessment and feedback will help you and your students determine their progress toward, and success in meeting, your LOs.

> *Reflect.*
>
> Brainstorm a list of answers to this question, "what are assessments good for and/or used for?" Challenge yourself to list at least five things from the teacher perspective and then five things from the student perspective. Let none of your items be "for a grade."

2.5.1 Types of Assessment

Assessment of student learning should give both the instructor and the learner useful information on the progress toward meeting the LOs. Two types of assessment are *summative assessment* and *formative assessment*. In a summative assessment task, students are asked to demonstrate mastery of the LOs, usually at the end of a unit or as the final product of the course. Instructors will evaluate the level to which the student succeeds and might assign a grade or performance score. Common summative assessments are final exams, term projects, or the final submission of a paper. More innovative summative assessments could be creating multimedia projects, fabricating something that can help teach others, or reporting on a level-appropriate research project. It is the summary of what the student learned and experienced, and what they can show you they can now do.

The purpose of formative assessment is to monitor the progress of learning and give an opportunity for feedback. A classic style of formative assessment is referred to as classroom assessment techniques (CATs), a term and method coined by Angelo & Cross (1993). They describe what formative assessments accomplish:

> Their aim is to provide faculty with information on what, how much, and how well students are learning, in order to help them better prepare to succeed—both on the subsequent graded evaluations and in the world beyond the classroom. (p. 5)

When instructors design formative assessments, like CATs, into their courses, they "become better able understand and promote learning, and increase their ability to help the students themselves become more effective, self-assessing, self-directed learners" (p. 4).

The qualities of a CAT are also the good characteristics of any formative assessment strategy. A good formative assessment is "learner-centered, teacher-directed, mutually beneficial, formative, context-specific, ongoing, and firmly rooted in good teaching practice" (p. 4).

Some popular and quick CATs are:

One-sentence summary (CAT 13; p. 183) Students are prompted to write a single sentence that summarizes a topic or concept. It sometimes takes the form of *who–what–when–where–why–how*.	**Example prompt:** In a single sentence, summarize one method that astronomers use to discover planets around stars (other than our Sun).
Invented dialogues (CAT 17; p. 203) Students synthesize high-level course concepts into a creative narrative, which takes the form of a conversation or journal entry of a character.	**Example prompt:** With a partner, write a series of short journal entries from the point of view of a cartoon character "photon" that is produced by a distant object and travels to Earth. Choose the wavelength of your photon character (infrared, visible, or X-ray) and briefly describe its origin, journey, and destination.
Misconception/preconception check (CAT 3; p.132) Students are asked a series of questions that focus on common misconceptions for the content.	**Examples:** Concept inventories (Bailey 2019) exist for many topics in astronomy—light, gravity, seasons, Moon phases, physics concepts, etc. Some teaching tools, like lecture-tutorials (Wallace & Prather 2019) and peer instruction (Mazur 1997) include activities to reveal misconceptions as well as help students overcome them.
Muddiest point (CAT 7; p. 154) Students write a lingering question or point of confusion on a notecard or in free text to a polling tool. Twists on this include engagement questions or general feedback about the course or activities.	**Example prompts:** • What are you still confused about from today's class? • What was something new you learned today? • What would you be most excited to learn about in the next class?

Formative and summative assessments work in partnership throughout a course. If you find yourself not able to decide what the label is (formative or summative), then do not label it, but do articulate the purpose(s) it serves. For example, a quiz can be summative and formative. In a summative sense, the quiz rounds out the unit by bringing together the concepts at a high level to meet a (T) unit-level LO. However, it is only one milestone among many leading up to a final high-level and rigorous take-home exam. In that sense, the quiz is formative and just one step toward a higher course-level LO. You can gauge progress toward the end goal and students can get feedback on how to improve or confirm they are doing all the right things.

When designing assessments, focus on the following:
- What is the assessment is telling you, and the student, about their progress?
- What are you, and the student, going to do with that information?
- What type and format of feedback are you going to give?
- What is the learner expected to do with the feedback?
- How does the assessment fit into the bigger picture of the course-level LOs?

2.5.2 Feedback Loops

Assessments give you and the learners an opportunity to monitor progress and incorporate feedback. There are a variety of ways to incorporate feedback on what they have done well, where they are still struggling, and how to move forward in their learning to improve. Feedback might come from you, fellow students, teaching assistants, an online system, or self-assessment. Forward-looking feedback helps students figure out how they might improve or what their next achievable step might be. A benefit for using formative assessments and a robust feedback strategy is that students are prone to be more engaged and motivated in their learning (Nicol & Macfarlane-Dick 2006). You are setting up a learning environment that shows that you care about their learning and are consistently asking them how they are doing in their progress. It is this instructor presence and sense of community that helps to motivate students.

A powerful way to help students learn is to provide guidance on how to be aware of one's own learning. Thinking about what one knows or thinks, and using that to be more self-aware about one's progress in learning, is referred to as metacognition.[7] Examples of this are the following:
- At the end of the class, ask students to write down what they are still confused about or what questions remain. (Angelo & Cross 1993).
- Give an assignment where students reflect on their study strategies and their performance on an exam. They can also reflect on what they got incorrect and reasons why. https://www.cmu.edu/teaching/designteach/teach/examwrappers/.
- After an in-class polling question, task students to compare answers with a classmate and give reasons why they think their answer is correct (Carl

---
[7] Metacognition, https://cft.vanderbilt.edu/guides-sub-pages/metacognition/.

Wieman Science Education Initiative (CWSEI) & The Science Education Initiative at the University of Colorado (CU-SEI) 2017).
- Promote a problem-solving strategy that requires students to first answer, "What is the problem asking?" and then write down "Here's what I know" and "Here's what I need to know" before putting pencil to paper to solve the problem (Angelo & Cross 1993).

When you examine learner progress regularly and frequently, you are better able to adjust instruction and give students what they need to move forward. You can also gain insight on where students get stuck or how an activity needs to change for next time. When students are asked to examine and reflect on their own progress and learning, they can have a clearer picture of what they do and do not understand, and where they need to focus their energy or get help.

2.5.3 Assessment Strategies

Using clear LOs as a guide, it is the instructor's responsibility to design an assessment that is relevant, meaningful, and will give feedback to the learner on their progress. For lower-level LOs in the (A) category discussed in Step 1: Topic-level Learning Objectives, a common formative assessment is a low-stakes quiz or a preclass question set to check that students completed a reading or video assignment. There is only minimal feedback, and it is usually generated by the course website as an auto-graded quiz or by students submitting lingering questions. For higher-level LOs in the (M) and (T) categories, the assessments should be more rigorous and offer richer feedback. They should aim to be more authentic to real-world (outside of the course) contexts. It is worth noting that not all assessments need to be "graded" or even be reviewed by the instructor. Some assessment strategies have students self-assess against a rubric, discuss work with peers in the class, or use adaptive technology.

So where do you find assessment strategies you can use in your course? There are few go-to books and online resources in an educational developer's bag of tricks, and now we will build up your box of pedagogical goodies.

Assessment Resources:
- *Classroom Assessment Techniques: A Handbook for College Teachers*(2nd ed., Angelo & Cross 1993). This book is rich in formative assessment activity implementation guides. The authors share their scholarly approach as background and justification for the 50 CATs techniques they outline.
- *Learning Assessment Techniques: A Handbook for College Faculty* (Barkley & Major 2016). In the same style as the CATs book, these authors provide robust context for 50 LAT techniques and guides.
- Carnegie Mellon University's Eberly Center for Teacher Excellence and Innovation provides overviews, justifications, and strategies for assessment in the college classroom, https://www.cmu.edu/teaching/assessment/index.html.
- Iowa State University's Center for Excellence in Learning and Teaching provides an overview of common CATs, http://www.celt.iastate.edu/teaching/

assessment-and-evaluation/classroom-assessment-techniques-quick-strategies-to-check-student-learning-in-class/.
- Internet search: "formative assessment techniques" or "formative assessment strategies" or "classroom assessment techniques." There are a plethora of resources online, and you might find more K–12 resources than college level. Do not be turned off by the K–12 flavor—much of what we do in higher education filtered up from the K–12 educators. Learning is learning, no matter the grade level.
- PhysPort[8] supports various astronomy concept inventories and diagnostic tests. The PhysPort website can also help analyze your data with easy to use tools: https://www.physport.org/assessments/?Subjects=91&.

If you have a teaching and learning center at your institution, they will likely have the books above to borrow. Your library or interlibrary loan might also be able to provide them.

2.5.4 Designing Assessments that Align

What do we mean by *align*? The assessments you design should directly address student progress and/or demonstrate success at meeting a particular LO. This means that the task you are asking the students to do should match what the LO is saying they should be able to do. Here are some examples of assessments that do not quite align with the LO.

Topic-level learning objective	The assessment task
Level: (M) Making meaning. Students will be able to describe why we see different phases of the Moon from Earth.	Label the following diagram with the correct phase of the Moon: 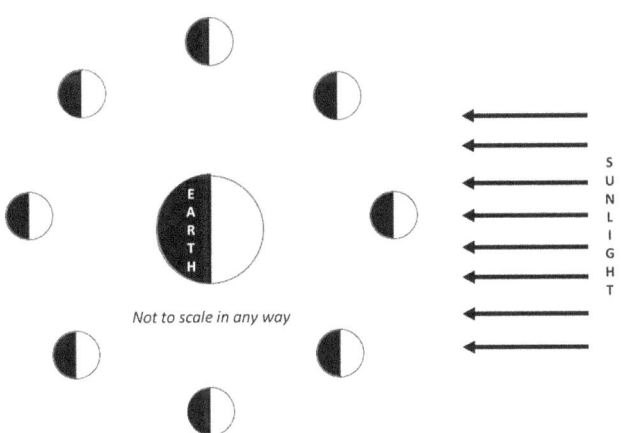

---
[8] PhysPort-Peer Instruction, https://www.physport.org/methods/method.cfm?G=Peer_Instruction.

(*Continued*)

What is the mismatch?
Students are being asked to label a diagram that is assessing whether or not they can memorize a diagram, not if they understand *why* there are different phases of the Moon.

Discussion
What other task/assessment might work better to align with the LO? Labeling a diagram, which is a memorization task, is generally considered an (A) level LO. If the instructor needs an (M) level LO, then the assessment task needs to be more complex. What are your ideas?

Learning objective	**The assessment task**
Level: (T) Transfer. Students will be able to compare and contrast the properties of different wavelengths of light.	Rank the following wavelengths of light in order of shortest wavelength to longest wavelength: gamma rays, infrared, visible, X-ray, microwave, ultraviolet, radio waves.

What is the mismatch?
For sure, a "ranking task" asks students to compare one thing to another; however, this assessment might only indicate if students have memorized a particular order of the properties.

Discussion
The instructor has labeled this LO as (T) so the assessment needs to be high level. What is a richer task to ask students to do where they can demonstrate some critical thinking on the properties of light? Or maybe the LO is not using the right wording and needs to be changed to be lower level. How might you change the LO so that the assessment above is more aligned with the task? Alternately, how might the question be elevated to be a more robust "compare-and-contrast" task?

Learning objective	**The assessment task**
Level: (A) Acquiring. Identify if a type of nebula absorbs, emits, and/or reflects light.	Describe the absorb, emit, and/or reflect processes for various types of nebulae.

What is the mismatch?
Consider if you were a student reviewing the LO for the unit, in preparation for a quiz or exam. How far would you go in understanding the mechanism? How might you study or practice? When confronted with the assessment task, would you be prepared for it?

Discussion
The assessment task is a much higher level than "identify." Students might focus on the properties or descriptions of nebulae in a memorization sense, and not "why or how" light will be reflected, absorbed, or reemitted. A lower-level objective might be: "Match the process (emit, absorb, and/or reflect) to the type of nebula." Alternately, the LO could be rewritten to reflect that students need to understand the how and why.

Frequently in course design workshops, the following concern is voiced, "But, if I am meant to do assessments/evaluations that match up to my LOs, in a very detailed and precise way...aren't I then *teaching to the test*?" A valid concern, and fear, particularly when some institutions are concerned with grade inflation. Suskie (2009) phrases a popular explanation well:

> In a way, good assessment *is* teaching to the test. Assessment is part of a process that identifies what we want students to learn, provides them with good opportunities to learn those things, and then assesses whether they have learned those things (p. 12).

One of the responsibilities of an instructor is to help facilitate learning, giving students opportunities and resources to meet the LOs. Students ultimately are responsible for their own learning and motivation to learn, but you—the—instructor should expect to set up the environment, activities, and support for them to be successful. If you want them to reach higher and understand deeper, you have got to let them know how to do that and provide opportunities for practice, assessment, and feedback. This chapter aims to help you do that.

In the next task, you will research and brainstorm formative and summative assessments for your course-level, unit-level, and topic-level LOs. You will use formative assessments frequently with your topic-level and unit-level LOs and might group things together. As you brainstorm and design an assessment strategy, you might find that your LOs need to be changed. That is a good thing and means that you are thinking about the alignment and what you *really* want students to do. You might also notice that some of the assessment strategies feel like learning activities—you aren't imagining it! It is true that sometimes these are interchangeable, or better yet, they serve multiple purposes in learning. An assessment can be a learning activity. A learning activity can be an assessment. You might also get some ideas for learning activities while thinking of assessment strategies. As previously mentioned, jot down off-task ideas on a sticky note and set aside for later.

Assessment and Feedback Guide.

Use these questions to examine your assessment strategy for each course-level, unit-level, and topic-level LO.
- *What is the purpose of the assessment?*
    You should be able to describe why the assessment is relevant, if it is more formative or summative, and how it will be timely to student learning or understanding progress.
- *Where and how do students get feedback, and what do they do with it? What do I do with feedback on student learning?*
    Remember that feedback might come from self-assessment or peers. If you cannot determine how or where feedback will be given or used when students participate in the assessment, then you might need to reconsider if the assessment is relevant and useful to the learning.

- *How does each assessment fit into the course-level LOs and course goals?*
  As you look at the hierarchy and nesting of the topic-, unit-, and course-level LOs, examine how the assessments weave into that framework or help hold it together. Do the assessments grow in rigor throughout the term?
- *If students have met the LO, what are some things they can show me? Compare to the products that will come from an assessment, do they match up?*
  If things do not match, you have options to rewrite the LO to be more relevant and/or redesign the assessment to be more relevant. Consider the ultimate purpose of the assessment to student learning and if you want to know progress, give an opportunity for feedback, or have it be a summative demonstration of their learning.

Task.

Use *Worksheet 7: Assessments and Feedback Strategies*[4] to describe a summative assessment for each course-level LO. Then, brainstorm assessment ideas for each unit-level and topic-level LO (or set of related LOs) and mark it as formative or summative. Identify places where you will get feedback on the progress of the learners and what you will do with that information. Then note where learners will get feedback and from whom (self, peer, instructor, system), and how it will help them learn.

Congratulations! You have completed Step 2!
Take a break from this chapter, worksheets, and notes. Return back in a few days and review your worksheets before heading into Step 3.

2.6 Step 3: Creating Learning Experiences

In Step 3: Creating Learning Experiences, you will consider how students are introduced to course content and acquire initial understandings, make meaning of ideas and concepts, transfer and deepen their understandings, and reflect on their learning. While exploring ideas and creating learning experiences, you might find that some of your assessments might very well be a learning activity, too. Likewise, learning experiences usually have built-in opportunities for formative assessment (feedback and reflection). Aim to be clear how everything works together and maps to the LOs.

2.6.1 Active Learning Primer

What is active learning? In general, an active learning approach to teaching will provide your students with varied opportunities to struggle with the content in front you and each other. The shared struggle or confusion is where the deeper learning can happen. They will confront misconceptions, integrate new understandings with prior knowledge, discuss what they think they know and what they do not know, and think critically about the course content. Brogt & Dokter (2019) emphasized why this type of engagement is critical:

> As revealed by the scholarship on teaching and learning, humans learn better through active engagement. In a class setting, this means "learning through activities and/or discussion in class, as opposed to passively listening to an expert. It emphasizes higher-order thinking and often involves group work" (Freeman et al. 2014, pp. 8413–8414). These results have been rigorously tested across disciplines, including astronomy (e.g., Prather et al. 2009) and for science majors and nonmajors alike (e.g., Kober 2015; Freeman et al. 2014; Springer et al. 1999). As specific examples of active learning in astronomy teaching are discussed throughout the rest of this book, we will not reiterate them here, but there are many astronomy-specific active-learning tools that have been developed and are ready-to-use, either by individual students, pairs, or small groups (p. 1–7).

Fink (2013) illustrates his essential components to promoting active learning which "combine to form an enlarged and more holistic view of the topic—one that includes getting information and ideas as well as experiences and reflection" (p. 118).

The first component, getting information and ideas, asks instructors to figure out how students will be exposed to or discover the course content, either with primary sources or secondary sources (or both). Secondary sources are your lectures (video or in class), textbook readings, or other media. Primary sources, however, allow students the opportunity to "read original sources and examine original data, that is, ideas and data that have not yet been fully analyzed and interpreted by others" (p. 120). Your decision on how to introduce course concepts to students will rely on your LOs and the general level of your course. Students in an introductory course might need more secondary sources at the beginning and can be introduced to level-appropriate primary sources for the (M) and (T) LOs. In the astronomy major and upper-level courses, you might consider having the majority of your content delivered via primary sources as you build up the professional skills of future scientists and researchers.

The second component, experiences, promotes constructing activities where students can make deeper meaning of the course content. What are the students actually doing or observing, and who are they working with? Initial meaning-making might involve discussions with in-class peers after a multiple choice polling question. There are also a variety of online simulations, applets, and citizen science projects waiting to have an instructional wrapper or activity built around the tool. Observing astronomers in action and using video chat to bring astronomers into the classroom are powerful and engaging strategies to help non-science-major students appreciate the field and develop a better grasp of the nature of science (Hickox & Gauthier 2014). Higher-level activities might involve analyzing or visualizing real astronomical data, projects involving communicating science to the public, collaboratively creating an observing plan, or being involved in a research project at your institution.

The third component for Fink's active learning philosophy involves reflection. As experts in their field, professors instinctively reflect on what they are learning and how it relates to, and might change, what they already know. Students however, need guidance and "time to reflect in order to decide what meaning to give" (p. 122) to the learning happening in the course. You can design these reflective moments by asking how new activities or concepts relate to other things in the course. A second type of reflection is prompting students to think about how they are learning, not just what they are learning. You might ask them to submit a lingering question about a class activity through an open-text in-class polling response. If one of your course goals focuses on the nature of science, you might ask students to submit journal entries throughout the term on how their worldview might be changing.

2.6.2 Choosing and Aligning Learning Activities

Learning activities can include passive tasks like reading, listening to a lecture, or watching a video, as well as more active tasks like creating a concept map, discussing questions with peers, and collaborating on a group research project. Passive tasks fit well with LOs that are in the *acquire knowledge* category. The passive task of watching a video might be followed with a formative assessment of self-quizzing or outlining their notes. Students benefit from mini-lecture or classroom lecture-capture videos by reviewing and revisiting material multiple times until they get what they need from it.

For (M) and (T) LOs, you will need to design activities that will help students practice new skills, create new connections between course topics, and think critically and deeply about the content. These activities might require collaboration between students and facilitation by instructors and teaching assistants. When students work together to learn, they help each other figure out where confusion lingers and can grow deeper understandings together. Collaborative strategies also help to promote a learning community, where individual students might not feel as isolated while struggling.

The balance you find between active and passive learning in your course will greatly depend on your own teaching philosophy and how much you internalize a learner-centered viewpoint. It isn't all or nothing! There is a place for lecture in the classroom. If you have not incorporated or experienced active learning in your classroom yet, then you might consider trying only one or two new things. In-class polling with peer discussion is a good entry point and fits well with (M) LOs. In future course offerings, you can add to your active learning repertoire where appropriate for you, your content, and your learners.

What are the final steps on alignment? While you are choosing and designing the learning activities, you will be assessing their relevance and fit to the topic-level and unit-level LOs, and how the experiences build up to the course-level LOs. Consider the complexity and rigor of the learning activities against your AMT-categorized LOs as you assess your course design plan for alignment. You will also want to make sure the learning activities and experiences build students' knowledge and skills up to the level of the unit-level and course-level assessments. Alignment helps everything in the course feel more intentional, relevant to student learning, and helps the course flow from one section to the next.

Examples of astronomy-related activities and experiences that go beyond textbook reading, short lectures, and problem sets include

- Helping students explore and relate various online citizen science projects like CosmoQuest[9] and Zooniverse[10] to course topics. Learners can work with real data, contribute to the scientific community, and make the content they are learning less abstract and more authentic (see Chapter 8 for more).
- Designing an opportunity for students to discover course content through exploration of multiwavelength imagery or tools like Chandra's openFITS[11] image-processing tool. Find out what students are curious about and give them a way to pursue answers.
- Allowing students to struggle with the course topics in pairs or small teams through higher-level in-class polling questions or lecture-tutorial-style worksheets.
- Developing open-ended questions for students to answer using online animations or simulations like PhET[12] (see Chapter 5 for more).
- Constructing multistep problems for in-class small group exercises that include regular stopping points to check in with teammates.
- Using a platform like WorldWide Telescope[13] for students to create presentations about our multiwavelength universe set in the backdrop of an interactive observable universe (see Chapter 9 for more).

2.6.3 Resources

The following resources are rich with activity ideas. Each addresses course design and learner-centered teaching methods a bit differently, so you will get multiple perspectives on the tasks and content in this chapter. Your own department might have a budget for teaching resources, and these would be a high-impact addition to a bookshelf.

Learning Activities and Experiences Resources:

- Barkley et al.'s (2014) *Collaborative Learning Techniques: A Handbook for College Faculty* has sections on implementing collaborative learning as well as example activities with guides.
- Angelo & Cross' (1993) *Classroom Assessment Techniques: A Handbook for College Teachers* is a double-duty guide book. Sometimes, formative assessment can also be a learning activity.
- Barkley & Major's (2016) *Learning Assessment Techniques: A Handbook for College Faculty* is another dual-purpose book. The learning assessment strategies in the guide can be used as a learning activity.

---

[9] https://cosmoquest.org/x/.
[10] https://www.zooniverse.org/.
[11] http://chandra.harvard.edu/photo/openFITS/.
[12] https://phet.colorado.edu/.
[13] http://www.worldwidetelescope.org/webclient/.

- Barkley's (2010) *Student Engagement Techniques: A Handbook for College Faculty* is like her LATs book with a section on conceptual frameworks, tips and strategies, and implementation guides for 50 different activities.
- Center for Astronomy Education classroom materials and workshops: https://astronomy101.jpl.nasa.gov/materials/.
- Design your own lecture-tutorial-style activities with this guide from the Science Education Resource Center at Carleton College: https://serc.carleton.edu/NAGTWorkshops/teaching_methods/lecture_tutorials/index.html.
- Online physics simulations from PhET: https://phet.colorado.edu/.
- Online astronomy simulations from the Nebraska Astronomy Applet Project: https://astro.unl.edu/naap/.
- Open-source night-sky visualization software, Stellarium: https://stellarium.org/.

Learning Activities Guide.

Questions to ask for each LO and/or course objective:
- *Does the activity address the level of the LO (acquire, making meaning, transfer)?*
  By participating in the activity, what will students be doing that will help them make progress toward the LO? Is it at the right level?
- *Is there flexibility in the activity for students at different skill levels?*
  Will those who need more time to show progress feel left out or become anxious? Will those who move quicker get bored or have something advanced they can do?
- *Is there an opportunity, and is it feasible, for students to collaborate and learn from each other?*
  Collaborative activities and learning experiences have built-in formative assessment and feedback as students discuss a problem, brainstorm a strategy, or create something together. They can help each other uncover misconceptions and gain clarity through alternate explanations and viewpoints.
- *How are students held accountable for participating or being engaged in the activity?*
  Certainly you would like to see students be self-motivated and engaged, but much of the time there needs to be some sort of accountability built into the activity. It might be they hand in a worksheet, complete a quick reflection, or get credit for showing up and being on task.

Task.

Use *Worksheet 8: Learning Activities and Experiences*[4] to brainstorm and outline learning activities and experiences for each LO or group of LOs. You will check for alignment, rigor, flexibility, collaboration opportunities, and individual accountability.

Congratulations! You have completed Step 3!
Once again, I suggest walking away from the chapter, worksheets, and notes. Return back in a few days and review your worksheets before heading into Step 4.

2.7 Step 4: Putting It All Together

In Step 4: Putting It All Together, you will examine the overall alignment of your course plan for your one course goal by reviewing all of your LOs, assessments, feedback, and activities. You will consider the flow of the course and connections between the units. Finally, you will reflect on how you will communicate your course plan to students and colleagues.

2.7.1 Checking for Alignment

At this "checking for alignment" stage, the iterative, reflective, and flexible nature of this course design process becomes obvious. You might go back and change a course goal or LO when you have another look at the assessments and activities. You might determine you have too many unit-level LOs or that your topic-level LOs ballooned to an unreasonable number and you need to pare it down. You might identify opportunities where you can merge topics or activities to get students thinking at a higher level more efficiently. You could even realize one of your "big ideas" or course goals is not attainable or realistic.

This adjustment will continue as you teach. However, by the time the course starts, your course map should describe how the learning activities and experiences help the students make progress toward the LOs, which connect with relevant and appropriate assessment and feedback plans. That is alignment.

Course Alignment Guide.

Questions to ask yourself as you review your course map:
- Are your course goals and course-level LOs written in student-friendly language?
- Do your course goals describe big-picture ideas and what you hope your students will remember most from the course?
- Do your course-level LOs have the proper level of rigor and speak toward the final assessments or products of the course?
- Do your topic-level and unit-level LOs make relevant connections to your course-level LOs? How do they relate to each other or nest within each other?
- Does the summative assessment plan clearly describe what students will do to show they have met your course-level LOs?
- What are the opportunities for formative assessment and instructor feedback as students make progress toward the course-level LOs?
- Are there specific places for students to figure out what they know and do not yet know, and then how to act on that information?
- Do your learning activities and experiences give students a chance to learn-while-doing or practice at high enough levels to meet your summative assessment expectations?

> *Task.*
>
> Use *Worksheet 9: Course Plan*[4] and the questions in the Course Alignment Guide to review your work on one of your course goals.

2.7.2 Finding the Flow

Throughout this course design journey, you have been asked to think about the alignment of the course goals, LOs, assessments, and activities at different scales. The smallest scale is at the topic level or the class-period level, which nests or weaves into the units that build up to the ultimate course-level LOs. This can be described as flow. The flow of a course can be viewed as the connective tissue that holds the entirety of the course together into one cohesive learning experience.

Flow also needs to exist at the microlevel of how a given class period or activity flows to the next throughout the week. It might seem obvious to you that pre-class video and next-day in-class group problem solving are linked and dependent on one another; however, students need to be told in a clear way. Being transparent and specific with students will help them find relevance and motivation. Give students opportunities to discover how last week's class topics relate to the assignment over the weekend and will build up to next week's more rigorous tasks. Build the connective tissue into all aspects of your course. You might do this with the sequence of activities, frequent reflection and assessment, or asking students to talk with peers about the connections at the end of a class period.

In this mock workshop, you were asked to focus on one course goal or course-level LO. In reality, you might have three to five course-level LOs where each breaks out into a few units. Your course structure might be tightly organized into an outline with nested bulleted lists. Or, it might be less of a hierarchy and more like a concept map of related ideas. Maybe your course makes use of various themes that weave together throughout the term. Whatever the style, it is your job to find clarity in the course design and clear up any tangles. If you have trouble determining the structure and flow of your course, focus on how you would describe the themes and topics of the course to someone else who might not be an expert in the field.

> *Flow guide.*
>
> Questions to ask yourself as you review your course plan:
> - How do the class-period or topic-level activities build up to and prepare students for more complex unit-level activities and assessments, and even higher to the course-level LOs?

- In what ways are you communicating to students the relevance between out-of-class and in-class activities and assessments?
- How are students finding and reflecting on the connections between the units in your course?
- Does your course plan or map communicate the structure and flow of your course in an obvious and transparent way?

***

Task.

Complete *Worksheet 10: Reflecting on Flow*[4] to answer the Flow Guide questions.

2.7.3 Communicating Your Course Plan

The course plan or map you create for yourself might look like a lesson plan with lots of details, to do lists, and planning notes. Though you would not share this level of detail with your students, you might share this course plan with graduate teaching assistants or undergraduate learning assistants. It is a living document that can be updated and shifted around throughout the term, particularly if you ask students for early and mid-course feedback.

The course plan, map, or outline you do share with students should not be intimidating and overwhelming. An approachable method is to share the high-level course goals, course-level LOs, and unit-level LOs in the syllabus and on your class website (e.g., Canvas, Blackboard, etc.). You can leave the class- or topic-level LOs for when they will encounter that material. In an effort to be transparent with your course design, consider listing or describing where progress is checked through formative assessments and clearly mark where summative assessments occur. Describing or outlining the activities, experiences, and assessments relevant to each unit- or course-level LO helps show students the path to success. As an example, in a physics course at Dartmouth College, the professor writes the class-level LOs on the board so students know "what they should be able to do" by the end of the collaborative problem-solving and laboratory activities. Students can self-check during class, keep an eye on the goals, and know that everything they are doing has a purpose.

You might not want to use the word "alignment" in your communications to students, but you can articulate the relevance of the learning activities to the assessments. It can motivate and engage students when they understand why they are doing something and how it will help them succeed. A well-communicated course plan can help with buy-in, particularly in courses where active and collaborative learning are the focus.

2.8 Conclusion

You have learned about and tried the main steps of an integrated course design method (Figure 2.1) by
- developing course goals and articulating specific LOs,
- creating a formative assessment and feedback strategy to evaluate student progress toward the LOs,
- creating a summative assessment strategy to evaluate student success with the high-level LOs,
- designing learning activities and experiences that help the student learn and practice, and
- developing a communication plan.

This was just a start, a taste of being structured and decidedly intentional in designing a course or learning experience. The next step is to branch out and work with all of your course goals, not just the one you used here. It can be an overwhelming and time-consuming process, so give yourself plenty of time before the term.

Please consider the advice from the beginning of the chapter:
- Seek out interested colleagues who can either work along you on their course, or can give you constructive feedback.
- Find your teaching and learning center or those at your institution who help faculty with teaching strategies and technology integration.

Thank you for joining me on this course design journey, in a format that is very much different from a live in-person workshop or consultation. I don't get to see how you (readers) are learning and progressing through the steps, and then hearing about how it went during the term. Wishing you the best in your teaching and course design futures!

Please visit the Course Design Workshop companion site where you can find more resources, worksheets, and reflections!

Reflect.

Consider answering the following questions:
1. How does your experience of using an integrated course design process compare to what you have done previously? Refer back to your first reflection in this chapter.
2. What did you find most useful about this experience?
3. What was most engaging for you?
4. What did you find most challenging?
5. Which aspects of this integrated course design process might you incorporate into your regular course and learning design practices?

> 6. What are your lingering questions?
>
> I'd love to know your answers to these reflection questions! Please consider visiting the Course Design Workshop site (https://sites.google.com/view/cdw-companion) to submit your answers and lingering questions. Knowing what has engaged or motivated you in the course design process, as well as hearing your challenges and lingering questions will help me improve this chapter on the next iteration. This is my way of getting some formative assessment!

Acknowledgments

I would like to show my appreciation for my teaching and learning colleagues at Dartmouth College. If it were not for them, this chapter would not really exist. The steps and ideas here come from many conversations, many faculty workshops and institutes, and many resources and articles shared on our Slack channel. An appreciative thank you to the wonderful faculty and students at Dartmouth College who are an inspiration to my daily work. A special shout out to Prue Merton who helped me through this writing project and gave me fabulous, useful, thoughtful, and encouraging feedback along the way. Thank you, Prue! I'd also like to thank Sanlyn Buxner for this opportunity. Lastly, I am sending a big wave through the air to all my astronomy education colleagues, whom I miss working and networking with at super-cold winter AAS meetings.

References

Anderson, L., Krathwohl, D., & Bloom, B. 2001, A Taxonomy for Learning, Teaching, and Assessing: A Revision of Bloom's Taxonomy of Educational Objectives (New York: Longman)

Angelo, T., & Cross, K. 1993, Classroom Assessment Techniques: A Handbook for College Teachers (2nd ed.; San Francisco, CA: Jossey-Bass)

Bailey, J. M. 2019, in Astronomy Education, Volume 1: Evidence Based Instruction for Introductory Courses, Evidence based instruction for introductory courses, ed. C. Impey, & S. Buxner (Bristol: IOP Publishing), p. 10-1

Barkley, E. F. 2010, Student Engagement Techniques: A Handbook for College Faculty (San Francisco, CA: Jossey-Bass)

Barkley, E., & Major, C. 2016, Learning Assessment Techniques: A Handbook for College Faculty (San Francisco, CA: Jossey-Bass)

Barkley, E. F., Cross, K. P., & Major, C. H. 2014, Collaborative Learning Techniques: A Handbook for College Faculty (San Francisco, CA: Jossey-Bass)

Brogt, E., & Dokter, E. 2019, in Astronomy Education, Volume 1: Evidence Based Instruction for Introductory Courses, Evidence based instruction for introductory courses, ed. C. Impey, & S. Buxner (Bristol: IOP Publishing), p. 1-1

Carl Wieman Science Education Initiative (CWSEI) & The Science Education Initiative at the University of Colorado (CU-SEI) 2017, Clicker Resource Guide, http://www.cwsei.ubc.ca/resources/files/Clicker_guide_CWSEI_CU-SEI.pdf

Fink, L. D. 2013, Creating Significant Learning Experiences: An Integrated Approach to Designing College Courses) (San Francisco, CA: Jossey-Bass)

Fink, L. D. 2005a, Idea Paper #42 Integrated Course Design, https://www.ideaedu.org/Portals/0/Uploads/Documents/IDEA%20Papers/IDEA%20Papers/Idea_Paper_42.pdf

Fink, L. D. 2005b, A Self-Directed Guide to Designing Courses for Significant Learning, https://www.deefinkandassociates.com/GuidetoCourseDesignAug05.pdf

Freeman, S., Eddy, S. L., McDonough, M., et al. 2014, PNAS, 111, 8410

Haave, N. 2014, Six Questions That Will Bring Your Teaching Philosophy into Focus, https://www.facultyfocus.com/articles/philosophy-of-teaching/six-questions-will-bring-teaching-philosophy-focus/

Hickox, R., & Gauthier, A. 2014, in 224th Meeting of the American Astronomical Society, Poster Session (Washington, DC: AAS)

Kober, N. 2015, Reaching Students: What Research Says about Effective Instruction in Undergraduate Science and Engineering (Washington, DC: National Academies Press)

Mazur, E. 1997, Peer Instruction: A User's Manual (Upper Saddle River, NJ: Prentice Hall)

Nicol, D. J., & Macfarlane-Dick, D. 2006, Studies in Higher Education, 31, 199

Prather, E. E., Rudolph, A. L., Brissenden, G., & Schlingman, W. M. 2009, AmJPh, 77, 320

Prather, E. E., & Wallace, C. S. 2019, in Astronomy Education, Volume 1: Evidence Based Instruction for Introductory Courses, Evidence based instruction for introductory courses, ed. C. Impey, & S. Buxner (Bristol: IOP Publishing), p. 3-1

Springer, L., Stanne, M. E., & Donovan, S. S. 1999, Review of Educational Research, 69, 21

Suskie, L. 2009, Assessing Student Learning: A Common Sense Guide (Bolton, MA: Anker Pub. Co.)

Weimer, M. 2012, Five Characteristics of Learner-Centered Teaching, https://www.teachingprofessor.com/topics/teaching-strategies/active-learning/five-characteristics-of-learner-centered-teaching/

Weimer, M. 2013, Two Activities that Influence the Climate for Learning, https://www.teachingprofessor.com/topics/for-those-who-teach/two-activities-that-influence-the-climate-for-learning/

Wiggins, G. P., & McTighe, J. 2008, Understanding by Design (Alexandria, VA: Association for Supervision and Curriculum Development)

Wiggins, G. P., & McTighe, J. 2013, Essential Questions (Alexandria, VA: Association for Supervision and Curriculum Development)

Astronomy Education, Volume 1
Evidence-based instruction for introductory courses
Chris Impey and Sanlyn Buxner

Chapter 3

Lecture-Tutorials in Introductory Astronomy

Edward E Prather and Colin S Wallace

Lecture-tutorials for introductory astronomy are designed to help instructors of introductory astronomy actively engage their students in developing their conceptual understandings and reasoning abilities across a wide range of astrophysical topics. The development of lecture-tutorials was informed by nearly two decades of research into common learning difficulties students experience when studying astronomy. The results from multiple studies provide evidence that lecture-tutorials can help students achieve learning gains well beyond what is typically achieved by lecture alone. Achieving such learning gains requires that an instructor understand how to effectively incorporate lecture-tutorials into his or her course. This chapter provides details into the best practices for the effective integration and implementation of lecture-tutorials—practices that we have developed through years of reflective practice from working with thousands of Astro 101 students and instructors. We also present a case study of how lecture-tutorials were used to promote the active engagement of learners in an Astro 101 megacourse enrolling over 700 students. This case study illustrates how the thoughtful implementation of lecture-tutorials can result in dramatic learning gains, even in the most daunting instructional environments.

Chapter Objectives

By the end of the chapter, readers will
- understand how to effectively integrate lecture-tutorials into their course,
- be able to respond to common student questions, and
- describe the evidence for the efficacy of lecture-tutorials.

3.1 Introduction

Imagine you have been assigned to teach a typical general education, college-level, introductory astronomy course (hereafter Astro 101). A large number of students enroll in the course—perhaps as many as a few hundred, depending on your institution. All of these students attend the same lecture section, which meets two to three times per week for at least 50 min at a time. Students sit in seats that are bolted to the ground in a stadium-style layout that focuses their attention toward the front of the lecture hall. Unlike your colleagues teaching introductory physics, your Astro 101 course has no breakout recitation sections or labs. You have limited teaching assistant (TA) support, if any. The vast majority of your students are non-STEM majors who, put off by their previous science and math classes, plan to make Astro 101 the final science course they ever take. A large percentage of your students are freshmen who are just learning how to succeed at college. Many of your students may be first-generation college students and/or come from at-risk populations that have disproportionately high DFW rates (the number of students who earn D and F as their final course grades or who withdraw from the course) in STEM courses. You know that there is a body of educational research that suggests that you should "actively engage" your students (Freeman et al. 2014), but the entire structure of the course seems designed to thwart any attempts to do anything other than just lecture at your students. What else could you possibly do?

Fortunately, there is a wide variety of pedagogical strategies that enable instructors to actively engage their students, even in the suboptimal classroom environment described above. These strategies include Think–Pair–Share (also known as Peer Instruction; Mazur 1997), Ranking Tasks (Hudgins et al. 2007), and Interactive Lecture Demonstrations (Sokoloff & Thornton 2001). In this chapter, we describe another instructional strategy that Astro 101 instructors can incorporate into their curricula to actively engage students' learning: *The Lecture-Tutorials for Introductory Astronomy* (Prather et al. 2005; Prather et al. 2013). Each lecture-tutorial is a two- to seven-page worksheet that addresses a single topic at a level appropriate for Astro 101 students. As described in more detail below, lecture-tutorials are designed to be completed in class by students working in collaboration with one or two of their peers. Each lecture-tutorial is a standalone activity that has been created to supplement lecture and, more importantly, be incorporated into class only after students have been taught about the topic covered by the lecture-tutorial; in this sense, they should be thought of as a postlecture activity. A single lecture-tutorial provides a sequence of questions that intentionally elicit and confront students' incorrect ideas (Clement et al. 1989), build upon their productive intuitions and beliefs (McDermott 1991), and guide their learning to help them develop more expert-like understandings of astrophysical topics. Lecture-tutorials often contain tables of data, figures, and other discipline-specific representations that students must reason about. Many of these representations have been specially designed to foster the learning of a particular topic, and may or may not correspond to typical textbook figures or to representations that are commonly used by experts in astrophysics; consequently, we refer to these specially created figures as pedagogical discipline representations (Wallace et al. 2016). Lecture-tutorials span the range of topics taught in Astro 101, from lunar phases and the seasons, to light and spectroscopy, to more advanced topics at the forefront of modern astrophysics, such as cosmology (Wallace et al. 2012), molecular excitations and synchrotron radiation (Wallace et al. 2016), and the detection of exoplanets via gravitational microlensing

(Wallace et al. 2016). The development of each lecture-tutorial is informed by research into how people learn, and common conceptual and reasoning difficulties experienced by Astro 101 students. Multiple studies show that students who use lecture-tutorials significantly improve their understanding of the associated astrophysical topics beyond what is typically achieved by lecture alone (Prather & Brissenden 2008, 2009; Prather et al. 2005; LoPresto & Murrell 2009; Wallace et al. 2012).

Of course, the success of lecture-tutorials, like any pedagogical strategy, depends on how it is used. While research has shown that the use of active-learning strategies can help students achieve high learning gains, our research provides compelling evidence that *how* an instructor implements active learning is perhaps the most important factor in determining how much his or her students learn (Prather et al. 2009; Wallace et al. 2018). Since the early 2000s, we have engaged in classroom research, worked with thousands of faculty in professional development workshops, and reflected on our own practices. These experiences have helped us significantly evolve our implementation practices in order to maximize the effectiveness of the lecture-tutorials. In this chapter, we will unpack many implementation issues and solutions in the hopes that this discussion will help other Astro 101 instructors create more successful classroom environments. We will also present a case study of an Astro 101 "megacourse" enrolling over 700 students as a way of demonstrating how a series of thoughtful pedagogical decisions can result in an active-learning classroom that uses lecture-tutorials to foster and support improved student learning.

Before we start our discussion, its critical to note that there are many more issues that one may encounter when implementing active-learning strategies in the classroom than we can possibly unpack and work through in this chapter. While we do not wish to scare off instructors thinking of moving toward active learning, one needs to be ready to deal with how to orient students to the active-learning classroom, how to motivate students to participate, how to establish classroom norms for collaborative groups, how to work with groups who are struggling or underperforming, how to monitor and provide real-time feedback to student on their success, and how to match course assessments to in-class experiences. In this chapter, we will address several key implementation issues that are specific to the effective use of lecture-tutorials.

3.2 Preparing to Implement Lecture-Tutorials

Our experience indicates that for lecture-tutorials to be effective, students must believe that lecture-tutorials will help them succeed at the course's homeworks, midterms, final exam, and other assessments. Consequently, instructors need to think carefully about how they will integrate lecture-tutorials (and any other pedagogical tool or strategy for that matter) into the different elements of their course. For example, the lecture-tutorial "Telescopes and Earth's Atmosphere" focuses on developing students' understandings of what types of electromagnetic radiation penetrate Earth's atmosphere and why some telescopes are located in space and others on mountaintops. Imagine an Astro 101 instructor giving a lecture on ray optics, different types of telescopes (e.g., Newtonian versus Cassegrain), and optical effects such as chromatic aberration, and then assigning this lecture-tutorial to his or her students. Even though both the lecture and the lecture-tutorial are superficially about "telescopes," the lecture did very little to prepare students for the reasoning tasks presented in the lecture-tutorial, leading students to view the lecture-tutorials as "a waste of time" and "irrelevant," especially if homework and exam questions focus exclusively on the non-lecture-tutorial content from the lecture. This poor alignment between lecture-tutorials and other components of the class will significantly degrade the effectiveness of using lecture-tutorials in the classroom.

Before adopting any piece of curriculum, textbook, or pedagogical strategy, instructors should determine the learning outcomes for the course, decide what evidence they need to gather in order to determine whether those outcomes have been achieved, design the assessments needed to collect that evidence, and then assemble a curriculum that will prepare students for those assessments (Wiggins & McTighe 1998). This process of "backward design" can—and should—be iterative, especially as an instructor gains experience with the course. An instructor who is trying to figure out what is reasonable to expect out of Astro 101 students can leverage the fact that many years of astronomy education research have produced valid and reliable assessments of students' understanding of light and spectroscopy, star properties, Newtonian gravitation, and cosmology, to name just a few topics (Bardar et al. 2007; Wallace et al. 2011; Bailey et al. 2012; Williamson et al. 2013). There are also classroom-tested questions that can be used for Think–Pair–Share (TPS) and/or for assessments that are available from the Center for Astronomy Education (https://astronomy101.jpl.nasa.gov/materials/). Perusing these TPS questions will illustrate that Astro 101 students are capable of engaging in sophisticated critical thinking that goes well beyond simple regurgitation of facts, as these questions involve multistep reasoning, and the interpretation and integration of complex astronomical scenarios, numerical ideas, and cognitive tasks. Engaging in the process of backward design helps an instructor set realistic yet challenging learning outcomes for his or her students, and it helps the instructor make sure that all aspects of the course—its goals, its assessments, and its curricula—are aligned with one another.

We will now work through an example to illustrate how the principles of backward design can be applied to the teaching of Astro 101 using lecture-tutorials. First, imagine that you wish to get your students to understand how we use observations of Doppler-shifted starlight in the process of detecting extrasolar planets. Figure 3.1 shows a question that we often use to assess our own Astro 101 students' understanding of this topic. Consider all the discipline ideas and relationships students must coherently use in order to answer this question and the intellectual effort required to unpack its representations. They must have a fundamental understanding of what "radial velocity" is. They must recognize that it is the star's radial velocity that is provided on the graph, not the planet's (despite the fact that this is explicitly stated in the stem of the question, it is still a common source of difficulty for many students and faculty). They must remember that negative radial velocities correspond to a star whose light is blueshifted due to its

Given the location marked with the dot on the star's radial velocity curve, at what location (A-D) would the planet be located at this time?

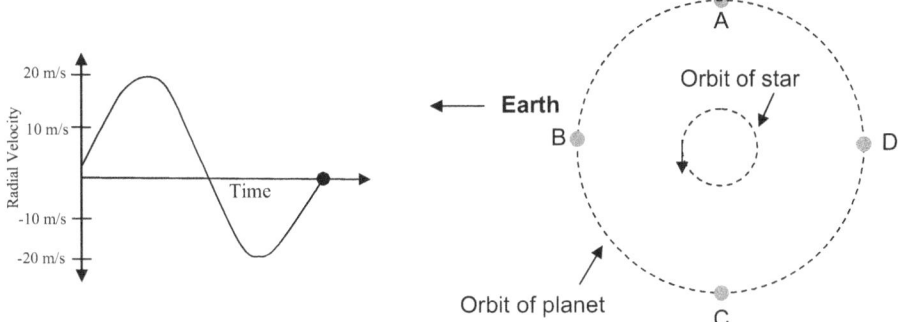

Figure 3.1. A sample question that probes students' understanding of Doppler shift and the detection of extrasolar planets from the radial velocities of their stars.

motion toward Earth and positive radial velocities correspond to a star whose light is redshifted due to its motion away from Earth. Students need to be able to take the orbital information coded in the instant identified on the star's radial velocity graph and correctly translate that into the correct position in the diagram of the star's orbit. They must understand that both the star and the exoplanet orbit a common center of mass, and that at any given time, the star and planet are located on opposites sides of this center of mass—which requires that the star and planet are always moving in opposite directions and complete their orbits in the same amount of time. Students must be able to correctly interpret the picture of the orbits of the star and planet, and determine how both are moving and where both are located at any instant in time relative to the identified location of Earth. This is a conceptually rich and challenging question whose surface features (e.g., the location of Earth, the time of the dot on the radial velocity curve, the direction of the star's motion, etc.) can be readily altered in order to create a large number of variants that are equivalent cases to the one shown but are prima facie novel to students. However, as we can attest from years of classroom instruction, it is *not* beyond the capabilities of Astro 101 students to correctly answer this question—but only if they have received ample time and intellectual engagement in order to develop their mental models on this topic beyond what is achieved from lecture alone.

For the sake of our example, now imagine you are an Astro 101 instructor who wants to use the question in Figure 3.1 because it aligns with and assesses one or more of your course-learning outcomes. You must consider how you will adequately prepare your students to be successful on a question like this. The lecture-tutorial "Motion of Extrasolar Planets" is specifically designed to help students develop the discipline knowledge, conceptual understandings, and reasoning abilities needed to answer the question in Figure 3.1. Additionally, students will probably benefit from a robust understanding of the Doppler shift, which is addressed in its own eponymous lecture-tutorial.

At this point, we must again emphasize that lecture-tutorials are not designed to be stand-alone activities that students engage with independent of other elements of the course; rather, they are meant to be done in class following a very targeted lecture on the topic. So, after deciding on your course-learning outcomes and the corresponding assessments, and after choosing the lecture-tutorials that will help students achieve those outcomes and perform well on the assessments, an instructor must construct classroom experiences that prepare students for the tasks contained in the selected lecture-tutorial. While we will refer to these classroom experiences as "lecture," because they typically take place in the lecture setting of an Astro 101 course, we do not mean to imply that an instructor should only be lecturing during this time.

There are two main goals for the lecture. First, the instructor must provide his or her students with the foundational knowledge they need as well as opportunities for those students to practice applying that knowledge. Second, the instructor must solicit from and provide to students feedback on how their understanding of the material is progressing. This sort of feedback is commonly referred to as formative assessment, as it is provided not for the purpose of assigning grades (although some instructors do award a small amount of participation credit); the intent is to help students gauge and reflect on their current state of understanding. Research shows that the metacognition afforded by formative assessment serves as one of the most powerful ways an instructor can improve student learning and close pernicious achievement gaps between students from different demographic groups (Black & Wiliam 1998).

In order to accomplish these two goals, an instructor should augment the traditional information-delivery aspect of lecture with instructional strategies that both actively engage students in developing their mental models on the topic and provide formative feedback. One effective active engagement instructional strategy we have implemented to supplement instruction is "50/50" and "Fill in the Blank" interactive lecturing. As an example, after a brief background lecture on the Doppler effect, a lecturer using the "50/50" and "Fill in the Blank" method could start off by telling the class "When the star is moving toward Earth, its light will be," and then pause. Students then shout out, simultaneously, "blueshifted." Alternatively, the instructor can provide a pair of choices for students, e.g. "When the star is moving toward Earth, will its light be blueshifted or redshifted?", and then pause. This interactive lecture could continue with "Will the lines in the spectrum for a star whose light is blueshifted appear at longer or shorter wavelengths?", and then pause. This "50/50" and "Fill in the Blank" interactive lecturing technique can be used multiple times during a lecture. The sequenced questions offer a quick and effective way for the instructor and students to gain real-time feedback on whether the students are building a coherent model of the foundational knowledge that is essential to be able to reason about the topic being studied. This interactive lecturing technique needs to be established as a class norm at the start of the semester. We inform students that during the lecture, there will be times when they know the next word or right answer to a 50/50 statement, and that we simply want the entire class to say their answer out loud when we pause. We have found this to be an incredibly effective method for helping students organize their knowledge, for providing feedback, and for motivating students to engage with the topic.

In order to evaluate whether the majority of students have developed the discipline understanding necessary to engage with the lecture-tutorial, we recommend instructors incorporate a series of TPS questions into their lecture. It is important that these TPS questions address the different representations, conceptual ideas, and reasoning abilities critical to doing the lecture-tutorial. Instructors who are interested in how to effectively implement TPS should consult the guidelines at https://astronomy101.jpl.nasa.gov/download/workshopfiles/Think-Pair-ShareHow-ToGuide.pdf. For a bank of TPS questions that align with the lecture-tutorials, instructors should visit https://astronomy101.jpl.nasa.gov/materials/. The feedback provided by the effective use of TPS questions can help an instructor adjust his or her instruction in real-time *before* starting the lecture-tutorial. More important, these TPS questions help students see how the different information presented in the lecture, covered in the lecture-tutorial, and featured on the course exams are all connected to one another. This awareness serves as a strong motivator for students to earnestly engage with the lecture-tutorial.

Once students have experienced an interactive lecture and responded to TPS questions on the key discipline ideas, we ask students to collaborate with their classmates on the lecture-tutorial. Every time you have students do a lecture-tutorial, we recommend that you provide them with the following instructions:

- *Work with a partner.* Lecture-tutorials are meant to be collaborative activities, so students should work with one or two of their classmates. Discourage groups of more than three students, because not every student may fully participate in larger groups. This is especially true for students located at the end of a row of several students who are working together.
- *Read the instructions and the questions carefully.* Many student questions are asked because students often fail to read the content of the lecture-tutorial question carefully enough to understand what is being asked. As we describe in the next section, whenever a student asks about a question, your first response should be for the student to read you the question in its entirety.
- *Discuss the concepts and your answers with each other. Take the time to understand the material now. It will help you on the exam.* Reinforce to students that the lecture-tutorial is not disconnected from the rest of the course; on the contrary, it is a critical part of their preparation for exams. We often tell students that by writing out their answers to the questions in the lecture-tutorial, they are authoring their own textbook—so they should be the best authors they can possibly be! Of course, this instruction will lose its force if your exams do not assess the concepts, skills, and reasoning abilities developed by the lecture-tutorials, so make sure that your exams do accurately and adequately reflect lecture-tutorial content.
- *Come to a consensus on your answer before your group moves on to the next question.* Because lecture-tutorials are collaborative activities, students must actually work together to complete them. We have conducted research that strongly suggests that student learning during a lecture-tutorial is driven by

the discourse they have with their classmates as they defend and debate their answers (Eckenrode et al. 2016). We cannot emphasize enough how important it is for students to participate in lively discussions of their reasoning while working through the lecture-tutorial. Note that a significant number of questions in a given lecture-tutorial will end with the phrase "explain your reasoning" to encourage these discussions. It is critical for faculty to set a high standard for student participation and level of discourse at the start of the course and continuously throughout the course. You can, and should, let your entire class and individual groups know when their level of engagement is not meeting your expectation. One easy-to-implement way to accomplish this is to tell the class that "it is too quiet" (or, alternatively, "it should be loud in here") while they are working on their lecture-tutorial. When a particular low-performing group asks for help, this is also a good time to remind them of your expectation of their level of discourse.

- *If you are stuck or not sure of your answer, check with a nearby group.* While we discourage groups of more than three students, different groups are certainly welcome to interact with one another. This furthers the opportunities for students to engage in discussion and debate with their peers, and it reduces the overreliance of students on the instructor to answer all questions that might arise.
- *If you are really stuck or do not understand what the tutorial is asking, raise your hand and ask for help.* While students are working on the lecture-tutorial, the instructor and TAs should be circulating around the room, listening to students' conversations, and responding to questions as they arise. For advice on how to address students' questions without relecturing to them, see the following section. If you are worried about having a student-to-instructor ratio that is too large for you to efficiently respond to every group with a question, read the case study below on teaching a megacourse and how we used undergraduate TAs to help offset this ratio issue.

We recommend projecting these instructions (shown in italic in the above bulleted list) on a PowerPoint slide that remains visible during the entire time students are working on the lecture-tutorial. You should also give these instructions verbally when students are ready to start their very first lecture-tutorial of the term. While you will not need to verbally repeat these instructions every time students do a lecture-tutorial, we have found that we usually need to re-emphasize some or all of these points several times throughout the semester.

After the time for the lecture-tutorial ends, we recommend that instructors spend some time debriefing the activity with students. Provide a few minutes for students to ask questions and get help with any conceptual or reasoning difficulties they experienced. You will probably need to help your students understand how to ask thoughtful questions such as "Can you clarify how the slope on a Hubble plot tells us whether the expansion rate of the universe is increasing or decreasing?", rather than just seeking a solution statement through a question like "What is the answer to question 18?" You may also want to quickly debrief the specific difficult or interesting answers to the lecture-tutorial's questions with the entire class at once using the "50/50" and "Fill in the Blank" methods mentioned above. We have found that including a thoughtful and targeted debrief plays a critical role in improving our students' attitudes and beliefs about doing the lecture-tutorial. Providing students the opportunity to ask questions, get clarification and feedback on whether their answers are correct, and whether they are prepared for exam questions, has a profound effect on students' willingness to participate in working collaboratively on the lecture-tutorials, and more importantly, on their self-efficacy (Bailey et al. 2017).

With all of the suggestions about implementation given above, understanding about how to manage time is perhaps the most challenging issue that instructors who wish to implement lecture-tutorials face, and so we will take a moment to discuss this issue. We strongly recommend starting each lecture-tutorial by telling students how long they have to work on the activity. We recommend estimating five to eight minutes per page, depending on the number of questions and complexity of the reasoning involved. You can always increase or decrease this amount of time based on how fast most students are progressing through the lecture-tutorial; however, it is important to give this time constraint so that students realize they must get to work and work efficiently, because they do not have an indefinite amount of time. Along these lines, you should keep track of when most students have completed a page, and then, when appropriate, say out loud to the class "if you are still on the first, second, etc., page, you are starting to fall behind." This feedback can be very helpful for groups, especially slower ones (including those who are not meaningfully engaging in the activity) to self-assess their efforts. When the vast majority of students are on the last page, we recommend asking students to "raise your hand if you are on the last page or are done," and then tell the class "you only have a few more minutes to go." By having a clear majority of students raise their hands, you are communicating to *all* students that most students were able to complete the lecture-tutorial in the afforded time, and that it is reasonable for you to wrap up the lecture-tutorial period in the next couple minutes. Of course, there will always be some students who do not finish. Do not make them feel bad—especially if they were giving earnest effort—but ask them to finish the lecture-tutorial outside of class—and invite them to work with you in your weekly "free help session" (typically referred to as office hours). In fact, its good practice to encourage all students to revisit the lecture-tutorial soon after class and take that time to better understand the questions, representations, tasks, and answers for the lecture-tutorial. Even students who finished the activity may have only jotted down the "bare bones" of an answer and explanation to each question, so in the spirit of being good authors of their textbook, they should flesh out their explanations while the material is still fresh in their minds.

While you may only want to do only a few of lecture-tutorials the first time you use them in a course, we have found through experience that many students will only take lecture-tutorials seriously when they are a regular component of the course and when they are introduced early in the course (within the first two or three classes). When used only infrequently, lecture-tutorials can seem like a strange addition to the course pedagogy; students are not completely sure of what the purpose of the activity is, what their behavior is supposed to be, how the activity relates to their overall grade and course success, and as a result, they may not engage as fully with the lecture-tutorial activities as students in courses where lecture-tutorials are a significant and regular part of the curriculum.

Because lecture-tutorials require approximately 10–20 min of class time, you may be worried about whether or not you actually have enough time in your class schedule to implement *Lecture-Tutorials*. This is where a thoughtful consideration of your goals for the class will help you decide how to efficiently budget your class time. For example, you may realize that you do not need to spend 50 min giving a traditional lecture on Kepler's 2nd law. Instead, you may be able to accomplish your astronomical content goals by giving a tightly focused and streamlined 15-minute interactive lecture (including 50/50 and TPS questions) on Kepler's 2nd law that helps students develop critical conceptual ideas and reasoning abilities, followed by 20 min on the associated *Lecture-Tutorial*. Additionally, when you take a more holistic look at your class schedule for the entire term, you may realize there are topics that you can de-emphasize or remove completely in order to make time for the *Lecture-Tutorials* on the topics you want to go deeper with and really engage your students about. Perhaps you have always devoted a lecture to planetary rings, only to retrospectively realize that you never cared enough about the topic to actually ask students meaningful questions about this topic on your exams. If it happens that a day spent on planetary rings does nothing to advance your goals for the course, then give yourself the freedom to drop the topic entirely. Alternatively, you may realize that rings are in fact important for your course goals, which may give you the impetus to develop the instructional experiences necessary to advance students' understandings and the assessment questions necessary to measure whether students have actually met your learning outcomes for this topic. Either way, a holistic look at how you use your time with students may allow you to develop a more cohesive and focused learning experience for your students.

Lecture-tutorials can be a powerful pedagogical tool, and they can help your students significantly improve their conceptual understandings and reasoning abilities over a wide range of discipline content. However, they should not be simply dropped into a course with little thought about how they will be implemented and how they align with the rest of the course. Research shows that an instructor's ability to effectively implement active learning is perhaps the most important factor in determining the learning gains of his or her students (Prather et al. 2009; Wallace et al. 2018). Lecture-tutorials are no exception. An instructor adopting lecture-tutorials needs to carefully consider all the issues related to their implementation described in this section. That being said, instructors should not be afraid to try lecture-tutorials in their classes. Most students appreciate when their instructor has set clear goals and is utilizing activities designed to explicitly help them learn. As with any active engagement strategy, one's implementation of lecture-tutorials gets better with practice. If you would like to get guidance and feedback on your implementation, consider attending one of the Center for Astronomy Education's professional development workshops (https://astronomy101.jpl.nasa.gov/workshops/) and/or interact with other Astro 101 instructors via the Astrolrner@CAE Yahoo Group (https://groups.yahoo.com/neo/groups/astrolrner/info).

3.3 Best Practices when Facilitating Collaborative Groups Working though Lecture-Tutorials

Inevitably, students will have questions as they work on a lecture-tutorial. In fact, this is a good thing, and something that lecture-tutorials were designed to promote, as students who are asking questions are students who are in a teachable moment. Be sure to constantly circulate around the room during the lecture-tutorial time. We find that students are more likely to ask questions when they see you nearby. When students ask a question, you must be ready to respond efficiently; you cannot spend too much time with an individual group, because you will probably have other groups of students with their own sets of questions. Your interactions with student groups must also keep the students actively engaged in the process of constructing their own understandings of the material. For these reasons, we strongly recommend that you not relecture information to students. Remember, lecture-tutorials are postlecture activities, so students have already heard your lecture on the relevant topic. Repeating the words you said earlier is probably not the most effective or efficient approach. Occasionally, you may find a group of students who somehow missed a key piece of knowledge from the lecture. If there is no way students could figure out that piece of information via asking them a set of 50/50 clarification questions, then you may need to just tell them a piece of information—but be concise, and resist going into full lecture mode. Students' need for help and the kinds of questions they will ask while doing their lecture-tutorial can come in many forms. We will now discuss several different methods we use to handle common interactions we have with student groups.

Students will often ask if their answer is correct. There are different ways you may want to respond to such a question. If the group is correct, and the question they are inquiring about is relatively simple, then it is perfectly fine to just tell the students they are correct and move on, as time is precious. However, for more difficult, sophisticated questions that will typically also ask students to explain their reasoning, it is important to ask a group member (and we suggest asking the student who appears least engaged from the group) to explain their reasoning for their answer—and only affirm their correct answer if they can provide a correct explanation. If they cannot provide a correct explanation and/or if their answer is incorrect, then be prepared to engage them in a series of questions as described in the following examples.

Most student requests for help will be along the lines of "we don't understand what is going on in this situation," or "what is this question asking," or "we don't even know where to begin with this question." Whenever students have a question related to the content and/or how to proceed down a particular reasoning pathway, your goal is to use a Socratic-style questioning technique to help guide your students' thinking along the right path. The number one instructional move we recommend starting with is to ask your students to read the lecture-tutorial question out loud and verbatim. This serves two purposes. First, it helps you make sure you know exactly which question they need help with. Second, and more importantly, some students do not read the questions in the lecture-tutorial very carefully before they call you over, so by having them read it aloud to you, we often find that someone in the group will figure out the answer to their question as it is being read aloud.

If simply reading the question aloud is insufficient, you have several different facilitation strategies that you can use. One thing to keep in mind is that you are trying to efficiently diagnose where your students are struggling and to get them back on the correct path, but again time is critical, so it is best to think of this as emergency triage and not surgery. You can explicitly ask students to describe what they find confusing about the given question or situation (and you should do this if they have not already made clear what the specific issue is beyond "We need help on number 5."). If your students are able to articulate the issue they are having, it can often be useful to have them reflect on their answer to a previous question in the lecture-tutorial that establishes critical information needed for the question they are asking about. In doing so, you may find that these students have made a particular reasoning error with the previous question, and now it is clear how best to help these students. The most common and effective facilitation strategy we see adopted by instructors is to ask targeted 50/50 questions to both diagnose students' conceptual or reasoning issue and to direct their thinking along a productive path (e.g., "If two stars are the same size, then will the hotter star give off more energy or less energy?"). As you work through your lecture-tutorials before class (which you definitely need to do), it can be helpful to anticipate which conceptual or reasoning issues your students may have with a particular question, and consider which variables you may need to frame in your 50/50 questions. You may need to ask students which variables or physical characteristics are important, and how they are related, for a given situation (e.g., "What two pieces of information do I need in order to determine the strength of the gravitational force between any two objects?" or "Which feature of the blackbody curve is directly related to the object's temperature?"). Depending on the specific circumstances, you may find that you need to mix and match these different facilitation and questioning strategies in order to help a group of students get unstuck. Throughout this process, however, never lose sight of the fact that your primary role is to be a guide who employs Socratic-style questioning rather than an authority who provides answers. By guiding students with questions, you are keeping them actively engaged in the material and holding them responsible for constructing their own knowledge, which decades of research show is necessary for deep and long-lasting understanding to develop (Redish 1994).

Sometimes you will find a group whose students are not exhibiting the types of collaborative behavior you expect during lecture-tutorial time. One student may be dominating and/or doing all of the work. One student may be completely disengaged and trying to hide his cell phone use. The students may not all be on the same question, which suggests that they are not coming to a consensus on their answers before moving on to the next question. They may not be writing down their answers and their reasoning. Confronting and addressing these kinds of unproductive behaviors can be uncomfortable for you and for them. However, it can be done in a positive way that expresses your pedagogical goals and expectations and/or demonstrates your care for their learning. Remind students that all members of their group need to be involved in collaborating and coming to a consensus on their answers, as it is the level of discussion and consensus-forming they foster in their group that will determine the level of improvement in their understanding that they will experience from doing the lecture-tutorial activity (Prather et al. 2005; LoPresto & Murrell 2009; Eckenrode et al. 2016). To try and get all group members to participate, you may want to direct your help and interactions to the group members who appear disengaged, who are not recording their answer, or who are working on a question different from the one you were called over to help out with. Imagine these different facilitation statements/questions that might be employed for the different issues we have raised: "I'll come back once each member of your group is working on this question," or "John, what did you write down for the question Maria is asking about?" or "Rosa, what do you think about the question that Marco just asked?" By not automatically responding to the group member that is working ahead or the dominant group member, you can pull the other students into the interaction, and communicate that your expectation is that all group members are involved in collaborating and coming to consensus. We also take the time to reinforce the idea that they are the authors of their own textbooks, so they need to write down abbreviated but cogent answers/explanations in class, and then revisit and evolve these explanations outside of class work. By doing this, they will set themselves up well when it comes time to study their lecture-tutorials while preparing for the exam. These messages are important for students to hear, and it is perfectly normal to have to repeat these to students throughout the term. No matter which form of sub-optimal group dynamic you observe, it is important to curb unproductive student behaviors as soon as possible. If some groups are allowed to exhibit these behaviors unchecked, then that sends an implicit message to the rest of the class that these behaviors are acceptable, which can inadvertently undercut much of what you are trying to accomplish with your implementation of the lecture-tutorials.

3.4 Case Study: The Astro 101 Megacourse

As described above, lecture-tutorials are one of several pedagogical tools and strategies that one can use to actively engage students in an Astro 101 class. The effectiveness of lecture-tutorials has been supported by multiple studies (Prather et al. 2005; Prather & Brissenden 2008; LoPresto & Murrell 2009; Wallace et al. 2012). In this section, we add another study to the literature on the effectiveness of lecture-tutorials by showing how the instructional model described above can be applied to an Astro 101 course with a mega-enrollment of several hundred students.

One of us (Prather) began teaching megacourses at the University of Arizona (UA) in the spring of 2010. While many previous reports on "large lecture" or "megacourses" discuss the challenges of teaching 100–300 students (e.g., Thanopoulos 2004; O'Moore & Baldock 2007; Kapp et al. 2011), the UA megacourses saw enrollments of 700–1400 students. To put this in perspective, an instructor teaching a single megacourse may could be responsible for educating 3%–5% of the *entire* undergraduate population of the UA in a single semester.

Figure 3.2. The view from the stage in Centennial Hall, the University of Arizona's performing arts center that also doubled as the classroom for the Astro 101 megacourse.

The challenges associated with teaching a megacourse are immense. The first issue is finding a classroom that can accommodate 1000 students. These UA megacourses were taught in Centennial Hall, the university's 2000 seat performing arts center, which is designed for theater, orchestral, and ballet performances (Figure 3.2). Not only are the seats in the performing arts center bolted to the floor and unable to rotate, they even lack desktops! The rows are packed so close together that an instructor cannot walk across a row to reach students who need help. The lighting is much dimmer than a normal classroom's. The instructor must lecture from a raised stage, where he or she is dwarfed by a gigantic screen upon which lecture slides are displayed. As with many Astro 101 courses, there are no breakout recitation or laboratory sections, and there are no prerequisites for enrolling, which means our student population is very representative of the entire UA undergraduate population— approximately one in five of which will drop out of college after just one year. This confluence of factors appears to be a "worst case" scenario for many instructors, yet we took up the challenges of trying to recreate in this environment the same high level of student collaboration, interactivity, and learning gains we had previously achieved in smaller class.

We were interested to see if the results and lessons learned from the astronomy education research we had conducted with our colleagues over much of the preceding decade would translate well into an Astro 101 megacourse. For the past 20 years, our research has uncovered many conceptual and reasoning difficulties that students experience with a wide variety of core topics in Astro 101. The results of this work have been used to inform the development of pedagogical tools and strategies, including lecture-tutorials, that explicitly address these difficulties. At the same time, we have worked in collaboration with many astronomy education researchers to create several validated and reliable assessments that instructors can use to measure their students' understandings on a wide variety of Astro 101 topics (Bardar et al. 2007; Wallace et al. 2011; Bailey et al. 2012; Williamson et al. 2013). All of this work has been disseminated to faculty across that nation via the Center for Astronomy Education's Teaching Excellence Workshops (https://astronomy101.jpl.nasa.gov/workshops/). These workshops have been designed to help faculty improve their abilities to effectively implement active learning (Prather & Brissenden 2008). Through iterative formative and summative research, and reflective teaching practice in our classrooms, and by listening to the thousands of faculty members that have attended our workshops, we have significantly evolved our classroom practices, instructional models, and pedagogical training experiences—and we would need the best versions of all of these elements in order to engineer an effective active-learning environment for the Astro 101 megacourse.

The instructional model described in the previous sections that combines interactive lectures, TPS, and lecture-tutorials was developed for and honed in classes that typically had enrollments of 150–200 students. While this enrollment is significantly smaller than the number of students in a single megacourse, 150–200 students is still a large number of students. Because our prior research demonstrated that lecture-tutorials and other aspects of this instructional model are successful in large classes, we had reason to believe that they would also work in a megacourse.

Several logistical issues had to be addressed in order to make the megacourse run effectively. For example, as described earlier, the rows in this theater are packed so close together that we would not be able to get to students who needed help. To solve this access issue, we blocked off every fifth row of the class to prevent students from sitting in those rows. These empty rows allowed us to move quickly and easily throughout the room in order to have access to students who raise their hands for assistance during collaborative group work, or to quickly bring a student a microphone when he or she had a question during lecture. Many classroom practices that are simple and can be taken for granted become significant challenges in a megacourse, such as handing out and picking up classroom materials (e.g., participation forms, activity sheets, homework, and surveys). To deal with this, we formulated an intricate flowchart detailing exactly where in the room each TA should go and which rows they were to hand out and pick up papers from so that all students could receive or submit their class materials in only a few minutes. Another difficulty with the megacourse was dealing with class testing. For midterm examinations, we reserved Centennial Hall at evening times outside of normal class time. This meant that we were not using normal class time for testing, which allowed us to efficiently maintain exam security and check students' IDs without having to worry about conflicting with other classes or scheduled performances. One aspect of this course that presented a unique challenge was how to accommodate office hours. Because between 10%–30% of students in our courses typically attend office hours, we had to schedule a 150 seat classroom multiple times per week and staff it with two or three TAs per meeting time. We also established and strictly enforced a zero-tolerance cell phone and laptop policy in order to prevent hundreds of students from texting and using Facebook, YouTube, Twitter, or other websites that distract the learning of their fellow students. Studies have shown that students who spend class time using these electronic resources lower their grades by as much as a full letter grade (Duncan et al. 2012). Even if only 10%–15% of our students use cell phones and laptops during class, that is still 75–110 illuminated screens in a dark room, which create a serious distraction for the rest of the class. Students who needed or wanted to use their electronic devices were told they could do so in a specified area of the classroom. To our surprise, only approximately 10 students actually used their laptops and tablets for note taking during a given semester.

By far, the biggest issue we had to address for the megacourse was making sure we had enough instructional staff to deal with the significant increase in the enrollment of this course. While all of the course's curriculum and assessments were already developed, and while a single individual could lead the lecture portion of the course, there was no way that one instructor and a single graduate TA (our normal ratio of instructional staff for a course of 150–200 students) could manage 700 or more students who were all working on a lecture-tutorial simultaneously. This is an issue faced by many Astro 101 instructors, who may have a large class and little or no TA support. While we were fortunate enough to have the Department of Astronomy provide two graduate TAs for these courses, this was nowhere near an adequate number of instructors. Our solution: hire approximately eight high-performing former Astro 101 students who took the class in a previous semester to return to the classroom as peer teaching assistants (PTAs). As undergraduates, these former Astro 101 students are significantly cheaper than a graduate student, because they can be hired for an hourly wage and no benefits. Note that while our PTA program bears some similarity with the Learning Assistant (LA) program popular at many university physics programs (Otero et al. 2006; Otero et al. 2010), it differs from the LA program in that we recruited almost exclusively nonmajors, and we were not focusing our efforts on creating future K–12 STEM teachers. In these respects, our program was more similar to the Supplemental Instruction (SI) Program (Arendale 1997). Students hired as PTAs had to pass through an in-person interview in which they were placed in mock teaching scenarios, which required them to demonstrate their content understandings, communication abilities, and pedagogical abilities to effectively and efficiently help Astro 101 students. PTAs received specific training throughout the term focused on developing their pedagogical content knowledge (Gess-Newsome & Lederman 1999). This was primarily done in weekly training meetings with the instructor, during which we reviewed the conceptual and reasoning difficulties associated with the coming week's lecture-tutorials and engaged in a version of situated apprenticeship (Prather & Brissenden 2008) in which we modeled authentic student difficulties and mentored the PTAs in how to use Socratic-style questioning techniques to help student groups overcome those difficulties. Having a well-trained cadre of PTAs proved to be absolutely essential for the successful implementation of lecture-tutorials in the megacourse.

Our efforts paid off, as evidenced by the performance of megacourse students on the Light and Spectroscopy Concept Inventory (LSCI; Bardar et al. 2007) as well as the Star Properties Concept Inventory (SPCI; Bailey et al. 2012). In addition to assessing content that is fundamental to the course, the LSCI and SPCI also cover concepts and reasoning tasks that are addressed by multiple lecture-tutorials. In this section, we report on data from the megacourses taught in spring 2010, spring 2011, and spring 2012 (the megacourse was not offered in the fall semester). The SPCI was only given to students in the spring 2011 course. Other assessments, surveys, and concept inventories were administered in other semesters for research projects that are beyond the scope of this chapter. Both the LSCI and SPCI were administered at the beginning and at the end of the semester so we could measure any learning gains achieved by students as a result of completing the course.

We only included data for students for which we had both their pre- and post-instruction responses. Furthermore, while we used Scantrons to collect our data in the spring 2010 course, in subsequent semesters, we used an online password-protected system. Students received a nominal amount of participation credit for completing both their pre- and post-responses to the concept inventories, although their grades were not affected by their responses to individual questions. For the spring 2011 and 2012 semesters, we removed the responses of all students who spent fewer than 10 minutes or more than 60 minutes on the LSCI post-instruction. We also removed the responses of all students who spent fewer than 4 minutes or more than 60 minutes on the SPCI. We looked at post-instruction times, because by that point in the semester, most students have developed the content knowledge to be able to really reason through the questions, as opposed to just guessing. Students who spend fewer than 10 minutes on the LSCI have less than 30 seconds, on average, to read, reason about, and answer each item, while students who spend an hour or more on one of these assessments are clearly taking much longer than intended to respond to the 26 items. We found empirically that students are able to finish the SPCI in less time than the LSCI (with a median time of 8.5 minutes for the SPCI, compared to 15.2 minutes for the LSCI), which is why we made the lower cutoff only 4 minutes instead of 10 minutes. By imposing these cutoffs, we removed 206 students with matched pre- and post-instruction responses from the spring 2011 LSCI data set, 74 students from the spring 2011 SPCI data set, and 117 students from the spring 2012 LSCI data set.

On the SPCI, the spring 2011 megacourse achieved an average normalized gain of $\langle g \rangle = 0.39$ with a standard deviation of $\sigma_{\langle g \rangle} = 0.19$ from $N = 307$ matched pre- and postinstruction responses. This value of $\langle g \rangle$ falls within Hake's "medium gain" region ($0.3 \leq \langle g \rangle < 0.7$; Hake 1998). To understand how the spring 2011 megacourse compares to other classes assessed with the SPCI, we compare our results to those presented in Bailey et al.'s (2012) validation study of the SPCI. The 334 Astro 101 students in Bailey et al.'s (2012) study had a pre-instruction average of 7.09 (with a standard deviation of 2.73) and a post-instruction average of 11.84 (with a standard deviation of 3.87). From these average scores, we calculate an average normalized gain of $\langle g \rangle = 0.25$. In contrast, the students in the spring 2011 megacourse had a pre-instruction average of 6.48 (with a standard deviation of 2.83) and a postinstruction average of 14.19 (with a standard deviation of 3.72). The fact that the students in the megacourse began with a lower pre-instruction average on the SPCI and ended with a higher post-instruction average than the students in Bailey et al. (2012) explains why the megacourse had the higher average normalized gain. These results indicate that students taught in an Astro 101 megacourse can significantly increase their understanding of topics related to star formation and stellar properties.

We now examine the results of all three megacourses on the LSCI. Table 3.1 shows the average normalized gains, their standard deviations, and the number of students N with matched pre- and postinstruction scores for each of the three semesters. Once again, all of these average normalized gains fall within Hake's "medium gain" region.

Table 3.1. Average Normalized Gains $\langle g \rangle$, Their Standard Deviations $\sigma_{\langle g \rangle}$, and the Number of Students N with Matched Pre- and Postinstruction LSCI Scores for the Spring 2010, Spring 2011, and Spring 2012 Versions of the Astro 101 Megacourse

Semester	$\langle g \rangle$	$\sigma_{\langle g \rangle}$	N
Spring 2010	0.42	0.24	357
Spring 2011	0.48	0.24	290
Spring 2012	0.43	0.26	288

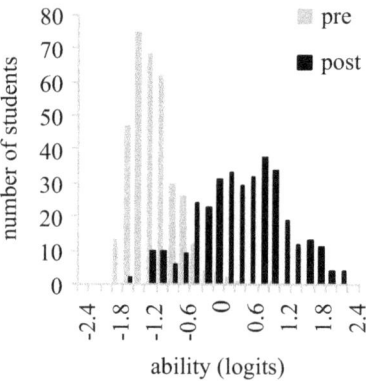

Figure 3.3. The pre- and post-ability histogram for the spring 2010 mega-course.

How do the average normalized gains of the megacourses on the LSCI compare with the average normalized gains of Astro 101 courses across the country on the LSCI? In a previous study, we calculated the average normalized gains on the LSCI for 69 classes, representing nearly 4000 students at 30 colleges and universities across the U.S., plus one in Ireland (Prather et al. 2009). Out of those 69 classes, only 19 (27%) had average normalized gains in the "medium gain" region—and only 10 (14%) of those classes had average normalized gains above 0.40. With average normalized gains above 0.40, we find that the three megacourses achieved some of the highest learning gains of Astro 101 classes in the U.S., as measured by the LSCI.

We also reanalyzed the LSCI data from Prather et al. (2009) plus the LSCI data from the megacourses using item response theory (IRT). As described in more detail in Wallace et al. (2018), IRT provides a way to estimate students' underlying abilities to reason about light and spectroscopy concepts, independent of the specific items to which they responded. Figures 3.3–3.5 shows the distribution of student abilities, pre- and post-instruction, for the spring 2010, spring 2011, and spring 2012 megacourses, respectively.

Note that in all three semesters there is a clear shift upwards in ability pre- to post-instruction. One important result of this IRT analysis is the discovery that, post-instruction, the majority of students possess abilities that are far beyond what

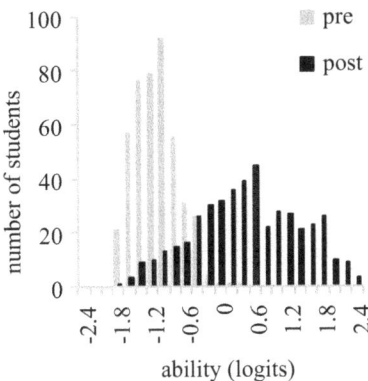

Figure 3.4. The pre- and post-ability histogram for the spring 2011 mega-course.

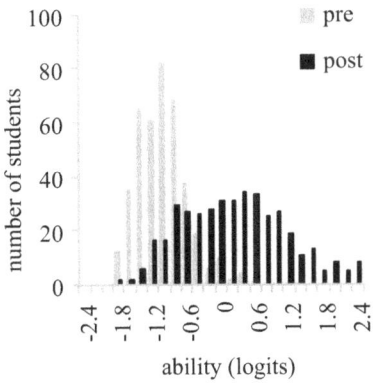

Figure 3.5. The pre- and post-ability histogram for the spring 2012 mega-course.

any student possessed pre-instruction. Additionally, the pre-instruction abilities represented in these three megaclasses are among the lowest in the entire national data set, whereas the post-instruction abilities are among some of the highest achieved by any student in the sample. These data provide powerful evidence that the proper implementation of lecture-tutorials, coupled with thoughtful solutions to the challenges facing active engagement in large-enrollment classes, can work together to significantly improve students' conceptual understandings and reasoning abilities, even in megacourses containing several hundred students.

3.5 Summary

Lecture-tutorials for introductory astronomy are grounded in 20 years' worth of research into the conceptual and reasoning difficulties experienced by students taking an Astro 101 course. They can serve as a valuable pedagogical tool to actively engage students, even in classrooms that have hundreds of student groups operating simultaneously. But as is the case with all forms of active engagement, an instructor's implementation is critical. In this chapter, we unpacked many of the instructional principles and practices we developed over many years to facilitate the effective use of lecture-tutorials. Instructors who are interested in using lecture-tutorials should carefully reflect on how all aspects of the course—its goals, student-learning outcomes, assessments, and curricula—fit together and mutually reinforce one another. As we have discussed throughout this chapter, effective implementation of lecture-tutorials is about more than just finding time for them in your class schedule. One must establish and communicate classroom and collaborative group norms, and adopt a backward-design approach to aligning assessments with all of the other aspects of the course, in order to establish a productive feedback loop between you and your students so that you can continuously work to foster an effective and vibrant active-learning environment. While implementing lecture-tutorials does require an investment in time, you do not have to figure out all of the nuances of the implementation strategy by yourself. By following the guidelines laid out in this chapter, you can avoid many of the mistakes we have made in the past or have seen others make. Taking the time to consider how your implementation is best suited to your institutional and classroom-specific context is critical. We strongly suggest that new and experienced faculty consider attending one of the many professional development workshops offered to help evolve faculty classroom practices, such as the Center for Astronomy Education's workshops (http://astronomy101.jpl.nasa.gov/workshops) and the Workshop for New Physics and Astronomy Faculty (http://www.aapt.org/Conferences/newfaculty/nfw.cfm). We find that faculty who take a scholarly and thoughtful approach to their teaching typically report experiencing greater enjoyment in their classroom and pride in their students' dramatic gains in knowledge and abilities.

Acknowledgments

The research and curriculum development efforts highlighted in this chapter have been supported by the National Science Foundation (grant Nos. 9952232, 9907755, and 0715517) and by the generous contributions of NASA's Exoplanet Exploration Program and Associated Universities, Inc.

References

Arendale, D. 1997, in Proc. 17th and 18th Annual Institutes for Learning Assistance Professionals: 1996 and 1997, ed. S. Mioduski, & G. Enright (Tucson, AZ: Univ. Learning Center), 1
Bailey, J. M., Johnson, B., Prather, E. E., & Slater, T. F. 2012, IJSEd, 34, 2257
Bailey, J. M., Lombardi, D., Cordova, J. R., & Sinatra, G. M. 2017, PRPER, 13, 020140
Bardar, E. M., Prather, E. E., Brecher, K., & Slater, T. F. 2007, AEdRv, 5, 103
Black, P., & Wiliam, D. 1998, Assessment in Education, 5, 7
Clement, J., Brown, D. E., & Zeitsman, A. 1989, IJSEd, 11, 554
Duncan, D. K., Hoekstra, A. R., & Wilcox, B. R. 2012, AEdRv, 11, 010108
Eckenrode, J. W., Prather, E. E., & Wallace, C. S. 2016, Journal of College Science Teaching, 45, 65

Freeman, S., Eddy, S. L., McDonough, M., et al. 2014, PNAS, 111, 8410
Gess-Newsome, J., & Lederman, N. G. 1999, Examining Pedagogical Content Knowledge: The Construct and Its Implications for Science Education (Dordrecht: Kluwer)
Hake, R. R. 1998, AmJPh, 66, 64
Hudgins, D. W., Prather, E. E., Grayson, D. J., & Smits, D. P. 2007, AEdRv, 5, 1
Kapp, J. L., Slater, T. F., Slater, S. J., et al. 2011, Journal of College Teaching and Learning, 8, 23
LoPresto, M. C., & Murrell, S. R. 2009, AEdRv, 8, 010105
Mazur, E. 1997, Peer Instruction: A User's Manual (Englewood Cliffs, NJ: Prentice Hall)
McDermott, L. C. 1991, AmJPh, 59, 301
O'Moore, L., & Baldock, T. 2007, EJEE, 32, 43
Otero, V., Finkelstein, N., McCray, R., & Pollock, S. 2006, Sci, 313, 445
Otero, V., Pollock, S., & Finkelstein, N. 2010, AmJPh, 78, 1218
Prather, E. E., & Brissenden, G. 2008, AEdRv, 7, 1
Prather, E. E., & Brissenden, G. 2009, AEdRv, 8, 010103
Prather, E. E., Rudolph, A. L., Brissenden, G., & Schlingman, W. M. 2009, AmJPh, 77, 320
Prather, E. E., Slater, T. F., Adams, J. P., et al. 2005, AEdRv, 3, 122
Prather, E. E., Slater, T. F., Adams, J. P., & Brissenden, G. 2013, Lecture-Tutorials for Introductory Astronomy (3rd ed.; San Francisco, CA: Pearson)
Redish, E. F. 1994, AmJPh, 62, 796
Sokoloff, D. R., & Thornton, R. K. 2001, Interactive Lecture Demonstrations (New York: Wiley)
Thanopoulos, J. 2004, Journal of Teaching in Int. Business, 15, 61
Wallace, C. S., Chambers, T. G., & Prather, E. E. 2016, AmJPh, 84, 335
Wallace, C. S., Chambers, T. G., & Prather, E. E. 2018, PRPER, 14, 010149
Wallace, C. S., Prather, E. E., & Duncan, D. K. 2011, AEdRv, 10, 010106
Wallace, C. S., Prather, E. E., & Duncan, D. K. 2012, IJSEd, 34, 1297
Wallace, C. S., Prather, E. E., Hornstein, S. D., et al. 2016, PhTea, 54, 40
Wiggins, G., & McTighe, J. 1998, Understanding by Design (Englewood Cliffs, NJ: Prentice Hall)
Williamson, K. E., Willoughby, S., & Prather, E. E. 2013, AEdRv, 12, 010107

Astronomy Education, Volume 1
Evidence-based instruction for introductory courses
Chris Impey and Sanlyn Buxner

Chapter 4

Technology and Engagement in the University Classroom

Douglas Duncan

This chapter summarizes reasons for making the role of students in the classroom more active and engaged in their own learning. First, evidence is presented that faculty typically overestimate the learning taking place in class and that deep or conceptual learning is much less than we would like. We then show how to increase student engagement and learning, and the role technology can play in achieving those goals. "Watch-outs" are presented—common failures in technology use that waste time and money. Results from astronomy and physics education research are invoked to show what uses of technology are likely to succeed—to increase student learning and engagement, and produce more positive attitudes—and what uses are likely to fail and come to be considered a waste of time and money. To succeed, clear learning goals must guide the adoption of technology, rather than "cool new technologies" determining what students and faculty do. A range of technologies, from simple colored cards to electronic student response systems ("clickers"), videos, "flipped classrooms," tutorials, and smartphone apps are reviewed, with an emphasis on better and worse uses of each technology. Finally, the importance of metacognition in student success is discussed, and resources that can improve metacognition and *how* students study and try to learn are presented.

Chapter Objectives

By the end of the chapter, readers will be able to
- describe how engaging students in "active learning" results in more effective student learning depending on how techniques are implemented,
- describe how using "backward design"—working backwards from the goals you are trying to achieve to choose and implement technology—will increases the chance that any technology you use will produce worthwhile results,

- give examples of different technologies of colored cards, "clickers," peer instruction, smartphone use, videos, "flipped classrooms," PHeT applets, online homework, classroom demonstrations, and tutorials, and describe how to implement them in the classroom,
- evaluate the effectiveness of *implementation* of technologies in your class, and
- communicate to students the importance of active learning with the support of different technologies.

4.1 Introduction: Why Engagement is Important, and How Technology May Increase or Reduce It

"Tell me and I forget, teach me and I may remember, involve me and I learn."

Ben Franklin said this over two centuries ago, and it remains true today. The push for greater student engagement in the classroom stems from the understanding that learning takes place in the mind of the student, not that of the teacher, and that deep and lasting learning requires thoughtful engagement. The National Research Council books *How People Learn* (2000) and *How Students Learn: Science in the Classroom* (Bransford & Donovan 2005) summarize research that can increase the effectiveness of science teaching, and they encourage faculty to base choices how they teach on research, rather than tradition, personal experience, or educational trends.

Many teachers look to technology to increase student engagement, especially in large classes. The present chapter presents research that shows which technologies increase student engagement and which reduce it. It also presents evidence showing that *how* technology is implemented has a dramatic effect on its effectiveness in engaging students and improving learning. This theme—"how you use the technology" is critical and explains why some instructors achieve large learning gains and others get no learning gains while using the same technology. The professor who years ago stood in front of the black or whiteboard while writing has his or her equivalent in the (poor) user of technology today.

Many instructors do not recognize the need for change in their classroom. They are often surprised at the lack of learning or superficial depth of learning by their students, and they consistently overestimate how much students learn from their lectures. Even when lectures are clear and interesting, the extent and depth of learning that takes place solely due to lecture is limited. Two important research results have caused many who teach astronomy to use methods aside from lectures alone. The methods, discussed below, are often mediated by technology. The first research result, by Lightman & Sadler (1993) demonstrates that teachers vastly overpredict the learning gains their students will achieve. Their survey contains data from 66 teachers who taught astronomy to K–12 students. The students answered questions on a variety of astronomy subjects (Figure 4.1) at the start and end of the semester (pre- and posttests). The questions were conceptual—they were written to probe thorough understanding (see the section on assessment below). Student gains were far, far less than teachers expected.

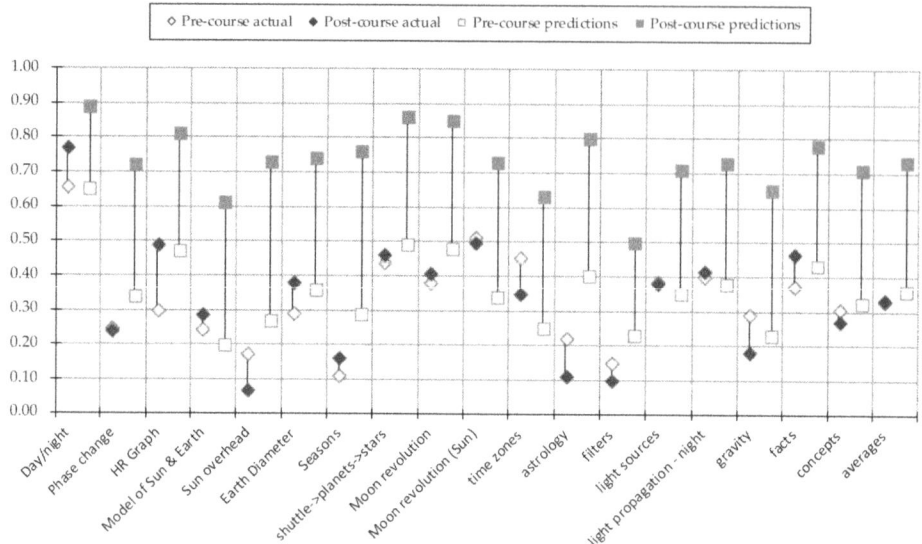

Figure 4.1. Reproduced from Lightman & Sadler (1993), with the permission of the American Association of Physics Teachers.

The second research result that causes many to augment their lectures is Hake's large 1998 study: "Interactive-engagement vs traditional methods: A six-thousand student survey of mechanics test data for introductory physics." Hake used a multiple-choice assessment called the Force Concept Inventory (Hestenes et al. 1992) that probes conceptual understanding more deeply than most tests, because the wrong answers are based on interviews with large numbers of students, and they represent commonly held misconceptions. In other words, the "wrong" answers are very tempting, and students need a thorough understanding of the correct answer to avoid the wrong answers. Hake also collected data from the Mechanics Baseline test (Hestenes & Wells 1992), which involves some quantitative problem solving. Results were presented as "normalized learning gains" in order to compare classes of different ability levels at different universities (Figure 4.2). The normalized learning gain, $\langle g \rangle$ is defined as the ratio of the actual class average gain $\langle g \rangle$ to the maximum possible average gain, i.e., $\langle g \rangle = (\%\text{<posttest>} - \%\text{<pretest>})/(100 - \%\text{<pretest>})$. A class where the pretest average was 25% and the posttest average was 50% would have $\langle g \rangle = 25\%$ (actual gain)$/75\%$ (possible gain) $= 0.33$. Results from over 6000 students in 62 introductory physics courses show a limit to conceptual or thorough understanding at $\langle g \rangle$ about 0.25; one might colloquially say that students "master" no more than about 25% of the concepts presented during a semester. Interactive engagement, including various technologies and approaches presented below, resulted in a range of scores, with most surpassing the results of even the best lecture courses.

In summary, active learning or interactive engagement is when the instructor stops talking and students do something such as working on a problem in small groups or discussing questions with each other, then using "clickers" or other means

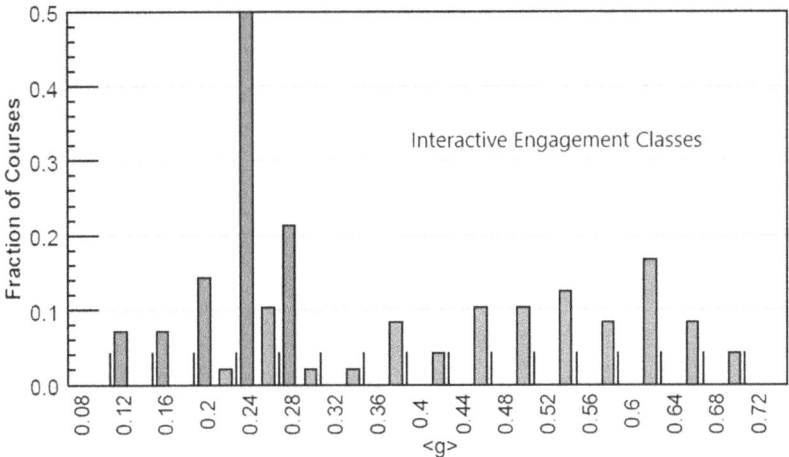

Figure 4.2. Normalized learning gains of students in traditional and interactive engagement classes. Reprinted from Hake (1998), with the permission of AIP Publishing.

to submit answers. Students in STEM courses where instructors use active learning do better on exams and tests specifically designed to measure conceptual understanding. Students in active-learning courses are also less likely to fail or withdraw. This is especially true for students from backgrounds that are underrepresented in STEM subjects or who are first in their families to go to college (University of Texas (Austin) Teaching Portal 2018).

That increased engagement can improve student satisfaction is important for majors and nonmajors. The rate of dropout of STEM college majors is roughly 50% (Seymour & Hewitt 1997; this includes students who switch to a non-STEM major). Unlike chemistry or physics, but like the Earth sciences, more than 90% of introductory astronomy students are non-STEM majors. They will not use astronomy in a formal way in their careers, and they will take few additional science courses. The attitude toward astronomy and science they develop in class is likely to remain with them. The social aspects of learning are important: most students enjoy interacting with other students, and they learn more when they do so (Vygotsky 1962; Bandura 1977). Surveys show that students who took a course with elements specifically designed to enhance their academic skills or social development enjoyed significant advantages over peers who did not have such an experience. Specifically, they were more challenged academically, reported more active and collaborative learning activities, interacted more frequently with faculty, perceived the campus environment as being more supportive, and gained more from their first year of college (Kuh et al. 2008).

Moreover, the ability to work in groups, to problem solve, and to communicate well is highly valued by 70%–80% of employers (National Association of Colleges and Employers 2018). This may be a consideration in choosing whether and how to use technology in your classroom.

Some technologies enhance engagement, cooperation, group work, and communication skills, and some do not. This is discussed below. In all cases, it is important to explain to students *why* they are expected to engage with each other and with the instructor, and what the purpose is of technology used in class (Duncan 2009). This is discussed in Section 4.8, The Importance of Metacognition.

The University of Texas Teaching Portal (https://cns.utexas.edu/teaching-portal) is an excellent resource for additional references justifying the need for student engagement as well as suggestions and recommended technology, as is the Carl Wieman Science Education Initiative (http://www.cwsei.ubc.ca/), which includes short videos of active teaching in action. As will be seen below, how the use of technology is designed and implemented makes a huge difference in its success, so the Wieman videos of technology and techniques in action are very useful. Two classrooms that supposedly "use the same technology" often use it very differently. Specifying the technology alone is not enough information to describe how effective a class using it will be.

4.2 Backward Design Makes Technology Use More Successful

If you do not know where you are going, you are unlikely to get there. That sounds like an obvious truism, but roughly half of those who teach introductory astronomy have never written down a summary of their class goals (Slater et al. 2001). Actually writing goals down does not take long, and it often results in a change to what and how you teach. If you are thinking of introducing technology into your classroom, *design backwards.* Begin by specifying the goals you are trying to achieve. Determining these in advance increases your chance of success. D. K. Duncan (unpublished) visited science museums throughout the U.S. and surveyed the processes by which they created educational experiences. The leading museums designed "backwards": they began with their goals for visitors and then selected the most appropriate technologies. A more common practice, seen in the less successful science museums, was to take the latest technology and see how it could be used for education. The "backward" design approach was more successful.

We live in a technological age, and many who teach astronomy have technical backgrounds. Many companies' business is to sell technology. The result is a steady stream of apps, devices, and other technology continuously being presented to those who teach. Simply adopting something that is cool or clever is not likely to improve student learning.

The adoption of technology should be driven by the goals you are trying to achieve. That is an example of what is called "backward design."

Descriptions of how to accomplish successful backward design in the educational realm can be found in "Understanding by Design" (Bowen 2018) and in the book by Wiggins & McTighe (2008). Backward design is focused on student understanding and the design of assessments that can measure their understanding. As Bowen warns, it is easy to have the misconception that learning *is* the activity when, in fact, learning is derived from a careful consideration of the meaning of the activity. For example, a computer technology that allowed students to manipulate the positions of the Sun, Earth, and Moon to study Moon phases could be very useful, but it may or may not result in student understanding of the phases. Thoughtful use of technology leading to understanding should be our goal, not merely use of technology.

In summary, backwards design proceeds as follows:
1. Determine goals—what should students learn, experience, and feel.
2. Decide what evidence would prove that students have achieved your goals, and design assessments to gather that evidence.
3. Plan lessons, technology use, and experiences to achieve specific goals.

An interesting example is provided by the University of Colorado's Fiske Planetarium, which at this writing is one of the highest technology planetariums in the U.S. Over 2000 college students take astronomy each year and visit the planetarium. Nearly all are shown where the Sun rises and sets in summer versus winter—the technology makes this easy. However, the goal is actually that students could point to the horizon and explain where the Sun would rise and set at different times of the year, and retain that knowledge throughout their lives. Giving the students big cardboard arrows asking them to stand where they thought the Sun would rise in summer greatly increased the degree of engagement, even though the added technology (cardboard arrows) was decidedly low tech compared to the $2M planetarium system. Students were seen to spread widely along the horizon, and then the Sun was allowed to rise, and they could judge their own performance along with the instructor. In this case, being able to point to the horizon where the Sun would rise was deemed better evidence of the desired learning than performance on a multiple-choice question. Not everyone who teaches has a planetarium, but anyone who uses any technology should think carefully about their goal for what students should achieve with the technology, and what assessment (discussed further below) would provide acceptable evidence that the goal or goals have been achieved.

4.3 A Range of Technologies

Listening to a lecture is a passive experience, and student engagement falls off quickly, cycling between attention and inattention. Making a "break" in the lecture draws students back into engagement (Bunce et al. 2010), and technology can be useful for doing so. More importantly, it can make the student an active participant in learning, not just a passive recipient.

1. Colored Cards

Cards that have A, B, C, D printed on them in different colors, that allow students to vote by folding them and holding up one color, have been rather widely used in astronomy teaching to promote student engagement. The Center for Astronomy Education and Center for Physics and Astronomy Education have been making them available since 2001.[1] Cards allow all students in a class to simultaneously register an

---
[1] Center for Astronomy Education (CAE), https://astronomy101.jpl.nasa.gov/.

answer to a question posed by the instructor, allowing much more participation than calling on individual students does. Individual students can still be asked to explain their reasoning after a class vote. Cards are inexpensive and require no batteries, which are advantages over "clickers."

2. Clickers

Clickers, or student response systems, are a relatively easy way to produce a significant change in student engagement and the classroom environment. Clicker technology has the advantage over colored cards that students are usually registered to a single clicker so their responses are recorded and available to the instructor. Responses may be used to give students credit, to diagnose their difficulties, or for research purposes. Clicker technology is quite mature and easy to use. Many tens of thousands of clickers have been used at CU Boulder since 2002, and some important patterns of success and failure have emerged (Duncan 2009). Some of the most important are the following:

1. A school should standardize with one brand of clicker. It is unreasonable to ask students to buy more than one, and they hate that.
2. It is essential to explain *why* you are trying to increase student engagement. The students who want to engage usually sit in the front. Many of those who sit at the back of class do not come in wanting to engage with you. You need to explain the advantage of engagement and using clicker technology if you want all students to experience the benefits.
3. How often you use this technology affects your success. If you make it a regular part of your class and treat it seriously, students will treat it as important.
4. If one of your goals is to increase engagement and participation, structure the reward for using clickers to support your goal. Duncan (2009) makes "clicker points" 10% of the class grade. He asks students a question about five times per hour class, gives two points for any answer and three points for the correct answer, and usually encourages students to talk with their neighbors before answering. Willoughby & Gustafson (2009) and James (2006) have studied grading incentives.
5. Stress that genuine, deep learning is not easy and that conceptual questions and conversations with peers help students find out what they do not really understand and need to think about further, as well as help you pace the class. Students tend to focus on correct answers, not learning. Explain that it is the discussion itself that produces learning and if they "click in" without participating, they will probably get a lower grade on exams than the students who are more active in discussion—"no brain, no gain."
6. If you are a first-time clicker user, start with just one or two questions per class. Increase your use as you become more comfortable.
7. Explain what you will do when a student's clicker does not work, or if a student forgets to bring it to class. Deal with that problem as well as personal problems that cause students to miss class by dropping 5–10 of the lowest clicker scores for each student.

8. Talk directly about cheating. Emphasize that using a clicker for someone else is like taking an exam for someone else and is cause for discipline. Explain what the discipline would be.
9. Watching even part of a class taught by an experienced clicker user, or the Wieman videos recommended above, is a good way to rapidly improve your skill with this technology. You will probably notice that if students are asked to discuss a question, the level of engagement and talking is extremely high (more than you have ever seen in class, if you have not seen peer discussion), and then it starts to die down. This means that most students have finished discussing your question. Talk may then pick up as students start to discuss other things. You will learn how long to let discussions run.
10. Experienced users use a mix of question difficulty. It is tempting to make questions too easy because both students and instructor feel good when most students get the correct answer. Learning is increased when questions are more challenging, however.
11. Trade good questions with other faculty members. A published resource of astronomy questions, some conceptual, is Green (2003), and an online version is at http://hea-www.harvard.edu/%7Epgreen/educ/ConcepTests.html.

Duncan (2009) lists the most common misuses of clicker technology that lead to failure. Avoiding known failure modes is very useful in successful technology use.

Some of the most powerful gains from the use of clickers come when they are used in peer instruction (Mazur 1997). Peer instruction is when students are expected to discuss and solve challenging conceptual questions with other students during class. Mazur and his colleagues have been industrious in collecting data over many years that demonstrate how the learning gains from peer instruction surpass that of any pure lecture class (Crouch & Mazur 2001). Peer instruction can be facilitated by the use of colored cards or by clickers. Lasry (2008) found that both clickers and colored cards used with peer instruction produced the same learning gains. Both were significantly more than traditional lecture classes.

The University of Colorado has had tens of thousands of clickers in use for more than 10 years, and colored cards before that. Assessment data shown in Figure 4.3 (S. Pollock 2007, private communication) replicate the results of Hake and Mazur.

This data shows larger learning gains for clickers than colored cards; however, clickers have been in use at CU for many years, and colored cards were only used for one year. As technology users get more practice, they usually incorporate and discover aspects of implementation that increase effectiveness, such as the list for clickers above, and their results usually improve, so this might explain the larger learning gains with clickers over cards.

When peer instruction first came to be widely used, some faculty wondered if it was simply a way that poor students copied what good students said. The work of Smith et al. (2009) demonstrates clearly that a scientific discussion between students produces genuine learning. This is true for both the student with the higher as well as the lower grade.

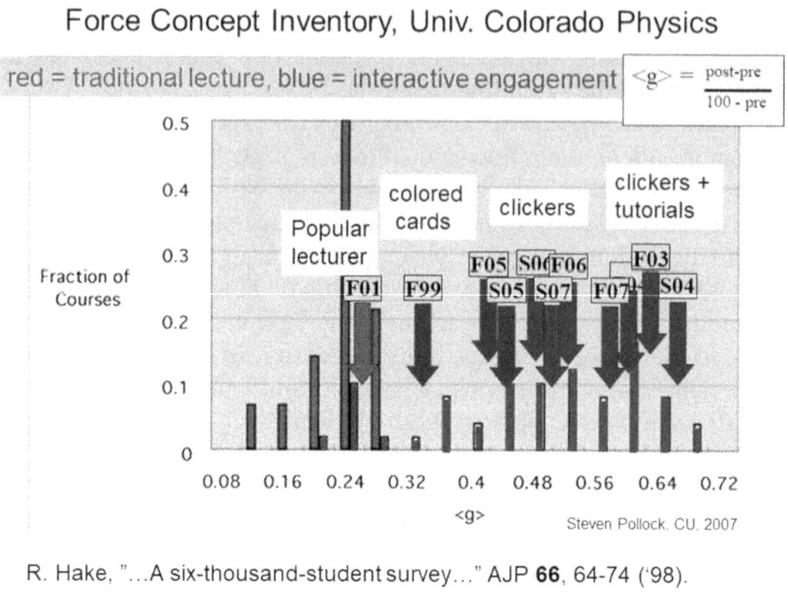

Figure 4.3. University of Colorado results superimposed on those of Hake (1998).

A benefit of peer instruction is that the "give-and-take atmosphere" encouraged by the use of clickers (or colored cards) makes the students more responsive in general, so that questions posed to the class as a whole during lecture are much more likely to elicit responses and discussion (Wood 2004). This makes for a more lively and enjoyable class.

Another extremely important benefit of peer instruction is that when students talk to each other, they make their assumptions and thoughts visible to you in a way that you would not otherwise know. Philip Sadler's Harvard PhD dissertation (1992) made clear how many astronomy-related ideas students learn when they are young, before ever taking a college astronomy course. If these preconceptions (which are often wrong, though they make sense to the students; they could be called misconceptions) are not addressed during instruction, students often cling to the ideas that they have believed in for a long time and do not learn what is taught in the astronomy class. Schneps & Sadler (1988) documented this in one of the most famous teaching-related videos of all time, "A Private Universe." That 20 minute video is available through the Annenberg Foundation and is highly recommended. Excerpts are also available on YouTube. While the students are discussing a peer discussion question, you, the instructor, walk around and listen to their arguments. This is one of the best ways to understand your students' reasoning processes. Nobel Laureate Carl Wieman, one of the founders of the large discipline-based (science) education research effort at the University of Colorado, is a fan of the children's book, *Fish is Fish*. For those not familiar with the story, two fishy friends have long wondered what is out on the land. One of the fish turns out to be a tadpole, and he promises his friend that he will go out on land and report back what he sees. He tells

Figure 4.4. "Birds" illustration from *Fish is Fish* by Leo Lionni, copyright © 1970 and renewed 1998 by NORAELEO LLC. Used by permission of Alfred A. Knopf, an imprint of Random House Children's Books, a division of Penguin Random House LLC. All rights reserved.

his friend that there are amazing creatures called "birds," and that they have feathers, and wings, and fly through the air. His friend thanks him: "Now I understand birds." Figure 4.4 shows what he thinks. This, of course, is what happens in the mind of your students when you teach them astronomy concepts. They take what you tell them, put it into their own context, and their beliefs are constructed from both sources.

The "reason for the seasons" is one of the concepts dramatized in "A Private Universe." If you have ever taught how the Earth's tilt causes the seasons, and then found students explaining that the Earth's tilt causes "part of the Earth to be closer to the Sun," you have seen an example similar to *Fish is Fish* where prior incorrect beliefs get combined with a correct explanation. Technology that gets students to talk and lets you listen to them talking is extremely valuable for identifying student beliefs and reasoning patterns. Students talk to each other in more unguarded ways than they talk to the instructor.

A perhaps surprising aspect of clickers observed at Colorado and elsewhere is that having more features on the clicker often produces less learning and more logistical difficulties. This is probably because the brain has a limited cognitive capacity and when part of it needs to pay attention to how to use a device, less is available to pay attention to the concept being taught (*Thinking Fast and Slow*, Kahneman 2011). This is true of any technology you adopt for student use. University of Colorado physics and astronomy faculty often meet with the iClicker company and each time lobby them to continue to offer a basic clicker with nothing on it besides A, B, C, D, E, and an on–off switch. Cognitive capacity is discussed more extensively in the section on video below.
3. Smartphone Apps—Does the Technology Increase or Decrease Student Engagement?

Nearly every college student carries a smartphone nowadays, and an application on the phone can serve a similar purpose to a clicker, at lower cost. A number of companies offer these, including iClickers' REEF Polling, which allows the use of any device with a browser or which can download it as an app. Learning Catalytics, which allows students to use any Wi-Fi-enabled device; TopHat, which allows students to use any Wi-Fi-enabled or texting device; and Squarecap, which allows students to use any Wi-Fi-enabled device. There is a potential problem with encouraging students to use their phone in class, however.

4.4 Technology that Reduces Student Engagement and Learning—Smartphones and Laptop Computers

Probably everyone who teaches has now observed the large amount of phone use, usually for texting, among college students. Duncan et al. (2012) found that roughly 75% of students at a large state university used their phones during class, and their grades were significantly lower than those of the students who did not use a phone. Additional data make this problem even clearer.

The methodology of Duncan, Hoekstra, and Wilcox included extensive classroom observation, anonymous student surveys, and many anonymous, private interviews. Two important results are that no faculty member saw even half of the texting taking place in their class, and that most students said that phone policy should be set by the instructor and that if there was no policy, it was fine to text when students wanted. Typical quotes from the anonymous student interviews include, "When you go to class, it's a time to sit down and text." "Sometimes people are texting all the time and it really gets annoying." "I would say that I probably send 16 text messages in a class, definitely." In 2009 Ophir, Nass, and Wagner (Ophir et al. 2009) tested Stanford undergraduates, documented the cognitive price that multitaskers play, and also documented that students far overestimated their ability to multitask. Students in the Duncan, Hoekstra, and Wilcox study also evidenced little appreciation for how their texting would interfere with learning astronomy. Ward et al. (2017) found that the mere presence of one's own smartphone (in a pocket or bag) reduces available cognitive capacity.

Patterson & Patterson (2017) show that taking notes on a laptop reduces students' grades compared to taking notes on paper. Sana et al. (2013) showed that students sitting behind laptop users had a large drop in their grades (Figure 4.5). A short observation of almost any college classroom (try it; sit quietly in the back of any classroom for just 5 minutes) shows a shockingly high percentage of laptop users have multiple windows open and are multitasking.

Given the substantial evidence that multitasking on smartphones or laptops reduces student grades and that students are not very aware of the impact, it is impossible for the author to recommend using smartphone apps in place of clickers or colored cards, at least until published data demonstrate that peer instruction mediated by phones produces the same significant learning gains as peer instruction mediated by cards or clickers. A comparative test of clickers versus phone apps is planned for the very large introductory chemistry class at the University of Colorado

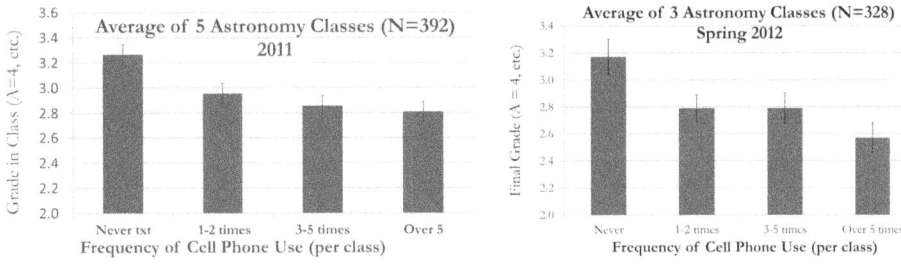

Figure 4.5. Grades vs. frequency of texting. Reproduced from Duncan et al. (2012).

in fall 2018. As of spring 2018, 10,000 clickers are being purchased by CU students each year, and no faculty member is known to have substituted a phone app for clickers.

Katz & Lambert (2016) experimented with giving students in an introductory psychology class a small amount of positive credit for putting their phones away. They argue that positive reinforcement is more effective than negative reinforcement and present comments in which college students confirm that view. D. K. Duncan (2015, unpublished) experimented with giving students in a 50 person astronomy class participation credit each time they put their phone on the desk in front of them and did not use it during class. By the end of the term, both Katz and Lambert's students and Duncan's students were extremely positive about the experiment. Many commented that engagement was greater, and they actually appreciated a break from immediate phone use. However, this approach seems infeasible in larger astronomy classes and ones without desks for each student. A possible approach is with the technology of an app called FLIPD (http://www.flipdapp.co/). The FLIPD app allows students to lock themselves out of phone use for the duration of a class, and it makes a report available to faculty showing which students were not using their phones during class. Using this app and giving a small amount of "positive reinforcement credit" seems a potentially promising approach for getting greater student engagement.

4. Science Videos

Videos can bring subjects into the classroom that students would otherwise not see. Ludwig et al. (2004) find that videos can raise student interest level, enhance understanding, and increase memorability. They can be dramatic, sometimes with professional production values, and often more up to date than a textbook. However, videos themselves are passive. Is the learning produced by watching videos more like a traditional passive lecture, or can it be like more active classrooms? This is a consideration in MOOCs, massive online courses that are being used more and more. There are also "flipped" classrooms, in which students are supposed to watch videos to learn subjects, then discuss the subjects and practice problem solving in class. How well does that work? How the technology is prepared and used affects the learning in both settings.

When students watch a video (or, for that matter, a lecture), they need to input audio and visual material into their brain, combine it with what they already know,

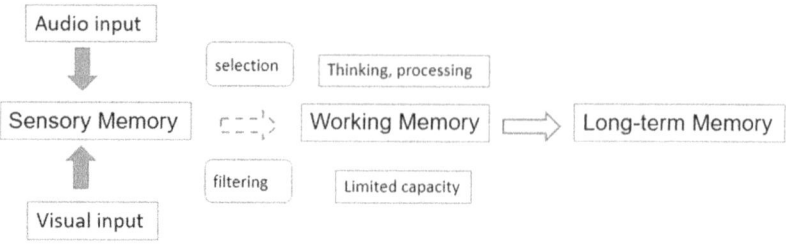

Figure 4.6. Learning is affected by limitations of cognitive load (Mayer & Moreno 2007).

and (ideally) encode it in an appropriate place in their long-term memory. Cognitive scientists (Sweller 1988, 1994; Moreno & Mayer 2007) often model this as follows. All of our brains do considerable filtering so that our "working memory" is not overloaded. Input includes intrinsic, germane, and extraneous factors. Intrinsic factors include information that must be processed, such as the vocabulary used, whether students recognize the objects in a video, or the operating system of any software the students use. Because these are not directly germane to the science lesson being taught, they need to be structured to take up as little of the students working memory as possible. That is why Colorado faculty choose "clickers" with the minimum number of functions. The germane load is the cognitive activity related to the lesson being taught (Figure 4.6). The extraneous load is anything else that the students notice and think about. This could include unnecessary information, items that a novice student recalls from memory but that are not germane, and music or background in a video that is not related to the concept. The PHeT applets discussed below pay enormous attention to intrinsic, germane, and extraneous load during development. Developers videotape many hours of college students using prototypes. (Students are paid to do this.) The apps are then constantly modified to reduce intrinsic and extraneous load.

The free, very widely used tutorials of the Kahn Academy (www.khanacademy.org) almost always use video and audio at the same time, making "input" more effective. In Kahn videos, when the teacher explains something, she or he writes it on the screen. Using both audio and visual parts of the brain is more effective than, for example, overlaying a printed explanation on a video, because both use visual input to the brain (Mayer & Moreno 2003). Screen recording and video editing software such as Camtasia make it relatively easy to create your own version of Kahn Academy lessons.

Various approaches exist to help students concentrate on the germane parts of videos and maximize their learning:
1. Keep it short. Video segments of approximately 5 minute duration maximize the attention of most viewers; at 10 minutes or longer, student attention drops significantly or they do not watch the entire video (Guo et al. 2014). A short segment also reduces cognitive load, and it should teach one or at most a few ideas.
2. Expect students to control the flow of the video, and insert breaks, comments, or questions that students must answer before they go on. This is

somewhat akin to clicker questions in class—it requires the viewer to become an active learner. Many learning management systems (e.g., Canvas) allow videos to be annotated, captioned, or stopped. Videos can also be tied to an assignment that requires students to write a response.
3. Signal what is important. Segmenting videos, and introducing each segment with a title, directs student's attention. Movies use sound to influence viewer's concentration; simple sound cues can sometimes be effective if not overdone. The same is true of arrows, which can be used to direct novices' attention to a part of a video that the instructor or expert wants them to notice.
4. Take out what is not necessary. As Brame (2015) points out, one needs to consider the intended audience for a video when making it. Experts and novices notice different things when watching a video or a demonstration. Information that may be extraneous for a novice learner may actually be helpful for a more expert-like learner, while information that is essential for a novice may serve as an already-known distraction for an expert.

The PhD work of Derek Muller presents a more fundamental challenge to those trying to teach science with videos. Muller dramatized his results in a TEDx talk available on YouTube (https://www.youtube.com/watch?v=RQaW2bFieo8). He made two videos explaining forces and motions. The first was very smooth and clear. It featured a "stop motion" scene of a basketball in mid-air and discussed the forces on the ball. Vectors were drawn on the picture to illustrate the forces. In the second video, when the ball is stopped, two people argue about the forces on the ball. One expresses a common but incorrect belief, the other disagrees with the first speaker and presents the correct answer. Students preferred the first video, calling it, "clear, concise, and easy to understand." Their learning gains were measured using the Force Concept Inventory, and the gains were essentially zero. They called the second video confusing. A student remarked, "I had to watch it more than once to decide who was right." These students' pre- and posttests revealed significant learning gains. This is the same methodology used in *Lecture-Tutorials for Introductory Astronomy* (Prather et al. 2012) in which "Student 1" and "Student 2" disagree, one presenting a commonly held misconception and the other a correct conception. Confronting conceptual difficulties, passing through a period of confusion and introspection, has been shown to increase learning significantly; lecture-tutorials have produced significant learning gains in classrooms throughout the U.S. Video producers should explore how technology might be used to enable videos to lead students in an active way through multiple conflicting ideas to correct ideas.

5. Flipped Classrooms

There is currently much "buzz" in educational circles about "flipped classrooms." Definitions vary, but typically a flipped classroom asks students to watch a video version of a lecture before class, and to spend class time discussing questions, working problems, and interacting with the teacher.

At the time of writing this review chapter, data are just beginning to document under what circumstances flipped classrooms increase student engagement and

learning. Reviews are given by Zainuddin & Halili (2016) and Goodwin & Miller (2013). Some aspects that are important include the following:
1. Quality of the out-of-class videos and a system that lets students control starting, stopping, and searching is important, for reasons discussed in the preceding section on videos;
2. Motivation of the students—they are supposed to do significant work alone, in advance. That requires motivation and discipline.
3. Giving students control of the video lecture allows self-paced learning.
4. In terms of Bloom's taxonomy (1969), the simpler stages of learning (memorization) are relegated to the videos, while more complex stages (understanding, analyzing, etc.) receive more time in class, with the instructor.

The four listed factors can increase engagement and learning. However, as with other technologies, implementation is critical. As Strayer (2012) puts it:

"[success is achieved when] teachers go beyond just replacing the lecture with an online learning event. Interactive technologies make it possible for educators to qualitatively reconceptualize the teaching and learning dynamic. By augmenting the fast-paced interaction and dialogue that happens in the face-to-face setting with an online learning environment that gives students space to take in new ideas, deliberate and carefully express their thoughts on the subject, teachers are able to create learning communities that are more connected and more stable than we have seen in the past."

However, achieving this dynamic as well as coherence and synergism between the in and out of the class parts of a flipped classroom is a significant challenge. It requires careful class design as well as the support of appropriate and dependable technology. Students know what to expect in a traditional class structure, and adapting to a new structure such as a flipped classroom is a challenge for them (Strayer 2012). As discussed in the Metacognition section below, it is important to directly discuss with students what they are expected to do and the reasons behind your methods.

Those researching published results of flipped classrooms should be careful to note the control group used in any study; it is often a traditional lecture classroom. As shown in the Hake and University of Colorado data presented above, interactive engagement methods in the classroom produce larger learning gains than traditional lectures. That is true both with and without a flipped classroom.

An important consideration in any assignment given to students is whether they will do it the way that you wanted and expected them to do it. (See the section discussing this below.) With respect to flipped classrooms, anecdotal comments expressed to Duncan by some college students included many who said that flipped classrooms saved them time but they did not think it improved their learning. "You fast-forward through the videos until you find the answer to a question you were asked, then you fast-forward to answer the next question" was an opinion expressed by multiple students. Many who teach put considerable thought into the structure and pacing of lectures (including where the breaks for questions and deliberation take place), and of course, students cannot "fast-forward" through your live lecture. They can through a video lecture. How students use out-of-class materials affects their success; this is also true in the use of online homework (Section 7).

Much more research is needed on the efficacy and dynamics of flipped classrooms.

6. PHeT and other online help

The free PHeT applets developed at the University of Colorado (http://phet.colorado.edu) have been used over 360 million times worldwide and translated into over 65 languages. This is almost certainly the most widely used science teaching tool in history. Founded in 2002 by Nobel Laureate Carl Wieman when he switched his research from atomic physics to research on university physics teaching (Discipline-based Education Research; DBER), the project achieves its remarkable success through careful attention to intrinsic, germane, and extraneous load during development. Well-funded, the PHeT project videotapes hundreds of hours of student use of prototypes, and continuously improves the interface to improve student learning. The PHeT applets are not lessons—they are tools. It is up to the instructor how to use them, but they are designed to make students an active participant in their own learning. Originally designed for college physics instruction, PHeT has branched out into chemistry, some biology, and some astronomy. Particularly useful in astronomy are the "Black Body," "My Solar System," "Gas Properties," and "States of Matter" applets. These can be used for demonstrations (though see warnings in the "Demonstration" section below), homework, or recitation activities. Recitation or homework settings are valuable because the simulations are designed for students' exploration and engagement, which take an unpredictable amount of time and often lead to questions not written by the instructor. Such "exploration" is more like actual science than answering questions with one expected correct answer. Many universities have a program called "Learning Assistants"[2] (highly recommended; https://www.learningassistantalliance.org/), which facilitates having discussion groups in classes that otherwise would not have them. PHeT applets and Tutorials (cf. the following section, Technology Made of Paper) are often used in learning-assistant-led recitations.

D. K. Duncan (2018, unpublished) uses the "My Solar System" app and asks students to make a solar system with two or three massive planets. Students are not told about the dynamics of multibody systems. They discover to their surprise how difficult it is to produce stability and not eject or change the orbits of one or more planets. This illustrates in a very convincing way the idea surprising to many students (and to professional astronomers until the last few decades; Gomes et al.

---

[2] A learning assistant, or LA, is an undergraduate student who, through the guidance of course instructors and a special pedagogy course, facilitates discussions among groups of students in a variety of classroom settings that encourage student engagement and responsibility for learning.

2005) that solar systems can go through periods of dynamical instability and drastic changes in planetary orbits.

The free Kahn Academy videos mentioned above cover many topics, including basic algebra, vectors, and other math useful in astronomy, as well as some astronomy topics. They can include quizzes that test students' achievement. They generally incorporate the four good approaches that help students concentrate on the germane parts of the videos, as enumerated in the previous section.

7. Online homework

Many astronomy textbooks come with online learning systems. For five consecutive years, Duncan surveyed introductory students as to the relative learning benefits of lectures, online homework, written homework, the textbook, planetarium and telescope use, and other class components. The online homework (e.g., "Mastering Astronomy") was rated highly, sometimes higher than the textbook. Students typically like the online homework. Such systems can present animations or videos that cannot be assigned with written homework, and they give immediate feedback. However, evidence that online homework increases student learning is surprisingly weak. Allain and Williams found little difference in students' learning gains when comparing students assigned written homework that was not graded to those using WebAssign (http://webassign.net). They found learning gains on a conceptual test, the Astronomy Diagnostic Test (Hufnagel et al. 2000), ranged from $\langle g \rangle$ (the normalized learning gain defined above) 0.05 to 0.15. In other words, learning gains were small.

Duncan regularly plots student grades versus time spent on the assigned Mastering Astronomy online homework. Class sizes range from 75–150 students. Two results appear year after year:
1. The correlation between time spent on the online homework and student grades is positive, but weak. Correlation coefficients $R^2 \sim 0.15$ are typical.
2. There is a wide range in time spent on the homework. The average is about half an hour but the range from 15 minutes to an hour is well-populated. (The online system records how much time students spend on the homework.)

Without tracking individual students, it is difficult to interpret the value of online homework. Some students go rapidly through the homework and guess; others use it more carefully and thoughtfully. However, some good students go through the homework rapidly because they know most of the answers. Research more carefully tracking the actual use of online homework would be valuable.

8. Demonstrations

Most physicists and astronomers love "cool" demonstrations. Using a beautiful Orrery or climbing a ladder and "doing the Galileo experiment" of dropping heavy and light objects can certainly get students' attention. But how much do they learn? As shown in "A Private Universe" when one student is called on to do a demonstration, the others can be passive and just watching, their thinking not challenged. Mazur (2011) presents evidence that demonstrations as usually performed produce little student learning. The problem is that when novices see a demonstration, they remember it in terms of their mental model, which may include misconceptions. Weeks later, they think the demo showed what they already believed. On some of the wrong answers that students gave Mazur, they actually said, "As shown in the demo." Mazur's work shows that predicting the outcome of a demonstration before doing it increases learning, but it does not solve the problem of misremembering what the demonstration showed.

9. Paper "Technology"

Is paper, or a "sticky note," a technology? No matter how classified, sometimes something written on a piece of paper is the approach that produces student learning and engagement. A very simple technique employed by many of the astronomy faculty at the University of Colorado is to reward with a "sticky note" (from a pad of sticky notes) students who answer a professor's question posed to the class, or who ask a good question. Students write their name on the note and leave it at the end of class, and it is worth a small amount of credit, for example, credit equal to answering one clicker question. This tangible reward significantly increases class participation, and even in a class of 100 or more students, a majority will participate and get a sticky note, especially if the instructor makes an effort to call on a variety of students and not always the same ones.

Some of the most thoroughly documented increases in the learning of astronomy students come from the use of "lecture-tutorials" (Prather et al. 2009; Wallace et al. 2011; LoPresto & Slater 2016). These are based on research with hundreds of introductory astronomy students that reveals something important and useful: certain misconceptions appear year after year. Knowing this research means that before your students walk in the classroom door, you can already know that many of them think the seasons are caused by our distance from the Sun, that the Big Bang was when galaxies exploded out into preexisting space, or that the Earth's mantle is liquid, because you see magma coming out of volcanoes. These ideas often make sense to the students holding them, and they are sometimes called preconceptions. Knowing students' prior ideas allows curricula to be developed that directly confront commonly held misconceptions. As originally developed by Adams et al. (2003) and further by Prather et al. (2013), lecture-tutorials are workbook chapters a few pages long that feature discussions between "Student 1" and "Student 2." One answers an astronomy question with a common misconception and the other presents the correct answer. Users of the workbook are asked to agree with one student or the other. (The PhD work of Muller, described in the previous section on Science Videos, was motivated by the lecture-tutorial approach.)

Conceptual learning gains produced with tutorials can be impressive. Figure 4.7 is from LoPresto & Slater (2016) and Figure 4.8 from Wallace et al. (2011). Learning gains from lecture alone are modest, averaging a gain from 42% correct to 47% correct in LoPresto and Slater's study. When tutorials and classroom voting/peer discussion were added 73% average correct was achieved.

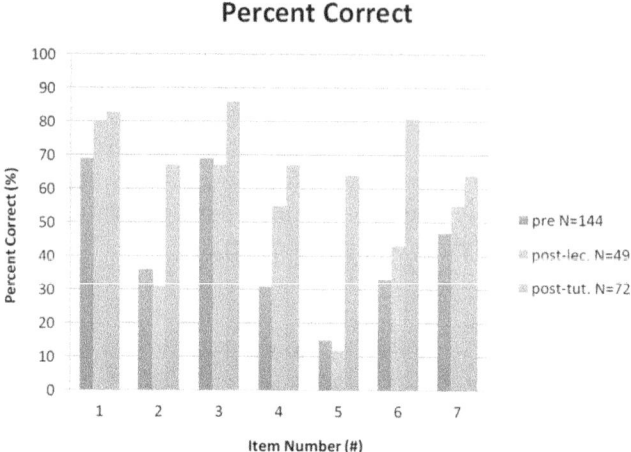

Figure 4.7. Lecture-tutorials (rightmost gray bars) produced large gains. Reprinted from LoPresto & Slater (2016). CC-BY 3.0.

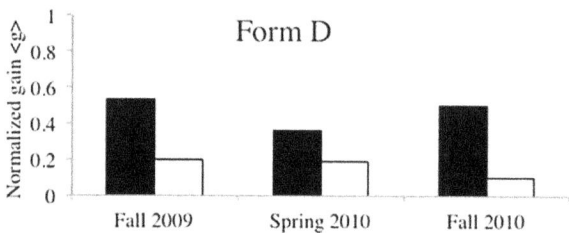

Figure 4.8. Normalized gains of lecture-tutorial (black bars) and non-LLT (white bars) students. From Wallace et al (2011), reprinted by permission of Taylor and Francis, Ltd.

For his PhD thesis, Wallace et al. (2011) researched students' conceptions of cosmology and developed four tutorials to confront misconceptions. Three of the four were quite effective, and the results from one of them are shown in Figure 4.8, presented in terms of the normalized gain $\langle g \rangle$ defined in the Introduction to this chapter. Much greater conceptual learning gains are present in the lecture-tutorial classes, and this was also substantiated through student interviews.

4.5 The Same Technology, Highly Different Outcomes: Why? Differences in Implementation

With tens of thousands of clickers in use at the University of Colorado, faculty members have heard thousands of student opinions about the use of clickers. A majority find that the technology leads to more engagement and more learning, and that they like it. A minority complain: "It sucks." "A waste of time and money." What is the difference? Implementation. Duncan (2009) has categorized uses of clicker technology that lead to success and those that lead to failure, based on student comments. Sociologist Hoekstra studied student views about classroom

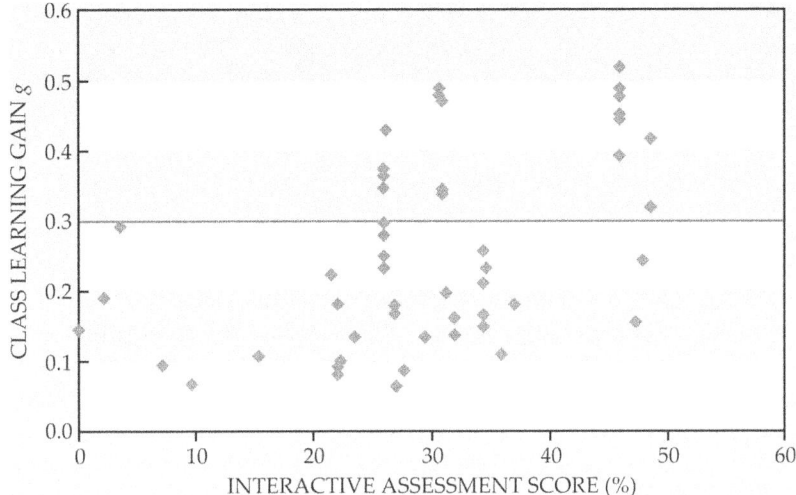

Figure 4.9. Highly interactive classes can produce large learning gains, but this is not guaranteed. Reprinted from Prather et al. (2009), with the permission of AIP Publishing.

technology for her PhD thesis (Hoekstra 2008). Comments to her in anonymous student interviews could be quite brutal, "Could someone please make my [x] teacher take a physics course so that she learns how to use clickers [effectively]?" This result cannot be emphasized too much:

How you implement a technology makes a huge difference to success.

Duncan (2009) found that it was essential that faculty members explain *why* engagement with the professor was good for students. It is easier for students to sit in the back of a class and not pay attention than to engage with the teacher via clickers or colored cards. The same students usually sit in the front of the class, wanting to engage, and the same students in the back, not wanting to engage. Unless the teacher explains the value of engagement, there is likely to be "pushback" against technology that increases engagement.

Prather at al. (2009; reproduced in Figure 4.9) conducted a national survey of astronomy classes conducted with various degrees of interactive engagement. Conceptual learning gains were measured with the Light and Spectra Concept Inventory (Bardar 2007), and those teaching were assessed for the degree of interactivity of their teaching. The highest learning gains were all in classes that engaged students more interactively. However, many supposedly interactive classes produced low learning gains. Prather et al. conclude that implementation makes a large difference in student learning.

Even technologies that look simple such as asking students to choose A, B, C, D, or E using a card or a clicker require practice by the instructor to determine how much time to give students to talk, how to encourage quiet students to participate, and how to convince a class that the use of the technology will benefit them and that it deserves their serious participation. It may seem obvious to an instructor that the student who listens to their neighbor in a peer discussion and then uses the remaining discussion time to send a text will not benefit much from peer discussion. However, students conditioned to thinking that science classes are all about "the right answer" rather than conceptual understanding will not be very thoughtful about their own learning unless you discuss that with them—see the section on Metacognition below.

4.6 Do Not Assume that Students Will Use It Like You Designed It

Students may use the very same technology but derive a wide range in learning gains, depending on how, and how thoughtfully, they use the technology. Those whose teaching incorporate online homework and tutorial systems often have the ability to track how long students spend on the work. If you find that one student spends 10 minutes on a lesson and another an hour on the same lesson, perhaps on a lesson that you designed to take about 30 minutes, you have a strong indication of varying degrees of thoughtfulness.

As discussed in the section on flipped classrooms, students have learned that they can "fast-forward" through the online lectures to find answers, and that is probably not the way the videos were designed to be used. Lecture-tutorials made of paper are usually used in the classroom. If students are assigned to do them on their own, at home, they can easily find all the answers online and complete them without thinking.

There is no substitute for testing a new technology as it is actually used by students, which may or may not be what you designed. The great success of the PHeT applets is in large part due to extensive observation of actual student use and improvement based on observation.

4.7 The Importance of Metacognition

When technology is introduced into teaching, it usually changes the way that students study and learn. Having metacognitive discussions with your students—getting them to explicitly think about their own learning—can help them use the technology in ways that you want them to and in ways most beneficial to their learning. CLASS, the "Colorado Learning Attitudes about Science Survey" (https://www.colorado.edu/sei/class/), can be used to reveal students' attitudes about how to learn science. Dr. Steven Chu has created an excellent series of five videos, available on YouTube, that demonstrate effective and ineffective ways to study (e.g., How to Get the Most Out of Studying "Beliefs That Make You Stupid": https://www.youtube.com/watch?v=RH95h36NChI) that can help students realize the importance of being engaged and focused when they try and learn.

One of the biggest differences between experts and novices is that experts constantly check their own thinking and their own work. Experts are thoughtful about their assumptions and sometimes solve a problem in more than one way to check their answers. They do not just "get answers"; they ask themselves if the answers make sense. These metacognitive skills need to develop for students to become experts (Perkins & Gratny 2010).

Experts usually believe that knowledge is something you incrementally gain, rather than something innate (a "fixed" mindset; Dweck 2007). Weimer's (2012)

"Deep Learning vs. Surface Learning: Getting Students to Understand the Difference" emphasizes the importance of developing students' metacognitive awareness. Lovett (2013) shows that teaching metacognition improves student learning and can particularly benefit minority students or other students that have less experience with learning difficult concepts.

4.8 Assessment: How Do You Know If You Reached Your Goal?

A full discussion of assessment is not the subject of this chapter, but it is useful to consider how assessment can help the implementation of technology succeed. Assessment comes in two forms, summative and formative. Summative assessments come at the end of instruction and can, for example, be used to assign grades. Formative assessments are used during instruction, and they can provide very useful information that allows "midcourse corrections," especially when you begin to use new technology and new teaching approaches.

Assessment can also be quantitative or qualitative (or mixed methods). As trained astronomers and physicists, many of us like quantitative assessments and surveys that can report means and standard deviations. However, it is the experience of the author that qualitative (or "ethnographic") assessments in which students anonymously give feedback about a class (or are observed) can be even more valuable, and this is particularly true when using new technology. The most important result of this kind of feedback is when students bring up topics that you never thought of asking about or surveying. It does not take a large sample to get extremely useful feedback from open-ended student comments. If there is an issue with your technology or your class, it will become apparent when roughly 10 or so students give comments.

A very nice summary of easy-to-use Classroom Assessment Techniques ("CATS," 2018) can be found at https://cft.vanderbilt.edu/guides-sub-pages/cats/.

References

Adams, J. P., Prather, E. E., & Slater, T. P. 2003, Lecture-Tutorials for Introductory Astronomy (San Francisco, CA: Pearson Education)
Allain, R., & Williams, T. 2006, JCSTe, 35, 28
Bandura, A. 1977, Social Learning Theory (Englewood Cliffs, NJ: Prentice Hall)
Bardar, E. M. 2007, AEdRv, 6, 75
Bloom, B. S. 1969, Taxonomy of Educational Objectives: The Classification of Educational Goals by a Committee of College and University Examiners: Handbook 1 (New York: D. McKay)
Bishop, J. L. 2013, in Proc. 120th American Society for Engineering Education Annu. Conf. and Exposition (Washington, DC: ASEE)
Bowen, R. S. 2018, Understanding by Design, (Nashville, TN: Vanderbilt University Center for Teaching), https://cft.vanderbilt.edu/understanding-by-design
Brame, C. J. 2015, Effective Educational Videos, http://cft.vanderbilt.edu/guides-sub-pages/effective-educational-videos/
Bransford, J. D., & Donovan, M. S. 2005, How Students Learn: Science in the Classroom (Washington, DC: National Academies Press)
Bunce, D. M., Flens, E. A., & Neiles, K. Y. 2010, JChEd, 87, 1438

Crouch, C. H., & Mazur, E. 2001, AmJPh, 69, 970

Duncan, D. K. 2009, Tips for Successful Clicker Use, http://www.cwsei.ubc.ca/resources/files/Tips_for_Successful_Clicker_Use_Duncan.pdf

Duncan, D. K., Hoekstra, A. R., & Wilcox, B. R. 2012, AEdRv, 11, 010108

Dweck, C. S. 2007, Mindset: The New Psychology of Success (New York: Penguin Random House)

Green, P. J. 2003, Peer Instruction in Astronomy (Upper Saddle River, NJ: Pearson Education)

Guo, P. J., Kim, J., & Rubin, R. 2014, in Proc. First ACM Conf. on Learning @ Scale Conf. (New York: ACM), 41

Gomes, R., Levison, H. F., Tsiganis, K., & Morbidelli, A. 2005, Natur, 435, 466

Goodwin, B., & Miller, K. 2013, Technology Rich Learning, 70, 78

Hake, R. R. 1998, AmJPh, 66, 64

Hestenes, D., & Wells, M. 1992, PhTea, 30, 159

Hestenes, D., Wells, M., & Swackhamer, G. 1992, PhTea, 30, 141

Hoekstra, A. 2008, Learning Media and Technology, 33, 329

Hufnagel, B., Slater, T., Deming, G., et al. 2000, PASA, 17, 152

James, M. C. 2006, AmJPh, 74, 689–91

Kahneman, D. 2011, Thinking, Fast and Slow (London: Macmillan)

Katz, L., & Lambert, W. 2016, Teaching of Psychology, 43, 340

Kuh, G. D., Cruce, T. M., Shoup, R., Kinzie, J., & Gonyea, R. M. 2008, Journal of Higher Education, 79, 540

Lasry, N. 2008, PhTea, 46, 242

Lightman, A., & Sadler, P. M. 1993, PhTea, 31, 162

LoPresto, M. C., & Slater, T. F. 2016, JAESE, 3, 59

Lovett, M. C. 2013, in Using Reflection and Metacognition to Improve Student Learning: Across the Disciplines, Across the Academy (Sterling, VA: Stylus), 18

Ludwig, T., Daniel, D. B., Froman, R., & Mathie, V. A. 2004, The Society for the Teaching of Psychology Pedagogical Innovations Task Force, http://teachpsych.org/resources/pedagogy/classroommultimedia.pdf

Mayer, R. E., & Moreno, R. 2003, Educational Psychologist, 38, 43

Moreno, R., & Mayer, R. 2007, Educational Psychology Review, 19, 309

Mazur, E. 1997, Peer Instruction: A User's Manual (San Francisco, CA: Pearson Education)

Mazur, E. 2011, Observing Demos Hurts Learning, and Confusion is a Sign of Understanding, https://computinged.wordpress.com/2011/08/17/eric-mazurs-keynote-at-icer-2011-observing-demos-hurts-learning-and-confusion-is-a-sign-of-understanding/

National Association of Colleges and Employers 2018, http://www.naceweb.org/

National Research Council 2000, How People Learn: Brain, Mind, Experience, and School, Expanded Edition, ed. J. D. Bransford, A. L. Brown, & R. R. Cocking (Washington, DC: National Academies Press)

Ophir, E., Nass, C., & Wagner, A. D. 2009, PNAS, 106, 15583

Patterson, R. W., & Patterson, R. M. 2017, Economics of Education Review, 57, 66

Perkins, K., & Gratny, M. 2010, in AIP Conf. Proc. 1289, Physics Education Research Conf., ed. C. Singh, M. Sabella, & S. Rebello (Melville, NY: AIP), 253

Prather, E. E., Slater, T. F., Adams, J. P., et al. 2004, AEdRv, 3, 122

Prather, E., Slater, T., Adams, J. P., & Brissenden, G. 2013, Lecture-Tutorials for Introductory Astronomy (3rd ed.; San Francisco, CA: Benjamin Cummings)

Prather, E. E., Rudolph, A. L., & Brissenden, G. 2009, PhT, 62, 41

Sana, F., Weston, T., & Cepeda, N. J. 2013, Computers & Education, 62, 24

Sadler, P. M. 1992, PhD dissertation, Harvard Univ.

Schneps, M., & Sadler, P. 1988, A Private Universe, https://www.learner.org/vod/vod_window.html?pid=9

Seymour, E., & Hewitt, N. M. 1997, Talking about Leaving: Why Undergraduates Leave the Sciences (Boulder, CO: Westview Press)

Slater, T., Adams, J. P., Brissenden, G., & Duncan, D. 2001, PhTea, 39, 52

Smith, M. K., Wood, W. B., Adams, W. K., et al. 2009, Sci, 323, 122

Strayer, J. F. 2012, Learning Environments Research, 15, 171

Sweller, J. 1988, Cognitive Science, 12, 257

Sweller, J. 1994, Learning and Instruction, 4, 295

University of Texas (Austin) Teaching Portal 2018, https://cns.utexas.edu/teaching-portal

Vygotsky, L. S. 1962, Thought and Language (Cambridge, MA: MIT Press)

Wallace, C., Prather, E., & Duncan, D. 2011, AEdRv, 10, 0107

Ward, A. F., Duke, K., Gneezy, A., & Bos, M. W. 2017, Journal of the Association for Consumer Research, 2, 140

Weimer, M. 2012, Deep Learning vs. Surface Learning: Getting Students to Understand the Difference, https://www.facultyfocus.com/topic/articles/teaching-professor-blog/

Wiggins, G. P., & McTighe, J. 2008, Understanding by Design (Alexandria, VA: Association for Supervision and Curriculum Development)

Willoughby, S. D., & Gustafson, E. 2009, AmJPh, 77, 180

Wood, W. B. 2004, Developmental Cell, 7, 796

Zainuddin, Z., & Halili, S. H. 2016, The International Review of Research in Open and Distributed Learning, 17, doi: 10.19173/irrodl.v17i3.2274

Astronomy Education, Volume 1
Evidence-based instruction for introductory courses
Chris Impey and Sanlyn Buxner

Chapter 5

Using Simulations Interactively in the Introductory Astronomy Classroom

Kevin M Lee

Educational research shows the efficacy of interactive pedagogies, leading to current efforts to replace instructor-centered lectures with new methods centered on the learner. Scientific computer simulations can play a critical part in this educational transformation, as they engage users in a visually vibrant exploration of phenomena, which encourages users to perform experiments and test their understanding of the underlying relationships. Simulation use can have a unique impact in astronomy where so much of the content is far beyond the experience of students. This paper will focus on a framework for interactive simulation usage in the classroom consistent with the recommendations of educational research and illustrate its use with two widely used simulations.

Chapter Objectives

By the end of the chapter, readers will be able to
- describe the value of simulations and the role they can play in the classroom,
- give examples of the importance of interactive learner-centered instruction and motivate the importance of interactive use of simulations in the classroom,
- describe a framework guiding interactive usage of simulations in the classroom;
- give examples of the framework applied to two simulations, and
- visualize how they could extend the process to other simulations.

5.1 Characteristics of Computer Simulations

Computer simulations are an exciting component of science education that recreate a modeled or modified version of a real situation. The report *Learning Science Through Computer Games and Simulations* (National Research Council 2011) discusses a wide variety of science simulations (as well as games) and their many genres and subgenres. Computer simulations can be described in terms of the parameters set forth by Clark et al. (2009), which include the degree of user control provided, the extent of the surrounding scaffolding framework, the manner in which information is represented, and the nature of the simulation modeling.

The archetypal computer simulation used today in the college astronomy classroom
- (A) only allows the user to control a limited number of variables, and this type of simulation is often labeled as "targeted." This approach focuses the user's attention on important variables of interest, and it has significant advantages in terms of efficient implementation and integration into the curriculum.
- (B) is relatively "stand-alone." It requires minimal supporting scaffolding (although some may be available, its use is not required). This approach provides considerable flexibility in how the simulation can be incorporated into the curriculum.
- (C) conveys information presented using the representations commonly found in the discipline of astronomy: solar units, spectral and luminosity classes, nuclei representations, etc.
- (D) involves objects and interactions between objects that users can manipulate through controlling variables (known as a behavior-based model).

Thus, in this paper, a simulation is considered a targeted stand-alone behavior-based model making use of standard astronomical symbolism and nomenclature. A few concrete examples will now be discussed as well as what is known from educational research regarding the affordances and constraints of simulation usage and areas where more research is needed.

Astronomy simulations allow students to visualize phenomena that typically cannot be directly visualized. This focus includes representations over an incredibly large physical extent (e.g., illustrating the rotation curve for the stars of Milky Way, mapping the locations of galaxies, etc.), the evolution of a system over very large or very small timescales (e.g., plate tectonics, stellar evolution, nuclear reactions, etc.), and showing the invisible (e.g., small particles, magnetic fields, dark matter, etc.). They are dynamic visual simulations of natural phenomena governed by graphical user interfaces that allow users to control input parameters and explore the effects of their manipulations on the model. Graphical outputs of data and numerical readouts update in real time and allow users to explore relationships between variables and equations and to view multiple representations concurrently. Simulations attempt to bridge the gap between the astronomy classroom and the universe. Lindgren & Schwartz (2009) discuss the special advantages that such simulations provide for harnessing a user's spatial learning.

One illustrative simulation that has been available on the web in one form or another for over 20 years depicts the stars of an eclipsing binary system moving in their orbits while simultaneously displaying the system's light curve. The simulation allows users to explore the implications of changing stellar parameters in the binary system and the resulting effects on the light curve. Asking students to predict how a specific change to the stellar or orbital input parameters will affect the light curve establishes a high bar for their understanding of an eclipsing binary system.

Redish (2001, p. 19) describes how simulations can help students build mental models of physical systems: "In some cases, students don't have the experience or imagination to put together what they are reading in their text and hearing from the lectures into a coherent, sensible picture. They memorize bits and pieces, but because these pieces are not linked into a consistent, self-supporting structure, they forget or confuse the parts. In physics, many of our coherent pictures are in the form of mental models—visions of interacting objects having qualities and measurable properties. Producing visualizations that display these characteristics can help students create these mental models." Clark et al. (2009, p. 3) echoed this sentiment, stating: "Well-designed digital games and simulations… are exceptionally successful at helping learners build accurate intuitive understanding of the concepts."

Simulation usage fits under a paradigm of science education known as constructivism, which postulates that students "learn by doing." Students actively construct understanding from their experiences, forging connections between new knowledge and their existing knowledge. Constructivism acknowledges the substantial preexisting knowledge that students bring with them to any instructional activity. It is important to elicit a student's existing understanding of a topic, making sure that they confront any misconceptions that they may possess before attempting to build upon their existing knowledge. Note that learners construct meaning not only through interactions with the intellectual content, but also through interactions with other people. Students collaboratively construct new knowledge through interaction with their peers as learning is a social activity. This collaborative learning process is often referred to as social constructivism (Klopfer et al. 2009).

Simulations engage students and faculty due to their dynamic visual nature. They spark students' interest and motivate students to develop an understanding of science processes and concepts by involving them in authentic investigations. Many researchers report that students often spend more time using a simulation than they would a textbook or web page (e.g., Wieman et al. 2010)

Despite the strengths and benefits mentioned earlier, simulations will never be a utopian solution in education. The evidence that simulations are effective for learning is limited and ultimately inconclusive, due to gaps and weaknesses in the research base (National Research Council 2011), and because there are so many types of simulations—the term means very different things to different people. It is also due to the efficacy of simulation usage, i.e., how well they are implemented and whether that usage is well aligned with sound pedagogy. For simulations to be effective classroom tools, they need guided facilitation from the instructor. The learning outcomes from simulations depend on how they are used.

5.2 The College Astronomy Education Landscape

Considerable research on student learning in introductory science courses reveals that faculty routinely overestimate the level of conceptual understanding achieved in their classes (Lightman & Sadler 1993). Many faculty simplistically believe that multimedia-rich enthusiastic lectures will guide their students to appreciate and understand the broad landscape of an exciting scientific discipline. The reality is that students too often struggle with unfamiliar vocabulary and naïve ideas that they bring to the classroom, which combine to result in a lower level of understanding of fundamental concepts than either faculty or students desire (National Research Council 2012). A generally accepted explanation for this low student achievement is the excessive reliance by faculty on lecturing as the mode of instruction. The lecture method allows students to assume passive roles in the classroom and often results in minimal cognitive engagement. Teaching by this method alone leads to low conceptual gains and contributes to exceedingly negative attitudes toward science, technology, engineering, and mathematics (STEM) fields, in general. This reality has created an urgent need to bring innovative and demonstrably effective approaches to teaching undergraduate STEM courses into the mainstream. The recent book *Reaching Students: What Research Says about Effective Instruction in Undergraduate Science and Engineering* (Kober 2015)—based on the results of the Discipline-Based Education Report (DBER; National Research Council 2012)—is entirely focused on "new ways of thinking about what to teach, how to teach it, and how to assess what students are learning."

Evidence in the educational research literature demonstrates that active learning works. The evidence culminated in a meta-analysis of 225 studies on student performance in science, engineering, and mathematics courses (Freeman et al. 2014) and was the largest and most comprehensive meta-analysis of undergraduate STEM education published to date. This meta-analysis showed that average examination scores improved by about 6% in active-learning sections, and that students in classes with traditional lecturing were 1.5 times more likely to fail than students in classes with active learning. Freeman et al. found that "active learning is the preferred, empirically validated teaching practice in regular classrooms." The NRC report *Learning Science Through Computer Games and Simulations* (National Research Council 2011) also discusses the weak science achievement of U.S. students: "Many experts call for a new approach to science education, based in cognitive research. In this approach, teachers spark students' interest by engaging them in investigations, helping them to develop understanding of both science concepts and science processes while maintaining motivation for science learning."

Nearly 250,000 undergraduates take an introductory astronomy survey course in the United States each year (Fraknoi 2001). Nearly half of students who take this Astro 101 course do so in one of more than 500 community and tribal colleges (Brissenden et al. 2006). However, far less than half of the course instructors have a formal degree in astronomy and even fewer have formal training in pedagogy (Fraknoi 2001). For many students, this course is their only course in astronomy, and it often marks the end of their formal science education. Introductory astronomy courses serve as a unique forum to highlight the intimate relationships between science, technology, and society, while also modeling effective instructional strategies for the numerous preservice teachers who enroll. Lawrenz et al. (2005) report that as many as 40% of students in introductory science survey courses eventually become certified teachers who will serve a critically important role for systemic change in science education in the near future. In combination, these issues illustrate that introductory astronomy is a critical component in the STEM education system that helps to improve the public's understanding of science, enhance the STEM career pipeline for future scientists and engineers, and support the preparation of future teachers.

For the half of student enrollment in astronomy courses that occurs at community colleges and small four-year colleges (Fraknoi 2001), the faculty face substantial obstacles. These science faculty are often asked to teach astronomy as one of many science courses that they are teaching, and where, until recently, few opportunities have existed for professional development in astronomy education. Moreover, because these faculties teach a variety of courses, their own educational background may not necessarily be in astronomy.

The institutions of astronomy courses are a bimodal distribution; there are large lecture hall classes at larger schools and small classes at community colleges. Laboratories accompany only about 30% of lecture courses, and they are typically (and correctly) focused on getting students out observing the sky. Although several institutions have made substantial use of undergraduate learning assistants and carefully studied the endeavor, recitations in introductory astronomy courses are still rare.

5.3 A Framework for Interactive Simulation Usage in the Classroom

I will specify a framework for interactive simulation usage in introductory astronomy courses to address the implementation challenges discussed previously and to be consistent with educational research on active learning. The framework acknowledges that most simulation usage will have to occur in the lecture classroom, due to the small numbers of laboratories and recitations in introductory astronomy (and will not address simulation usage in homework settings). The framework should be useful to introductory astronomy instructors regardless of the idiosyncrasies of their instructional setting.

Optimal usage of a simulation involves each student (or pair of students) running their own copy of the simulation and exploring it with appropriate guidance and scaffolding. HTML5 simulations are becoming more prevalent, and mobile devices that can run simulations are commonly found in the hands of college students. At least 19 of 20 students own a laptop or a smartphone, and 3 in 10 students own a laptop, a smartphone, and a tablet (Brooks & Pomerantz 2017). However, it is probably still several years away until students are using their own devices in a classroom to run simulations. This issue is complicated by instructors' concerns that the negative of the distractions of mobile devices outweigh the positive of enabling activities (Duncan et al. 2012)

I will discuss how instructors can lead students through interactive usage of a simulation at the front of a classroom, where they are likely to have the only copy running. This paper will describe a guiding framework for implementing interactive simulation usage in a lecture classroom of any size. Instructors are encouraged to only make use of these types of questions until they feel confident with their implementation. Ideas on how to push further down this path of simulation interactivity can be found on the Science Education Resource Center at the Carleton College website (SERC 2018) under Teaching with Simulations and on the PhysPort website (PhysPort 2018) under PhET Interactive Simulations. A list of the tenets of our framework is as follows (Figure 5.1):

- Instructors must first have a clearly stated list of objectives of what they hope to accomplish by using the simulation. Whether simulation usage is effective can only be evaluated in terms of the stated goals and how that fits within the overarching goals of the curriculum.
- Instructors must practice with a simulation. Substantial preparation is needed before guiding students at the front of a classroom. It is recommended that instructors make a short, bulleted outline of the capabilities of the simulation that they plan to explore. This outline should serve as a reminder (at a glance) of what they want to explore, but it should not be something that instructors will be tied to and reading in class, which could stifle interactivity. The first requirement for getting students to be interactive is that the instructor must be interactive.
- Instructors should be mindful that students need an introduction to a simulation and time to gain comfort and familiarity with its interface. The capabilities of the simulation, which variables can be manipulated, and where one looks to observe the resulting manifestations all have a learning curve, and the instructor must serve as the students' guide.

- Overview of Capabilities
  - Go over what is shown in all 3 panels
  - Animate – Talk through readouts
- Panel 1
  - VQ: Good Question 1
  - VQ: Good Question 2
  - Demo Future Growth
- Panel 2
  - VQ: Good Question 1
  - Demo maximum and minimum value
  - WQ: Written Question 1
- Panel 3
  - Show for all planets
  - "Now" for largest value
  - WQ: Written Question 2
- Talk through lack of realism on Panel 3 features

Figure 5.1. Hypothetical simulation usage plan.

- Instructors need to incorporate considerable interactivity during their progression through the capabilities and science of the simulation. Little will be accomplished if an instructor simply lectures on the simulation. It is generally assumed that the simulation will be used to provide feedback on whatever question students are asked.

Let us consider several categories of interaction prompts.

Verbal Questions (VQ) are delivered to the entire class for students to answer. These questions should be carefully worded, have clearly defined simple answers stated in the question, and are most appropriate for verifying student knowledge of declarative information and surface-level conceptual information (the lower levels of Bloom's taxonomy). Instructors are encouraged to indicate to students with an identifiable and replicable vocal inflection that a question is being asked. Use your classroom voice!

It is also desirable to manage the timing of students' verbal responses (although compliance will never be perfect). Some type of synchronization is necessary or an enthusiastic student in the front row will yell out the answer before many students have had a chance to think about the question. I recommend having a protocol (clearly stated to students early in the term and regularly reinforced) regarding how quickly students should answer a question. One approach is to direct students that when a verbal question is posed to the class, they should count to three—1001, 1002, 1003—before stating an answer. Often a group of highly interactive students sitting near the front of the room quickly get their responses synchronized.

Verbal questions must be very carefully worded with clearly defined possible answers (delivered while pointing to the relevant simulation GUI element to be manipulated if appropriate). You may wish to deliver the answer choices in a slow-paced regular cadence.

Examples of effective questions that could match a simulation include:
- "When I increase the radius of the star, will the luminosity of the star *increase*, *decrease*, or *stay the same*?" (delivered while pointing to the relevant stellar radius slider for future manipulation)
- "When I increase the temperature of the object, will the peak of the blackbody curve move to a wavelength that is *higher*, *lower*, or *stay the same*?" (delivered while pointing to the temperature slider and then the curve peak)

One can envision less specific versions of these same questions that would elicit a variety of interpretations and responses from students and be very difficult to synchronize. Examples of less desirable, unfocused questions include:
- "What happens to the star if I make it bigger?"—Will students interpret this as pertaining to the star's mass or radius? How will they know to focus upon luminosity (and not on surface temperature)?
- "How does the blackbody curve change if I change temperature?"—Will students focus upon Wien's Law, the Stefan–Boltzmann Law, or something else? Is the temperature increasing or decreasing?

There are no strict rules regarding the delivery frequency of verbal questions. However, if an instructor is talking for 5 minutes and not involving their students, they have likely lost a good portion of their audience.

Identifying Times (IT). A related type of simple interaction that can often be used in conjunction with verbal questions is to have students indicate when a certain situation or configuration occurs. This is not useful for all simulations, but is especially useful in those with orbital motion. Examples include:
- "I am going to animate the simulation. Yell 'NOW' when the planet Mars reaches opposition."
- "We can see star trails in the simulation due to Earth's rotation. Yell 'NOW' when the star Sirius rises."
- "As we progress through the year, the midday altitude of the Sun varies. Yell 'NOW' when it reaches its maximum value for this observer's latitude."

Occasionally, a student will yell prematurely, but that can be an instructive moment when you explain what the correct trigger should have been. Note that the synchronization issue described earlier for verbal questions is automatically handled by this form of interactivity.

Written Questions (WQ) are directed at groups of students. These are higher-level questions that do not have simple answers (the middle levels of Bloom's taxonomy). Students will brainstorm together, try to reach consensus, and then report back to the class when they volunteer and are called upon. They may be asked to make a prediction, describe a process, specify an algorithm, or create a list meeting a specified criterion, to mention a few possibilities.

These questions are best thought out in advance, typed up beforehand, and then projected (or at worst, typed live). This approach will ultimately save time by not having to repeat the question and redirect students who answered a different question. Going over the answers to the written questions takes a bit longer, but again, most of this work should be done by the simulation.

Examples of solid questions include:
- "A blacksmith takes a horseshoe and places it in a forge and increases its temperature. Describe the resulting changes in the horseshoe's blackbody curve. You may do this verbally or use a diagram (or both). Make sure you make use of the relevant blackbody laws."
- "You are given the longitude and latitude for a position on Earth. Specify a procedure for determining the terrestrial coordinates of its antipodal point."
- "You are viewing an eclipsing binary system along the plane of its orbit. The two stars are the same temperature, but one star is twice as large as the other. Describe the shape of the system's light curve."

Other overarching goals to have when using a simulation are:

Forging connections (FC). This occurs when instructors connect something from the real world (or their world) and attempt to visualize it in the simulator. This has as much of a retention of information motivation as it does an interactivity motivation. It is hoped that student retention of information will be greater when they have forged a connection between the simulation and some other piece of knowledge or experience, which can be especially true if the simulation experience is connected to other people.

One such example concerns the author making a presentation on a simulation at the AAPT Winter National Meeting held in Anchorage, Alaska, in January of 2006. The simulator illustrated the Sun's path across the sky in a horizon diagram for any latitude on any day of the year. Demonstrating that day's path of the Sun in the simulator was an important part of the presentation that helped the audience appreciate what they had seen that day in the Alaskan sky.

On several occasions in class, students have brought up locations and dates when they were traveling (typically near the equator or a pole) and noticed how the path of the Sun differed compared to that for a middle latitude. For example, an exchange student from Finland told the class about laws requiring car headlights to be on during the day—and that happened over 15 years ago, so it forged a connection in the author's mind. These experiences should encourage other students to recognize that they could simulate the path of the Sun for other locations and dates they have visited, as well as reinforcing the seasonal dependence of sunlight near the poles.

Simulation limitations (SL)—Every simulation illustrates some subset of the reality of the universe. This simplification is especially common in astronomy where the number of objects, the physical scale, and the timescales involved cannot be realistically conveyed within the monitor real estate and desktop computer processing power commonly available. If students can recognize the limitations of a simulation, instructors will have gone a long way toward training students to be critical consumers and to be aware that simulations can not only address misconceptions, but also create them.

As an example of this, note that the NAAP eclipsing binary simulator displays stars as simple circular disks and calculates light curves accordingly. Several 100-level students have noted the lack of limb darkening (as the stars section of the course is right after the Sun section). Several 200-level students have noted that there are no deformation effects when the stars are in close proximity. Ellipsoidal stars would be difficult to model in the simulator; however, limb darkening would be easy to include. It was intentionally omitted to make light-curve shape interpretation straightforward and further the educational goals of the simulation that were perceived to be more important.

5.4 Implementing the Framework: Example 1—The NAAP Lunar Phase Simulator

This section will discuss implementation of the interactive simulation usage framework with the Nebraska Astronomy Applet Project's Lunar Phase Simulator (available at http://astro.unl.edu). The simulation allows control of three simultaneous representations: (a) a view looking down on the Moon's orbit around Earth, (b) the appearance of the Moon as seen from Earth, and (c) the positions of the Sun and Moon in the observer's horizon system. Note that representations (b) and (c) assume that our observer is at an unspecified midlatitude in the northern hemisphere (~40°N). Although the simulation has features that could be categorized as high-level concepts (e.g., a lunar landmark useful in discussing synchronous rotation and illustration of the angle between the Moon and Sun in the horizon diagram), it is especially useful for supporting a general geometrical understanding of lunar phases and the times they are present in the sky. This paper will focus on those capabilities. The simulation also has the capability to hide representations (b) and (c) to facilitate interactivity. Because those features are not generally present in simulations, they will not be discussed here.

A sketch of one possible usage plan is shown in Figure 5.2. In the classroom, we would begin with a quick description of the three representations shown and then click "animate" to illustrate the cycle of lunar phases.

VQ: The Moon will move through a complete cycle of phases. Is the time for a complete cycle *27.3 days*, *28 days*, or *29.5 days*?

Stop animating at either gibbous (or crescent) phase.

VQ: How much of the entire surface of the Moon is illuminated: *less than half*, *half*, or *more than half*?

VQ: How much of the surface of the Moon that we see is presently illuminated: *less than half*, *half*, or *more than half*?

- Overview of Capabilities
    - 3 Representations
    - Animate – period of LP? Days? Sidereal/synodic?
- Illumination (gibbous)
    - VQ: Entire surface?
    - VQ: Surface we see?
- Waxing phases
    - First half of cycle
    - VQ: Illuminated on RHS/LHS?
- Simplifications
    - Sun & Moon on CE
    - 8 possible times
    - Phases in middle of range
- Meridian times
    - VQ: Time on Meridian?
    - VQ: Rising - 6
    - VQ: Setting + 6
- IT: "NOW" for meridian/rising/setting
- 2 WQ

Figure 5.2. Usage plan for the lunar phase simulator.

Discuss with students that half of the entire surface of the Moon is always illuminated, but the percentage of the Moon that we see illuminated varies due to geometry, which is the source of lunar phases.

Draw student attention to the three waxing phases.

VQ: During the first (or second) half of the cycle of lunar phases, we see waxing (or waning) phases. Are these phases illuminated on the *right-hand side* or the *left-hand side*?

This simulation illustrates the Sun and Moon as always on the celestial equator. It is useful to discuss with students the band of the ecliptic in the horizon diagram, but it does not help them to become familiar with lunar phases. Similarly, phases are always shown as exactly in the middle of the position range for a particular phase and that there are only eight possible answers regarding times in the simulator (3, 6, 9, and 12 am and pm) when using the pull-down menu in representation (b).

It is important to make sure that students understand how the times zones on Earth are due to the direction of the Sun, with noon being directly toward the Sun, midnight opposite the Sun in the simulation, and 6 pm and 6 am distinguished by the counterclockwise direction of the rotation. Then meridian times can be seen by picturing a line between the center of Earth and the center of the Moon, and noting the time zone on Earth that the line traverses. The rising time for that particular phase occurs 6 hours earlier than the meridian time and the setting time 6 hours later.

VQ: At what time is the full Moon on the meridian?

VQ: At what time does the waning crescent rise?

If you have properly emphasized that the only "acceptable" answers are 3, 6, 9, and 12 am and pm, you will typically be OK with this less structured format. Note that the identifying times format works well here (and there are many possibilities).

IT: I am going to animate the simulation, yell "NOW" when the first quarter is on the meridian.

IT: Yell "NOW" when the waning gibbous sets.

It is useful to have some type of capstone question that makes use of most of the concepts previously covered. This example question involves identifying the position (meridian of longitude) on Earth corresponding to the time 1:30 am and picturing a tangent plane at that location (holding a meterstick up to the screen if possible). One can also simply move through the phases using the pull-down menu and note which ones are above the horizon in the horizon diagram (Figure 5.3).

The Lunar Phase Simulator also presents an excellent opportunity for encouraging students to scrutinize the realism of a simulator, and a WQ that accomplishes this is shown in Figure 5.4. Note that Fact A is depicted in a reasonable manner in

> *WQ: Your new job has you walking home from work at 1:30 am. What phases of the moon can you see on your walk home? What phases can you never see?*

Figure 5.3. A written question useful as a lunar phases capstone.

> *WQ: We have already covered the scale of the Earth–Moon system in the course. We learned that:*
> A) *the diameter of the moon is roughly one quarter that of Earth*
> B) *the radius of the lunar orbit is roughly 30 times the diameter of Earth*
>
> *Discuss with your neighbors how realistically these known facts regarding the Earth–Moon system are depicted in the simulation – and why you think that might be the case.*

Figure 5.4. A written question focusing on simulator realism.

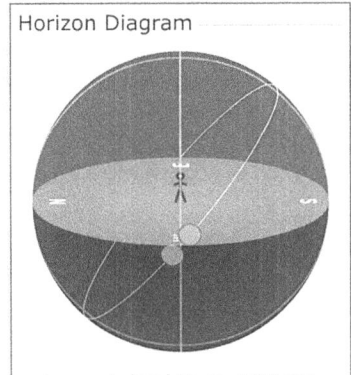

Figure 5.5. A thin waxing crescent on the western horizon. Credit: NAAP Lunar Phase Simulator University of Nebraska, https://astro.unl.edu.

the simulator—basically because it could be easily accomplished. Fact B is not depicted accurately—the radius of the lunar orbit is about three to four times the diameter of Earth rather than 30 times, simply due to space limitations as the lunar orbit needs to fit on the computer screen. Simulations that accurately reflect the true scale of the Earth–Moon system are not particularly useful as the Moon has to be quite small at a large distance from Earth. One could similarly explore the simulator's incorrect depiction of sidereal and synodic periods and it not showing the Earth–Moon system's revolution around the Sun. This synodic feature was implemented in an early version of the simulator, and it interfered with student learning of introductory phase concepts.

The Lunar Phase Simulator also presents a unique cultural opportunity for forging a connection (Figure 5.5). The importance of lunar phases in the Muslim calendar is discussed by Ahmad & Shaukat (1995). Ramadan is a month of fasting during daylight hours, and it lasts until the next lunar month begins. As soon as the new crescent Moon is seen (by an official observer), the month of Ramadan ends, and a great feast occurs. However, if the new crescent is not spotted, the fasting goes on for another day. Note that the first thin crescent of the lunar month is difficult to see in the sky, especially as the Moon at this phase has a small angular separation from the Sun. Thus, a window of opportunity occurs in the early evening when the Sun is below the western horizon and the Moon is lightly above the horizon, which may allow this small crescent to be spotted in the darkening sky. Ahmad & Shaukat (1995) describe people climbing on roofs in the early evening and looking to the western horizon in the hopes of spotting this thinnest crescent, which would allow a celebration to begin (Figure 5.5).

5.5 Implementing the Framework: Example 2—The PhET Gravity and Orbits Simulator

The PHeT Gravity and Orbits simulator (available at https://phet.colorado.edu) allows us to explore the Earth–Moon system from an entirely different perspective—the Newtonian physics of the lunar orbit. It is useful to start the simulation with Earth and the Moon in "To Scale" mode and illustrate to students that realism is not always that useful before changing to "Model" mode (Figure 5.6).

Start with the Moon orbiting Earth and "Path" checked. Let the Moon orbit for a while and then stop it exactly at the bottom of the page as is shown in Figure 5.7.

VQ: In what direction is the Moon moving right at this instant, *horizontally to the right*, *vertically toward Earth*, or *diagonally in between those two*?

Check velocity to reveal the answer and emphasize that the velocity is always tangent to the path. Newton's first law states that a moving object will move in a straight line unless some force is acting on it. Explain that here the force of gravity exerted by Earth redirects the Moon into its approximately circular path. The instructor can illustrate to students what would happen in the absence of gravity.

- To-Scale
- Model
- Earth-Moon -Path
    - Stop at bottom
    - VQ moving?
        - Check Velocity
        - Gravity Off
            - 1stLaw
    - VQ Greater Grav ?
        - 3rdlaw
    - VQ Greater acc?
        - 2ndLaw
    - VQ Earth moving?
- Sun-Earth-Moon -Path
    - WQ moon path?

Figure 5.6. Usage plan for the gravity and orbits simulator.

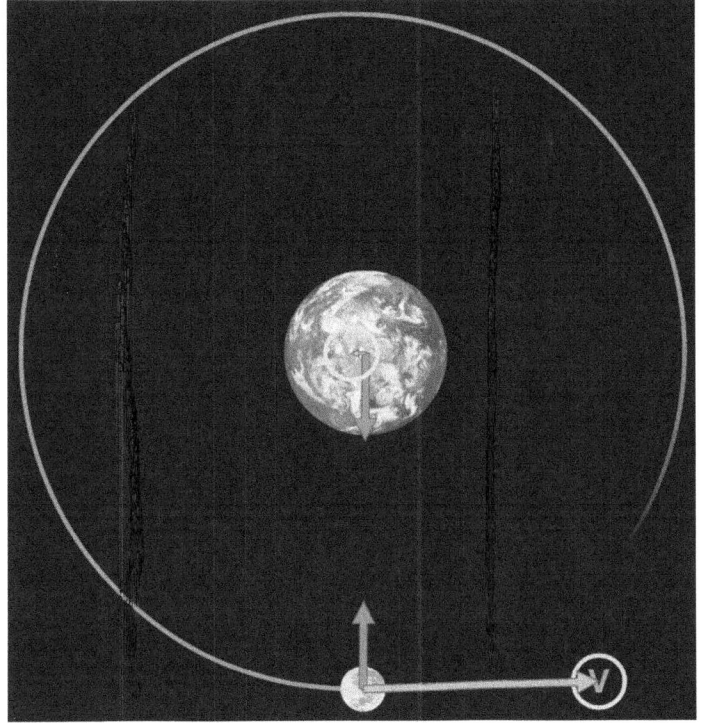

Figure 5.7. Earth and Moon in motion about Earth–Moon barycenter on the western horizon. Credit: PhET Interactive Simulations, University of Colorado Boulder, https://phet.colorado.edu.

Animate the system, and just when the Moon gets to that spot at the bottom of the page, toggle "Gravity" to off.

VQ: Which object has the greater gravitational force on it, *Earth*, or *the Moon*, or are they *the same*?

Check the "Gravity" force, which then shows both gravitational force vectors and that their sizes are equivalent. Repeat the question and discuss Newton's third law.

VQ: Which object presently has the greater acceleration, *Earth*, *the Moon*, or are they *the same*?

You can discuss Newton's second law completing the set. Put the Moon in orbit around Earth on its orbital path once again.

VQ: Is Earth moving, *yes* or *no*?

Zoom in (using the plus sign in the upper left of the simulation) and turn on the grid to make Earth's motion apparent. Note that if "velocity" is checked, a small velocity vector for Earth can be seen, but it is subtle, and the instructor will likely have to point it out to students because of Earth's cloud cover.

VQ: What is Earth moving around? Is it Earth's center? *Yes* or *No*?

VQ: I repeat, what is Earth moving around? Is it the center of mass of the Earth–Moon system? *Yes* or *No*?

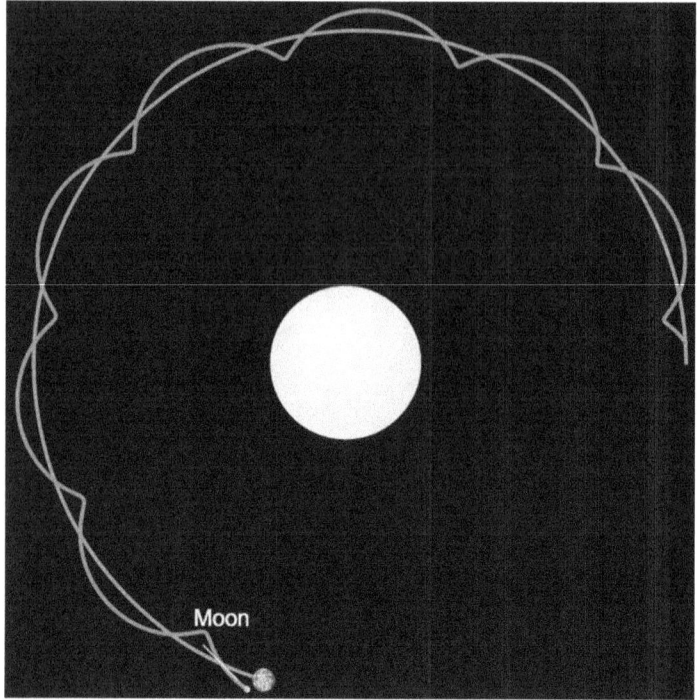

Figure 5.8. A thin waxing crescent on the western horizon. Credit: PhET Interactive Simulations, University of Colorado Boulder, https://phet.colorado.edu.

Because Earth is about 80 times as massive as the Moon, it does make sense that the center of mass is within Earth.

Add humor to keep the students' attention. Note that larger objects can typically destroy smaller ones in this simulation. Click on and grab Earth and drag it over the Moon, destroying it. Note that each of the four object configurations as well as the entire simulation has a reset curved arrow.

Finish up the Sun–Earth–Moon object configuration with all options unchecked.

WQ: I am about to animate the simulation with "Path" checked, which will illustrate the path of the Moon through space. Describe what the path of the Moon will be.

Click "Path" to illustrate the chartreuse path shown. Note that the Moon orbits the center of mass of the Earth–Moon system (which orbits the center of mass of the Sun–Earth system). The majority of your students will never have used a Spirograph, so be wary of generation-dependent humor (Figure 5.8).

5.6 Conclusions

Although educational research on the learning gains from simulation usage is a work in progress, educational research shows they are important tools for engaging and motivating students. Simulations are especially impactful in astronomy because so much of the subject matter is far beyond students' experiences. Simulations help students develop mental images of phenomena of which they are unfamiliar.

Interactive simulation usage in the classroom accomplishes more than lecturing over a simulation, and it is an achievable first step for many astronomy instructors. Many other valuable steps can follow involving students working directly with simulations individually or in small groups.

References

Ahmad, I. A., & Shaukat, S. K. 1995, Mercu, 24, 38

Brissenden, G., Prather, E. E., Slater, T. F., Greene, W. M., & Thaller, M. 2006, AAS Meeting 208, 17.05

Brooks, D. C., & Pomerantz, J. 2017, ECAR Study of Undergraduate Students and Information Technology, 2017, Research Report (Louisville, CO: ECAR), https://library.educause.edu/~/media/files/library/2017/10/studentitstudy 2017.pdf

Clark, D. B., Nelson, B., Sengupta, P., & D'Angelo, C. 2009, in Games and Simulations: Genres, Examples, and Evidence, http://sites.nationalacademies.org/cs/groups/dbassesite/documents/webpage/dbasse_080068.pdf

Duncan, D. K., Hoekstra, A. R., & Wilcox, B. R. 2012, AEdRv, 11, 010108

Fraknoi, A. 2001, AEdRv, 1, 121

Freeman, S., Eddy, S. L., McDonough, M., Smith, M. K., Okoroafor, N., Jordt, H., & Wenderoth, M. P. 2014, PNAS, 111, 8410

Klopfer, E., Osterweil, S., Groff, J., & Haas, J. 2009, The Instructional Power of Digital Games Social Networking Simulations and How Teachers Can Leverage Them (Cambridge, MA: Massachusetts Institute of Technology)

Kober, N. 2015, Reaching Students: What Research Says about Effective Instruction in Undergraduate Science and Engineering (Washington, DC: National Academies Press)

Lindgren, R., & Schwartz, D. L. 2009, IJSEd, 31, 419

Lawrenz, F., Huffman, D., & Appeldoorn, K. 2005, JCSTe, 34, 40

Lightman, A., & Sadler, P. M. 1993, PhTea, 31, 162

National Research Council 2011, Learning Science Through Computer Games and Simulations, Committee on Science Learning: Computer Games, Simulations, and Education ed. M. A. Honey, & M. L. Hilton (Washington, DC: National Academies Press)

National Research Council 2012, Discipline-based Education Research: Understanding and Improving Learning in Undergraduate Science and Engineering, ed. S. R. Singer, N. R. Nielsen, & H. A. Schweingruber (Washington, DC: National Academies Press)

PhysPort 2018, PhET Interactive Simulations, https://www.physport.org/methods/method.cfm?G=PhET

Redish, E. 2001, in Physlets: Teaching Physics with Interactive Curricular Material, ed. W. Christian, & M. Belloni (Upper Saddle River, NJ: Prentice-Hall)

SERC 2018, Teaching with Simulations, https://serc.carleton.edu/sp/library/simulations/index.html

Wieman, C. E., Adams, W. K., Loeblein, P., & Perkins, K. K. 2010, PhTea, 48, 225

Astronomy Education, Volume 1
Evidence-based instruction for introductory courses
Chris Impey and Sanlyn Buxner

Chapter 6

Practical Considerations for Using a Planetarium for Astronomy Instruction

Michelle Nichols, Christine Shupla, Steve Kortenkamp, Matthew Wenger, Wayne Schlingman, Patrick Durrell and Mark SubbaRao

Planetariums are unique and useful tools for teaching astronomy, along with other topics extending beyond the sky. This chapter includes an overview of topics commonly taught in the planetarium. Planetariums can be found in a variety of colleges, museums, and K–12 schools, making them additional and accessible resources for your astronomy courses. We provide ideas, resources, and case studies of using the planetarium for instruction.

Chapter Objectives

By the end of the chapter, readers will
- be able to describe ways planetariums can be and are used for instruction in introductory courses,
- develop ideas on how to access a planetarium for instruction, and
- be able to give practical examples of how to utilize and work with a local planetarium to enrich classes.

6.1 Introduction

Tools for modeling the sky have existed for centuries in many mechanical forms such as globes, orreries, perforated spheres, and other devices. The modern projection planetarium, utilizing a device or system to display representations of the night sky and related imagery on the inside surface of an overhead dome, was invented by the Carl Zeiss Company in Jena, Germany in 1923. The first planetarium in the western hemisphere, the Adler Planetarium & Astronomical Museum in Chicago, Illinois, opened in 1930 May (Figure 6.1).

Since that time, approximately 4000 fixed-dome (i.e., permanent structure) planetariums have been constructed worldwide. In addition, portable (i.e., mobile)

Figure 6.1. Optomechanical Zeiss star projector at the Adler Planetarium in Chicago, ca. 1955. Credit: Adler Planetarium, Chicago.

planetariums have been developed for use as educational tools for students, educators, and the general public. Hundreds of fixed-dome and portable planetariums in the United States are located on or near community college, college, and university campuses, with many others associated with school districts, museums, science centers, and other facilities.

With the introduction of digital fulldome planetariums in the late 1990s, the challenges inherent in an optical projector to convey the true three-dimensional nature of the cosmos were overcome, and many theaters now contain a powerfully engaging ability to display complex spatial relationships that exist in astronomy, such as eclipses, solar system dynamics, the spatial distribution of stars compared with traditional constellation patterns, and maps of the entire universe of galaxies (e.g., SDSS, GAMA, 2MASS).

Now that modern astronomy and astrophysics can be presented using real data, not only of the cosmological content, but also planetary and stellar science, planetariums have the capability to enable a deeper student understanding of the cosmos.

It is the view of the authors that the planetarium can be an engaging instructional tool for college classes. Whether a planetarium projector or projector system is integrated into a classroom or is a stand-alone facility that is occasionally used as part of the astronomy curriculum, there are many ways to make effective use of this immersive, three-dimensional setting to teach a wide variety of astronomical topics.

The purpose of this chapter is to share experiences and insights of those working with college students in planetariums, including best practices and resources for engaging students in different unique experiences related to learning in the planetarium.

6.2 Instruction in a Planetarium

There is more to using the planetarium than just showing the constellations—after all, astronomy is much more than the night sky! This is not to downplay the importance of showing the night sky and the constellations. Even at the college level, one of the first things Astro 101 students (most of whom are not physics or astronomy majors) want to learn about is the night sky and where to find certain constellations. For many who use a planetarium, one of the first great moments in teaching introductory astronomy in a planetarium is turning down the lights and showing what the night sky would look like from a truly dark location. While Astro 101 is so much more than the constellations, this first look at the night sky is a memorable experience and a way to inspire students to search for the features and shapes they saw in the planetarium. This aspect of learning is extremely important—our desire for students to look up and create their own personal experiences. While more planetariums are increasingly "going digital," even 50 year-old star projectors show a beautiful night sky.

A natural question to ask is: why should an instructor consider using a planetarium rather than utilizing, for example, slides and/or video presented on a flat-screen monitor? Several recent studies have shown that students have better retention of information and affective outcomes when engaged in a planetarium versus seeing the information in another instructional setting (Brazell & Espinoza, 2009; Türk & Kalkan 2015; Yu et al. 2015). In a study conducted by Zimmerman et al. (2014), students ages 11–17 who watched a planetarium show in a dome setting showed better retention of information to a statistically significant level versus those who were presented the same information via a computer; the students who watched the flat-screen presentation showed no statistically significant increases. In addition, students showed better retention of information to a statistically significant level when tested six weeks after the initial planetarium experience; students who only experienced the information via a computer retained less information. Exactly why this is the case is not entirely clear, but the reasons could include "the novelty of the dome environment, fewer distractions in an enclosed environment, and longer-term memory storage from multiple sensory inputs (e.g., direct and peripheral vision)" (p. A-12).

A comprehensive review of planetarium research can be found in Slater & Tatge (2017). As they point out, "the planetarium in and of itself in isolation is not a magical silver-bullet for solving all of astronomy education's challenges for improving learning and attitudes. Instead, planetarium education programs need to use the same educational theory-driven, research-confirmed best practices in science education to help enhance learners' cognition and affect." (pp. 122–123).

Thus, actively engaging students in the planetarium is as important as using its technological capabilities.

College faculty have used planetariums to enhance lecture instruction by demonstrating course concepts as well as conducting full astronomy labs. Students can make observations of the Sun's position throughout the day and year, observe and record lunar phases, note the changing apparent magnitude of a variable star, and more. The instructional possibilities depend on the type of planetarium technology being used. This chapter will discuss currently available planetarium systems and describe the instructional affordances and limitations inherent in each. The chapter then concludes with instructional case studies of how a planetarium can be used for single-class activities as well as an example in which the planetarium theater at the Flandrau Science Center at the University of Arizona is used to teach semester-long astronomy classes.

6.3 "Classic" (Optomechanical) Planetarium

Early large planetariums (e.g., the Deutsches Museum in Munich and the Adler Planetarium in Chicago) were places to see faithful reproductions of the night sky. In the 1960s, in large part thanks to the space race, many planetariums were built at colleges, community colleges, universities, high schools, and even elementary schools. The existence of these facilities is evidence that planetariums can be used as teaching tools for the basics of astronomy in a classroom-like setting. The early optomechanical star projectors ("starballs") were designed to project stars and constellations and demonstrate the motions of celestial objects (including the Sun, the Moon and the visible planets) in an immersive domed environment.

Planetariums can show the night sky (including stars, planets, the Sun, and the Moon) from anywhere in the world, and at any time, especially dates of historical significance. Even traditional optomechanical star projectors found in many smaller planetariums can show much more than the constellations. One of the more difficult concepts in Astro 101 courses is the motion of celestial objects in the night sky due to the rotation of the Earth and as the Earth revolves around the Sun. For many students, passively observing two-dimensional diagrams of how a star moves across our sky (along with the cardinal directions) due to the rotating and revolving Earth does not translate well to their understanding. In contrast, a demonstration in a planetarium where students can actively take part by making predictions on what they will see and where (and when) is much more effective.

Many traditional optomechanical planetariums also include one or more projectors that can be used to display images or video in one or more sections of the dome. They may also include additional special effects projectors.

Topics that can be covered in a classical planetarium include constellations, cardinal directions, seasons, motion of the sky (daily, yearly, etc.), celestial mechanics (motions of planets, retrograde motion, precession), moon phases, eclipses, sidereal time, ecliptic and celestial sphere, coordinate systems, astronomical history, cultural astronomy, forensic astronomy, celestial navigation, astronomical

Figure 6.2. The digital immersive the Arne Slettebak Planetarium at The Ohio State University. Credit: Wayne Schlingman.

predictions (future planet and star positions, etc.), and sunrise/sunset locations and times.

6.4 Digital Planetariums

With the introduction of digital planetarium systems, the instructional potential for planetariums has taken a leap forward. Over the past 20 years, planetariums of all sizes (including small portable planetariums) have increasingly updated their equipment with video projection systems to either complement or replace optomechanical projectors. These systems typically allow for digital coverage over most, if not all, of the dome, creating a truly immersive experience (Figures 6.2 and 6.3).

These immersive systems are referred to as "fulldome systems." Fulldome digital systems come in a variety of complexities—from single projectors operated by a single computer to large, multiprojector systems requiring a large rack of computers. Many small projectors have resolutions from 1024×1024 (1K) pixels on the dome, up to 2K and even 4K. Large systems of 8K–10K resolution are currently available for domes of any size.

Teaching Astro 101 in a planetarium with fulldome systems opens up a wide range of possibilities, allowing the use of digital media and models in real time, as well as the more standard static images, animations, and videos. While many of these digital resources can be displayed with any traditional digital projector, the ability to project them on a dome in a relevant context (such as showing the *Hubble Space Telescope* in its correct orbit) adds an extra dimension to what is possible. This cannot be understated with the many great visualizations and data sets available in astronomy. In addition to real-time display and navigation, there are many fulldome videos (videos that are pre-rendered to conform to the shape of the dome and surround the audience) with content that can be used for teaching in the Astro 101 classroom.

Figure 6.3. Imagery on the dome at the digital immersive Grainger Sky Theater at the Adler Planetarium in Chicago. Credit: Adler Planetarium, Chicago.

There are also hybrid systems, in which a star projector is used in tandem with a digital system, projecting the near-realism of the night sky with the starball, and using the digital system to overlay images, constellation outlines, and videos to complement what is being displayed on the dome. As of this writing, the digital night sky from smaller or medium-sized digital planetariums does not rival the night sky of the starball, although the quality of the digital sky is always improving. With a hybrid system, one can truly get the best of both worlds.

Planetariums are not limited to covering topics in observational astronomy, and a wealth of resources is available to augment many different college course topics. Digital planetarium systems are installed with proprietary libraries of visualizations, covering wide-ranging subjects from stellar evolution to relativity to space weather. High-resolution 3 dimensional images of the surfaces of the planets, moons, asteroids, and comets can be used to show students the latest results from planetary missions. The use of old, static images of the major planets can be replaced with a realistic view of the surface of Mars from orbit, or a flyby of a near-Earth asteroid or comet nucleus. Programming does not need to be limited to astronomy concepts. In fact, any data visualization at a sufficiently high resolution, optimized for a dome-shaped screen, is fair game for display in a planetarium, from the geological history of Earth to biological processes and more.

Digital systems have the ability to display astronomical data and results on the dome. Many fulldome systems now include large image and video databases and highly developed software that can incorporate data from online sources: http://www.data2dome.org/. Planetariums project some of the imaging and spectroscopic data from the world's largest observatories effectively on the dome. Even smaller systems can display 3D (position and distance) data for galaxies from the Sloan Digital Sky Survey, for instance, to show large-scale structure in the universe. Volumetric models of the Milky Way and nebulae can be used to show the structure of these objects. Want to show the locations of open clusters and globular clusters in our Milky Way, the different regions of our Galaxy? The aftermath of galaxy collisions? These can be done with the push of a button. Orbital ephemerides can be used to illustrate the distribution of orbits of objects. With continually updated databases, it is possible to show students the very latest discoveries and information, and place them in the correct cosmic context relative to Earth's location in the universe.

In addition, planetarium users have developed pathways to create and share content with other planetariums via the cloud, so even planetariums that do not have sufficient internal resources to develop their own content can benefit from the work of others. Large-scale organized efforts are now offering feeds of visualizations from content providers such as NASA and the European Southern Observatory, often providing resources the same day that new research is presented to the public and the media.

Whether your college/university has a small optomechanical projector, a fulldome visualization system, or something in between, instructors should take advantage of the many benefits of immersing your students in the beauty of the night sky. That "wow" factor carries a lot of weight in encouraging and motivating student-driven exploration of astronomy.

6.5 Portable Planetariums

Portable planetariums were created over 40 years ago to enable educators to share the night sky with audiences who did not otherwise have easy access to a fixed-dome planetarium. While these started as analog projectors and inflatable domes, they have expanded to include computerized systems with video projectors and a variety of dome types. The newer systems have greater versatility, allowing both pre-recorded shows and live presentations on a variety of topics, and incorporating video animations and live manipulation of three-dimensional images. Portable planetariums are a wonderful tool for engaging students; the visual nature of the system allows presenters to virtually transport their audiences to different times of the night and year, and to locations across the solar system and beyond. College instructors can contact local museums and educational institutions to request a portable planetarium for use with their students.

6.5.1 About Portable Planetariums

Portable planetariums can be transported to different institutions for presentations and set up as needed. In general, they require a large space (at least 20 feet by 20 feet) and a high ceiling (Figure 6.4). Most should not be used outside. All except handmade versions require electricity, but this is usually confined to a single outlet or power strip.

Planetarium domes now come in an array of sizes and entrances. The domes are usually constructed of heavy fabric or vinyl; they are inflated using a powerful fan, which is kept running throughout its use. (Some models have only a partial-dome or panorama held up mechanically, allowing audiences to walk up without entering a

Figure 6.4. A Digitarium planetarium set up in a school gym. Credit: Lunar and Planetary Institute.

structure; these are primarily used for demonstrations at conferences and will not be covered further in this article.) Entrances may be through a tunnel, a zipper, or an inflated "airlock" to hold in some of the air.

While the dome may instill fear initially among those concerned about being trapped, the domes are not airtight and are open on the bottom to the floor, creating a hemispherical tent rather than a bubble. Audience members in wheelchairs can enter first under the side of the dome; this does allow a fair amount of the air to escape, so the dome will need time to re-inflate before the others enter. In the event of an emergency, all participants can quickly be evacuated by "flipping the dome"—lifting up high on the side opposite the fan and allowing the material to collapse on the other side of the participants.

The visuals are usually created by a projector. Originally these were small lamps covered with a film cylinder to project stars; these are extremely easy to set up and use. Most portable planetarium systems today use a video projector and computer, connected with a curved or fisheye lens or a mirror to allow the image to cover the inside of the dome; these require training to set up and use.

6.5.2 Advantages and Disadvantages

Like any planetarium, a portable dome enables instructors to share the night sky, seasons, phases, planetary exploration, stars, galaxies, and even cultural stories with audiences. The sense of motion as the presenter flies an audience over the cratered surface of the Moon or Mars or through the Milky Way can be exciting, engaging even jaded college students. As in traditional domes, the 360° visualizations can be particularly useful in helping participants with complex spatial reasoning, such as demonstrating the Sun's changing position in the sky over the day and through different seasons, or the lunar phases as the Moon's position changes with respect to

Figure 6.5. Families taking a journey across the solar system in a portable dome. Credit: Periwinkle Foundation.

the Sun. The sensation of flying over an alien terrain or through a distant galaxy can inspire a memorable sense of awe (Figure 6.5).

The smaller size and portability can also be a benefit. The cozy setting can inspire a sense of familiarity and personal connection—of talking around a campfire or sharing stories with friends, rather than the impersonal lecture hall experience. A portable planetarium can be brought to different institutions and events, for outreach or public engagement at STEM nights, club meetings, and community celebrations. A portable planetarium can be set up as needed in a large room, auditorium, or gym, then removed.

Portable planetariums are considerably more affordable than a permanent planetarium; they range from around $20,000 up to $100,000 for the complete system (dome, projector, computer, and fan; Figure 6.6).

There are disadvantages. A portable planetarium can only hold a limited number of people—most will fit 20–30. The electrical cords can present a tripping hazard. Participants usually sit on the floor or on cushions, rather than chairs, which can be challenging for some audience members. A large number of people entering or exciting will cause most portable domes to partially deflate, requiring a wait time between presentations. Some participants may feel a sense of claustrophobia, and the changing visuals may make some slightly queasy.

Figure 6.6. An ePlanetarium dome set up on the White House lawn for a special event. Credit: Lunar and Planetary Institute.

6.5.3 Sources and Resources for Portable Planetariums

There are only a few companies that sell portable planetariums, including Starlab, ePlanetarium, Digitalis, Go-Dome, and Emerald. Additional planetarium companies sell projectors that can be used in portable domes.

The International Planetarium Society has assembled a variety of articles about portable domes: https://www.ips-planetarium.org/page/portableresources.

6.6 Ancillary Planetarium Resources

In addition to the resources available to show in planetarium theaters themselves, there are a host of other auxiliary opportunities connected to and associated with planetariums that professors and students can take advantage of. Many planetariums are located at institutions such as science museums, science centers, and natural history museums that may have exhibits, public events, classes, or programs that may support and augment what is being taught in class (Figure 6.7). In addition, many of these facilities host sky observing nights for the public, using portable telescopes or an on-site observatory.

Observing nights are a great opportunity for students to experience practical observational astronomy programs that might dovetail with the more theoretical or experimental topics covered in their classes. Finally, many science museums and planetariums welcome assistance by volunteers. Students interested in furthering their knowledge and lending a hand at these institutions should be encouraged to connect with volunteer coordinators or managers.

Figure 6.7. Solar observing via Adler Planetarium's Scopes in the City telescope outreach program, 2018. Credit: Adler Planetarium, Chicago.

Even if you do not have access to a planetarium, commercial and open-source planetarium software can give students some of the same learning experiences available from a planetarium presentation. Some software, including Stellarium, Starry Night, and WorldWide Telescope are intended for use on desktop or laptop computers. As with projection or digital planetarium systems, planetarium software can be used to explore objects in the solar system and motions of the stars, Sun, and planets, and to understand concepts such as celestial mapping and the ecliptic. Although the immersive experience can be lacking, in some cases planetarium software can provide superior instruction because students can use the program to conduct specific tasks, working on projects or activities individually or in small groups. (For instance, one instructor had students use the software to observe specific astronomy targets from different locations on Earth to determine which observatory facility would be best positioned for studying the target.) Instructors have also assigned class projects where students were required to create their own planetarium presentations using the software.

In addition to the above, fee-based and free apps are also available to show representations of the night sky in the past, present, and into the future on tablet computers and mobile phones. These apps can utilize GPS capabilities of phones or tablets to enable augmented reality, allowing users to sweep across the entire sky, investigating what can be seen in all directions, effectively turning mobile phones into miniature planetariums wherever a user is located. Apps are available for a variety of mobile phone operating systems, and some can even be used with a headset for immersive VR experiences.

Case Studies

Like any other learning setting, the planetarium can be utilized for direct instruction, peer engagement, and other active learning. The three case studies below show different ways that instructors have used the planetarium for teaching astronomical concepts. The first is an example of using the planetarium for a single class period as a way to augment a traditional lecture with a fulldome demonstration and peer instruction. The second is an example of using the planetarium to collect data for a lab activity. The final case study is a description of an entire course taught in the planetarium theater.

Case Study 1: Seasonal Changes in Constellations

At the Fiske Planetarium at the University of Colorado Boulder, summer students were given a lecture on the reasons for the seasons, including the relationship between Earth and the Sun, and how the sky changes during the year. In addition to showing traditional slides and videos, the instructor augmented the lecture by having students watch the sky change on the planetarium dome as well as fly through the system and look at it from different angles. The students were then asked to complete a lecture-tutorial on the topic (see Chapter 3) engaging in peer instruction. At various points during the lecture and after the lecture-tutorial, students used clickers to vote on their predictions. The digital projection system allowed students to see those responses on the dome in real time. Having the entire dome set up to be a teaching workspace allowed for graphs, examples, astronomical images, and questions to be visible at the same time. This ability for students to combine information across delivery methods encouraged discussion and understanding of the topic.

Case Study 2: Nighttime Lab in the Planetarium

An instructor at The Ohio State University used a planetarium theater so that Astro 101 students could collect data for astronomy lab activities. The first was a sky measurement activity on constellations. Even though this activity could have been completed outside, inclement winter weather necessitated the use of the controlled indoor planetarium setting. The instructor projected the night sky onto the dome, and students were able to measure positions and angles in the sky using their fists and fingers at arm's length as protractors. Students used red lights and binders to write down their measurements and the entire class was able to complete the activity without interruption during a single daytime class period. Doing the lab in the planetarium also made the activity more accessible to those with vision and mobility impairments. Additional lab activities facilitated in this setting included data collection for observations of Moon phases and planet motions that would normally take place for many nights over the course of a month.

Case Study 3: An Entire Course in the Planetarium

The Flandrau Planetarium at the University of Arizona has been used to teach introductory astronomy classes on and off for several decades. Despite the extraordinary visual and acoustic capabilities of modern digital planetariums, there are many logistical challenges involved with teaching an entire course in one of these domed circular classrooms. Comfortable, reclined seats tend to encourage napping of even the most well-rested students. Hard flat surfaces for writing notes or typing on laptops are often inadequate or entirely absent. Even when the planetarium is not in dark fulldome mode, the lighting conditions for reading and writing may not be consistent across all seats throughout the dome. Furthermore, these lighting conditions, as well as the curved arrangements of seats, conspire to make misuse of laptops and cellphones quite distracting to other students and especially to a mobile instructor, although it is easy in most fixed domes with a cove lighting system to introduce modest lighting at relevant moments when the students need to use written materials. Drawbacks such as these are among the most frequently cited by students in end-of-semester feedback. However, students responding to surveys still overwhelmingly prefer the uniqueness of the planetarium environment to standard university classrooms.

One strategy for dealing with these logistical challenges is to openly acknowledge them to our students on the first day of class and set informed behavioral and physical boundaries. For example, the back row of seats may be roped off, laptop-free sections can be designated and enforced, and a smartphone prohibition can be attempted to at least promote discreteness.

Once the logistical issues are understood, designing an active-learner-centered course for a planetarium is not necessarily any more challenging than in a traditional classroom. Here, we describe the basic structure of two general education Earth and planetary science courses taught at the University of Arizona (UA). These courses typically enroll about 100 students each semester and are held entirely within UA's 150 seat Flandrau Planetarium (Figure 6.8).

Flandrau runs the Uniview digital planetarium software, but we emphasize that the fulldome system is not used during an entire class period. The Uniview system allows for deeper exploration of important concepts in planetary science using its immersive 3D perspective. The system is typically used for 10–15 minutes periodically during a class to supplement or preview a more thorough discussion. In addition to the fulldome digital system, Flandrau also has a high-definition computer projector configured to accurately display 2D material onto the rounded dome. This system is used more regularly than the fulldome system. An instructor can use both projection systems simultaneously, or instantaneously switch back and forth between the two and control the room lighting at the same time.

Basic components of the courses taught in Flandrau are broken down into familiar curriculum sections, such as in-class participation, term projects, exams, and written homework assignments. The typical daily in-class work involves a think–pair–share approach and utilizes Turning Technologies clickers. Depending on the content for the particular day, these activities may involve anywhere from 8 to 15 instances, during a 75 minute class, when students either read or listen to a

Figure 6.8. Flandrau Science Center and Planetarium, on the campus of the University of Arizona in Tucson. Built in 1976, Flandrau was converted to a fulldome digital planetarium in 2015. The Great White Shark fulldome movie now showing helps demonstrate the diversity of immersive experiences available with digital planetariums. Credit: Steve Kortenkamp.

prompt and then have an opportunity to respond, discuss, and respond again if warranted. Other occasional in-class work involves individual or small-group activities such as using dice to understand probabilities and half-life. Generally, the groups are limited to two-three students to allow for easy collaboration in the fixed planetarium seats, but also to avoid detrimental dynamics found in larger groups.

Oddly enough, it is in conducting the term projects that teaching in a planetarium can be especially helpful. These out-of-class experiential learning opportunities involve students using their smartphone cameras to make observations and/or videos related to fundamental concepts taught in each course. Below we briefly describe three of these projects and how the Uniview system is used to enhance student learning:

(1) The Sun Project.

Students use their smartphones to record images of sunrise and sunset once per week for 10–12 weeks. All images are taken from the same observing location (e.g., top of campus parking garage). Students submit weekly progress reports of their Sun images, selfies at the observing location, and observing notes to the Learning Management System (LMS). In class, the Uniview fulldome system is used to simulate the changing location and time of sunrise/sunset during the semester, along with deeper coverage of the reasons for the observed changes. In class, students use their phones to time the amount of daylight during a given simulated day, then convert to hours of daylight for a real day (simulated time might be 20 minutes s^{-1}). In their project, students measure the real amount of daylight each week between their sunrise and sunset images. The project concludes with each student constructing time-lapse animations from their images to demonstrate the changing location of sunrise and sunset along the horizons during the semester, as well as the change in the amount of daylight as the seasons change. The planetarium simulations allow for a more accurate demonstration of the concepts involved than is possible in a traditional classroom, and the work of gathering their own observations provides mental and physical discomfort that is often needed to reinforce their learning.

(2) The Moon Project.

With the aid of a dozen simple nontracking Dobsonian telescopes, students use their smartphones to take images of the moon once each evening for 16 straight days. Observations are made together as a group on a grassy mall outside the Flandrau planetarium. Daily progress reports are submitted to the LMS, including Moon images, selfies at the telescope, and brief comments on the experience. This smartphone astrophotography project is greatly assisted by the reliably clear skies over Tucson, AZ. In class, the Uniview system is used to simulate the view from campus over the same period. By greatly enlarging the size of the moon on the dome, students can also take simulated lunar images that coincide with their telescopic images. After their images are obtained, the students produce a time-lapse animation demonstrating the changing phase of the Moon during the two-week period. Their time-lapse animations also clearly reveal lunar libration. Concepts related to their findings, such as spin–orbit resonances and eccentric orbits, are demonstrated in class using Uniview.

(3) A Model Solar System.

Students use their smartphones to produce a documentary-style narrated video tour of a model solar system accurately scaled to size and distance. They build the model sun, planets, and large moons. They also write a script for their narration based on concepts from class. Preliminary models, plans, and script, as well as a more detailed progress report are submitted to the LMS. In class, the Uniview system is used to demonstrate relative sizes and orbital spacing of planets and moons. In addition, throughout the semester, Uniview is used to help realistically demonstrate the limitation of human exploration of space and the vast extent of robotic exploration of the solar system. Emphasizing these distinctions is a required part of the documentary the students make (e.g., " humans have explored this far from Earth"— student holds Earth and Moon about 20 cm apart in a typical model—"while robots have gone ...").

The final planetarium-related activity is student homework. Students write homework solutions in what is referred to as Student on the Street (SOS) structure. This means that important concepts in the homework need to be explained using analogies and examples that a nonscience SOS would understand. Occasionally, an assignment is randomly selected and a real-life SOS is interviewed literally on the street outside Flandrau. The SOS interview is conducted on camera, with the student whose work was selected operating the camera, and the encounter is streamed live back into the planetarium theater.

Although the curriculum described above is not restricted to a planetarium classroom, having access to a planetarium for every class allows for deeper learning experiences for students taking the class. Using the planetarium in this way also enhances its profile on campus beyond the traditional uses of public outreach and entertainment.

6.7 How to Get Started

If you are wondering how to get started using a planetarium for instruction or working with your local planetarium, here are a few useful tips. The easiest way to start is by planning a class trip to the local planetarium or setting up a visit from a group with a portable dome. You can treat this as supplementary instruction, timing the trip to coincide with relevant course content, depending on the exhibits and shows that are available at the planetarium. If you have a planetarium on your campus, reach out and talk to the director or manager. Most campus planetariums welcome instructors teaching a class or two. This can be done by presenting a single topic or utilizing a premade show. If you have specific topics that you are required to cover, planetariums may be able to adjust the narrative of their shows, allowing topics that might otherwise not be in the show to be discussed; this is more likely for live presentations than for pre-recorded shows. In some circumstances, it may even be possible to work with planetarium staff to plan a fulldome show on a topic that is of interest to a suitably sized group. A well-developed set of content can be made into a fulldome show that can be given to a variety of groups. This is more likely to be possible at a campus facility than a public planetarium.

Resources for Teaching in a Planetarium

The International Planetarium Society (IPS) has a variety of resources:

For instructors who want to get started, there are several resources to start with, including free planetarium shows: https://www.ips-planetarium.org/page/fulldomemasters.

For information about traditional and portable planetariums, consider contacting your regional planetarium association (https://www.ips-planetarium.org/page/affiliates). Many school districts, museums, and permanent planetariums have portable planetariums, and some are available to be booked for outreach programs (usually for a fee). A planetarium finder is available from the IPS here: https://www.ips-planetarium.org/default.aspx.

In addition, an extensive listing of planetariums is available at the Loch Ness Compendium: http://lochnessproductions.com/ldco/ldco.html features traditional domes and http://lochnessproductions.com/lfco/lfco.html features domes with fulldome video.

The Data 2 Dome Collaboration is a project designed to promote a set of common standards for digital content (file formats and metadata) that will allow easy sharing of visualization resources, including astronomical data sets. It will allow astronomy data providers, science center professionals, and software vendors to work together to advance the state of the art in big data visualization: http://www.data2dome.org/.

If you are interested in more support for instruction, Spitz SciDomes use Starry Night and David Bradstreet's fulldome curriculum that was built to provide shows to specifically teach Moon phases, eclipses, basics for the night sky, and much more: https://www.spitzinc.com/planetarium/educate/fulldome-curriculum/.

Ohio State is starting to produce shows with classroom pre- and postvisit content and inventories for K–12 groups coming to the planetarium: https://planetarium.osu.edu/.

The Lawrence Hall of Science (LHS) also has a variety of resources available for instruction and planetarium show creation. The Planetarium Activities for Successful Shows website is available here: http://www.planetarium-activities.org/, and the LHS Planetarium Educator's Workshop Guide is available for free online and has excellent information about the theory and practice of audience participation planetarium programs, entertaining and educational, actively involving visitors: http://static.lawrencehallofscience.org/pass/digital/PDFs/PlanetariumEducatorsWorkshopGuide2015.pdf.

Lawrence Hall of Science Planetarium Activities for Student Success shows have also been converted to digital format and contain a set of 12 "shows" designed to be taught by a teacher in a dome. These are available here: https://www.skyskan.com/products/ds/interact and come complete with teacher guide and all digital materials.

Instructional guides are available from NSTA, The National Science Teachers Association: https://common.nsta.org/search/default.aspx?action=browse&text=planetarium&price=&type=&subject=&topic=0&gradelevel=&sort=1&page=0&dep=&coll=&author=.

Another Resource for Instructors: Planetarium and Astronomy Education Conferences

The International Planetarium Society hosts conferences for planetarium professionals every two years: https://www.ips-planetarium.org/page/conferences.

The Astronomical Society of the Pacific has annual meetings with strands that focus on education and outreach: https://astrosociety.org/get-involved/events/annual-meeting/.

Live Interactive Planetarium Symposium, or LIPS, is held once a year and focuses on interactive shows with live presentations: http://lipsymposium.org/LIPS/.

The immersive media entertainment, research, science, and arts conference https://www.imersa.org.

Regional Planetarium Conferences

MAPS (Mid-Atlantic Planetarium Society): https://www.mapsplanetarium.org.
GLPA (Great Lakes Planetarium Association): https://glpa.org.
GPPA (Great Plains Planetarium Association): http://www.spacelaser.com/gppa/.

PPA (Pacific Planetarium Association): http://www.ppadomes.org.

RMPA (Rocky Mountain Planetarium Association): http://www.wacdomes.org/index.php?option=com_content&view=article&id=12&Itemid=112.

SEPA (Southeastern Planetarium Association): https://www.sepadomes.org.

SWAP (Southwest Association of Planetariums): http://www.swapskies.org/index.shtml.

References

Brazell, B. D., & Espinoza, S. 2009, AEdRv, 8, 010108

Slater, T., & Tatge, C. 2017, Research on Teaching Astronomy in the Planetarium (Berlin: Springer)

Türk, C., & Kalkan, H. 2015, JSEdT, 24, 1

Yu, K. C., Sahami, K., Sahami, V., & Sessions, L. C. 2015, JAESE, 2, 33

Zimmerman, L., Spillane, S., Reiff, P., & Sumners, C. 2014, JRAEO, 1, A5

Astronomy Education, Volume 1
Evidence-based instruction for introductory courses
Chris Impey and Sanlyn Buxner

Chapter 7

Authentic Research Experiences in Astronomy to Teach the Process of Science

Travis A Rector, Andrew W Puckett, Michelle M Wooten, Nicole P Vogt, Kim Coble and Catherine A Pilachowski

"Research-based science education" (RBSE) is an instructional model that integrates scientific research with education by giving introductory-level undergraduate astronomy students an opportunity to do authentic research with real data. RBSE is a course-based undergraduate research experience (CURE) in astronomy. Its goals are threefold: (1) to teach that science is a process of discovery, not just a body of knowledge, (2) to improve attitudes toward science and STEM careers, and (3) to develop critical thinking, teamwork, and goal-driven work skills that are important in any career path.

The RBSE curriculum discussed in this chapter consists of five authentic research projects in astronomy: recovering asteroids, searching for classical novae in M31, studying semiregular variable stars, identifying active galactic nuclei in the Faint Images of the Radio Sky at Twenty centimeters (FIRST) survey, and measuring the photometric redshift of distant galaxies in the NOAO Deep Wide Field Survey (NDWFS). Each project uses real astronomical data from professional observatories to investigate authentic research questions for which the answers are not known. In other words, in order to learn science, students are given the opportunity to actually *do* science. We present the overall importance of engaging undergraduate students in research-based projects and provide resources for astronomy instructors to find and implement projects with their own students.

Chapter Objectives

By the end of this chapter, readers will be able to
- describe the benefits and characteristics of classroom undergraduate research experiences,

- describe authentic research-based science education projects that students can engage in as part of introductory astronomy courses, and
- find and utilize astronomy research projects that will build students' knowledge, skills, and experience in different astronomical topics.

7.1 Introduction

Promoting research experiences for all undergraduate students, both inside and outside the classroom, is deemed important by the National Academies (National Research Council 1996), the American Association for the Advancement of Science (Project 2061), and researchers of science teaching and learning (Sadler & McKinney 2010 and references therein). RBSE (and CUREs in general) is a method of instruction that models the processes of scientific inquiry and exploration used by scientists. It is "research based," integrating scientific research with education. It brings the excitement of true discovery to classrooms by giving students the opportunity to do science, not just study established results through lectures removed from the actual research process. Students participate in research projects, utilizing research-class telescope observations, analyzing data, and interpreting the results. They personally explore and work together as collaborators in a cooperative environment. The benefits of students' participation in CUREs include learning from mistakes, increasing confidence and competence in the science process, improving science writing, deepening understanding of content knowledge, increasing interest in scientific careers, and developing critical thinking skills (Wooten et al. 2018).

CUREs integrate research and education, illustrating science as it is done by scientists, and have been developed in several other fields including geology (Barnett et al. 2005; Bhattacharyya 2009) and biology (Campbell et al. 2012). They incorporate teaching strategies that model scientific reasoning. These include focusing on an in-depth project, engaging in self-organization and reflection, using computers as tools for data analysis, and creating student logs and concept maps for assessment. Characteristics common to CUREs include the following:

1. Multiple scientific practices that are driven by students or the instructor are enacted.
2. Discovery, or the process by which new knowledge or insights are obtained, is driven through student–instructor interactions. The outcomes of the process are unknown, and the findings are novel.
3. The broader relevance or importance extends beyond the course, and students' work often presents opportunities for action beyond the classroom (e.g., publication in professional journals or impacting the local community).
4. Collaboration occurs among students, teaching assistants, and instructors in the course, where the instructor acts as guide and mentor.
5. Iteration is built into the process, and there is an inherent risk of generating "messy" data.

CUREs are used in college introductory science courses because, for many students, this is their last formal exposure to science. They enable students to experience the rewards of research soon enough to pursue science as a career—most scientists chose their career because of a passion for research. Traditionally, an opportunity to participate in research usually comes only to STEM majors, and not before the junior year. Even if students do not pursue STEM degrees, CUREs develop skills that are helpful in any career, such as teamwork and interpretation of data to draw a conclusion. For those who become teachers, it leverages the concept of scientific discovery to a broader audience of learners. The importance of an undergraduate research experience in career selection is also well established (e.g., Hathaway et al. 2002; Russell et al. 2007). Ninety percent of students who intend to pursue graduate studies in physics participate first in a research project, as compared to 65% of those who plan graduate studies in other fields and 68% of the students who plan to enter directly into the workforce (Mulvey & Nicholson 2002).

Over the last 12 years we have developed and tested the effectiveness of RBSE projects at six partner institutions. This group includes two large "research one" universities (Indiana University-Bloomington (IUB) and University of Washington in Seattle), two medium-size teaching universities (University of Alaska Anchorage and Chicago State University), and two community colleges (Pima Community College in Tucson, AZ, and Truckee Meadows Community College in Reno, NV). A "RBSE-U" network of instructors from the partner institutions was developed to foster collaboration and to share innovation. Student gains in understanding the process of science, changes in attitudes toward science and STEM careers, and gains in critical thinking were assessed with various tools, the results of which are given in Wooten et al. (2018). The curricula were also improved based upon student and faculty feedback.

7.2 The RBSE Curriculum

The RBSE curriculum consists of five authentic research projects developed for Astro 101 students. Each project contains (1) real scientific data, (2) curricula to teach the necessary data-analysis skills and relevant science content, and (3) introductory exercises that model the research pedagogy. Each focuses on a topic accessible to students to which they can make a valuable scientific contribution. Most can be extended, so that students can build upon the work of prior cohorts. It is emphasized that RBSE research projects are based upon authentic scientific questions, not static activities. In each case, the "answers" are not known, and they address outstanding problems in astronomical research.

Students performing authentic activities are more likely to develop their inquiry and communication skills and become better lifelong learners (Edelson 1998). Each project therefore has introductory exercises that teach important research skills, i.e., how to approach a problem like a scientist. These exercises also cover the topical material necessary for the project. For example, to do the Nova Search project students complete several structured activities to learn how to search for novae, to measure their locations, and to precisely determine their brightness using aperture photometry with in-field calibration ("standard") stars. We call these "toolbox" activities (instead of "cookbook"), because students learn the techniques they will use to complete the project in a manner similar to that advocated by Brown et al. (1989). Students also learn skills that are valuable in other contexts, e.g., to visually display and interpret data in the form of a graph or chart.

The research projects currently require software to be installed on users' computers. Image-based projects use ImageJ, a free generic image-processing program developed by the National Institute of Health. Our Polaris plugin adds to ImageJ the necessary functions of aperture photometry, astrometry, and timing for a range of FITS data files, including the pixel-specific timing of images from the Sloan Digital Sky Survey (SDSS). For spectroscopic projects, we use GEAS spectroscopy tools (Vogt et al. 2013). Written in HTML5, these web applications enable students to analyze spectra entirely online (i.e., without the need to download and install software or data sets).

Each project has been designed to match areas in content and pedagogy commonly taught in introductory college astronomy courses. For example, the skills and science content for the "Spectroscopy of Semiregular Variable Stars" project include:

The Nature of Light:	The Nature of Stars:	Tools of Astronomy:
• The electromagnetic spectrum	• Properties of the Sun	• Image processing
• Optics and telescopes	• Solar variability	• Data analysis
• Cameras and CCDs	• The Sun as a star	• Astrometry
• Motion of the sky	• Stellar evolution	• Aperture photometry
• Celestial coordinates	• Types of variable stars	• Hertzsprung–Russell diagram

Thus, students learn scientific content knowledge in the context of the research project. They are more likely to retain this knowledge because they use it as part of the project. It therefore becomes relevant to the students, rather than merely a set of abstract facts they were told to learn.

7.3 The Projects

Currently, the RBSE curriculum consists of five research projects:

1. "Recovery" Observations of Asteroids

Students inspect images from the WIYN 0.9 m, SkyNet, or SDSS telescopes to search for known asteroids at risk of becoming "lost." Roughly one-fifth of all discovered asteroids are lost when, over time, uncertainties in their orbital parameters increase to the point that finding them again near their predicted locations becomes unlikely. Students "recover" asteroids and refine their orbits by analyzing images of predicted locations and searching for objects that have moved from one image to the next. If an object's orbit suggests a possible impact with a planet, students learn how to calculate these odds as well. An important aspect of the project is that students participate in an iterative approach to refining an asteroid's orbital parameters. The objective of this project is to help them understand that much of the scientific enterprise is devoted to improving the accuracy of knowledge.

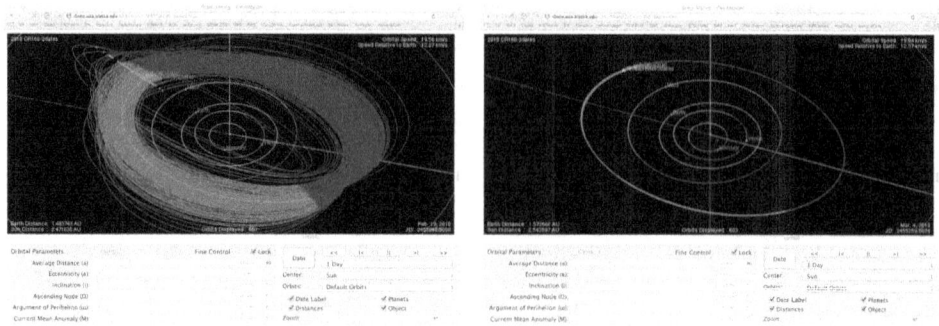

Figure 7.1. OrbitMaster visualizations of over 600 potential orbits of asteroid 2010 CR$_{160}$, showing reduced uncertainties based on our students' work. The left panel shows orbits based on initial observations by La Sagra Observatory, along with data taken 12 days later by the Astronomical Research Observatory on Skynet. The right panel shows orbits refined using serendipitous Spacewatch observations from 13 days later still. The La Sagra and Spacewatch observations were not known to be of the same object until after our students "linked" them by submitting to the MPC their measurements of the intervening ARO images a few weeks later (Holmes et al. 2010).

Once found, an asteroid's location is measured using ImageJ with a custom-made plugin called Polaris. A separate program called Find_Orb is then used with past observations to generate a new best-fit orbit along with hundreds of alternate possible orbits. Students confirm that they have improved knowledge of the orbit by showing that the range of possibilities has been reduced. They then submit their astrometric observations to the IAU Minor Planet Center (MPC) database, resulting in publication in *Minor Planet Circulars* (e.g., Holmes et al. 2010).

The current version of this project requires three separate programs, one of which only runs on a PC (Find_Orb), meaning this project can currently only be done on PC computers. However, recent progress toward platform independence has been made through the development of our online OrbitMaster visualization tool, based on the previous OrbitViewer tool developed by AstroArts Inc. and NASA/JPL (Figure 7.1).[1] Hundreds of possible orbits can now be visualized and compared from both before and after the students' contributions. OrbitMaster now also enables hands-on investigation of Kepler's laws, automatic detection of Earth impacts and close approaches, and updated relative speeds due to Earth's gravity.

2. Nova Search

Images of the Andromeda Galaxy (M31) are obtained regularly (monthly to weekly) with the WIYN 0.9 m telescope. Students are looking for a "nova," flaring caused by a thermonuclear reaction on the surface of a white dwarf star due to mass exchange with a gravitationally bound partner. Students find novae by "blinking," or rapidly comparing, images taken of the same location on different dates (Figure 7.2). Stars in the short-lived nova phase will flare and be detectable for a few months to over a year. Because of the complex environment of M31, identifying novae is most reliably done by eye (Soraisam et al. 2017).

---

[1] http://www.astroarts.co.jp/products/orbitviewer/index.html. This program is free software; you can redistribute and/or modify it under the terms of the GNU General Public License as published by the Free Software Foundation.

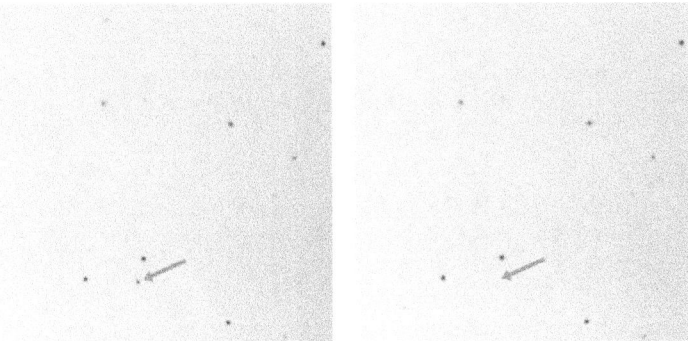

Figure 7.2. Two images near the center of the Andromeda Galaxy taken in 1995 August (left) and 1997 July (right). The images are inverted so stars look black and the night sky is white. If you look closely (see arrow), you can see a nova was erupting in 1995 August in the lower-left corner of the left image. By 1997 July, that nova had faded from view.

Students examine the novae they discover with ImageJ. If a nova is seen in more than one image, students generate a light curve by plotting its brightness over time. Students have investigated a range of questions, such as: is there a relationship between the distance of a nova from the galactic center and its rate of decay? Do the locations of novae correlate with *Chandra* X-ray sources? Is there a correlation between peak brightness and rate of decay? There is debate in the literature on these and other questions (e.g., Ciardullo et al. 1990; Yungelson et al. 1997).

3. Spectroscopy of Semiregular Variable Stars

An unconventional class of stars, known as semiregular variables, or "RV Tauri stars," exhibits complex changes in brightness as well as dramatic spectral changes over timescales of years. Students analyze spectra taken one to two times a year with the Kitt Peak Coudé Spectrograph to determine each star's current spectral class and surface temperature (Figure 7.3). Using photometry from the American Association of Variable Star Observers (AAVSO) database and astrometry from the Hipparcos catalog, students determine brightness and distance, and then calculate luminosity and size. Determining what correlations exist between varying stellar temperature, luminosity, and radius will improve our understanding of RV Tauri stars, including their physical state and why they change, and how they are related to other types of stars (e.g., Bjorkman et al. 2000).

4. Active Galactic Nucleus Spectroscopy

Several telescopes, including the Kitt Peak 2.1m, have been used to obtain spectra of over 2000 optical counterparts to FIRST radio sources (White et al. 1997) and in X-ray surveys. These objects are believed to be active galactic nuclei (AGN) because of their luminous radio and X-ray emission. The primary goal is to determine the nature of each object: is it a quasar, a radio galaxy, or something altogether unexpected? Students also analyze each optical spectrum to determine a redshift, and thus distance, for each object. FIRST radio images are then downloaded to measure the radio flux density and angular size (Figure 7.4). Once a distance is determined, students can calculate the intrinsic luminosity at optical, radio, and X-ray wavelengths, as well as physical size.

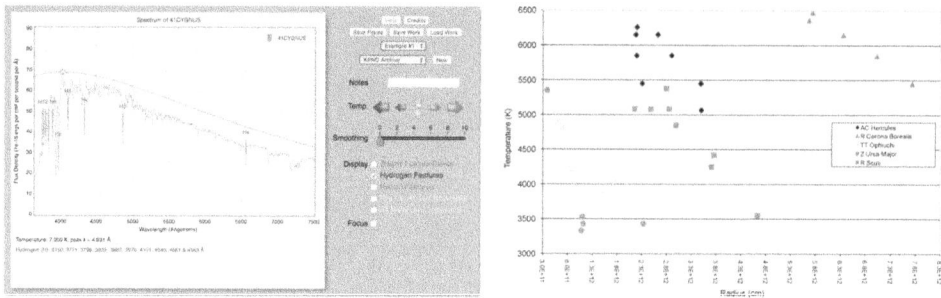

Figure 7.3. Students analyze a spectrum (left) with a GEAS spectroscopy tool to determine a star's spectral class during a particular epoch. Multiple epochs for five sample variable stars are plotted on a temperature vs. radius graph (right) to illustrate their complex behavior.

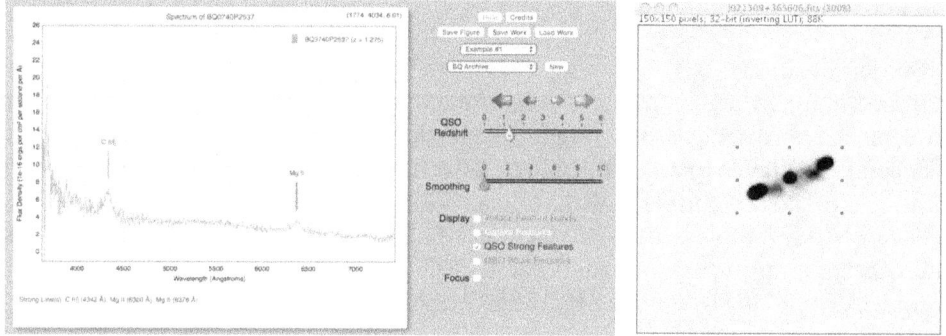

Figure 7.4. Quasar optical emission lines are identified, a redshift is measured, and optical flux density and luminosity are calculated with a GEAS spectroscopy tool (left). FIRST maps provide a radio luminosity and physical size (right).

The survey nature of this project allows students to investigate many different research questions, e.g., are quasars more numerous than radio galaxies? Is there a relationship between an object's physical size and its luminosity? For each class of object, students can also generate a "luminosity function," a histogram of the number of objects as a function of luminosity.

5. *Photo-z (Photometric Redshifts and Stellar Evolution)*

This project is intended for students with a good understanding of photometry and spectroscopy drawn from the other RBSE projects. Students search for distant galaxies in the NOAO Deep Wide Field Survey (NDWFS), using aperture photometry for red galaxies in three filters. Galaxy "colors" (the difference in brightness between filters) are plotted on a color–color plot (Figure 7.5). Each "track" shown represents a theoretical model for a galaxy in which star formation occurs for a different amount of time (with redder tracks representing galaxies for which star formation has long since ended). A galaxy's position on each track depends on its redshift. Thus, the redshift (distance) and star-formation history of a galaxy can be estimated from its location. The long-term goal of the project is to identify distant galaxies by searching regions near quasars in the survey area.

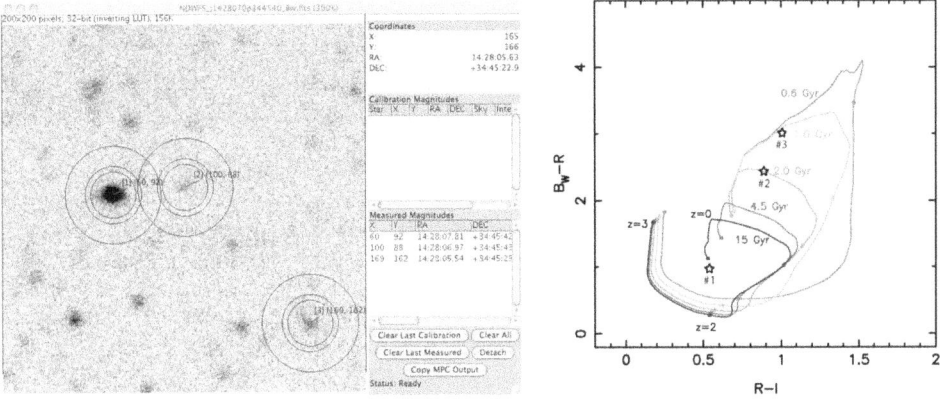

Figure 7.5. Aperture photometry in three filters of three galaxies discovered in the NDWFS (left) allows them to be plotted on a color–color diagram (right). Each "track" shows a galaxy with a different star-formation history. A galaxy's position on a track depends on its redshift and history. Three example galaxies are shown.

7.4 Student Discoveries

Students utilizing the RBSE curriculum have made several important scientific discoveries. For example, over a thousand students have participated in the *Nova Search* project over the last 12 years. They have inspected 169 images, finding 116 confirmed novae in M31. This is more than any other single effort (e.g., Shafter & Irby 2001). The latest student results from this project are presented in Shafter et al. (2015).

As part of the "Spectroscopy of Semiregular Variable Stars" research project, a group of students has been spectroscopically monitoring semiregular variable stars (e.g., RV Tauri-class stars). The periodicity of RV Tauri and semiregular types is not as well behaved as other variables such as Cepheids, and a single cycle takes between months and years. Long-term monitoring of these objects with the KPNO Coudé Feed spectrograph has revealed considerable new insights into their behavior. Three posters on results from this project were presented by Hernandez et al. (2013), Pugh et al. (2013), and Kurgatt et al. (2013) at the 221st meeting of the American Astronomical Society (AAS). Student work has also led to published papers (e.g., Howell et al. 2009).

Finally, students participating in the recovery observations of asteroids have, in the last four years, generated 700 astrometric measurements, recovering 122 asteroids and Kuiper Belt objects. Students have determined that none of these objects are (thankfully!) a threat to the Earth or other planets.

7.5 Student Gains

As part of our RBSE instructional program, we also assessed students' conceptions of the scientific process and what it was like to participate in an authentic scientific research project (Wooten et al. 2018). In brief, we find that participation in the RBSE curriculum has the potential to significantly increase students' perceived confidence in participating in science. Furthermore, participation in experiences wherein results were contributed to the scientific community more often led to students' nuanced perceptions of science processes, including increased understanding of the role of analysis and the utility of scientific communities and collaborations.

7.6 Other Resources and Programs for Authentic Research Experiences in Astronomy Classes

The RBSE curriculum is not unique in its use of real astronomical data in the introductory astronomy classroom. Here we briefly describe other programs and resources that support engaging students in astronomical research. There are programs that offer an opportunity for students to execute their own astronomical observations using robotic telescopes, including the Skynet Robotic Telescope Network, https://skynet.unc.edu/, and the MicroObservatory Robotic Telescope Network, https://mo-www.cfa.harvard.edu/OWN/index.html. Other programs give you access to archival data including SDSS Voyages, https://www.sdss.org/education/, which includes both premade activities and research challenges. Instructors are also making use of archive data in creating their own projects (e.g., Clarkson et al. 2016) as well as providing astronomy labs that help prepare students to engage in research, http://astronomy.nmsu.edu/geas/oview/geas.shtml (Vogt et al. 2013). Lastly, the NASA/IPAC NITARP program, https://nitarp.ipac.caltech.edu/page/other_epo_programs, maintains a thorough list of opportunities for teachers and students to use real astronomical data.

7.7 Conclusions

The learning objectives invoked by many science educators often focus on gains in student content knowledge regarding science concepts. But authentic science is a process of discovery, not just a body of knowledge. In recent years, there have been several calls for teaching to better reflect how science is done (e.g., Handelsman et al. 2004). To this end, the CUREs and the RBSE curriculum seek to engage students in the process of scientific research in an astronomy-content-rich context, emphasizing the discovery-oriented work of a scientist. The outcomes examined in this chapter reveal that introductory science students, majors and nonmajors alike, have the potential to do the work of scientists and contribute meaningful results to science.

The RBSE curriculum is free to use by anyone, and we welcome instructors who are interested in incorporating the projects in their teaching. Documentation and data sets for the current research projects can be found at these websites:

http://rbseu.uaa.alaska.edu/	(UAA website)
http://www.astro.indiana.edu/catyp/rbseu/	(IUB website)

Acknowledgments

We thank the many thousands of students who have participated in the RBSE curriculum, as well as the RBSE-U instructors, in particular Ana Larson, Dan Loranz, and Erin Dokter. We also acknowledge the original RBSE development team of Suzanne Jacoby, Jeff Lockwood, and Don McCarthy. This work was supported by the National Science Foundation grants #0618849 and #0920293.

References

Barnett, M., Kafka, A., Pfitzner-Gatling, A., & Szymanski, E. 2005, JCSTe, 34, 50
Bhattacharyya, P. 2009, JCSTe, 39, 43
Bjorkman, K. S., Miroshnichenko, A. S., & Krugov, V. D. 2000, AAS Meeting 196, 05.03
Brown, J. S., Collins, A., & Duguid, P. 1989, Educational Researcher, 18, 32
Campbell, T., Der, J. P., Wolf, P. G., Packenham, E., & Abd-Hamid, N. H. 2012, JCSTe, 41, 74
Ciardullo, R., Ford, H. C., Williams, R. E., Tamblyn, P., & Jacoby, G. H. 1990, AJ, 99, 1079
Clarkson, W. I., Swift, C., Hughes, K., et al. 2016, AAS Meeting 228, 214.17
Edelson, D. C. 1998, in International Handbook of Science Education, Vol. 1, ed. B. Fraser, & K. Tobin (Dordrecht: Kluwer), 317
Handelsman, J., Ebert-May, D., & Beichner, R. 2004, Sci, 304, 521
Hathaway, R. S., Nagda, B. A., & Gregerman, S. R. 2002, Journal of College Student Development, 43, 614
Hernandez, G., Walter, D. K., Cash, J., Howell, S. B., & McKay, M. 2013, AAS Meeting 221, 354.04
Holmes, R., Dankov, K., Vorobjov, T., et al. 2010, MPC, 69402, 2
Howell, S. B., Johnson, K. J., & Adamson, A. J. 2009, PASP, 121, 16
Kurgatt, C., Walter, D. K., Howell, S. B., Cash, J., & Eleby, J. S. 2013, AAS Meeting 221, 354.06
Mulvey, P. J., & Nicholson, S. 2002, Physics and Astronomy Senior Report: Classes of 1999 and 2000, AIP Report, Pub No. R-211.31, June 2002
National Research Council 1996, National Science Education Standards (Washington, DC: National Academies Press)
Pugh, B., Walter, D. K., Howell, S. B., & Cash, J. 2013, AAS Meeting 221, 354.05
Russell, S. H., Hancock, M. P., & McCullough, J. 2007, Sci, 316, 548
Sadler, T. D., & McKinney, L. 2010, JCSTe, 39, 43
Shafter, A. W., & Irby, B. K. 2001, ApJ, 563, 749
Shafter, A. W., Henze, M., Rector, T. A., et al. 2015, ApJS, 216, 34
Soraisam, M. D., Gilfanov, M., Kupfer, T., et al. 2017, A&A, 599, 48
Vogt, N. P., Cook, S. P., & Muise, A. S. 2013, American Journal of Distance Education, 27, 189
White, R. L., Becker, R. H., Helfand, D. J., & Gregg, M. D. 1997, ApJ, 475, 479
Wooten, M. M., Coble, K., Puckett, A. W., & Rector, T. 2018, PRPER, 14, 010151
Yungelson, L., Livio, M., & Tutukov, A. 1997, ApJ, 481, 127

though
Chapter 8

Citizen Science in Astronomy Education

Laura Trouille, Thomas Nelson, Julie Feldt, John Keller, Marc Buie, Carie Cardamone, Bethany Cobb Kung, Karen Masters, Kate Meredith and Kelly Borden

Citizen science has proven to be a unique and effective tool in helping science and society cope with the ever-growing data rates and volumes that characterize the modern landscape. It also serves a critical role in engaging the public with research in a direct, authentic fashion, and by doing so promotes a better understanding of the processes of science. As the field of citizen science matures, there are a growing number of quality opportunities for instructors to engage their students in authentic research through citizen science. Citizen science in classroom settings provides unique opportunities to engage students in the process of scientific discovery while making real and valued scientific contributions and is well aligned with research-supported educational practices. In this chapter, we provide a brief overview of the history and current state of citizen science and highlight a few key results from the literature around the impact of engagement in citizen science on learning and attitudes. We then present case studies of curricula incorporating citizen science into undergraduate introductory astronomy courses for non-STEM majors (i.e., Astro 101). This article is not meant to provide an exhaustive list of existing efforts; rather, we focus on two specific citizen science approaches and platforms: online data processing through Zooniverse and data gathering and analysis through the Research and Education Collaborative Occultation Network (RECON). We hope these examples serve as inspiration for joining the growing community of instructors bringing citizen science into their classrooms.

Chapter Objectives

By the end of the chapter, readers will be able to
- describe the breadth and diversity of citizen science opportunities available for instructors and their students,

- give examples and best practices to follow in incorporating citizen science into their classrooms, and
- discuss the literature around the positive impacts of incorporating citizen science in the classroom, as well as the open questions and opportunities for further research.

8.1 Overview

Citizen science—the involvement of the general public in research—has a long history. An early example is Edmund Halley's study of timings during the 1715 total solar eclipse, which included observations from a distributed, self-organized group of observers (Pasachoff 1999). Works by Dawson et al. (2015) and Shuttleworth (2018), among others, have linked modern-day efforts to their 19th century antecedents, for example, highlighting the role played by networks of amateur meteorological observers in establishing that field of study (i.e., by 1900, more than 3400 observers were contributing data to a network organized by George Symons, producing data on a scale that could not be matched by the professional efforts of the time).

In recent decades, citizen science has gained renewed prominence, boosted in part by technological advances and digital tools like mobile applications, cloud computing, and wireless and sensor technology, which have enabled new modes of public engagement in research (Bonney et al. 2016) and facilitated research projects that investigate questions from data at scales beyond the professional research community's resource capacity (Miller-Rushing et al. 2012).

In 2015, professional citizen science organizations were created in Europe, Australia, and the United States. In the U.S., the Crowdsourcing and Citizen Science Act of 2015 was introduced to encourage the use of citizen science within the federal government and, that same year, the first Citizen Science Association Conference was held (though some consider the 2012 European Space Agency side event on citizen science the first CSA gathering). CitizenScience.gov currently lists over 400 active citizen science projects. Participation in citizen science today ranges from hands-on data collection, tagging, analysis, and research projects (e.g., iNaturalist.org, Laurie 2018; eBird.org, Sullivan et al. 2009; and CitSci.org, Wang et al. 2015) to contributing in-person data and participating in hands-on data analysis (e.g., the Denver Museum of Science Genetics of Taste Lab, Boxer & Garneau 2015) to a growing number of co-created environmental monitoring projects using low-cost sensors with community members working in collaboration with researchers (e.g., the LA Watershed Project[1]) to online data processing efforts, of which Zooniverse.org is one example and described in more detail below.

Online citizen science, which has become a proven method of distributed data analysis, enables research teams from diverse domains to solve problems involving large quantities of data, taking advantage of the inherently human talent for pattern recognition and anomaly detection. For example, the EternaGame.org

---
[1] https://www.epa.gov/urbanwaterspartners/diverse-partners-brownfields-healthfields-la-watershed.

(Lee et al. 2014) online gaming environment (which is the next generation of the FoldIT platform; Cooper et al. 2010) challenges players to design new ways to fold RNA molecules to find solutions for diseases like tuberculosis. These new molecular structures are then synthesized and tested in Stanford's medical labs. As another example, Eyewire (Kim et al. 2014) and their recently released NEO online citizen science game connects citizen science with data collected by the Allen Institute for Brain Science and Baylor College of Medicine as part of the Intelligence Advanced Research Projects Activity's Machine Intelligence from Cortical Networks program (MICrONs). There are also growing numbers of online crowdsourced transcription efforts in the humanities, including From the Page,[2] Veridian (Daniels et al. 2014), Smithsonian Transcript Center,[3] and Transcribe Bentham (Causer et al. 2018). Furthermore, while not the focus of this chapter, we note the parallel track of "volunteer/distributed computing" efforts, like SETI@Home,[4] which harness computing resources for distributed computing and/or storage.

Within this growing citizen science ecosystem, astronomy has had a long history of leadership, as noted above. This leadership has continued into recent decades with the great breadth and depth of projects available. In the remainder of this chapter, we will focus on efforts through Zooniverse and RECON, but we wanted to provide a list of other astronomy-related citizen science platforms and programs here and strongly encourage readers to explore the myriad of opportunities available:

- Aurorasaurus—NASA (http://aurorasaurus.org/).
- Cameras for All-Sky Meteor Surveillance [CAMS]—SETI Institute (http://cams.seti.org).
- Citizen CATE—National Solar Observatory (https://eclipse2017.nso.edu/citizencate).
- Cosmoquest—(https://cosmoquest.org).
- Distributed Electronic Cosmic-Ray Observatory (https://wipac.wisc.edu/deco/app).
- Globe at Night—National Optical Astronomy Observatory (https://www.globeatnight.org).
- QuarkNet (https://quarknet.org).
- Radio JOVE—NASA (https://radiojove.gsfc.nasa.gov).

See CitizenScience.gov and SciStarter.org for comprehensive listings of citizen science projects and platforms not only in astronomy but also across the disciplines.

In parallel with this renaissance in citizen science efforts, there has been an explosion in citizen science efforts carried out in formal classroom settings. Citizen science provides unique, hands-on opportunities to engage students in the process of scientific discovery while making real and valued scientific contributions and is well aligned with research-supported educational practices (Jones et al. 2010; PCAST 2012; Freeman

---

[2] https://fromthepage.com.
[3] https://siarchives.si.edu/collections/siris_sic_14645.
[4] https://setiathome.berkeley.edu.

et al. 2014). In geoscience and biology courses for majors, there is a strong tradition of incorporating research experiences where the students efforts feed into a larger, existing citizen science project (e.g., CASPiE, Quardokus et al. 2012; Genome Education Partnership, Shaffer et al. 2014; Sea-Phages, Caruso et al. 2009; eternaGame.org; fold. It; eBird: Surasinghe & Courter 2012; etc.). There is also a growing number of citizen-science-based research experiences in non-major geoscience, biology, and astronomy courses (e.g., Trautmann 2013; Dickinson et al. 2012; smallWorldInitiative.org; citizen-science-integrated biology courses at Brandeis, University of Delaware's water biomonitoring efforts, etc.) and broader cross-campus initiatives (e.g., citizenscience.bard.edu). In Astro 101, a notable example is Slater et al.'s use of a backwards faded scaffolding approach in which students carry out multiple citizen-science-based mini inquiries throughout the semester (Slater et al. 2011).

Numerous studies have outlined the positive impacts of public participation in scientific research, including increases in long-term environmental, civic, and research interests (e.g., Dickinson & Bonney 2012 and references therein); the empowerment of communities to influence local environmental decision-making (Dickinson & Bonney 2012; Newman et al. 2012); the increased representation of women and minorities in the scientific process (Groulx et al. 2017); increases in confidence (Raddick et al. 2010, 2013; Masters et al. 2016; Greenhill et al. 2014), scientific literacy (Cronje et al. 2011; Crall et al. 2013; Jones et al. 2016; Trumbull et al. 2000), domain knowledge (Brossard et al. 2005; Masters et al. 2016); and increases in understanding that scientific progress is a collective process (Ruiz-Mallén et al. 2016).

In the sections below, we describe a few examples of the use and impact of citizen science in formal astronomy classroom environments. This article is not meant to provide an exhaustive list of existing efforts; rather, our goal with sharing these few examples is to provide an inspiration point for others to build from. Along these lines, we have chosen two different citizen science approaches from which to pull examples: (1) Zooniverse, an online platform for data processing and analysis, and (2) RECON, a coordinated telescope observing network for data gathering.

8.2 Astro 101: Zooniverse-based Citizen Science Opportunities

There is a critical need to support the development of a scientifically and data literate society, crucial to our country's health and economy (National Research Council 1996, 2003, 2010). Each year hundreds of thousands of non-science majors take introductory astronomy courses (Fraknoi 2001; Chen & Solder 2013) to fulfill their science requirement for graduation. These students later take on a range of roles in society, from lawyers to teachers and community leaders to policy makers. Introductory science courses like Astro 101 are often these students' last formal exposure to science, yet they generally provide little insight into how science actually works or exposure to key 21st century skills of data handling and analysis. Scientific literacy and data literacy skills serve non-STEM majors by empowering them to feel confident using evidence-based reasoning to solve personally meaningful problems in their everyday lives: when reading the news, voting on policy decisions that impact them and their communities, etc. (Feinstein et al. 2013). Introductory science courses like Astro 101 are also often the last formal opportunity for science identity development and positive impacts on attitudes toward science and scientists. In the subsections below, we first provide details on the Zooniverse platform and then describe two models for engaging Astro 101 students in citizen science through Zooniverse.

8.2.1 Zooniverse

Zooniverse.org is the largest platform for online citizen science, host to over 80 active projects with 1.7 million registered participants around the world. It is unique among online citizen science platforms as a result of its (1) shared open-source software, experience, expertise, and input from users across the disciplines, (2) reliable, flexible, and scalable application programming iInterface (API), which can be used for a variety of development tasks, (3) free, do-it-yourself (DIY) "Project Builder" (also known as the Project Builder Platform) capabilities as described below, and (4) the scale of its existing audience. Zooniverse partners with hundreds of researchers across many disciplines, from astronomy to zoology, cancer research to climate science, history to the arts. At a time when citizen science is gaining prominence across the world, Zooniverse has become a core part of the research infrastructure landscape. Since the launch in 2007 of the Galaxy Zoo project (Lintott et al. 2008; Fortson et al. 2012), Zooniverse projects have led to over 150 peer-reviewed publications, enabling significant contributions across many disciplines, such as in ecology (Swanson et al. 2016; Matsunaga et al. 2016; Arteta et al. 2016; Anderson et al. 2016), humanities (Williams et al. 2014; Grayson 2016), biomedicine (dos Reis et al. 2015), physics (Barr et al. 2016; Zevin et al. 2017), climate science (Hennon et al. 2015), and astronomy (Lintott et al. 2008; Fortson et al. 2012; Johnson et al. 2015; Marshall et al. 2015; Schwamb et al. 2018).

Thus, these projects have established a track record of successfully engaging a disparate crowd of volunteers and producing reliable results used by the wider scientific community. We note that lack of specialist knowledge or misclassification can lead to errors within data produced by citizen scientists (Freitag et al. 2016). In the Zooniverse model, however, consensus results are created based on numerous classifications (e.g., 15+ individuals classify each subject), which mitigate the impact of any one individual's errors. A rigorous approach to assessing and ensuring data quality within citizen science projects is particularly important when those data are used in a classroom context. Mitchell et al. (2017) found that in undergraduate use of the Australian phenology citizen science program, ClimateWatch, only 31% of students agreed with the statement that "data collected by citizen scientists are reliable" at the end of the project, whereas the rate of agreement was initially 79%. This result is particularly harmful in a society where science is already widely mistrusted and the processes of science are misunderstood.

The number of projects supported by Zooniverse has recently experienced rapid growth, an acceleration that is the result of the launch in July 2015 of the free Project Builder Platform (zooniverse.org/lab), which enables anyone to build and deploy an online citizen science project at no cost, within hours, using a web browser-based toolkit. The Project Builder supports the most common types of interaction, including classification, multiple-choice questions, comparison tasks, and marking and drawing tools. Figure 8.1 provides screenshots of the Project Builder editor interface and an example of the resulting public-facing web page. The Project Builder front-end is a series of forms and text boxes a researcher fills out to create the project's classification interface and website. All Project Builder projects come with a landing page, classification interface, discussion forum, and "About" pages for

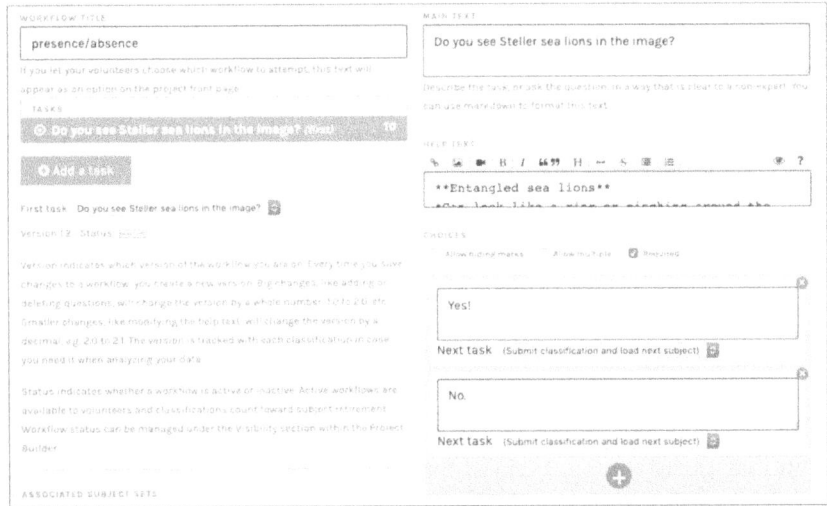

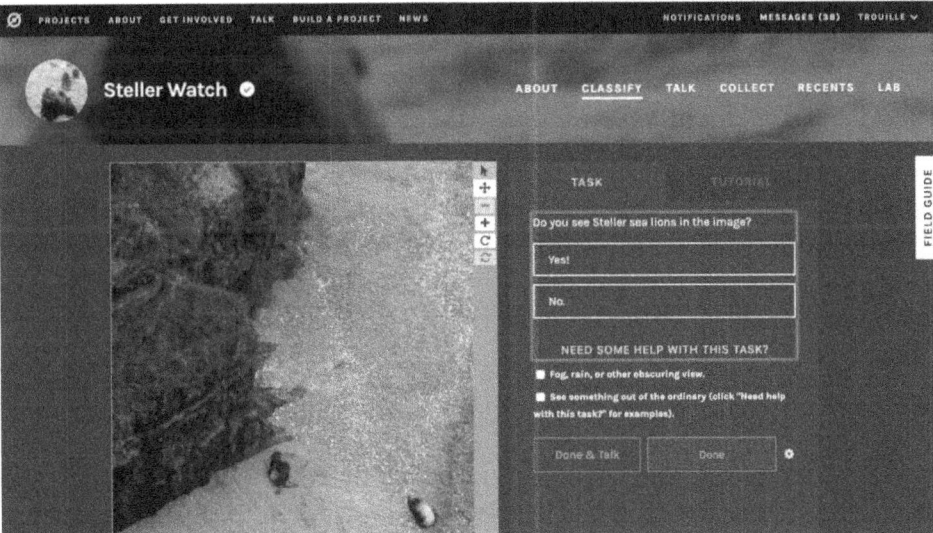

Figure 8.1. Screenshots of Zooniverse's free Project Builder Platform. The first image shows the project builder interface. The second image shows the website the project builder can immediately view as they upload their content. Credit: Zooniverse.

content about the research, the research team, and results from the project. The Project Builder is transformative; prior to its development, a typical online citizen science project required months to years of professional web development time. Zooniverse went from launching 3–5 projects a year to launching 26 in 2016, 44 in 2017, and over 50 in 2018.

Within the landscape of citizen science use in formal classroom environments, Zooniverse has two key characteristics we take advantage of here: (1) an extremely low barrier to entry and (2) projects across the disciplines that produce quality data that are easy to understand and use. In many citizen science projects and approaches, instructors must spend considerable time and effort training students so that they are able to make meaningful and quality contributions. In contrast, a student can provide useful and valued classifications to a Zooniverse project within minutes of entering the site. In terms of ease of access, by working within an online citizen science platform, we provide a complementary approach to field-work-based citizen science experiences. Through Zooniverse, students can contribute to the data processing, gain access to the classification results and additional relevant metadata, and pursue research projects in the context of professional researchers actively working with those same data. This removes geographic barriers as well as resource constraints for institutions with limited access to active researchers and/or who are unable to sustainably carry out field work.

8.2.2 Improving Student Attitudes toward Science with a Citizen Science Assignment

Students in introductory science classrooms often feel that they inherently lack the ability to "do science." We frequently hear students in introductory astronomy label themselves as "not a science (or math) person." It is also not uncommon for students to admit that they have "always been bad at science" or simply state that they "don't like science." The cause of these negative attitudes toward personal scientific proficiency are, of course, complex and can vary by the individual student (Osborne et al. 2003). Many students will have struggled with content in previous science and mathematical courses and, therefore, enter the college-level introductory science classroom having already developed an unfortunate aversion to science and strong doubts about their own scientific capabilities. Furthermore, such students are often in our classrooms not because of any innate interest in the subject matter but, instead, because general curricular requirements dictate that students must complete a science course in order to graduate.

How can we challenge and stretch our students while simultaneously bolstering their scientific self-confidence and repairing their attitudes toward science in general? Citizen science engages people without any specialized knowledge to take part in scientific research and highly values their contributions. This means that even students in an introductory science course can contribute to real scientific research studies. This contrasts with typical introductory science laboratory exercises in which students either simply reproduce well-known results or conduct more independent research projects which, however, do not produce results that contribute to general scientific knowledge (because they are only "published" in class and/or because the scope of such projects is highly limited by both student expertise and time). Students can easily differentiate between authentic and inauthentic work, and we hypothesized that students would have a positive reaction to engaging in authentic science through citizen science. Below we describe one model for engagement with online citizen science and the resulting impact on attitudes.

It is worth noting that developing authentic projects for the introductory classroom from scratch is incredibly challenging and time consuming, so much so that it is an unrealistic prospect for many faculty members. Because the citizen science projects on mature platforms such as Zooniverse have already been developed and vetted (as well as maintained) by other scientists, citizen science can be leveraged by any faculty member to quickly and easily bring authentic scientific research into the introductory science classroom.

Example: Low-barrier Approach to Citizen Science in Astro 101. With these goals in mind, authors Cardamone and Cobb Kung developed a Zooniverse-based citizen science student assignment to be completed by students primarily outside of class time over the period of about one month, with the expectation that students would spend between 5 and 10 total hours on the project during that month. The assignment was used in a number of introductory astronomy courses at George Washington University (Washington, DC) and Wheelock College (Boston, MA), with class sizes ranging from about 15 to 60 students. A similar assignment, however, could be used in any introductory science course, regardless of topic or class size.

Curricular design. The assignment required each student to individually contribute to a Zooniverse project over approximately four weeks and to briefly reflect on those contributions. Meanwhile, the students worked in peer groups to understand and articulate the scientific purpose of a common citizen science project. The assignment was introduced in class by describing how citizen science allows for the collaboration between professional scientists and the wider public. Connections were made to how these collaborations enable new scientific research and discoveries, and improve public understanding of both science and the scientific process. It was emphasized that everyone can participate in citizen science, as the projects are designed so that no specialized knowledge or skills are required. Indeed, citizen science harnesses the unique power and creativity of the human brain unmatched by even the best computers to recognize patterns and anomalies. Finally, students were told that they would be contributing directly to ongoing scientific research by participating in a citizen science project of their choice.

The students begin working on the assignment by exploring and then selecting a Zooniverse project in the "physics" or "space" categories (see Zooniverse.org/projects). They were limited to these general categories due to the topic of the courses, but as the Zooniverse hosts projects across the disciplines—including biology, climate change, nature, medicine, history, and social science—the assignment can be utilized in many different types of introductory science courses. Students could choose a particular Zooniverse project that was most aligned with their interests and values to provide them with a sense of agency and to increase their motivation in participating in the project (Christenson et al. 2012). Project choices were limited to those less than 50%

completed, so that it was likely to continue running for the entire time period of the assignment. Once students had individually selected a project, they formed groups of approximately four students around their shared interest in contributing to a particular Zooniverse project. The students were also encouraged at this early stage to begin to explore the science background of the project and its specific scientific goals.

Over the ~4 weeks of the assignment, students worked individually, making multiple visits to Zooniverse to contribute to their project. Students contributed to their project a minimum of eight times, ideally visiting the citizen science project two to three times per week, with each visit being approximately 15 minutes in length, but no two visits being on the same day. This assignment can be modified to be completed in shorter or longer time spans and require more or fewer visits, though we would encourage students to be required to make at least five visits because most students took several visits to become accustomed to their projects and confident in their classification abilities. Students kept a log of their work, recording visit dates and start/stop times, as well as a brief reflection for each visit. They were encouraged to note images or data they encountered that were particularly interesting, surprising, or confusing. Reflections were only required to be a few sentences in length, though some students were quite verbose. Some students kept these logs electronically, while others logged their visits on paper. Once they had completed their visits, students were asked to take a screenshot of their Zooniverse "recent projects" page that showcased the overall number of classifications they contributed to the project.

The project culminated with each student group producing a creative video presentation demonstrating their understanding of their particular Zooniverse project. Students were encouraged to use any video technique they found most appealing, including filming themselves, making animations, or providing narration over images. Students were required to answer four key questions with the video: (1) What are the overarching science goals that the citizen science project is trying to achieve? (2) What was the specific task (or tasks) that you did as a participant in this project? Reflect on the task. Was the task easy or hard? Was the task interesting or not? What did you enjoy the most and the least about the task? (3) Did you encounter anything surprising? Confusing? (4) How did your participation help the project meet its science goals? (In other words, how do the citizens' contributions to citizen science actually advance scientific knowledge?)

Outcomes: In order to assess the impact of this assignment on the students, analysis was performed on their logs and final video submissions and using a voluntary pre- and postassignment survey focused on two key questions: (1) does participating in citizen science increase a student's positive attitude toward science, in particular moving from viewing the scientist as "other" toward scientist as "self," and (2) does participating in citizen science increase a students' knowledge of the process of science?

Most student groups were able to accurately describe the scientific goals of their project, to demonstrate the project tasks, and to articulate how they contributed to advancing knowledge. The videos also included rich reflections of the students' experiences, with many comments that indicated they found their work on the projects interesting, such as: "I enjoyed the project as I got to learn about astronomical anomalies, participate in the scientific process, and view pictures many people will never get to see." Students frequently commented in their logs on the challenge and uncertainty involved in contributing to citizen science, for example: "This was my first attempt at contributing to science, and it was quite a confusing experience." Fortunately, students tended to become more confident in their contributions after several visits. Students reflected on new insights into the scientific process: "The classification process makes me appreciate the tedious but essential work that helps the science move forward. Not all of it is glamorous and exciting but it is a necessary part of furthering our knowledge of the universe." Students also expressed a feeling of ownership in their contributions, such as "I feel proud to have contributed to this body of work."

Changes in students' attitudes toward science and knowledge of the process of science were uncovered by comparing the results of a brief online survey completed before the introduction of the assignment with the results of the same survey administered again at its conclusion. Preliminary findings indicate that students had a more positive attitude toward science following the assignment, as they were more likely to agree that "participating in science is fun" and less likely to agree with the statement that "participating in science is boring." Students also showed a slight increase in self-efficacy, as they were less likely to agree that "only a few specially qualified people are capable of understanding science" and more likely to agree that "nearly everyone can understand science (if they work at it)." They were also more likely to agree that they themselves were "capable of learning science" and "making contributions to scientific knowledge." This aligns well with the fact that interest in contributing to scientific knowledge was the strongest motivator for citizens participating in the Galaxy Zoo Project (Raddick et al. 2010).

8.2.3 Engaging Students in Authentic Research through Citizen Science

The above section provided an example of integrating citizen-science-based assignments into Astro 101 courses with relatively minimal effort, both for the instructors and for the students, and seeing positive student impact. Preliminary results suggest that students both begin to see themselves as capable of contributing to science and gain a more positive attitude toward science. The following example takes this general model of participation in an active online data processing citizen science effort and expands it to include using that experience as the foundation for students to pursue their own research questions with the data the community has generated.

Example: Small Group Research Projects through Citizen Science in Astro 101. Through classroom.zooniverse.org,[5] Astro 101 students engage in a citizen-science-based research experience that is aligned with what scientists actually do, including opportunities to grapple with failure and experience the inherent messiness of science (Szteinberg 2007; Ford & Wargo 2007; Bonney et al. 2009). The project addresses undergraduate students' lack of experience in aspects of designing investigations that

---
[5] Funded by National Science Foundation award #1524189, #1525725, and #1524321.

are important to practicing scientists, including distinguishing between, generating, and manipulating both data and evidence (Lyons 2011); asking scientifically fruitful questions (Karelina & Etkina 2007; Slater et al. 2008); and making predictions, observations, and explanations (Tien et al. 2007; Kastens et al. 2009; Teichert et al. 2017). They engage with their peers in in-depth discussions to collaboratively generate a testable question, carry out data analysis, and draw evidence-based conclusions. Their research experience is divided into distinct milestones, highlighting the practices developed with each step, and revisiting and building on those practices throughout the semester. This approach avoids common pitfalls of active-learning activities in lecture-based courses—confirmatory exercises in which students follow explicit procedures to arrive at predetermined conclusions—and addresses the shortcomings cited in studies in which students show little to no improvement in their understanding of the research process despite the research experience (e.g., Yasar & Baker 2003).

Traditional labs in introductory science courses still generally involve following prescribed steps to reproduce known results, rather than engaging students in experiments that involve authentic scientific practices and the possibility of discovery (Buck et al. 2008; Kloser et al. 2011; PCAST 2012). The National Research Council, the National Academies, and the American Association for the Advancement of Science emphasize that the best way to foster students motivation and interest in science, engage students in performing scientific inquiry, and improve their understanding of the nature of science is through authentic research (National Research Council 1996, 2003, 2010). Embedding authentic research within introductory science courses benefits students in numerous ways. Authentic research experiences not only lead to better understanding of specific course content (Lyons 2011), but have been shown to support students in improving their understanding of the nature of science more generally (Larson-Miller 2011), in asking more scientifically fruitful questions (Karelina & Etkina 2007; Slater et al. 2008), and in making predictions, observations, and developing explanations (Tien et al. 2007). Furthermore, universities face the challenge of serving an increasingly socially, economically, and ethnically diverse undergraduate population, many of whom lack critical preparation for college-level STEM courses. Motivating, engaging, and supporting the learning of all students who enter college science classrooms is an imperative (National Research Council 2003, 2010). Research into the impacts of authentic research experiences on marginalized student groups is limited, but those studies that do exist indicate that these types of experiences can improve retention and outcomes for female students (Kingery 2012), urban students (Chapman 2013), minority students (Gregerman 2008), and special-needs students (Melber 2004).

Curricular design: The classroom.zooniverse.org curricular design and approach was informed by best practices developed through the growing number and network of course-based undergraduate research experiences (CURE[6]). This work also builds on existing efforts in incorporating citizen-science-based research experiences in non-major and major astronomy, geoscience, and biology courses (see the

---

[6] https://serc.carleton.edu/curenet/index.html.

"Overview" section, Section 8.1). The design mirrors the Bell et al. (2010) steps in the inquiry process and is informed by the "Science and Engineering Practices outlined in the Next Generation Science Standards." Below we list the assignments we developed for the course within a quarter system (also adapted for and implemented within a semester system). We follow CURE best practices and lessons learned from incorporating citizen science experiences into undergraduate classrooms. These include (1) using quality data and exposing students to how to assess data reliability and validity, (2) a low barrier to technical expertise for data collection, generation, and analysis through a user-friendly interface, (3) a diverse, but constrained, set of variables for developing hypotheses and a data set that lends itself to multiple, unique research questions and multiple pathways for analysis, and (4) course assessments that reflect authentic scientific communication and incorporate peer review.

In-class activities: The ~3.5 hours of in-class activities provide the students with a guided use of the platform and data analysis tools they will use in their research projects:
- Introduction: in-class, 30 minute activity during first week of the course introducing citizen science, Zooniverse, and the data analysis platform, guiding students in collecting/inputting data (hometown information, eye color, etc), manipulating the class data, and analyzing the results using the ZooTools data analysis platform.
- Data reliability: before class, students submit 20 classifications to GalaxyZoo.org. (See Figure 8.2 for a screenshot of the Galaxy Zoo landing page.) The in-class, 30 minute activity compares individual, class, and full Zooniverse classification results to expose how multiple classifications for each subject provides a quantitative measurement of the uncertainty and how to use that for data reliability/validity.
- Claims, evidence, and reasoning: two in-class, 60 minute activities using ZooTools to identify and discuss trends in a data set relevant to the core topics typically covered in the first half of the course (e.g., the H–R diagram). Provides scaffolding for using ZooTools as well as for the key plots effort in the research project experience.
- Survey of citizen science opportunities: this 20 minute in-class or out-of-class activity provides exposure to the myriad of in-person and online citizen science opportunities available through major platforms like Zooniverse, Ebird.org, and iNaturalist.org, as well as through the SciStarter.com and CitizenScience.gov repositories with hundreds of projects to participate in.

Research Project Milestones: Students work in small groups over the course of 15–20 hours to carry out their research projects, with opportunities for feedback at each of these milestones.
- Background: near the start of the course, students watch a short "Pinball Process of Science" video and a short video providing additional background on Zooniverse. We also provide links to additional background information and reference materials.

- Introductory activity: student groups carry out a 3 hour mini research experience with the Galaxy Zoo curated data set (Figure 8.2). This curated data set is a random subsample of 25,000 Sloan Digital Sky Survey galaxies in the local universe (specifically a subset of the data used in Masters et al. 2010). We included a limited set of metadata (e.g., mass, redshift, local density, etc.) from Masters et al. (2010) for each galaxy. Groups address the question, "Are all spiral galaxies blue and are all elliptical galaxies red?" (which was the topic of Masters et al. 2010).
- Research question and hypothesis: in their small groups, students discuss, debate, and ultimately agree on which research question they will pursue as a group for their full research experience. To guide them in this process of identifying a valid research question, the students carry out a short, 20 minute activity applying a rubric to assess the validity of research questions.
- Key plots: the groups use our online platform, ZooTools (described below) to analyze the classification results in the context of their research question, including comparing results for the individual, group, class, and full Zooniverse. From these analyses, students identify key plots and statistical analyses that highlight their conclusions best (Figure 8.3).
- Video: the culminating experience is for the students to create short 4 minute videocasts presenting their research question, plots, analysis, and results.

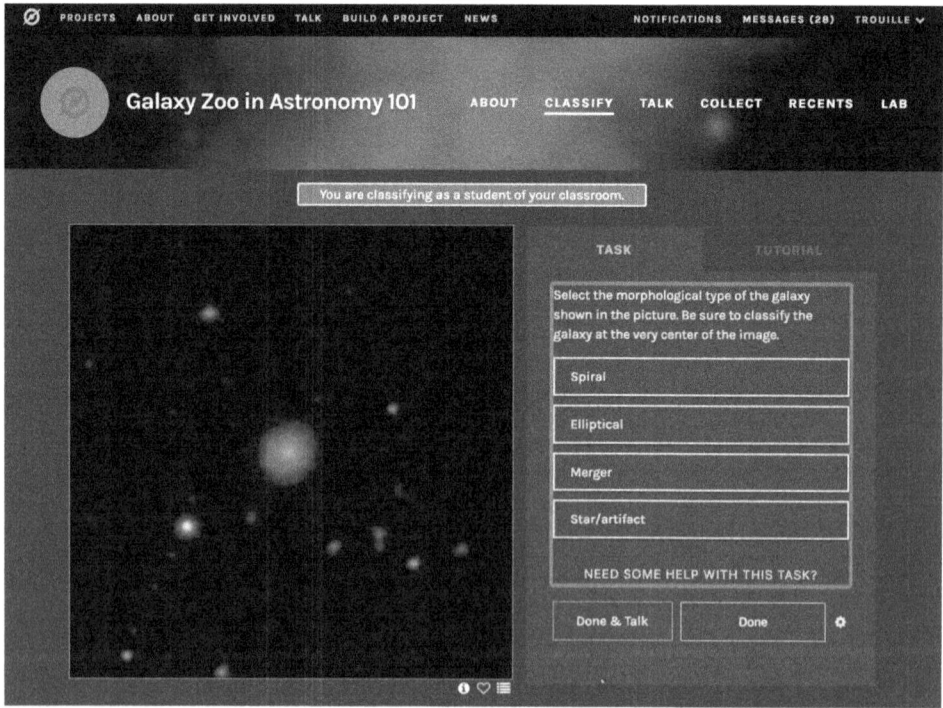

Figure 8.2. Screenshot of the Galaxy Zoo interface used in the Astro 101 in-class activity to showcase how online citizen science works and the processes followed to ensure data reliability. Credit: Zooniverse.

Students use free, easy-to-use software like Screencast-o-matic to simultaneously capture screen and voice recording to create their video. We provide students with a guideline for effective presentations in this format, as well as rubrics for self-assessment, group assessment, and assessment of other groups.
- Peer review: each student provides a peer review for three other videos.

These out-of-class assignments lead the students through the research experience, from classifying galaxies to working in their small research groups to identifying a valid research question, analyzing the data, and communicating their results. This provides students a first-hand experience of the process of authentic scientific research, insight into the true nature of science, and an understanding of basic statistics, essential for a scientifically literate citizen.

All curricular materials and instructional guides are available at https://classroom.zooniverse.org.

ZooTools, the data analysis platform: A major goal of this effort was to make the data analysis aspects of the research experience as accessible as possible to all students, no matter their background in working with data. To this end, we chose to base the classroom.zooniverse.org data analysis tools on Google's Sheets' infrastructure. The Google Suite has been adopted by high schools and universities around the world. In order to make Google spreadsheets even more user-friendly, we created custom, add-on data analysis tools and interfaces to facilitate the students' use of this spreadsheet-based data analysis platform. Our custom Zooniverse add-ons to Google Sheets, hereafter referred to as ZooTools, allow students to more easily apply filters to the full, curated Zooniverse project data set and access basic statistics

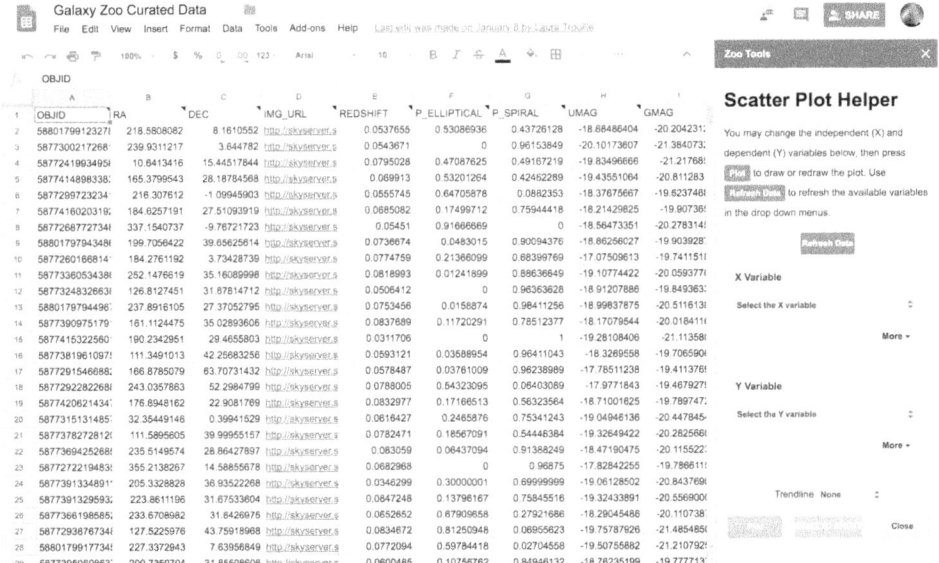

Figure 8.3. Screenshot of the ZooTools interface with the curated Galaxy Zoo data set used in this effort and the scatter plot widget (one of several user-friendly widgets within ZooTools for creating different plot types). Credit: Zooniverse.

(e.g., minimum, maximum, mean, median, standard deviation, etc.). ZooTools also provides a more user-friendly interface for creating plots (e.g., scatter plots, histograms, pie charts, etc.). Figure 8.3 provides a screenshot of the ZooTools interface within Google Sheets. Thus, through classroom.zooniverse.org, the students access our custom ZooTools with a curated Galaxy Zoo data set that includes the classification results and additional metadata of interest (e.g., the galaxy mass, color, distance, environmental density, etc.; values made available via the open data philosophy of the Sloan Digital Sky Survey). We note that the ZooTools code is open source and can easily accommodate data from other major citizen science efforts; we encourage other platforms, e.g., eBird.org, iNaturalist.org, etc., to explore using ZooTools and our curricular framework with their data.

Outcomes: In iteratively developing, assessing, and improving these curricular materials, five instructors at a range of R1, small liberal arts colleges, and community colleges (Northwestern University, University of Minnesota, University of Pittsburgh, University of St. Thomas, and Oakton Community College) supported 725 students in carrying out authentic Galaxy-Zoo-based research experiences through 10 Astro 101 course iterations between 2016 September 1 and 2018 June 15.

T. Nelson et al. (2019, in preparation), to be submitted to the Journal of Geoscience Education, provides an overview of the curriculum, the activities, the feedback from instructors on ease of use and implementation, and the impact on the students. The article presents the results from our pre-/postsurveys and student focus group interviews, including the gains in student understanding of the nature of science and the processes astronomers follow to carry out their research. Student quotes provide illustrations of the survey results, for example, "[Analyzing] the data taught us how easily scientific data can be manipulated and how important it is to know what data set was used and if any data was excluded in reaching a conclusion." We also found significant gains in recognizing the creative nature of research, as illustrated by this quote, "Through conducting this research project, we found that the nature of science has deep roots in creativity."

The article also summarizes the overwhelmingly positive feedback from our pilot instructors and students around ease of implementation (e.g., the clarity of the training and teacher guides, the facility in incorporating these materials into the existing curriculum, their value added, etc.). By implementing at a range of institution types, we have identified how best to adapt these materials to each and created a set of best practices in adapting these core materials to a given institution type, discipline, and course structure. For example, implementation within a community college course must take into account satisfying course credit transfer rules, including upholding existing course objectives and topical requirements.

Because the program includes ~3.5 hours of in-class activities and 15–20 hours for the small group research projects, we explored different models for adapting to quarter and semester systems, lecture versus lab + lecture, and different curricular and institutional constraints. For example, in the Northwestern University Astro 101 lecture course, the research project replaced the 20 hour term paper, worth 20% of the grade, that students had previously submitted. On the other hand, in the

Oakton Community College Astro 101 lecture + lab course, we used three, 3 hour lab periods and 8 hour of out-of-class time (both because this fits better within the course structure and to reduce the required out-of-class group time, which is more of a burden on community college students to accommodate).

The pilot testing also confirmed the astuteness of using Google Sheets + ZooTools—the user-friendliness and simplicity of these tools enabled students' comfort level and ability to carry out the data analysis. This is key for the mostly nonscience majors in these courses to be able to focus on experiencing the processes of science, rather than getting stuck on the data analysis tool itself (a common pitfall for incorporating research experiences into these classrooms).

Sustainability: The Zooniverse team has had good success over the past 10 years of maintaining the Zooniverse.org research projects, infrastructure, and associated curricular materials. Furthermore, we expect Galaxy Zoo to remain active into the foreseeable future, with new data ingested every six months or so. A strength of this effort is that Zooniverse has over 70 active projects; with two to four new projects launching each month (many in astronomy, climate change, and ecology/biodiversity), ZooTools can easily ingest new data sets, and the curricular framework can easily adapt to accommodate new projects in these research areas. We anticipate faculty will create their own Zooniverse projects based around their own research questions and data, and incorporate these projects into this curricular framework and toolkit to use with their students.

8.2.4 Mixing Hands-on Activities with Online Citizen Science

The Planet Hunters Educators Guide[7] is a curriculum developed by Zooniverse educators in conjunction with NASA/JPL introducing students to citizen science and the science behind Zooniverse's popular PlanetHunters.org project. With a heavy emphasis on models to guide student exploration, these lessons were developed to be used independently or to be used as a unit. While the content was originally designed for middle-school classrooms, the materials are relevant and can scale appropriately for Astro 101 courses. Educators have also adapted the Planet Hunters Educators Guide for use in high school, after-school clubs, and informal education settings.

The curriculum begins by introducing students to crowdsourced science by exploring citizen science projects across different platforms including GalaxyZoo.org, the Monarch Larva Monitoring Project,[8] and the GreatSunflower.org. In the second activity, students are introduced to the concept of the "habitable zone" as they identify conditions needed to sustain life on Earth and then determine which other moons and planets in our solar system may also harbor life. Next, students delve into the possibility of life beyond our solar system as they explore known exoplanets and determine if they are within their star's habitable zone. In the third activity, students compare characteristics of different star types and use models to determine habitability zones around these different types of stars.

---

[7] https://www.planethunters.org/#/education.
[8] https://monarchlab.org/mlmp.

In activities 4–6, students are introduced to the advantages and disadvantages of different exoplanet detection methods, create models to understand the transit method of exoplanet detection, and begin to analyze light-curve data on Planet Hunters. Through activities 7–9, students become research astronomers as they learn to use light-curve data to assess the habitability of exoplanets. Students begin by creating their own light curves using models to simulate planets transiting a star. They use these data to calculate characteristics of an exoplanet, including how close the planet is to its star and how long it takes to make one trip around the star (i.e., its orbital period). Then, using light curves from Planet Hunters, students are guided through the calculations necessary to determine the orbital period, radius, mass, semimajor axis, density, and surface temperature for their Planet Hunters exoplanet. Finally, just as NASA creates artistic representations of the objects we can indirectly see, students create visualizations of the exoplanets they have been analyzing.

8.3 Astronomical Citizen Science Data Collection Projects

In addition to the above examples of citizen science data analysis and data mining investigations, several astronomy citizen science efforts have engaged students, teachers, and members of the public in the collection of data to help address scientific investigations. In addition to the RECON Project described below, these include but are not limited to Radio JOVE (https://radiojove.gsfc.nasa.gov/), Citizen CATE (https://eclipse2017.nso.edu/citizen-cate/), and SETI CAMS (http://cams.seti.org/).

This type of citizen science research represents another important part of the scientific process, the collection of research data aligned with an investigation. In particular, citizen science data-gathering efforts are highly relevant in cases where data cannot be gathered without a geographically distributed network of collection sites. In cases in which resource and time limitations make it difficult or prohibitive for a small research team to gather data from multiple locations to address a research question, data collection efforts can be conducted by a distributed network of citizen science volunteers who can then provide their data to a central researcher for analysis. Depending upon the scope and requirements associated with accomplishing the research goal, this type of effort can require significant recruitment and coordination efforts. However, distributing data collection responsibilities across a network can allow for otherwise inaccessible research investigations.

8.3.1 Description of the RECON Citizen Science Project

RECON, the Research and Education Collaborative Occultation Network http://tnorecon.net/, is a citizen science astronomy research investigation supported by the National Science Foundation involving over 55 communities stretching across the western United States from Canada to Mexico (Buie & Keller 2016). The research goal of this investigation is to measure the sizes, shapes, moons, rings, and other characteristics of trans-Neptunian Objects (TNOs) down to 100 km in diameter using stellar occultation measurements. A stellar occultation occurs when an object within our solar system (planet, moon, asteroid, etc.) passes in front of a distant star and effectively casts a shadow from that star over Earth's surface. By positioning an array of telescopes in the occultation path and recording the start and end times of the occultation for each location on Earth, researchers can use the known velocity of the solar system object to generate a profile map of the size and shape of the object. This is a commonly used astronomical technique for studying objects throughout our solar system.

The observational challenge faced in the study of outer solar system objects is that the predicted location of the occultation shadow track has a large uncertainty. These uncertainties arise from our estimates of the orbital elements of TNOs. Distant objects like these have orbits extending out beyond Neptune and have only been measured for fractions of their 250+ year orbits around the Sun. This, along with the geometry involved with the alignment of Earth and the distant TNO and even more distant target star, currently results in substantial cross-track uncertainties in the predicted occultation path. The design of RECON was driven by the size of the uncertainty region. By using a large, fixed network, we can relax the required uncertainty for a successful observation. A traditional approach would require uncertainties comparable to the size of the object. RECON is a citizen science approach to deal with this challenge by establishing a picket-fence array of telescopes stretching 2000 km across the US with roughly 50 km spacing. This enhances the probability that at least two of the telescope sites involved will be within the shadow path of a 100 km sized object, resulting in the minimum number of chords required to approximate the size and shape of the occulting body. With the large ground-track coverage, this experiment also covers a much larger area to search for secondary bodies that might be missed by a smaller, more targeted deployment.

In 2008, when the RECON concept was first conceived, establishing such an array of remotely or robotically controlled telescopes was not practical. While the International Occultation Timing Association (IOTA) has a long-standing and well-coordinated network of amateur astronomer citizen scientists, the IOTA community is not distributed densely or regularly enough to accomplish the research goal of systematically measuring 100 km TNOs and searching for binary objects. Thus, the RECON Project has followed the approach of recruiting teachers, students, and community members from roughly 55 targeted communities located between Yuma, Arizona, and Oroville, Washington, to serve as citizen scientists to help in recording occultation data (Figure 8.4). Communities were identified using online geographic software (e.g., Google Maps), and RECON teams were recruited through email, phone, and site visits to local secondary schools and libraries in each community. Telescopes and camera equipment were shipped to participants, and training was provided via three four-day long intensive occultation astronomy workshops for representatives from each team. RECON teams are asked to participate in between six to eight occultation campaigns per year and receive support from the project leadership team throughout the project. Data are recorded electronically and transmitted via the internet to the central data repository, where they are then analyzed by project leadership working with undergraduates.

The RECON Network involves over 50 communities across the western United States. Through support from the NSF, green sites received both telescopes and

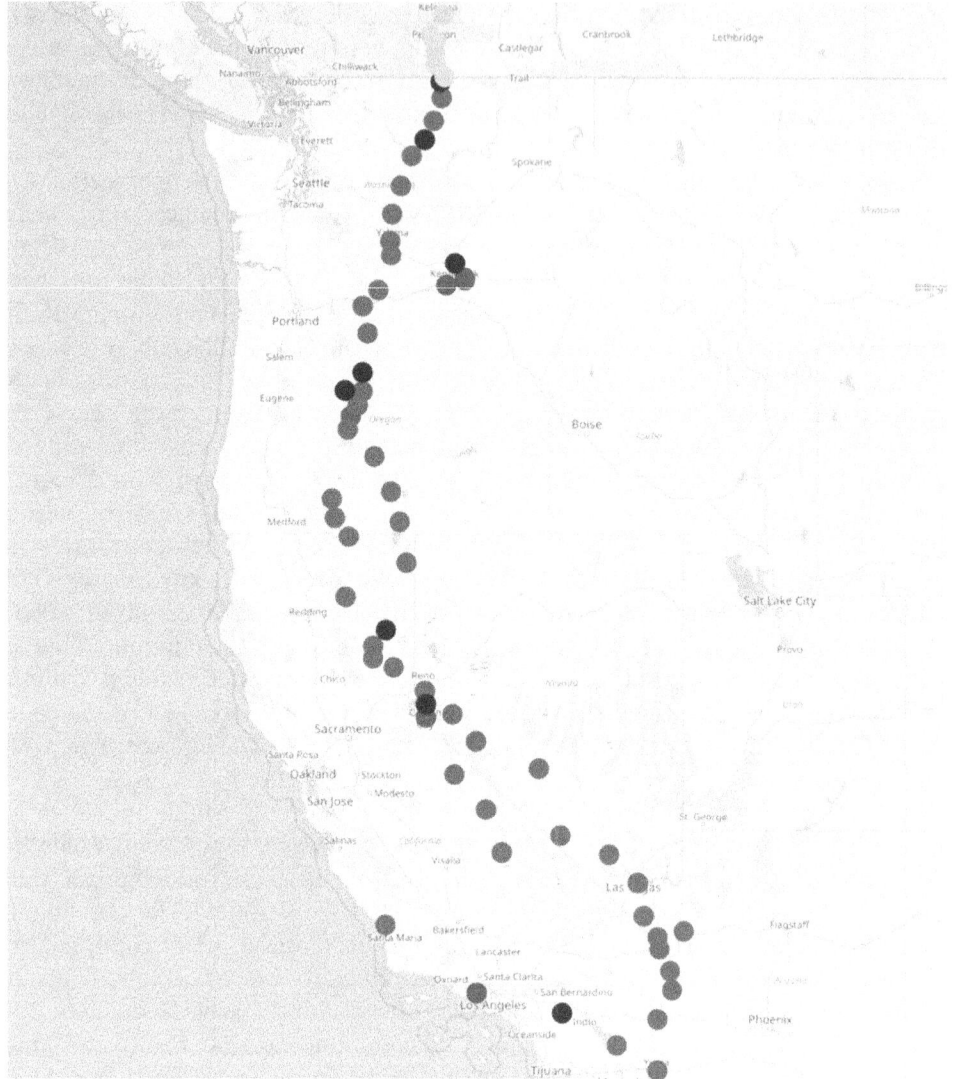

Figure 8.4. A map showing the extent of the RECON telescope network. Note that, in the past year, researchers from the Dominion Astrophysical Observatory have helped to create an international extension of the network, called CanCON, which includes six additional telescope sites north of the border between the U.S. and Canada. Credit: RECON and Map Data © OpenStreetMap contributors.

cameras, blue sites received cameras that were added to existing telescopes, and purple sites contributed their own telescopes and cameras. Recently, yellow sites were added by collaborators in Canada, creating an international extension of the network called CanCON.

The RECON project is an example of a data collection citizen science effort that has engaged over 200 teachers, students, and community members in occultation research. Over the course of the project, an average of 85 adults, 46 K–12 students, and nine college students participate in each full network occultation campaign. The project has successfully measured a Centaur (Buie et al. 2015), a classical Kuiper Belt Object (Benedetti-Rossi et al. 2016), along with additional measurements of Pluto and other TNOs (in preparation).

8.3.2 Citizen Science Insights from the RECON Project

Described below are two significant lessons learned from establishing and maintaining this coordinated research network. First, for RECON, face-to-face interactions were essential to expediting the recruitment process. While email and phone contacts were useful in setting up connections with teachers and community representatives, physical visits to the targeted communities provided a valuable opportunity to emphasize the value of the project to the research community as well as the local community. The concept of stellar occultations was abstract enough that being able to answer questions about the project in person was also a considerable advantage. The leadership team of this project traveled to all of the locations in the network to explain the project and recruit team members.

Second, because many RECON participants did not have prior experience working with telescopes, hands-on training was required. The project team provided three four-day workshops (for the northern, central, and southern regions of the network) to both explain the science of the project and to train team members on the use of RECON telescope and camera equipment. In addition, continued follow-up and individualized support has been important for sustaining project. Since the initial training in the spring of 2015, the project has provided three follow-up science team meetings for representatives from all communities. These team meetings have brought together teachers, students, and community member representatives from each team to provide additional training, share results, and conduct curricular discussions. These meetings have also provided a venue for bringing on new team members over the course of the project. This has been particularly useful given that the project has experienced an annual teacher attrition rate of 5%–10% since initial training events.

The above insights are generalizable to other citizen science efforts in which specific geographical sites are required to accomplish the scientific investigation. For example, the Citizen CATE project required locating telescopes along the midline of the path of totality for the 2017 solar eclipse. There are many citizen science data collection efforts in which the specific location of the data collection site is not predetermined and researchers can rely on a random distribution of volunteers to collect useable data (e.g., Project BudBurst, https://budburst.org/, Radio JOVE, https://radiojove.gsfc.nasa.gov/).

Through citizen science research efforts, participants are engaged in many science and engineering practices (NGSS Framework). With both Zooniverse and RECON, participants are involved in, among other practices, planning and carrying out investigations; analyzing and interpreting data; developing and using models; and obtaining, evaluating, and communicating information. Project participants also engage in troubleshooting and engineering practices of defining problems and designing solutions. While the RECON project leadership was initially responsible for identifying the central research question and planning the coordinated network to observe TNOs, citizen science team members have contributed to refining and improving the research effort throughout the project. There are other community-based citizen science efforts in which students and community members play even larger roles in asking initial research questions and planning full research investigations about local community issues. For example, in the East Bay Academy for Young Scientists (http://static.lawrencehallofscience.org/ays/), with support from the Lawrence Hall of Science, K–12 students identify local environmental and societal issues, fully develop research investigations, and present results of findings at research conferences, thereby participating deeply in the full process of scientific investigation. Through citizen science, participants grow in their understanding, skills, and identities as researchers contributing to our scientific understanding of the world.

8.4 Summary

Citizen science has proven to be a powerful research tool, enabling researchers to solve problems involving large quantities of data (e.g., Carvajal et al. 2018), discover rare or unusual objects (e.g., Boyajian et al. 2016), have important impacts on environmental and social justice issues (e.g., Theobald et al. 2015), and more. In parallel to the rise in quality and impactful citizen science projects over the past decade, there has been an explosion in opportunities to incorporate citizen science into formal and informal education. Citizen science provides instructors an opportunity to engage students in the process of scientific discovery while making real and valued scientific contributions in ways that are well aligned with research-supported educational practices.

Our goal for this chapter was not to provide an exhaustive listing of citizen science uses in astronomy classrooms, but rather to focus on a few examples in order to highlight best practices and guiding principles. Many of these principles mirror those developed through the CURE efforts, including (1) using quality data and exposing students to how to assess data reliability and validity, (2) a low barrier to technical expertise for data collection, generation, and analysis through a user-friendly interface, (3) a diverse, but constrained, set of variables for developing hypotheses and a data set that lends itself to multiple, unique research questions and multiple pathways for analysis, and (4) course assessments that reflect authentic scientific communication and incorporate peer review.

In order to showcase some of the diversity in citizen science opportunities, we highlighted examples from two distinct platforms and approaches: (1) the Zooniverse platform for online citizen science and (2) the RECON coordinated telescope observing and research network. Within the Zooniverse context, we shared two models for student engagement. In Section 8.2.2, we described the impact of students contributing regularly to one of the Zooniverse astronomy-based projects over the course of a month and reflecting on that experience. This is an approach that takes minimal effort on both the instructor and students but has real impact on student attitudes. In Section 8.2.3, we build on this base model and add a more in-depth research component to the experience (using a curated Galaxy Zoo data set), as well as exposure to the full Zooniverse ecosystem of projects across the disciplines and of the broader ecosystem of citizen science opportunities listed through citizenscience.gov and SciStarter.org. In Section 8.2.4, we provided an example of extending hands-on classroom experiences with online citizen science. In Section 8.3.1, we provided an overview of RECON, an astronomy research investigation involving a coordinated network of citizen science observers. Highlighted in Section 8.3.2 were the importance of personalizing the interaction between researchers and volunteers and providing training and support for participants. Depending upon the project, these goals can be accomplished online but can also benefit from in-person interaction.

We hope these examples serve as a useful starting point and inspiration for instructors looking to incorporate citizen science into their classrooms.

References

Anderson, T. M., White, S., Davis, B., et al. 2016, RSPTB, 371, 20150314
Arteta, C., Lempitsky, V., & Zisserman, A. 2016, in Proc. 14th European Conf., Computer Vision – ECCV 2016, ed. B. Leibe, J. Matas, N. Sebe, et al. (Basel: Springer), 483
Barr, A. J., Kalderon, C. W., & Haas, A. C. 2016, arXiv: 1610.02214
Bell, T., Urhahne, D., Schanze, S., & Ploetzner, R. 2010, IJSEd, 32, 349
Benedetti-Rossi, G., Sicardy, B., Buie, M. W., et al. 2016, AJ, 152, 156
Bonney, R., Cooper, C. B., Dickinson, J., et al. 2009, BioSc, 59, 977
Bonney, R., Phillips, T. B., Ballard, H. L., & Enck, J. W. 2016, Public Understanding of Science, 25, 2
Boxer, E. E., & Garneau, N. L. 2015, SpringerPlus, 4, 505
Boyajian, T. S., LaCourse, D. M., Rappaport, S. A., et al. 2016, MNRAS, 457, 3988
Brossard, D., Lewenstein, B., & Bonney, R. 2005, IJSEd, 27, 1099
Buie, M. W., & Keller, J. M. 2016, AJ, 151, 73
Buie, M. W., Olkin, C. B., Merline, W. J., et al. 2015, AJ, 149, 113
Buck, L. B., Bretz, S. L., & Towns, M. H. 2008, JCSTe, 38, 52
Caruso, S. M., Sandoz, J., & Kelsey, J. 2009, CBE-Life Sciences Education, 8, 278
Carvajal, M. A., Alaniz, A. J., Smith-Ramírez, C., & Sieving, K. E. 2018, Diversity and Distributions, 24, 820
Causer, T., Grint, K., Sichani, A. M., & Terras, M. 2018, Digital Scholarship in the Humanities, 33, 467
Chapman, A. 2013, PhD thesis, Univ. South Florida
Chen, X., & Soldner, M. 2013, STEM Attrition: College Students' Paths Into and Out of STEM Fields, Statistical Analysis Report, NCES 2014-001 (Washington, DC: U.S. Department of Education)
Christenson, S. L., Reschly, A. L., & Wylie, C. 2012, Handbook of Research on Student Engagement (New York: Springer)
Cooper, S., Khatib, F., Treuille, A., et al. 2010, Natur, 466, 756
Crall, A. W., Jordan, R., Holfelder, K., et al. 2013, Public Understanding of Science, 22, 745
Cronje, R., Rohlinger, S., Crall, A., & Newman, G. 2011, Applied Environmental Education & Communication, 10, 135

Daniels, C., Holtze, T. L., Howard, R. I., & Kuehn, R. 2014, Journal of Electronic Resources Librarianship, 26, 36

Dawson, G., Lintott, C., & Shuttleworth, S. 2015, Journal of Victorian Culture, 20, 246

Dickinson, J. L., Shirk, J., Bonter, D., et al. 2012, Frontiers in Ecology and the Environment, 10, 291

Dickinson, J. L., & Bonney, R. 2012, Citizen Science: Public Participation in Environmental Research, (Ithaca, NY: Comstock Pub. Associates)

dos Reis, F. J. C., Lynn, S., Ali, H. R., et al. 2015, EBioMedicine, 2, 681

Feinstein, N. W., Allen, S., & Jenkins, E. 2013, Sci, 340, 314

Ford, M. J., & Wargo, B. M. 2007, SciEdu, 91, 133

Fortson, L., Masters, K., Nichol, R., et al. 2012, in Advances in Machine Learning and Data Mining for Astronomy, ed. M. J. Way, J. D. Scargle, K. M. Ali, & A. N. Srivastava (London: Chapman and Hall), 213

Fraknoi, A. 2001, AEdRv, 1, 121

Freeman, S., Eddy, S. L., McDonough, M., et al. 2014, PNAS, 111, 8410

Freitag, A., Meyer, R., & Whiteman, L. 2016, Citizen Science: Theory and Practice, 1, 12

Grayson, R. 2016, British Journal for Military History, 2, 160

Greenhill, A., Holmes, K., Woodcock, J., et al. 2014, AJIM, 68, 306

Gregerman, S. 2008, in Linking Evidence to Promising Practices in STEM Undergraduate Education (Washington, DC: National Academy of Science)

Groulx, M., Lemieux, C. J., Lewis, J. L., & Brown, S. 2017, Journal of Environmental Planning and Management, 60, 1016

Hennon, C. C., Knapp, K. R., Schreck, C. J., III, et al. 2015, BAMS, 96, 591

Johnson, L. C., Seth, A. C., Dalcanton, J. J., et al. 2015, ApJ, 802, 127

Jones, M. T., Barlow, A., & Villarejo, M. 2010, Journal of Higher Education, 81, 82

Jones, M. G., Childers, G., Andre, T., Corin, E., & Hite, R. 2016, in Proc. ESERA 2015, Science Education Research: Engaging Learners for a Sustainable Future, ed. J. Lavonen, K. Juuti, J. Lampiselkä, A. Uitto & K. Hahl (Helsinki: Univ. Helsinki), Part 8, 150

Karelina, A., & Etkina, E. 2007, PRPER, 3, 020106

Kastens, K. A., Agrawal, S., & Liben, L. S. 2009, IJSEd, 31, 365

Kim, J. S., Greene, M. J., Zlateski, A., et al. 2014, Natur, 509, 331336

Kingery, K. 2012, PhD thesis, Purdue Univ.

Kloser, M. J., Brownell, S. E., Chiariello, N. R., & Fukami, T. 2011, PLoS Biology, 9, e1001174

Larson-Miller, C. 2011, PhD thesis, Univ. Nebraska–Lincoln

Laurie, S. 2018, iNaturalist Research-grade Observations, iNaturalist.org, https://doi.org/10.15468/ab3s5x

Lee, J., Kladwang, W., Lee, M., et al. 2014, PNAS, 111, 2122

Lintott, C. J., Schawinski, K., Slosar, A., et al. 2008, MNRAS, 389, 1179

Lyons, D. 2011, PhD thesis, Univ. Wyoming

Marshall, P. J., Verma, A., More, A., et al. 2015, MNRAS, 455, 1171

Masters, K., Cox, J., Simmons, B., & Lintott, C. J. 2016, JCOM, 15, A07

Masters, K. L., Mosleh, M., Romer, A. K., et al. 2010, MNRAS, 405, 783

Matsunaga, A., Mast, A., & Fortes, J. A. 2016, Future Generation Computer Systems, 56, 526

Melber, L. 2004, Teaching Exceptional Children Plus, 1, 4

Miller-Rushing, A., Primack, R., & Bonney, R. 2012, Frontiers in Ecology and the Environment, 10, 285

Mitchell, N., Triska, M., Liberatore, A., et al. 2017, PLoS One, 12, e0186285

National Research Council 1996, National Science Education Standards (Washington, DC: National Academies Press)

National Research Council 2003, BIO2010: Transforming Undergraduate Education for Future Research Biologists (Washington, DC: National Academies Press)

National Research Council 2010, Adapting to the Impacts of Climate Change (Washington, DC: National Academies Press)

Newman, G., Wiggins, A., Crall, A., et al. 2012, Frontiers in Ecology and the Environment, 10, 298

Osborne, J., Simon, S., & Collins, S. 2003, IJSEd, 25, 1049

Pasachoff, J. M. 1999, A&G, 40, 18

President's Council of Advisors on Science and Technology (PCAST) 2012, Engage to Excel: Producing One Million Additional College Graduates with Degrees in Science, Technology, Engineering and Mathematics, Executive Office of the President, https://www.energy.gov/sites/prod/files/Engage%20to%20Excel%20Producing%20One%20Million%20Additional%20College%20Graduates%20With%20Degrees%20in%20STEM%20Feburary%202012.pdf

Quardokus, K., Lasher-Trapp, S., & Riggs, E. M. 2012, BAMS, 93, 1641

Raddick, M. J., Bracey, G., Gay, P. L., et al. 2013, arXiv: 1303.6886

Raddick, M. J., Bracey, G., Gay, P. L., et al. 2010, AEdRv, 9, 010103

Ruiz-Mallén, I., Riboli-Sasco, L., Ribrault, C., et al. 2016, Science Communication, 38, 523

Schwamb, M. E., Aye, K. M., Portyankina, G., et al. 2018, Icar, 308, 148

Shaffer, C. D., Alvarez, C. J., Bednarski, A. E., et al. 2014, CBE-Life Sciences Education, 13, 111

Shuttleworth, S. A. 2018, Science Museum Group Journal, 3, 150304

Slater, S. J., Slater, T. F., & Lyons, D. J. 2011, PhTea, 49, 94

Slater, S. J., Slater, T. F., & Shaner, A. 2008, JGeEd, 56, 408

Sullivan, B. L., Wood, C. L., Iliff, M. J., et al. 2009, Biological Conservation, 142, 2282

Surasinghe, T., & Courter, J. 2012, Bioscene: Journal of College Biology Teaching, 38, 16

Swanson, A., Kosmala, M., Lintott, C., & Packer, C. 2016, Conservation Biology, 30, 520

Szteinberg, G. 2007, PhD thesis Prudue Univ.

Teichert, M. A., Tien, L. T., Dysleski, L., & Rickey, D. 2017, JChEd, 94, 1195

Theobald, E. J., Ettinger, A. K., Burgess, H. K., et al. 2015, Biological Conservation, 181, 236

Tien, L. T., Teichert, M. A., & Rickey, D. 2007, JChEd, 84, 175

Trautmann, N. M. (ed) 2013, Citizen Science: 15 Lessons that Bring Biology to Life, 6–12 (Arlington, VA: NSTA Press)

Trumbull, D. J., Bonney, R., Bascom, D., & Cabral, A. 2000, SciEd, 84, 265

Wang, Y., Kaplan, N., Newman, G., & Scarpino, R. 2015, PLoS Biology, 13, e1002280

Williams, A. C., Wallin, J. F., Yu, H., et al. 2014, in Proc. 2014 IEEE Int. Conf. on Big Data, IEEE Big Data 2014 (Piscataway, NJ: IEEE), 100

Yasar, S., & Baker, D. 2003, in National Association for Research in Science Teaching, https://eric.ed.gov/?id=ED478905

Zevin, M., Coughlin, S., Bahaadini, S., et al. 2017, CQGra, 34, 064003

Astronomy Education, Volume 1
Evidence-based instruction for introductory courses
Chris Impey and Sanlyn Buxner

Chapter 9

WorldWide Telescope in Education

Patricia Udomprasert, Alyssa Goodman, Edwin Ladd, Stella Offner
Harry Houghton, Erin Johnson, Susan Sunbury, Julia Plummer, Erika Wright
Philip Sadler, Philip Rosenfield and Curtis Wong

The American Astronomical Society's WorldWide Telescope (WWT) is a visualization program that enables a computer to function as a virtual telescope—bringing together archival imagery from the world's best ground- and space-based telescopes for the exploration of the universe. It is a powerful resource for astronomy education. In this chapter, we describe curricula developed by the authors that use WWT in teaching key topics in Astro 101 and K–12 science, including parallax, Hubble's Law and large-scale structure in the universe, seasons, Moon phases and eclipses, and life in the universe. We also demonstrate how WWT can be used in open-ended student research projects. Where available, we share education research results showing student-learning outcomes from these WWT-based resources.

Chapter Objectives

By the end of the chapter, the reader will be able to
- describe overall features and capabilities of the American Astronomical Society's WWT,
- provide specific examples of how WWT has been used to teach key astronomy concepts in different educational settings (both Astro 101 and K–12 science),
- describe a summary of research on learning outcomes for students who have used WWT-based curricula, and
- use links to resources on how to get started with WWT and where to access the curricula.

9.1 Introduction

Astronomy 101, or introductory college astronomy for nonmajors, can play a seminal role in creating a scientifically literate public. Fraknoi (2001) estimates that

250,000 college students take an Astro 101 course each year. For many nonscience majors, this is the last science class they will take as part of their formal education (Prather et al. 2009). Many students in Astro 101 classes will go on to become K–12 teachers. How they are taught basic astronomy concepts and other higher level ideas commonly emphasized in Astro 101 classes, such as the nature of science, will influence how they teach them (Thomas & Pedersen 2003), contributing to a science literacy cycle (good or bad) that has the potential to perpetuate for generations.

Studies show that students learn best in interactive environments (e.g., Prather et al. 2009; Lawrenz et al. 2005) that address their misconceptions (e.g., Sadler et al. 2009) and that include multiple models of instruction, such as videos and visualizations, which can break up the monotony of lectures (Slater et al. 2001). Visualizations are a particularly powerful way to clarify complex ideas, especially for topics where the objects are too large or too small to observe in everyday settings, like those in atomic physics or astronomical phenomena (Lee et al. 2010). Visualizations help students learn by making "complex information accessible and cognitively tractable," and they "allow us to perceive, and to think about, relations among items that would be difficult to comprehend otherwise" (Uttal & O'Doherty 2008, p. 53). This chapter shows how the American Astronomical Society's WWT can be used as an effective tool to address these teaching needs.

9.1.1 WorldWide Telescope and Its History

WWT[1] is an astronomy visualization program that offers unparalleled access to the world's store of online astronomical data. At a 2005 meeting in Chicago, Visualization of Astrophysical Data: Bringing Together Science, Art, and Education, Wong presented his vision for "The Universe Project," which builds on Jim Gray's SkyServer (Gray & Szalay 2002). Wong's vision would essentially bring all known astronomical data in the public domain together into a beautiful "sky browser," akin to a web browser. Several professional astronomers were captivated by Wong's presentation and offered to help if Wong found a way to work to bring his dream to reality. Less than a year later, at Microsoft Research, Wong, with software architect Jonathan Fay, began work on a prototype that eventually came to be called "WorldWide Telescope" (WWT), in dedication to Jim Gray. The prototype was intended to allow its users to create "guided tours" of the universe that would take other users from place to place on the sky, along a path set up and narrated by the tour creator (Wong 2008). The user could stop the tour at any time to look around and explore, and then return to the tour by just pressing "play" again. After seeing the prototype, Goodman, one of the consulting astronomers on WWT, was amazed at the research-quality tool that had been built, largely by Fay, for what Wong intended as a purely educational purpose. So much data, with so many links to underlying information—research articles, raw data, Wikipedia entries—had been assembled, that Wong and Fay had essentially created the kind

---

[1] All versions (download, web-based, API) of WorldWide telescope are open source (under the MIT license) and free for noncommercial use.

of "virtual observatory" that professional astronomers had dreamed about for the previous decade.

With funding from Microsoft Research, and collaboration with Goodman and many other astronomers and outreach specialists, Wong and Fay continued work on WWT, until its first public release in 2008. Since 2008, the program has acquired many new features, including a three-dimensional view that helps users visualize NASA planetary surface data, our solar system, the Milky Way, and the universe, as well as get a sense of the vast range of scales relevant to the study of the universe. As Wong envisioned, WWT users can tell stories through "Tours," multimedia presentations that take the user through a set of "slides" that smoothly connects and animates different views specified by the tour author. The tours have different audio tracks for narration and music. Once downloaded, WWT tours can be edited by any user. Figure 9.1 shows a screenshot of WWT, with a small number of its key features highlighted. WWT was designed with personal inquiry, exploration, discovery, and explanation in mind, and those features have been demonstrated to excite STEM learners (Landsberg et al. 2010). Full details of WWT's 10 year history are reported by Rosenfield et al. (2018).

WWT was highlighted in the 2010 National Academy Decadal Survey of Astronomy (National Research Council 2010, p. 105) as *"a significant contribution to the public understanding of Astronomy,"* calling it *"a corporate version of previously under-funded efforts of astronomers to accomplish similar ends, [that] coordinates the world's public-domain cosmic imagery into one resource, allowing people on home PCs to explore the cosmos as if they were at the helm of the finest ground and space-based telescopes."* WWT is an ideal platform for widely usable

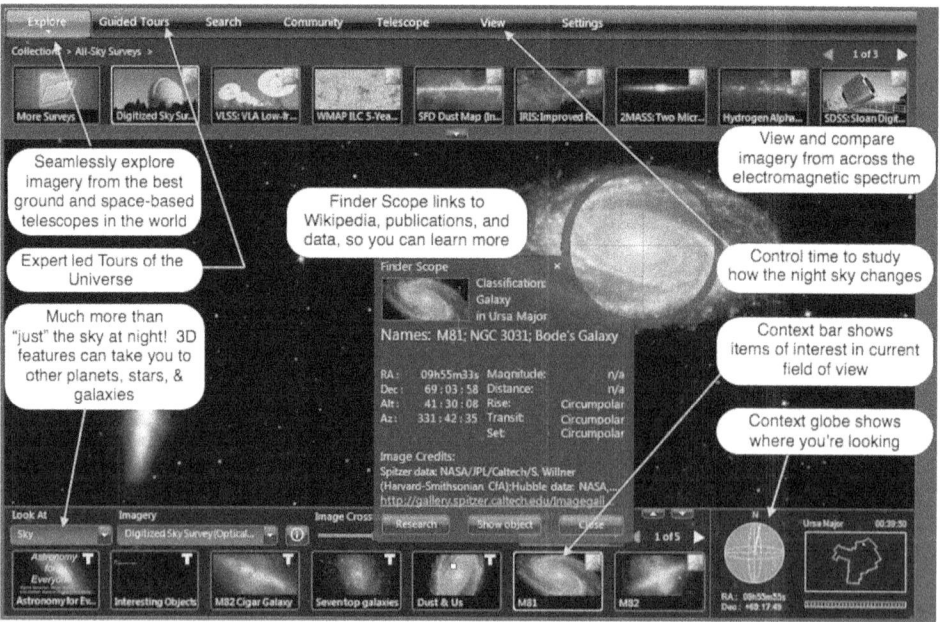

Figure 9.1. Annotated screenshot of WWT, showing a view of the night sky. We highlight features relevant to astronomy education. Credit: WWT Ambassadors; Udomprasert et al. (2012).

and interactive labs because it is a free resource available to any institution or any member of the public, with the potential to reach an ever-broadening and diverse audience, including populations that are traditionally underserved in STEM education. WWT was originally a (free) Windows-only program, which has now expanded to include a WebGL (web-based, platform-independent) version, as well as several services to support software developers to embed WWT in their own projects. Today, the user base of WWT is in the tens of millions, and all versions of the software are freely accessed at http://worldwidetelescope.org. In 2014, Microsoft Research migrated WWT to be an open-source resource, under management of the American Astronomical Society, giving developers and users more opportunities to tailor the program to suit one's needs.

The WWT Ambassadors (WWTA) program was founded in 2009 to bring WWT into formal and informal educational environments. The WWTA program has reached tens of thousands of learners in K–12 classrooms and at public venues like planetaria and science festivals (e.g., Rosenfield et al. 2014, 2018; Goodman et al. 2012; Udomprasert et al. 2012). Educational materials created as part of WWTA are hosted at wwtambassadors.org.

9.2 Samples of WWT in Astronomy Education

Given the wealth of features available in WWT, there is a learning curve associated with its use in education. To address this concern, the authors have developed a series of WWT-based curriculum resources that cover a broad range of topics that might be taught in a typical Astro 101 or high school astronomy course. The available materials can be implemented as is or adapted to suit the needs of one's own students. For a general overview on getting started with WWT, please see the resources assembled at http://www.worldwidetelescope.org/Learn/.

9.2.1 WWT in College Introductory Astronomy Courses

WWT has been used in college Astro 101 courses in a variety of ways. Ladd has incorporated extensive WWT tours into lab-based activities to help students visualize complex topics that are challenging to understand through static, two-dimensional diagrams typically shown in astronomy textbooks. Offner frequently displays a brief WWT tour relevant to the topic of that lesson, both to help give students context for what they will be learning about that day and to show students examples of what can be presented in WWT. Offner's students create their own WWT tours as part of a research project that takes place throughout the semester. We share details of these use cases in this section.

9.2.1.1 WWT Bucknell Introductory Astronomy Labs

With NSF funding,[2] Ned Ladd led the development of two lab activities for an introductory astronomy course at Bucknell University—the Parallax Lab[3] and the

---

[2] NSF award #DUE-1140440.
[3] https://wwtambassadors.org/bucknell-wwt-parallax-lab.

Hubble Law & Structure of the Universe Lab.[4] Both involve hands-on activities and a guided investigation in the astronomical realm via a WWT tour. The goal for both labs is to bridge students' experiential understanding in the lab environment and all terrestrial scales to the larger astronomical size scale. The WWT components for these labs are currently available for the Windows client only,[5] but plans are in place to produce a platform-independent version in the future.

Both lab activities are part of a semester-long course that presents extrasolar astronomy in three 50 minute lectures and one three-hour lab section per week. Lab sections average approximately 20 students. Typically, the lab activity runs with the following characteristics:

- Students complete a prelab reading assignment and quiz before the lab period. The reading assignment is approximately a page and a half long. The quiz consists of four questions based on the reading.
- In the lab, students typically work in groups of two. Students work in pairs at computers for the WWT component and in groups of four to six for the hands-on component and subsequent calculations.
- At the end of the lab period, students complete a quiz that is based on components of the WWT tour, measurements and calculations, and conclusions they have reached during the lab.
- The lab staffing usually consists of one instructor and one undergraduate TA who is not necessarily (and not usually) a physics and astronomy major.

The Parallax Lab

The Parallax Lab activity begins with a guided visualization of the spatial distribution of stars in the local universe using WWT's rendering of the Hipparcos catalog (Perryman et al. 1997). While real astronomical parallax involves measuring the visually imperceptible shifts in the apparent positions of stars over the course of a year, the software allows students to visualize astronomical parallax exaggerated in scale and compressed in time. Using WWT's capability to view the universe from any perspective, students see how the apparent positions of nearby stars change as they "fly" from the Earth to a star in the Orion constellation and then back home.

A quantitative presentation of parallax is then provided using the Big Dipper asterism. Students measure the changes in the apparent positions of the Big Dipper stars when viewed from two vantages points—Earth and a "friend's" location some 6 parsecs from Earth. This large separation between viewing locations (*much* larger than the changes in position due to Earth's motion around the Sun) makes the shifts in the apparent positions of the stars easily noticeable. Students use the parallax concepts to determine the relative distances to the stars in the Big Dipper and discover that one of the Big Dipper's stars is much farther from Earth than the rest. Figure 9.2 shows a view of our solar system and the Big Dipper stars from a far-away vantage point. You can see that most stars in the Big Dipper happen to be

---

[4] https://wwtambassadors.org/bucknell-wwt-hubble-lab.
[5] Materials for both labs are available at http://wwtambassadors.org/wwt-astro-101-labs/.

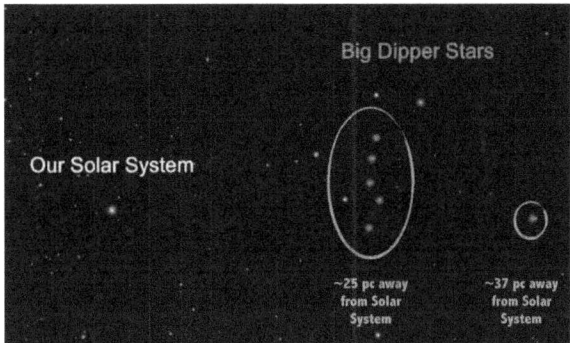

Figure 9.2. Screenshot from the WWT Bucknell Parallax Lab, showing an "overhead" view of the Big Dipper and our solar system. Credit: WWT Bucknell Labs; Ladd et al. (2015).

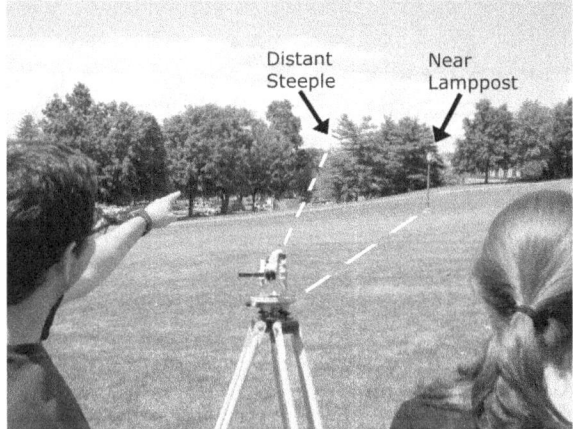

Figure 9.3. Students measure the angular separation between a church steeple and a lamp post in a hands-on activity that is analogous to the parallax measurements of stars. Credit: Ladd et al. (2015).

similar in distance from our solar system, but one star is significantly farther than the others.

With this grounding in the astronomical concept of parallax, students then move to the terrestrial environment and examine the parallax effect on campus-sized scales. In an open location with clear sightlines to landmarks such as street lamps, church steeples, and radio towers, they lay out a 2 m radius circle representing the orbit of Earth around the Sun. They then use a small terrestrial telescope to measure the apparent angular separation between a nearby object (e.g., a lamp post on campus) and a distant object (e.g., a radio tower on a distant hilltop) as a function of position on their circular "orbit." Using the geometry of the orbit, the measured change in angular separation, and their understanding of parallax, they then calculate the distance to the nearby landmark (Figure 9.3).

Students are given an opportunity to reflect on the quality of their measurements and how the uncertainties in their distance estimates scale with the distance to the measured object. Upon completion of the outdoor measurements, they then return to the classroom for an exit quiz, which prompts them to connect their terrestrial measurements to the concept of astronomical parallax.

The Hubble Law and Large-scale Structure of the Universe Lab

The Hubble Law lab starts with a hands-on activity and introduces the concept of an expanding universe with a physical model of a large "Slinky" spring and paper clips (Figure 9.4). The spring represents the expanding universe (in one dimension), while the paper clips attached to individual coils represent galaxies participating in that expansion. By taking measurements of the distances between "galaxies" with the spring stretched to various lengths, students can construct the velocity–distance Hubble law relationship and see that this relationship holds for observers located in any of the universe's galaxies. The universality of this relationship reinforces the idea that large-scale galaxy motions are the product of a single process—the homologous expansion of the universe. Students then use this understanding to determine the age of the universe.

They then turn to WWT and use the Hubble law as a tool for measuring the distances to galaxies in our real universe. After a short WWT tutorial on the Doppler effect, students use WWT's embedded data links to download several galaxy spectra from the Sloane Digital Sky Survey catalogue. They determine the recession velocity for each galaxy with the aid of a Microsoft Excel spreadsheet and then estimate a distance to each galaxy using the Hubble law relationship.

Each lab group determines the distances for three to four galaxies (all purposely chosen to be close to each other in the sky), and then the results from all lab groups are combined into a single data set that lists galaxy sky position (in R.A. and Dec.) and the Hubble-law-determined distance. Students then visualize this data set within WWT, examining in particular how the galaxies mapped in 3D look like a pencil beam and are clustered along the line of sight (Figure 9.5). WWT's ability to allow students to change perspectives is particularly useful here, as students can "fly" through their data set to see its structure directly. Their data set is then combined with much larger and more comprehensive data sets (such as the full Sloan Digital Sky Survey catalog), and students can see the full three-dimensional structure of the universe (Figure 9.6).

This investigative approach naturally leads to questions of structure formation in an expanding universe, and a closing WWT tour provides context for how structure develops as a competition between gravity and expansion. A lab-ending quiz ties

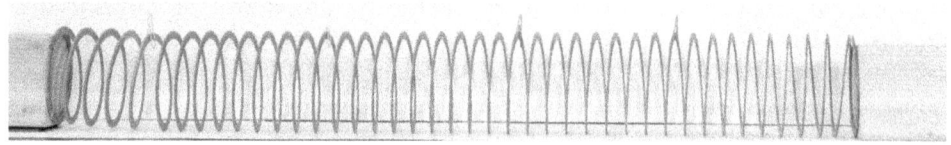

Figure 9.4. In the Bucknell Hubble Law Lab, students use paper clips on a Slinky spring to represent galaxies in our expanding Universe. Credit: Ladd et al. (2016).

Figure 9.5. Screenshot from the WWT Bucknell Hubble Law Lab showing a map of galaxies with distances determined by students who measured redshifts in their spectra. Credit: WWT Bucknell Labs; Houghton (2018).

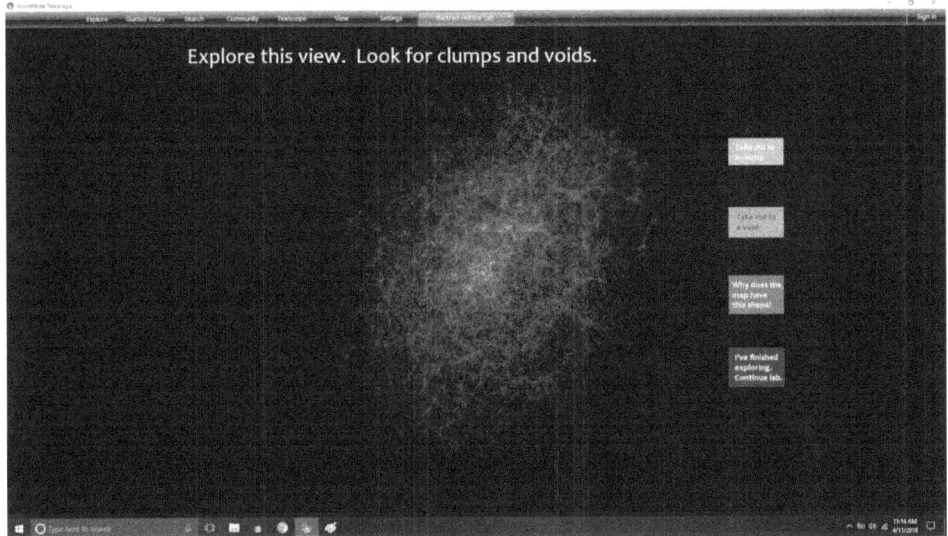

Figure 9.6. Screenshot from the WWT Bucknell Hubble Law Lab showing galaxies mapped by the Sloan Digital Sky Survey. Students can explore large-scale structure in our universe. Credit: WWT Bucknell Labs; Ladd et al. (2016).

together the concepts developed in the tabletop model with the further development afforded by WWT.

We have piloted both lab activities in introductory astronomy classes designed for nonmajors at Bucknell University. Assessment involved both quantitative pre- and postactivity testing, as well as qualitative analysis of student responses to open-ended questions on these topics. Preliminary analysis indicates that students are able to extend the conclusions developed in their hands-on modeling activities to the astrophysical environment; however, they still find these phenomena nonintuitive and difficult to generalize, even after completing the lab activities. We speculate that the very large change in scale, from the lab environment to the size of the universe, makes the transfer of their terrestrial intuition to the astrophysical realm difficult (Ladd et al. 2015). Uttal & O'Doherty (2008) describe a phenomenon called "Representational Insight," which is "the process of coming to understand that, and how, a representation stands for something else." They describe studies (e.g., DeLoache 1989) which show difficulties students have in relating models to their referents (the things the model represents). Detailed and realistic views in WWT help bridge this gap between the hands-on models and the real-life objects in space that they represent.

As of this writing, both the Parallax and Hubble Law Labs require the desktop version of WWT to be run on Windows computers. Bucknell students worked in pairs at PCs in a computer lab where the necessary WWT tour files were installed in advance by instructors. As the open-source WWT community continues to develop the functionality of the WWT web client, we hope that these lab materials will someday be accessible on all platforms.

9.2.1.2 WWT in UMass Amherst Astronomy 101

At the University of Massachusetts at Amherst, Astronomy 101 ("The Solar System") is a general education class for nonastronomy majors. The majority of the students who enroll are freshmen, and most students go on to a non-STEM major. The course objective is to "help students develop critical reasoning skills and achieve an appreciation for what science is and how it happens." In her teaching of the course, Offner includes WWT, which serves a unique role by allowing students to visualize and interact with professional astronomy data. WWT resources described in this section can be found at https://wwtambassadors.org/astro-101-tours.

Students use WWT to carry out a final class project, in which they work in groups of two to three to research and produce a WWT Tour on an astronomy topic of their choice (e.g., asteroids, NASA space missions, dwarf planets). Sample screenshots from student projects are shown in Figure 9.7. This allows the students to explore an interest in greater depth, be creative, and to participate in the larger astronomy community. Some of the student presentations are shared online at wwtambassadors.org.

WWT Project Structure

The project is structured into three components with intermediated deadlines in order to keep students accountable and supply feedback prior to the final deadline.

Topic Selection: First, the students choose a partner and pick first and second choice project topics. Offner gives students a list of ideas and also encourages them to brainstorm on their own. At the end of a week, each group submits a (one-page) document that describes each presentation topic and outlines what questions their tour will address. Offner assigns the groups to topics based on stated preference and to maximize the range of topics.

Tour Script: Over the next three weeks, students research their topic and write a 3.5–4.5 minute narration to accompany the tour. The script contains (1) an introduction to the topic, (2) a description of the topic importance, (3) the answers to the questions posed in topic overview, (4) a brief conclusion, and (5) a list of citations. The students are encouraged to write for an audience who is interested in learning more about astronomy but who has not taken any astronomy class. This

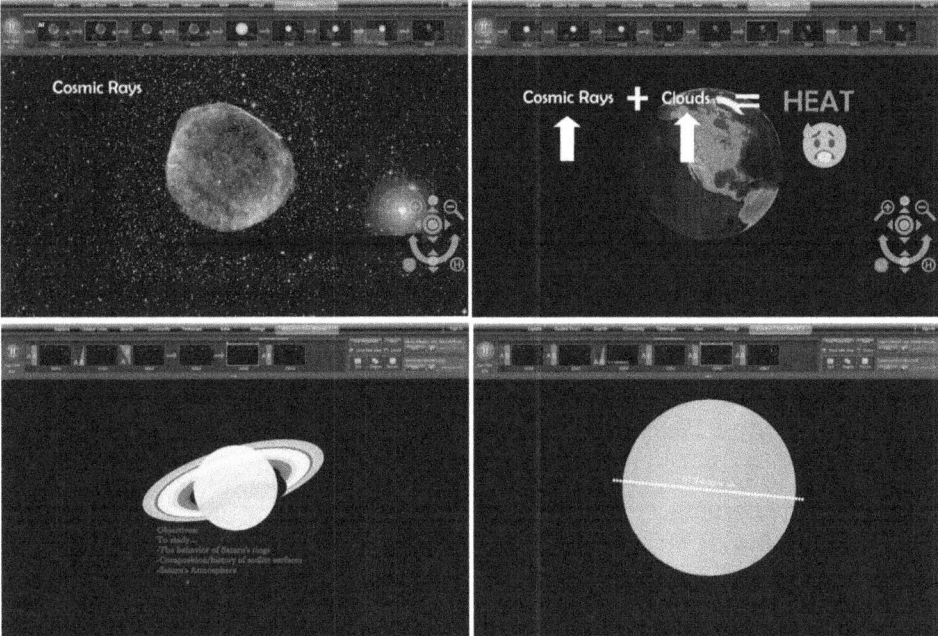

Figure 9.7. Screenshots from WWT tours made by Astro 101 students at the University of Massachusetts at Amherst. Credit: Stella Offner and UMass Amherst students.

allows Offner to give feedback and suggestions, which helps to increase the accuracy and clarity of the final presentation.

WWT Presentation: In the final three to four weeks, the students develop a WWT tour illustrating their narration. The tour is required to include (1) music, (2) an introduction slide with the title and author names, (3) use of WWT functionality including time evolution, zooming, and at least two different WWT data types, and (4) a closing slide with credits. The credits slide must list citations for all external materials imported into the tour, including music and images.

WWT Training

Offner implements several strategies to train students in WWT functionality. First, at the beginning of each class, she plays silent tours on that day's lecture topic. (These tours use WWT to illustrate key concepts in Astro 101, and they are also available for download at wwtambassadors.org). Students watch the tour as they filter into class and get a sense of the available WWT data, views, and functions. Second, as homework, Offner assigns a WWT tour for students to watch and answer questions about. Students often install WWT on their own computers, but it is also available in several computer rooms in the campus library. When the presentation component is assigned, she gives an in-class, hands-on tutorial about creating a WWT tour. She encourages students to bring their laptop and follow along. She plays several tours in class, including the "Ring Nebula" tour by a 6 year old boy named Benjamin, and she asks students what they like and dislike about the tours.

Finally, she holds WWT help hours before the project deadline to help student troubleshoot tour issues. Instructions for tour-making and training are available at https://wwtambassadors.org/creating-wwt-tours.

At the time of implementation, WWT tour-authoring could only be done in the WWT desktop client. In order to ensure that students all had access to the software, Offner had WWT installed on several computers in the university library. It is now possible to author tours in the WWT web client, so instructors can assign tour-making projects in their class to students who do not have access to a Windows computer. Note that the web client's tour-authoring tools are still limited compared to those available in the desktop client, but the WWT development team is continually improving the feature parity between the web and desktop clients.

9.2.2 WWT in K–12 Education

The WWT activities described in this section were developed for and tested in middle-school environments. Because nonscience majors in introductory college science classes begin with roughly the same prior knowledge as middle-school students (Bisard et al. 1994), these curriculum resources can still be highly relevant in courses at the high school and Astro 101 level. WWT tour files are easily edited by the user, so an Astro 101 instructor could choose to renarrate some of the components in a style that would be more suitable for older students.

The WWT Seasons and Moon Phases and Eclipses Labs were developed as part of an NSF-funded program called "Thinking Spatially About the Universe," which emphasizes spatial thinking skills as part of the astronomy curricula.[6] Both combine WWT-based visualizations with hands-on models to help students connect the Earth-based and space-based views that are needed to understand these phenomena. The Life in the Universe Lab was developed with funding from the John Templeton Foundation.[7]

9.2.2.1 WWT Seasons Lab
The eight-session WWT Seasons Curriculum[8] asks students to
  (a) describe, from an Earth-based perspective, how the Sun appears to move in the sky throughout a day, and how that daily movement changes through the year;
  (b) describe, from a space-based perspective, how the Earth rotates about its own tilted axis and revolves around the Sun; and then
  (c) explain how the space-based explanation accounts for their Earth-based visual experience.

Lab activities give students multiple opportunities to practice distinguishing between these two perspectives, while integrating evidence gathered from both physical and virtual models. Yu et al. (2015) showed that learning outcomes for seasons are improved significantly when students view the same visualizations in a planetarium

---
[6] NSF award #DRL-1503395 & 1502798.
[7] John Templeton award #58380.
[8] https://wwtambassadors.org/seasons.

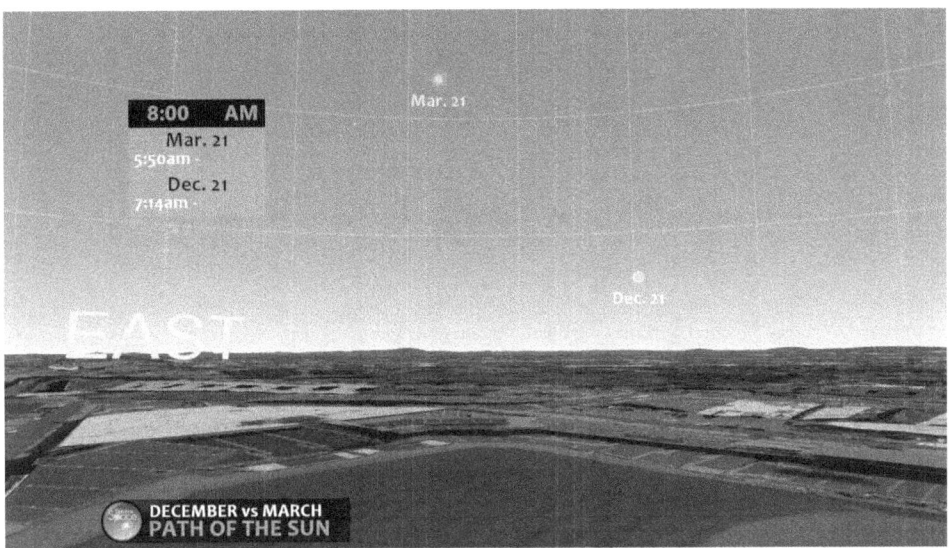

Figure 9.8. Screenshot from the WWT Seasons Lab, showing a comparison of the Sun's path through the Boston sky in March vs. December. Credit: WWT ThinkSpace; Houghton (2018).

rather than on a flat 2D monitor. In a planetarium view, students can experience immersively how the Sun appears to move in our sky. When watching the same path on a flat 2D monitor, students have to mentally construct where the Sun is in the sky based on the visualization, a task which adds to the students' cognitive load. However, many introductory astronomy classes do not have access to a planetarium. Blending physical models with the virtual views helps to better contextualize for students what is happening in the sky. In the ThinkSpace labs, students watch the Sun move through the sky in a WWT view for four specific dates (the solstices and equinoxes). Students note where the Sun was at sunrise, midday, and sunset, then they transfer those locations to a clear plastic hemisphere "sky trackers." They connect those three points with a dry erase marker, to show how the Sun appears to move in the sky on that particular day. Figure 9.8 shows a sample view in WWT, comparing the locations of the Sun on December 21 and March 21 close to sunrise.

Figure 9.9 shows the plastic hemisphere used to transfer data from the WWT views to a model "sky." Before watching the WWT views, the instructor asks students to predict the path of the Sun for "today." Roughly 97% of the 481 middle-school students who participated in the study predict that the Sun rises due east, goes straight overhead at midday, and sets due west (shown in Figure 9.9 as the path marked in RED). For comparison, Figure 9.9 shows the actual path of the Sun for Boston on December 21 (marked in green). Students are very surprised to observe how different the actual path is than what they had thought prior to watching the view in WWT. Unless students correct their idea of how the Sun appears to move in the sky (and recognize that the Sun's apparent path is different throughout the year), it is not possible for them to grasp how the Earth's tilted axis can be the main cause of seasonal changes on Earth (rather than a changing Earth–Sun distance).

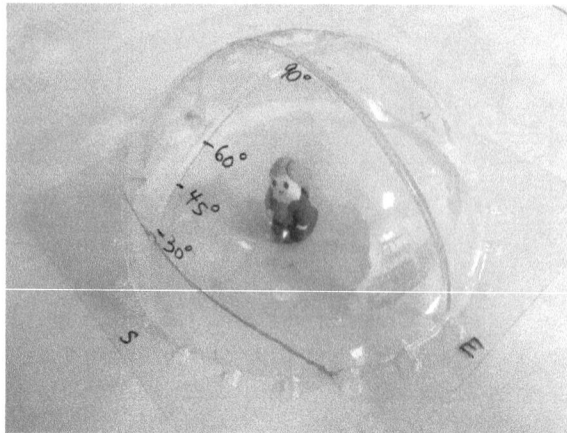

Figure 9.9. Students transfer "observations" of the Sun from WWT to a physical model of a figurine's sky. In red, we show the typical student's prediction of how the Sun moves the sky "today." In green, we show the actual path of the Sun in December for Boston. Credit: ThinkSpace; Philip Sadler; Lillian Simcoe.

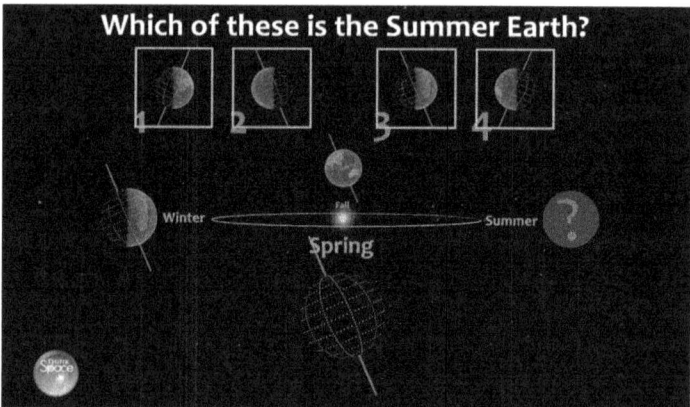

Figure 9.10. Screenshot from the WWT Seasons Lab showing how the Earth's axis is tilted and always points in the direction of the star Polaris. Here, students are invited to choose the image they think represents the summer Earth. Credit: WWT ThinkSpace.

After students have observed the Earth-based perspectives of how the Sun moves in our sky, they are introduced to the space-based perspective or Earth orbiting the Sun with a tilted axis, as in Figure 9.10. Next, the instructor helps students connect the space and Earth-based views to show how the tilted axis impacts the midday Sun angle at each season. For example, in Figure 9.11(left), Boston is marked on the globe by a red dot. The user can zoom in to that location in WWT, showing an Earth-based observer looking in the direction of the Sun, which is at a very low sun angle of 24 degrees, in Figure 9.11(right).

Figure 9.12 shows a view students can manipulate in WWT, to understand why the total hours of daylight we experience at a particular location on Earth changes throughout the year, and why different parts of Earth experience different lengths of

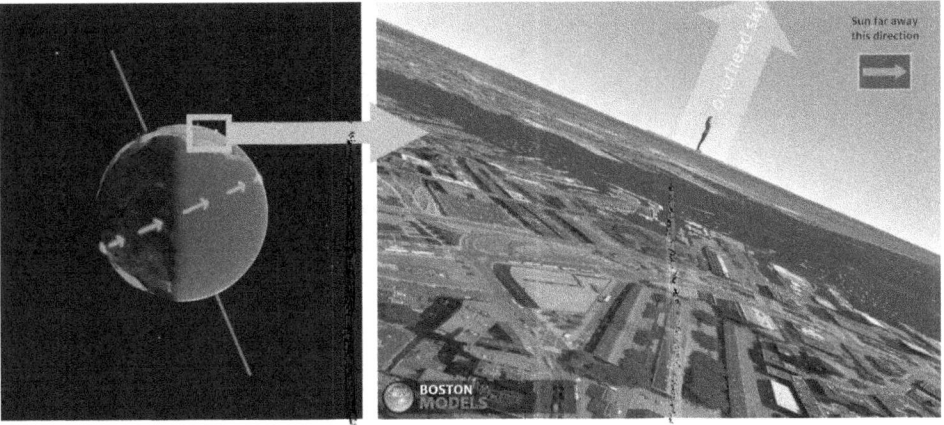

Figure 9.11. Screenshots from the WWT Seasons Lab showing a zoomed in view of the Boston ground, and how our location on Earth determines the angle of the Sun in our sky. Credit: WWT ThinkSpace; Houghton (2018).

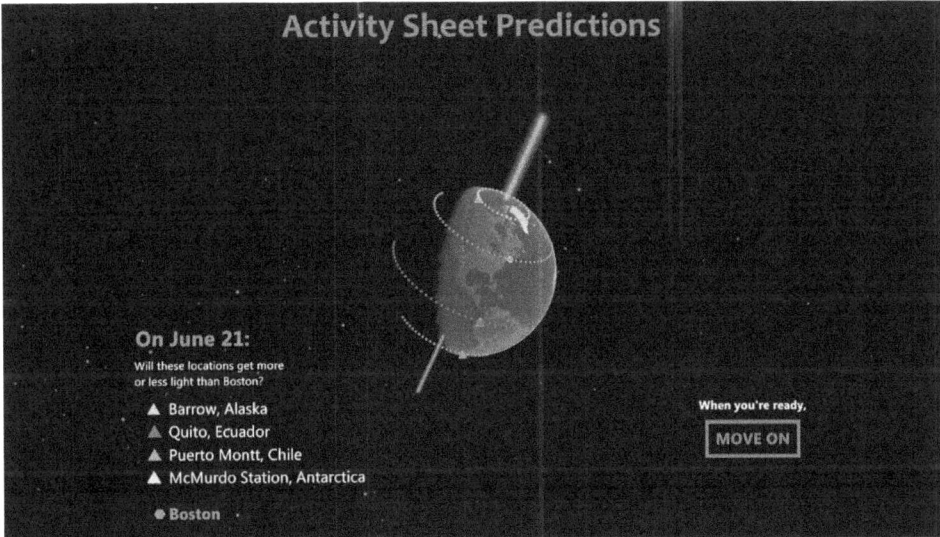

Figure 9.12. Screenshot from the WWT Seasons Lab showing a view of the Earth that students can manipulate, to explore how different cities experience different amounts of daylight and darkness on this date. Credit: WWT ThinkSpace.

daylight hours on a given day. This visualization in WWT is a powerful aid in helping students see explicitly how Earth's tilted axis tips one hemisphere preferentially into the daytime side of Earth, lengthening the amount of daylight hours in that hemisphere for that time of year. In the final lesson, students learn about the shape of Earth's orbit and explore whether distance changes between the Earth and Sun can lead to the seasons we experience on Earth.

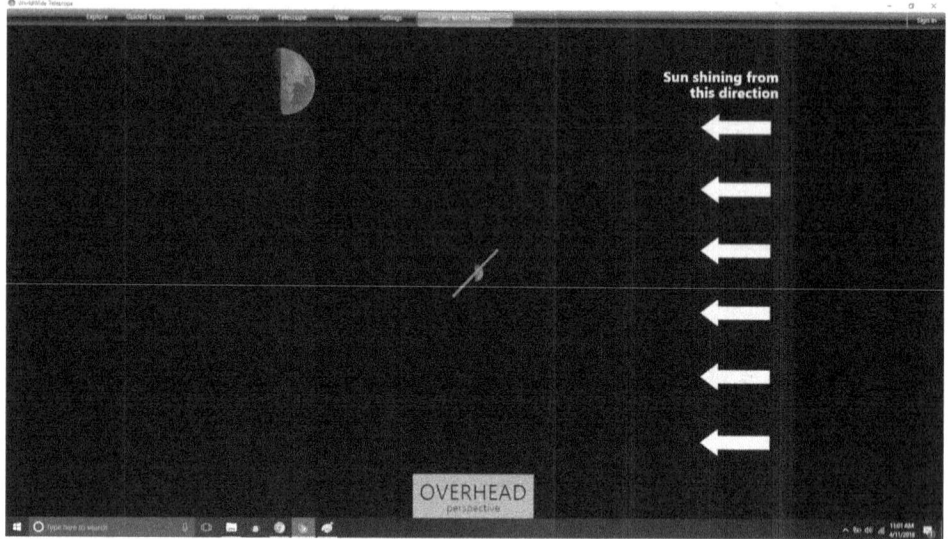

Figure 9.13. Screenshot from the WWT Moon Phases Lab demonstrating how to connect the overhead perspective of the Earth–Sun–Moon system with the part of the Moon that is visible from Earth. Credit: WWT ThinkSpace.

9.2.2.2 WWT Moon Phases and Eclipses Lab

Like the WWT Seasons lab, the WWT Moon Phases and Eclipses Lab[9] engages students with a blend of hands-on physical and virtual models to explore why Moon phases and eclipses occur. Again, the emphasis is on connecting the overhead space-based perspective with the Earth-based perspective, to understand how a half-lit Moon can appear in different phases, depending on how much of the lit-up side is facing Earth. We teach students a four-step method to determine what phase a viewer in the northern hemisphere on Earth would see, when given an overhead view of the Moon in a particular location in its orbit around Earth.

1. Shade the half of the Moon that appears dark from overhead. (The half that is facing the Sun is lit up).
2. Draw a line to divide the Moon into the half facing Earth and the half facing away from Earth.
3. Identify how much of the side facing Earth is lit up.
4. Identify whether the lit-up side would appear to the right or left, to a northern hemisphere observer.

Figure 9.13 shows a screenshot from the WWT tour that helps guide students through these four steps.

Students can manipulate the view in WWT to see how a half-lit Moon appears as a crescent to a viewer on Earth, when most of the lit-up half of the Moon is facing away from Earth. (See Figure 9.14.) Students also work with physical models,

---

[9] https://wwtambassadors.org/moon-phases.

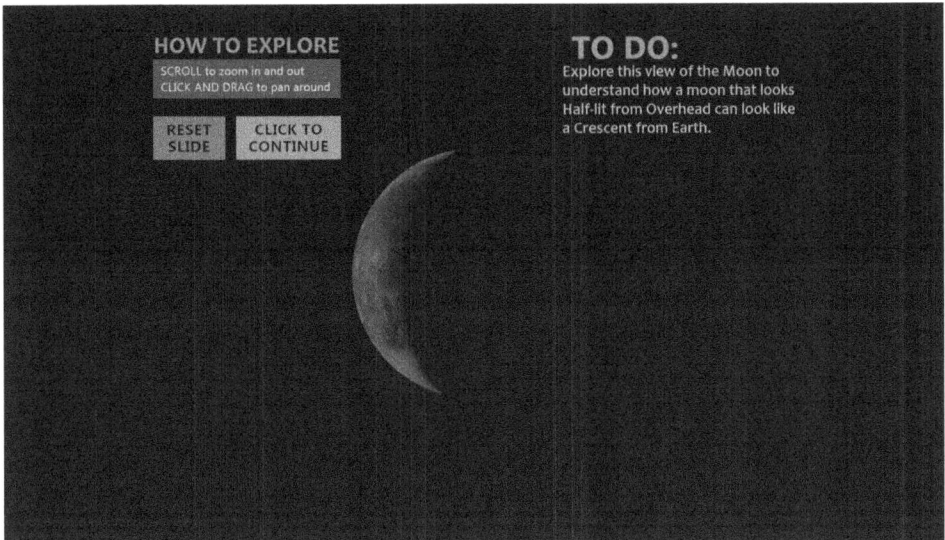

Figure 9.14. Screenshot from the WWT Seasons Lab showing a view of the Moon that students can investigate to see how a half-lit Moon can appear to have different phases depending on how much of the lit-up side is facing the viewer. Credit: ThinkSpace; Houghton (2018).

observing the "space-based" overhead view (which is half-lit/half-dark) and seeing how that compares with the "Earth-based" view.

To help students understand eclipses, especially why lunar eclipses do not happen every month, the lab activities emphasize the concept of scale. Because almost all images of the Earth and Moon together are shown out of scale, students have a strong tendency to imagine that the Earth and Moon are much closer together than they really are. This lab uses a traditional physical model activity, where a lamp is placed in the middle of the room to represent the Sun, and students stand around the lamp in a big circle. Each student's head represents the Earth at a different time of year, and they each hold a 1.5″ diameter foam ball to represent the Moon. Because they are limited by the length of their arm, the distance they can hold the Moon away from their head is far too close, and many students have trouble making a full Moon because their head (Earth) blocks light from the Sun, and they inadvertently create a lunar eclipse instead of a full Moon. Most students eventually figure out that they can create a full Moon by lifting their foam ball high enough, so it is above their head, but then they are concerned that they are holding the moon at such an unexpectedly high angle. In WWT, students can view a correctly scaled view of the Earth–Moon system in WWT and recognize that at the correct orbital distance, the small 5° tilt of the Moon's orbit is enough to prevent the Earth from blocking the Moon during most months. (The students would need a 15 ft long arm to hold the Moon at a correctly scaled distance). In WWT, students can then choose a viewing date when we know an eclipse will happen and see how, on that specific date, the Earth, Sun, and Moon align.

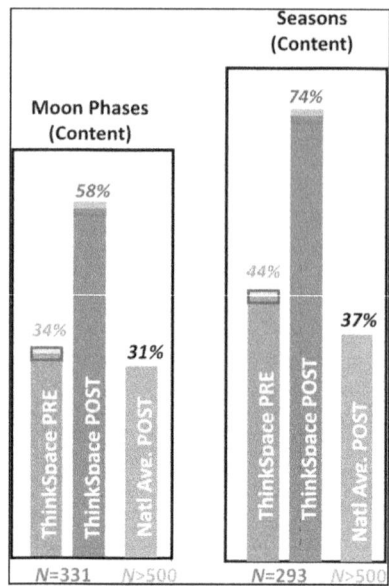

Figure 9.15. ThinkSpace prep (green) vs. postcontent (blue) scores for Moon phases and seasons, compared with national averages of delayed post-"business as usual" instruction from Sadler et al. (2009; gray). Credit: WWT ThinkSpace.

9.2.2.3 Learning Outcomes from WWT Seasons and Moon Phases Labs

The ThinkSpace team partnered with nine middle-school science teachers in the Greater Boston area and offered the ThinkSpace labs as a replacement to their existing curriculum. A research team member led instruction to minimize variability of teacher implementation. All students ($N \sim 890$) completed written pre- and postassessments that include both spatial skill tasks and science content questions. Roughly half the student participants are from suburban school districts with a predominantly high socioeconomic status population, while the remaining half are from urban school districts with 55% and 29%, respectively, of students from economically disadvantaged populations. Here, we only describe general learning outcomes from the written science content assessment.

The science content questions include distractor-driven multiple-choice (DDMC) questions drawn primarily from the MOSART (Misconceptions-Oriented Standards-based Assessment Resources for Teachers) test bank, of which the Astronomy and Space Science Concept Inventory (ASSCI) is the most relevant subset (Sadler et al. 2009).

Science Learning Outcomes. ThinkSpace students had significant pre- to post-content learning gains. Figure 9.15 shows the average MOSART pre- versus postcontent scores for each lab. Comparisons between the pre- and postscores for the Moon phases and seasons yield a Cohen's $d = 1.2$, 95% CI [1.1,1.4] and $d = 1.5$, 95% CI [1.3,1.7], for the two respective curricula.

Each MOSART assessment question (Sadler et al. 2009) has been field-tested with $N > 500$ middle-school students nationally, postinstruction (and sometimes with a

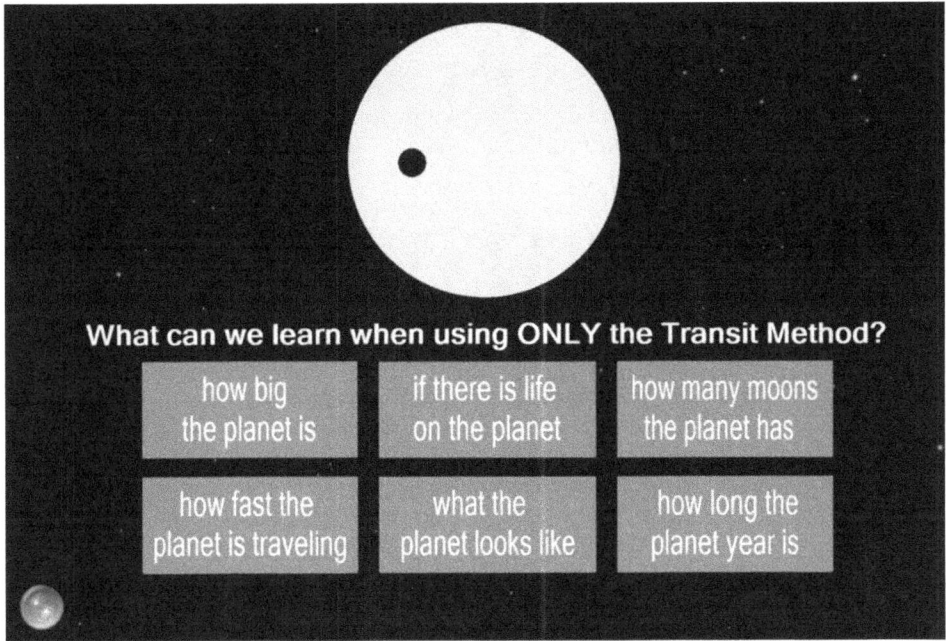

Figure 9.16. Screenshot from the WWT Life in the Universe Lab showing how astronomers detect planets around other stars by measuring dimming in the light when a planet passes in front of the star. Credit: WWT LITU.

long delay). Figure 9.1 shows the average delayed postscore for the MOSART national sample. The ThinkSpace scores are significantly higher, but we note that the ThinkSpace postassessments were given immediately following instruction, rather than at the end of the school year for the MOSART national sample.

9.2.2.4 WWT Life in the Universe Lab
The WWT Life in the Universe Lab[10] gives students an opportunity to explore current topics in astronomical research. The lab gives an overview of "our place in the universe," starting with Earth in the solar system, our solar system's place in our Milky Way galaxy, and leading out to the exploration of other galaxies beyond ours. Students then learn about the search for extrasolar planets, with an emphasis on the transit method. WWT visualizations help students understand how the transit method works, and they show where in the Milky Way extrasolar planets have already been discovered. Students learn about the "Goldilocks" zone and explore what makes a planet "habitable." Finally, they consider distance scales in our own galaxy and calculate how long it would take to communicate with or travel to meet life elsewhere in the universe, if it exists. Figures 9.16 and 9.17 show sample screenshots from the WWT Life in the Universe Lab.

---

[10] https://wwtambassadors.org/life-universe.

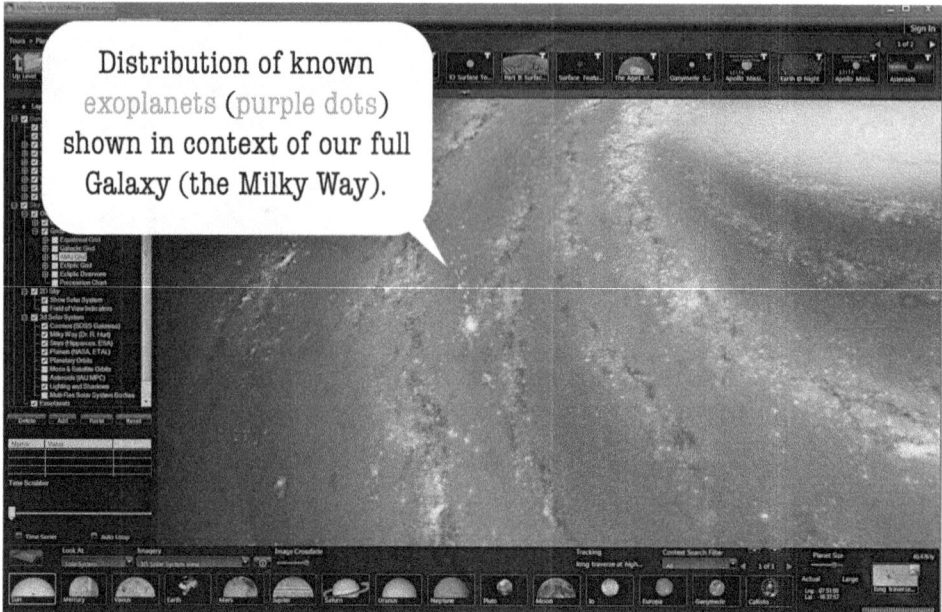

Figure 9.17. Screenshot from the WWT Life in the Universe Lab showing the distribution of known exoplanets in our galaxy. Credit: WWT LITU.

9.2.2.5 Outcomes for the WWT Life in the Universe Lab

Figure 9.18 shows pre and post Likert results from student surveys, where participants self-reported their level of curiosity, interest, and self-identity in science. We had matched pre- and postsurvey data for 35 students. t-test comparisons of the pre- and postsurveys show that students had statistically significant increases for almost every question asked, with mostly moderate effect sizes. Cohen (1988) defined effect sizes as "small, $d = 0.2$," "medium, $d = 0.5$," and "large, $d = 0.8$". Education research projects that achieve medium or large effect sizes are generally considered highly successful.) We see especially significant gains in participants' ability to see themselves as successful in science, and in their interest in and curiosity in science.

9.2.3 Technology Requirements for Running the WWT K–12 Labs

During pilot testing of the WWT Seasons, Moon Phases, and Life in the Universe Labs, the WWT Ambassadors team brought banks of Windows laptops to schools, so students could access all the features needed in the WWT desktop client. We recognize that the requirement of installing WWT on Windows computers is a barrier to broader adoption of the curriculum materials, so the team has converted most of the WWT content into web-accessible versions. In most cases, the WWT visualizations have been converted to video, with the downside being that WWT's trademark interactivity is lost. In portions of the lab where interactivity is critical for understanding the concepts (such as Session 7 of the Seasons Lab), we have created a simplified version of the WWT content that runs on the web client, allowing broader

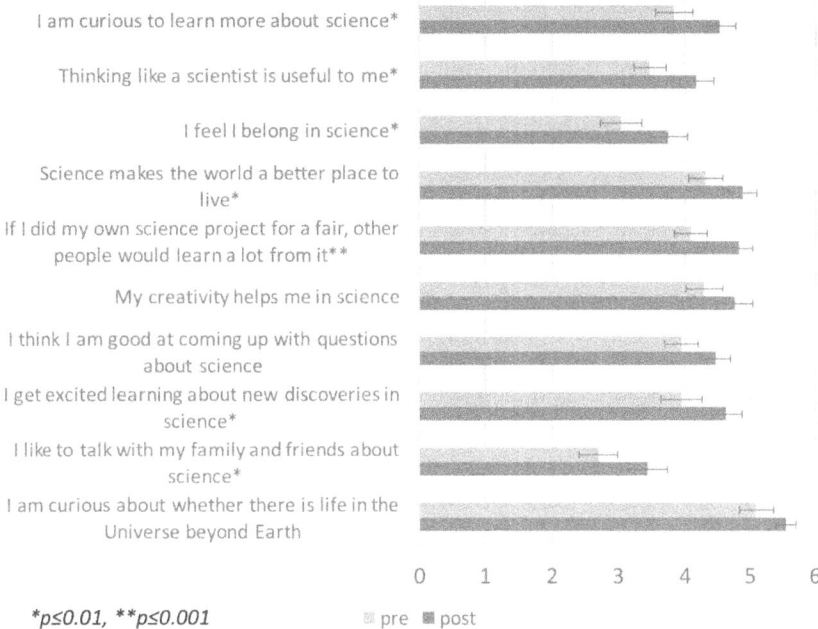

Figure 9.18. Pre/post Likert scores rating participant perception of science identity for middle-school students who experienced the WWT Life in the Universe curriculum. Credit: WWT LITU; Houghton et al. (2019).

access while still giving students the opportunity to control what they are looking at in WWT. Portions of the Seasons and Moon Phases Labs have been ingested into PBS Learning Media as slideshows, which provides over a million K–12 educators with easy access to these materials. They can be found at pbslearningmedia.org.

9.3 Discussion and Future Developments

This chapter has presented examples of WWT-based curriculum resources that cover a broad variety of topics in a typical introductory astronomy course at the college or high school level. All materials are free to download and use. Instructors can modify existing WWT tour files to suit the needs of their own classes, or create new lessons to teach topics that have not been covered yet. The WWT Ambassadors website (wwtambassadors.org) can serve as a clearinghouse for new or updated versions of WWT-based curriculum materials. We encourage users to become part of the WWT community by joining the discussion forum[11] or contributing to the WWT GitHub[12] repository.

Until 2017, the WWT Windows desktop client was required for tour-authoring and to access many of the 3D views used in a majority of the existing curriculum

---

[11] https://wwt-forum.org/.
[12] https://github.com/wwt.

materials. As of early 2018, the WWT web client is nearing feature parity with the desktop client, and before long, the WWT Parallax, Hubble Law, Seasons, Moon Phases, and Life in the Universe curricula will be accessible through the platform-independent web client. WWT visualizations can be embedded into other web pages and online learning platforms through the API, making their power and beauty more easily accessible to large numbers of students. As more and more universities join online learning platforms like edX and Coursera, there is a growing need for innovation in instructional design that works well online. Early research has shown that talking-head video, which just mirrors in-class lectures, bores learners (who typically watch at double speed). The updated WWT web client will offer a platform upon which we, and others, can experiment with fully online versions of the interactive materials, and the efficacy of those materials online can be compared with "live" in-person use of the same curriculum.

As an open-source project, WWT can now be integrated into other data analysis and visualization software, such as Glue,[13] a program for multidimensional linked-data exploration, and pyWWT,[14] which allows users to embed an instance of WWT into their Python projects. This will open up new avenues for development of interactive online labs that focus on visualization of real astronomy data.

New astronomical facilities (for example, the *James Webb Space Telescope*, *Gaia*, and the Large Synoptic Survey Telescope) will provide a wealth of new data that can be incorporated into WWT-based educational resources. As we move deeper into the 21st century, students will benefit from an understanding of how scientists make sense of "big data." Visualizations like WWT will play a critical role in this field.

We encourage the reader to become part of the WWT educational community, and we look forward to seeing WWT implemented in online astronomy classes in ways we have not yet envisioned.

Acknowledgments

This material is based upon work supported by the National Science Foundation under grants Nos. DUE-1140440 (Bucknell WWT Labs), AST-1510021 and AST-1650486 (Univ. Mass Amherst Astro 101 Projects), and DRL-1503395 and 1502798 (ThinkSpace Seasons & Moon Phases Labs). Any opinions, findings, and conclusions or recommendations expressed in this material are those of the author(s) and do not necessarily reflect the views of the National Science Foundation. Life in the Universe (LITU) is supported by the John Templeton Foundation under grant number 58380.

We are grateful to our students, our partner teachers, and all their students, for participating in the field testing of these WWT-based curricula and offering us valuable feedback.

---

[13] http://glueviz.org.
[14] https://github.com/WorldWideTelescope/pywwt.

References

Bisard, W. J., Aron, R. H., Francek, M. A., & Nelson, B. 1994, JCSTe, 24, 38
Cohen, J. 1988, Statistical Power Analysis for the Behavioral Sciences (Hillsdale, NJ: Lawrence Erlbaum Associates)
DeLoache, J. S. 1989, Cognitive Development, 4, 121
Fraknoi, A. 2001, AEdRv, 1, 121
Goodman, A., Fay, J., Muench, A., Pepe, A., Udomprasert, P., & Wong, C. 2012, in ASP Conf. Ser. 461, Astronomical Data Analysis Software and Systems XXI, ed. P. Ballester, D. Egret, & N. P. F. Lorente (San Francisco, CA: ASP), 267
Gray, J., & Szalay, A. 2002, Communications of the ACM, 45, 50
Houghton, H. 2018, WorldWide Telescope: The Universe in Your Hands AstroBeat, 164, https://wwtambassadors.org/publications/worldwide-telescope-universe-your-hands
Houghton, H., Udomprasert, P., Sunbury, S., Wright, E., Goodman, A., Johnson, E., & Bishop, A. 2019, in ASP Conf. Ser., Advancing Astronomy for All (San Francisco, CA: ASP)
Ladd, E. F., Gingrich, E. C., Nottis, K. E. K., Udomprasert, P., & Goodman, A. A. 2015, in ASP Conf. Ser. 500, Celebrating Science: Putting Education Best Practices to Work, ed. G. Schultz, S. Buxner, L. Shore, & J. Barnes (San Francisco, CA: ASP), 191
Ladd, F., Udomprasert, P., Nottis, K., & Goodman, A. 2016, in Proc. 2016 Int. Conf. Education and New Developments, Building a Three-dimensional Universe From the Classroom: Multiperspective Visualization for Non-science Undergraduates, ed. M. Carmo (Lisbon: World Institute for Advanced Research and Science), 246
Landsberg, R. H., Subbarao, M. U., & Dettloff, L. 2010, in ASP Conf. Ser. 431, Science Education and Outreach: Forging a Path to the Future, ed. J. Barnes, D. A. Smith, M. G. Gibbs, & J. G. Manning (San Francisco, CA: ASP), 314
Lawrenz, F., Huffman, D., & Appeldoorn, K. 2005, JCSTe, 34, 40
Lee, H. S., Linn, M. C., Varma, K., & Liu, O. L. 2010, JRScT, 47, 71
National Research Council 2010, New Worlds, New Horizons in Astronomy and Astrophysics (Washington, DC: National Academies Press)
Perryman, M. A. C., Lindegren, L., Kovalevsky, J., et al. 1997, A&A, 323, L49
Prather, E. E., Rudolph, A. L., & Brissenden, G. 2009, PhT, 62, 41
Rosenfield, P., Fay, J., Gilchrist, R. K., et al. 2018, ApJS, 236, 22
Rosenfield, P., Gaily, J., Fraser, O., & Wisniewski, J. 2014, CAPJ, 15, 35
Sadler, P. M., Coyle, H., Miller, J. L., et al. 2009, AEdRv, 8, 010111
Slater, T., Adams, J., Brissenden, G., & Duncan, D. 2001, PhTea, 39, 52
Thomas, J., & Pedersen, J. E. 2003, School Science and Mathematics, 103, 319
Udomprasert, P. S., Goodman, A. A., & Wong, C. 2012, in ASP Conf. Ser. 457, Connecting People to Science: A National Conf. on Science Education and Public Outreach, ed. J. B. Jensen, J. G. Manning, M. G. Gibbs, & D. Daou (San Francisco, CA: ASP), 149
Uttal, D. H., & O'Doherty, K. 2008, in Visualization: Theory and Practice in Science Education, ed. J. Gilbert, M. Reiner, & M. Nakhleh (New York: Springer), 53
Wong, C. 2008, in ASP Conf. Ser. 389, EPO and a Changing World: Creating Linkages and Expanding Partnerships, ed. C. Garmany, M. G. Gibbs, & J. W. Moody (San Francisco, CA: ASP), 227
Yu, K. C., Sahami, K., Sahami, V. A., & Sessions, L. 2015, JAESE, 2, 33

Astronomy Education, Volume 1
Evidence-based instruction for introductory courses
Chris Impey and Sanlyn Buxner

Chapter 10

Measuring Students' Understanding in Astronomy with Research-based Assessment Tools

Janelle M Bailey

Research-based assessment tools can help an instructor better understand students' prior knowledge about astronomy topics as well as measure change in that understanding over time. Eight assessment tools appropriate for Astro 101—three diagnostic tests and five concept inventories—are described here, including information about their development and typical use. I also provide practical tips for using the assessments, including information about how to give them and whether or not to grade them. All of the instruments can be accessed through the PhysPort online resource.

Chapter Objectives

By the end of the chapter, readers will be able to
- describe the difference between diagnostic tests and concept inventories,
- give examples of research-based assessments and their development, and
- find and administer assessments related to introductory astronomy.

10.1 Introduction

As scientists, we want to test things to see whether changes to conditions or inputs make a difference in outcomes. This is not easy—or even always possible—when it comes to astronomy, but there are ways to do this in our astronomy teaching. Assessment tools (or instruments) such as diagnostic tests and concept inventories can help an instructor know what students entering our courses understand about astronomy before the class begins, allowing us to tailor instruction for maximum impact. When we use the tool again at the end of the course, we may be able to measure learning over a period of time on a set of specific topics and make some judgments about the effectiveness of our instruction. This chapter will describe several assessment tools developed for astronomy content, their design and quality, and how they can be used in the classroom.

10.2 Diagnostic Tests and Concept Inventories

I will talk about two different types of assessment tools in this chapter. Though somewhat different in design and scope, they have commonalities in use. All are intended to identify what students know about the content prior to or after instruction, and when paired (having the same students take the test at the beginning and end of the class) can measure change in knowledge over time. *Diagnostic tests*, the first tool type, are broad in scope, covering many different topics within a content area (here, astronomy). On the other hand, *concept inventories* (the second type) are narrower, focusing on a single topic such as light or stars. In the following sections, I will further define the type of instrument, then present astronomy-related instruments in approximate chronological order of development. Each instrument description will include information about its design and development process, as well as typical results of use. Unless otherwise noted, the tools have been designed with a typical college-level introductory astronomy survey course (a.k.a. "Astro 101") in mind.

10.2.1 Some Definitions

Before diving in, it might be helpful to define some common terms that are used when researchers report on tools like those described in this chapter. Each definition provided in Table 10.1 also includes a source (often one used elsewhere in the chapter) for more information, though of course these are not the only resources that discuss these terms.

10.2.2 Diagnostic Tests

Diagnostic tests are instruments that are designed to assess students' broad understanding of a general domain. They tend to include multiple topics within that domain, such as those that might be covered in a survey course like Astro 101. Topics might be taken from K–12 national standards documents such as the *Benchmarks for Science Literacy* (American Association for the Advancement of Science (AAAS) 1993), *National Science Education Standards* (NSES; National Research Council (NRC) 1996), or more recently the *Next Generation Science Standards* (NGSS; NGSS Lead States 2013). Other sources of topics include surveys of what is commonly taught (Slater et al. 2001), agreement about what should be taught (Partridge & Greenstein 2003) in target courses, or common misconceptions about the content. Table 10.2 provides a few examples of how content in the standards documents and related sources is related to an item in three diagnostic tests—the Astronomy Diagnostic Test (ADT) 2.0, the Astronomical Misconceptions Survey (AMS), and the Test of Astronomy Standards (TOAST)—that will be described in greater detail below.

Table 10.1. Operational Definitions of Common Terms

Term	Operational definition	For more information
Concept inventory	A research-based, typically multiple-choice instrument that focuses on a relatively narrow topic or set of related concepts, which can be used to gauge students' understanding on that topic.	Bailey (2009)
Cronbach's alpha	A measure of the internal consistency of an instrument—that is, do takers of the instrument respond to different questions in the same way? This measure of reliability can be used on multiple-choice instruments or scales (e.g., 1 = strongly disagree to 5 = strongly agree). Alpha typically varies between 0 and 1, with higher numbers corresponding to greater internal consistency.	George & Mallery (2009)
Diagnostic test	A research-based, typically multiple-choice instrument that can be used to gauge students' knowledge about a set of topics. These may be broader than concept inventories in scope (e.g., covering all topics in a course).	Halloun & Hestenes (1985)
Distractors	In a multiple-choice question, distractors are the wrong answers.	Sadler (1998)
Effect Size	A measure of the magnitude of a statistical relationship.	Tabachnick & Fidell (2007)
Kuder–Richardson Formula 20	A measure of internal consistency of an instrument that is used for dichotomous items (e.g., true/false), based on estimating the instrument as all possible halves.	Allen & Yen (1979)
Misconception	A notion held by someone (e.g., a student) that is considered incorrect with respect to the established knowledge of the field. Sometimes misconceptions are distinguished as being around topics that students have learned in formal education but are incorrect, compared to alternative or naïve conceptions that develop naturally from the student's interactions with the world.	Driver & Easley (1978)
Paired	Data that come from the same person taken at different points in time. See also repeated measures.	George & Mallery (2009); Tabachnick & Fidell (2007)
Preinstructional knowledge	What someone understands about a topic before receiving formal instruction on it in the given situation. In the case of Astro 101 courses, we typically think of this as what they know about	Driver & Easley (1978)

(*Continued*)

	astronomy at the start of the course, which may have been learned from K–12 schooling, family, or personal interests.	
Reliability	The extent to which an instrument can yield similar results, regardless of who administers the test and to whom. All measures of reliability, such as Cronbach's alpha and Kuder–Richardson Formula 20, are technically estimates.	George & Mallery (2009)
Repeated measures	When an instrument (e.g., a concept inventory) is administered to the same group of students at multiple time points, such as at the start and end of a course. Also called a within-subjects design.	George & Mallery (2009); Tabachnick & Fidell (2007)
Test bank	A group of test items from which the instructor can make a selection to create a personalized instrument.	Sadler et al. (2009)
Validity	An overall judgment of the extent to which a test measures what it claims to measure. There are multiple types of validity to consider, and these may change under different circumstances. Often, validity has been considered a property or characteristic of the test, but Kane (1992) considers it to be an argument to be made about the interpretation of test results.	Allen & Yen (1979); Kane (1992)

10.2.2.1 Astronomy Diagnostic Test

The first big instrument to be developed for the Astro 101-style course was the Astronomy Diagnostic Test (ADT; Hufnagel et al. 2000; Hufnagel 2002; Zeilik 2003). Prior to this, Sadler (1998) had created an assessment for a high school curriculum project called Project STAR, but it was neither widely available nor had it been tested with undergraduate students (Hufnagel 2002). Building on the Project STAR instrument and earlier work by Zeilik et al. (1998)—the Misconceptions Measure, later called the ADT 1.0—a group of researchers set out to adapt and test the instrument that became known as the ADT 2.0. One of the main objectives for writing the ADT 2.0 was to apply "standard psychometric principals, e.g., Miyasaka and Ryan (1997)" (Hufnagel 2002, p. 48), including having only a single concept per question, avoiding jargon, and writing questions such that the correct answer could be known prior to reading the multiple-choice options.

Topics on the ADT 2.0 include the apparent motion of the Sun, scale of the solar system, lunar phases, distance scales, seasons, global warming, nature of light, gravity, stars, and cosmology, comprising 21 content questions (an additional 12 questions probe students' background and attitudes; Hufnagel 2002, pp. 49–50). Each item has between three and five choices (one correct and the remaining two to four distractors based on known student difficulties). The number of choices is based

Table 10.2. Samples of Source Topics and Related Items

Item Source	Assessment Item
Stars produce energy from nuclear reactions, primarily the fusion of hydrogen to form helium. These and other processes in stars have led to the formation of all the other elements. [9–12] (NRC 1996, p. 190)	ADT 2.0 (Hufnagel 2002, p. 49) Where does the Sun's energy come from? A. The combining of light elements into heavy elements. B. The breaking apart of heavy elements into lighter ones. C. The glow from molten rocks. D. Heat left over from the Big Bang.
Because the Earth turns daily on an axis that is tilted relative to the plane of the Earth's yearly orbit around the Sun, sunlight falls more intensely on different parts of the Earth during the year. The difference in heating of the Earth's surface produces the planet's seasons and weather patterns. (AAAS 1993, p. 69)	TOAST (Slater 2014, p. 12) Imagine that Earth was upright with no tilt. How would this affect the seasons? A. We would no longer experience a difference between the seasons. B. We would still experience seasons, but the difference would be *less* noticeable. C. We would still experience seasons, but the difference would be *more* noticeable. D. We would continue to experience seasons in essentially the same way we do now. AMS (True/False version; LoPresto & Murrell 2011, p. 15) The change of seasons is caused by the varying distance between Earth and the Sun. AMS (Multiple-choice version; LoPresto & Murrell 2011, p. 16) What causes summer to be hotter than winter? A. Earth is closer to the Sun in summer. B. The daylight period is longer in summer. C. The Sun gets higher in the sky in summer. D. [Both B and C above]. E. [All of the above].

on the nature of the question—for example, the question "How does the speed of radio waves compare to the speed of visible light?" only has three viable options (radio is faster than visible light, they are the same, or radio is slower than visible light), whereas "When the Moon appears to completely cover the Sun (an eclipse), the Moon must be at which phase?" has five options (four named phases and "at no particular phase").

Table 10.3 shows some of the basic testing characteristics of the ADT and other instruments that have been reported in the literature (discussions of these other

Table 10.3. Summary of Test Development Characteristics

Instrument	Test sites	N courses	N students	Cronbach's alpha	CTT, IRT[a]	References
ADT	National	97	pre = 5346, post = 3842	pre = 0.65, post = 0.76	Neither	Deming (2002)
AMS	Local	5	paired = 133	n.r.[b]	Neither	LoPresto & Murrell (2011)
TOAST	National	5	pre = 1066	pre = 0.83	CTT	S. J. Slater (2014)
LPCI	Local	n.r.[b]	pre = 324, post = 78	pre = 0.54, post = 0.55[c]	CTT	Lindell (2001)
LSCI	National	14	pre = 548, post = 368	post = 0.77	CTT	Bardar et al. (2007)
SPCI	Local	7	paired = 417	pre = 0.470, post = 0.763	CTT	Bailey et al. (2012)
GECI	Local	6	paired = 332	pre = 0.60, post = 0.79	CTT	Keller (2006)
NGCI	National	n.r.[b]	pre = 925, post = 743	post = 0.84	CTT	Williamson et al. (2013)

[a] CTT (classical test theory) or IRT (item response theory) refers only to the main instrument development publication listed in the References column; both the LSCI and SPCI subsequently have been analyzed through IRT (Wallace et al. 2018 and Wallace & Bailey 2010, respectively).
[b] n.r. = not reported.
[c] Lindell used the Spearman–Brown equation to predict reliability if there were more items (25) on the instrument, which yielded projections of 0.67 and 0.68 for pre- and posttest, respectively.

instruments, as well as more about the nature of the table itself, are presented in forthcoming sections). Here we see that one common measure of reliability, Cronbach's alpha, was 0.65 on the ADT 2.0 pretest and 0.76 on the posttest (Deming 2002). Generally speaking, a value of 0.7 or greater is considered acceptable (George & Mallery 2009), although pretests with high item difficulty (Deming 2002) or a homogenous population, such as Astro 101 students who have never taken an astronomy course (Wallace & Bailey 2010), may yield lower results and so may not be of major concern to researchers.

The original intent of the ADT 2.0 was to provide instructors with a way to gauge what students understand about astronomy prior to instruction (Hufnagel 2002), although it has subsequently been used as a pre-/posttest to measure changes in understanding over the course as well (Alexander 2005; Brogt et al. 2007c; Deming 2002). Both Deming (2002) and Brogt et al. (2007c) investigated the results of the ADT 2.0 with large national data sets of thousands of students. Deming's national sample yielded a pretest average score of 32.4% and an average posttest score of 47.3%. Brogt et al. did not report full-sample values (instead they were broken up by class style—lecture, lecture + lab, etc.) but weighted averages across the class styles were comparable to Deming's results. Alexander (2005) compared the results on a modified ADT 2.0 (one question was omitted due to lack of course coverage) over a traditionally taught course and then a subsequent course that incorporated several active-learning strategies, finding that the latter led to higher gains and larger effect sizes on the ADT.

10.2.2.2 Astronomical Misconceptions Survey
LoPresto & Murrell's (2011) Astronomical Misconceptions Survey (AMS) was developed in two formats—true/false and multiple choice—each with 25 items. The items are based on common misconceptions identified from both the research literature and the authors' instructional experience. Many topics are included in the AMS, though few are addressed by multiple questions. Unique topics in the AMS (compared to the ADT or other instruments) include questions relating to the nature of astronomy versus astrology, the invention of the telescope, and the purpose of putting telescopes on a mountain. In its true/false version, all of the questions are false. The multiple-choice version uses common misconceptions as distractors (i.e., incorrect options). For example, the true/false item "Black holes are giant holes that move through space and suck in everything they encounter" (LoPresto & Murrell 2011, p. 15) becomes in the multiple-choice version:

Which of the following is not true about a black hole?
  a. It is a mass for which the escape velocity has reached the speed of light.
  b. It is surrounded by an event horizon.
  c. It is a giant hole moving through space sucking up everything in its path.
  d. [All of the above are true].
  e. [None of the above are true] (p. 16).

LoPresto & Murrell (2011) used the true/false version of their instrument as the pretest & found an average score of 50.3%, "which could be interpreted as random guessing" (p. 15). They gave the posttest in true/false for some sections the course, yielding an average score of 72%. In other sections, they used the multiple-choice version, where the average posttest score was only 47%. Subsequent uses of the instrument led the authors to classify items into categories of major misconceptions, minor misconceptions, or not misconceptions, based upon the percentage of correct responses in each format at both pretest and posttest, and with reasonable agreement across both formats. Although these findings are cited in works by others, it does not appear that the AMS has been used in other research studies.

10.2.2.3 Test of Astronomy Standards
The Test Of Astronomy STandards (TOAST; Slater 2014) is a diagnostic test that intends to serve as a general content assessment for introductory astronomy. Using three previously mentioned sources of important topics (AAAS 1993; NRC 1996; Partridge & Greenstein 2003) to develop the content coverage, Slater (2014) identified "three meta-criteria and 11 criteria" (p. 7) for the instrument. These are physical laws and processes (including gravity, electromagnetic radiation and its production, and fusion and the formation of heavy elements), the structure and evolution of the universe (evolution of the universe, stars and stellar evolution, evolution and structure of the solar system, seasons, and scale), and patterns in the sky (yearly patterns, daily patterns, and lunar phases). There are 27 items[1] in the instrument, predominantly taken from existing instruments such as the ADT 2.0 or some of the concept inventories described below; additional items were modified from unpublished instruments or created for the TOAST when needed. For example, one of the cosmology items was newly developed:

The Big Bang is best described as
  a. The event that formed all matter and space from an infinitely small dot of energy.
  b. The event that formed all matter and scattered it into space.
  c. The event that scattered all matter and energy throughout space.
  d. The event that organized the current arrangement of planetary systems (Slater 2014, p. 19).

Slater (2014) found a pretest reliability of 0.83 (see Table 10.3) and a pretest average score of 44% when used with introductory astronomy students. Slater et al. (2015) further describe various item characteristics of TOAST items, again using pretest data only. Researchers have begun to use the TOAST as a pre-/posttest to assess instruction (e.g., Heyer 2012; Stork 2014; French & Burrows 2017). French & Burrows (2017), for example, found pre- and posttest averages of 37.2% and 61.6%, respectively.

---
[1] Here, and for subsequent instruments, the number of items refers only to content-related items, omitting any questions such as gender or college major.

10.2.2.4 Summary of Diagnostic Tests
Diagnostic tests such as the ADT, AMS, and TOAST are ideal for getting a broad sense of students' prior knowledge (pretest, taken at the start of a course) and can provide some feeling for their learning within a course such as Astro 101 when then paired with a posttest (taken at the end of the same course). They typically include a range of topics that are covered in survey courses but may be limited to only one or two questions per topic. These instruments are unlikely to give you detailed information about deep student learning or on information such as more general problem solving or critical thinking skills.

10.2.3 Concept Inventories

Research in science education has shown that many students have common sense ideas (i.e., misconceptions or alternative conceptions) that do not align with the scientific explanations (Driver & Easley 1978). Halloun & Hestenes (1985) developed an instrument that could be used as a placement exam, to evaluate instruction, or to diagnose misconceptions in physics. The Mechanics Baseline Test (Halloun & Hestenes 1985; Hestenes & Wells 1992) and its descendant the Force Concept Inventory (FCI; Hestenes et al. 1992) were created to measure students' basic understanding of mechanics, and specifically force and motion, with these known common sense ideas as item distractors. Because of the nature of the typical first-semester introductory physics course, the FCI can often be used in a manner similar to the diagnostic tests described above—indeed, most of the content of such a course is limited to mechanics (Halloun & Hestenes 1985).

This focus on a narrower content area is primarily what distinguishes the concept inventory from the broader diagnostic tests such as the ADT 2.0 and TOAST described above. One feature of concept inventories is that they tend to be written in students' natural language rather than following a strict adherence to scientific terminology (Bailey 2009), though this can be the case with the diagnostic tests as well. An example of this is the use of "white" as a choice in a question about star colors despite scientific understanding that white is the result of the addition of all colors of light (Bailey 2006; Bailey et al. 2012). Additionally, like the FCI and the diagnostics tests described here, concept inventories are all "distractor-driven multiple-choice instruments" that use known misconceptions or student difficulties to create the distractors (Sadler et al. 2009, p. 2). For example, research has shown that students may believe that radio waves and visible light travel at different speeds (Zeilik et al. 1998). As a result, a question about this might ask about relative speeds of these two forms of electromagnetic radiation (Bardar 2006; Bardar et al. 2007).

There are several concept inventories that address topics in astronomy that might be included in an Astro 101 course. Unlike the introductory mechanics courses in physics, however, none of the concept inventories will be as comprehensive as the FCI. One word of caution, however: if your course covers several or all of these topics, you should *not* either give out all of these instruments to your course (lest your students get really tired of taking "tests" and come to hate you!) or pull out bits

Figure 10.1. Item from the Lunar Phases Concept Inventory (Lindell 2004, p. 2).

and pieces from each one to make a new, custom test (as this destroys any arguments to be made about each instrument's validity and reliability).

10.2.3.1 Lunar Phases Concept Inventory

The Lunar Phases Concept Inventory (LPCI; Lindell 2001, 2004; Lindell & Olsen 2002) was originally designed to first identify undergraduate students' understanding of lunar phases and then to evaluate the effectiveness of an instructional activity on the topic. The LPCI consists of 14 items around the appearance of the Moon and the period of its cycle; orbital motions and timescales; motions of the Moon; the relationship between the phase and the positions of the Sun, Earth, and Moon; the relationship between the phase, location in the sky, and time of observation; and the cause of phases (Lindell & Sommer 2003). An example of a question that addresses the appearance of the Moon can be seen in Figure 10.1—note that in this case there are more than the typical four or five potential responses due to the nature of the question. The LPCI initial reliability scores were somewhat lower than desired (pretest 0.54 and posttest 0.55), but Lindell (2001) predicted acceptable reliabilities if the instrument had more items; see Table 10.3. Initial use of the LPCI yielded an average pretest score of 35.4% and an average posttest score of 76.2%. A more recent version of the LPCI (Lindell 2004) is available from its author.

Although originally designed for and used with college students, the LPCI has been used by several researchers with middle-grade students (Sherrod & Wilhelm 2009; Wilhelm 2009) and with preservice elementary and middle school teachers who may be expected to teach this topic (Wilhelm et al. 2008). (The changing appearance of the Moon is a common elementary standard and the cause of the phases often appears in middle-grade standards; see, for example, AAAS 1993; NRC 1996; NGSS Lead States 2013.) Additionally, Mulholland & Ginns (2008) modified the LPCI to be used with preservice teachers in the southern hemisphere. They converted some questions to a southern hemisphere perspective but retained

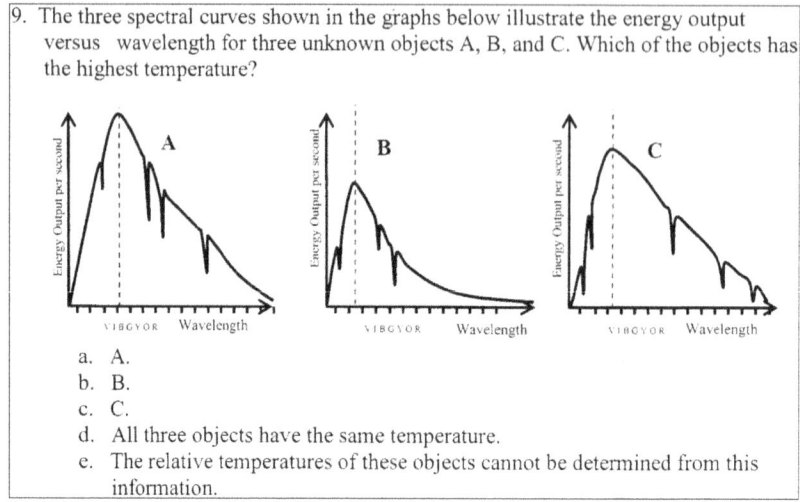

Figure 10.2. Item from the Light and Spectroscopy Concept Inventory (Bardar 2006, p. 173).

some northern-hemisphere-based questions, for a total of 24 items with an average pretest score of 34% and an average posttest score of 52%.

10.2.3.2 Light and Spectroscopy Concept Inventory
The Light and Spectroscopy Concept Inventory (LSCI; Bardar 2006; Bardar et al. 2007) addresses a notable amount of content that is covered in the typical Astro 101-style course. This includes the nature of the electromagnetic spectrum; Doppler shift as an indicator of motion; blackbody radiators, including the relationship between temperature and peak wavelength and the relationship between temperature, surface area, and luminosity; and the physical processes behind and the features of continuous, absorption, and emission spectra. The LSCI contains 26 items, an example of which is shown in Figure 10.2. Cronbach's alpha for the LSCI posttest was 0.77 (see Table 10.3), and the field-test average scores were 23.9% pretest and 38.7% posttest (Bardar 2006).

The LSCI has been used in a large number of courses to compile a national data set (Prather et al. 2009; Schlingman et al. 2012; Wallace et al. 2018). Prather et al. (2009) used the LSCI to compare different styles of instruction and found that the pretest scores for different courses clustered around 25%. Posttest scores were not reported. Rather, normalized gains (i.e., a measure of actual gain as compared to potential gain, calculated as $\langle g \rangle = (\text{post\%} - \text{pre\%})/(100\% - \text{pre\%})$) were described and ranged between −0.07 and 0.50—using the 25% average as the pretest score, this would correspond to a posttest range of 20%–62%. Schlingman et al. (2012) conducted a classical test theory analysis of the national data set, while Wallace et al. (2018) completed an item response theory analysis of it. These two approaches can provide different information about the test as a whole as well as individual items within it. Classical test theory is the more common approach for analyzing concept inventories, as seen in Table 10.3, although use of IRT has been growing (Wallace &

Bailey 2010; Wallace et al. 2018) and is the analysis used for nearly all large standardized testing programs such as the GRE® (Carlson & von Davier 2013).

10.2.3.3 Star Properties Concept Inventory
The Star Properties Concept Inventory (SPCI; Bailey 2006; Bailey et al. 2012) was created to assess students' understanding of the properties and formation of stars, including nuclear fusion and stellar mass, luminosity, temperature, and lifetime. Version 3 (published in Bailey et al. 2012) contained 23 items but more recent analyses, including one by Wallace & Bailey (2010), has led to a 22 item Version 4 that is available from Bailey. A sample item addresses the mass–lifetime relationship of stars:

Star C has a lifetime of 50 million years, while star D has a lifetime of only 10 million years. What can you say about the masses of these stars?
   a. Star C has the greater mass.
   b. Star D has the greater mass.
   c. Stars C and D have about the same mass.
   d. There is not enough information given to answer this question (Bailey 2006, p. 241).

Note that the original version of this question (as presented in Bailey 2006) used labels C and D for stars but these have been changed to W and Z in Version 4. The reliability of the SPCI Version 3 pretest was 0.47—lower than ideal—but the posttest was 0.76, which is satisfactory (Bailey et al. 2012). Pretest and posttest averages for introductory astronomy courses in the field test were 31% and 51%, respectively.

The SPCI has been used in several subsequent studies. LoPresto & Murrell (2009) used the SPCI to compare two instructional approaches, a traditional instructor-centered approach and a collaborative student-centered structure using lecture-tutorials. Scores were similar to the field testing, with a pretest average of 26% and posttest averages of 57% for the lecture course and 63% for the interactive course. Wallace & Bailey (2010) conducted an item response theory analysis of the instrument and suggested revisions that have been taken into account for Version 4. Bailey et al. (2017) used the SPCI to measure changes in content knowledge while also evaluating students' self-efficacy for and interest in learning about stars, finding that classes with the largest gains in self-efficacy also had the largest gains in knowledge, and that instructional design that included mastery experiences with feedback, verbal persuasion, and vicarious experiences through peer instruction was common across those courses. Finally, Oğuzhan Dinçer & Çobanoğlu Aktan (2017) translated the SPCI into Turkish and conducted an analysis of its properties. The 22 item version has a reliability of 0.82.

10.2.3.4 Greenhouse Effect Concept Inventory
Another concept inventory with more applicability to the planetary science aspect of astronomy is the Greenhouse Effect Concept Inventory (GECI; Keller 2006). This instrument contains 20 items designed to assess students' understanding of energy flow through Earth's atmosphere and the resulting effects. This is a somewhat different

focus from previous research efforts on this topic, which had typically focused on the cause of the greenhouse effect (Keller 2006). A sample item is as follows:

Which of the following most strongly affects Earth's overall surface temperature?
  a. Heat released by factories and other industrial activities.
  b. The destruction of the ozone layer allowing more sunlight into the atmosphere.
  c. The flow of different forms of energy through the atmosphere.
  d. Air pollution trapped in the atmosphere by gases.
  e. Sunlight being magnified and focused by gases in the atmosphere (Keller 2006, p. 408).

Cronbach's alpha for the GECI was reported as 0.60 pretest and 0.79 posttest. To my knowledge, the GECI has not been used for other research purposes, perhaps because it has not been published outside of Keller's dissertation.

10.2.3.5 Newtonian Gravity Concept Inventory

The most recent published concept inventory in astronomy education is the Newtonian Gravity Concept Inventory (NGCI; Williamson 2013; Williamson et al. 2013). The 26 items on this instruments span four concept domains: directionality of gravitational forces, the force law (e.g., role of distance or mass), independence of other forces, and thresholds (e.g., "There is no distance for which the force of gravity suddenly stops"; Williamson et al. 2013, p. 5). A sample item from the NGCI is presented in Figure 10.3. The posttest version has a Cronbach's alpha of 0.84; pretest mean scores ranged across field-test sites between 37% and 59%, while posttest mean scores varied between 49% and 71%.

The NGCI has not yet been adopted widely, in part due to its relative newness. Williamson et al. (2016) extended the research on the NGCI by using it in introductory college, algebra-based physics courses, and argued that this is an appropriate use, further describing some differences in understanding between this population and the original introductory astronomy population.

---

2. Two astronauts are floating in space very far away from any planets or stars. What is the direction of the gravitational force that they experience, if any?

   a. Toward each other, because there is a gravitational force between them.
   b. Away from each other because they are pulled by distant planets and stars.
   c. They experience a gravitational force, but its direction cannot be determined.
   d. They do not experience a gravitational force because there is no large object nearby.

Figure 10.3. Item from the Newtonian Gravity Concept Inventory (Williamson 2013, p. 272).

10.2.3.6 A K–12 Tool
The astronomy concept inventories described here, like the diagnostic tests, have been designed with the Astro 101 course in mind. Sadler (1998) developed and tested an assessment instrument for the Project STAR curriculum project. Later, Sadler et al. (2009) developed the Astronomy and Space Science Concept Inventory, actually a set of more than 200 questions that were then used to create three tools for different grade bands within K–12. As such, its development process and use are quite a bit different from what has been described here so far. One of the key aspects that Sadler et al. (2009) looked at was the ability of K–12 teachers to predict their students' scores on these questions; typically, teachers significantly overestimated their students' understanding of astronomy content.

10.2.3.7 Summary of Concept Inventories
Concept inventories are more focused on narrower topics than diagnostic tests, and as a result, may give an instructor more information about deep content understanding within that topic area compared to diagnostic tests when used in a similar pretest/posttest manner. They provide a relatively fast and easy way of gauging students' understanding. Compare this to methods such as open-ended written responses, projects, or student interviews that may provide a better grasp of students' understanding but are much more time intensive to administer and score.

10.3 Instrument Development and Quality

Although the instruments described in the previous sections vary in the details, the development of these instruments follow many common steps. All have undergone a rigorous iterative process of testing and revision, typically with large numbers of students (whether at a single institution or multiple institutions). All (except the true/false version of the AMS) are distractor-driven instruments (Sadler et al. 2009), with incorrect choices based on existing and/or newly conducted research on student ideas. In most cases, qualitative methods (such as interviews and open-ended questions) were used prior to or in early stages of instrument development to get a better sense of students' typical understanding about the topic. This systematic approach to question development, testing, and refinement—one that often takes several months or even years (all five of the concept inventories described here were created as doctoral dissertation projects)—is a critical piece of the validity arguments made about these instruments.

Lindell et al. (2007) analyzed the development process of a dozen physics and astronomy concept inventories. Because of when the work was completed, this analysis only includes the ADT and the LPCI of the astronomy instruments described here. The authors investigated the methods used for the development processes, as described in publications or in personal communications with the developers. Categories of comparison included how the concept domain was determined, test specifications, reporting of item statistics, size and location of field testing, validation studies, and reporting of reliability statistics. Table 10.3 summarizes some of the main development characteristics of the instruments described in this chapter. It is not a comprehensive exploration of the development details, but the comparison was inspired by the review done by Lindell et al. (2007). They found that there was not a consistent methodology employed in the development of the instruments they analyzed, and I would maintain that the current group of astronomy instruments also has several differences despite many commonalities. Lindell et al. (2007) argued that the community needs to develop guidelines for the development of concept inventories. Three of the four concept inventories described in this chapter (LSCI, SPCI, and GECI) were in concurrent development just before their review and so could not incorporate their recommendations.

Another way of looking at instrument quality is provided by PhysPort. The PhysPort[2] online resource portal, developed by the American Association of Physics Teachers in collaboration with Kansas State University and funded by the National Science Foundation, hosts many assessments across physics and astronomy, including the instruments discussed here (but excluding the K–12 instruments by Sadler 1998 and Sadler et al. 2009). Each instrument is rated as having one of four levels of research validity, based upon the extent to which seven criteria are met. The criteria are

- based on research into student thinking,
- studied using student interviews,
- studied using expert review,
- studied using appropriate statistical analysis,
- research conducted at multiple institutions,
- research conducted by multiple research groups, and
- research published in peer-reviewed publication (McKagan 2018).

"Gold star" instruments have met all seven criteria, while "silver" have met five or more; "bronze" have met three or more, and "research-based" instruments have met at least one criterion (McKagan 2018). The ADT and SPCI are classified as gold star as of this writing; the LSCI, NGCI, TOAST, and GECI are silver; the LPCI is bronze; and the AMS is research-based. Using McKagan's list, let us look at why the ADT is classified as gold star.[3]

- *Based on research into student thinking*: The original ADT (Zeilik 2003; Zeilik et al. 1998) and version 2.0 (Hufnagel 2002) used prior research as well as new interviews to develop content.
- *Studied using student interviews*: Sixty student interviews as well as 30 written responses to question stems only were used to assess reliability (Hufnagel 2002).
- *Studied using expert review*: In addition to the authoring team, feedback was solicited from other astronomy education experts (Hufnagel 2002).

---

[2] http://physport.org.
[3] I should note that this is my interpretation of why PhysPort has classified the ADT as gold star; the details of their decision are summarized at https://www.physport.org/assessments/assessment.cfm?I=36&A=ADT under the "Research" tab.

- *Studied using appropriate statistical analysis*: Analyses included reliability measures, item discrimination and difficulty, normalized gain, and two additional measures of gain (Brogt et al. 2007c; Deming 2002; Hufnagel 2002).
- *Research conducted at multiple institutions*: Data were collected from 68 instructors teaching 97 classes across 31 states (Deming 2002).
- *Research conducted by multiple research groups*: After the initial analysis presented by the authoring team (Deming 2002; Hufnagel et al. 2000), Brogt et al. (2007c) completed an additional analysis of the original data set. Although the original authors were part of this study, the first two authors were new to the project.
- *Research published in peer-reviewed publication*: The development process and results were published in *Publications of the Astronomical Society of Australia* (Hufnagel et al. 2000) and *Astronomy Education Review* (Brogt et al. 2007c; Deming 2002; Hufnagel 2002).

The robust development and testing process of the diagnostic tests and concept inventories described here are important to consider: compare this to the common process of writing exam questions a short time before it is given or simply taking questions from other sources (e.g., other instructors, textbook question banks). While such sources have some questions that look great on the surface, testing might show that they are confusing to students or may mask true student understanding by not probing the right kinds of information. Having an instrument that is not able to measure what we want to measure is problematic in any science, and so the careful selection of research-based assessment instruments is critical to being able to make valid inferences about student learning. That being said, the purpose of these instruments is different from that of a unit, midterm, or final exam, as discussed in the next section.

10.4 Using Diagnostic Instruments in Astronomy Courses

There are two primary ways to use instruments such as those described here in courses such as Astro 101. Both assume that you have an interest in doing some sort of systematic evaluation of something happening in your course—something research like, even if you do not go so far as to publish your results.[4] The first is to better understand what your students know or do not about astronomy or a particular topic within it at the start of the course. Diagnostic tests such as the ADT, TOAST, and AMS can give a broad overview of students' strengths and weaknesses on the topics covered, whereas concept inventories provide more focused attention on the selected topic. In this mode, you should give the instrument on the first or second day of the course, prior to any content instruction. It should be ungraded—or

---

[4] Note that if you do have an interest in publishing your results, there are many considerations and approvals that need to be sought. Such a discussion is beyond the scope of this chapter, but see, for example, discussions on human subject research by Brogt and colleagues (Brogt et al. 2007a, 2007b, 2008) and research guidance such as by Slater et al. (2015) or the series of articles in "Getting Started in PER" found at http://www.per-central.org/per_reviews/volume2.cfm.

perhaps given for participation or attendance points—but ask students to give it their best effort, as it will help you design the most effective instruction for them. Most instructors do not typically look to see whether a given individual student knows question 2 and not question 7; rather, they look at trends across the course (such as identifying topics that have high percentage of correct responses and so can then be given less instructional time, or ascertaining the common wrong answers on topics that might be particularly difficult for students). In fact, some instructors may notice after a few semesters of giving the same instrument that these general trends are common enough that they can be applied consistently without needing the diagnostic every time.

The second way to use concept inventories and diagnostic tests is as a pre/posttest comparison over a unit of instruction, typically either a section of the course (e.g., stars for the SPCI) or over the full semester (Bailey 2009). This can be done to measure student learning on the topics of the instrument or to compare outcomes to other courses using the same instrument. The pretest, as described in the previous paragraph, should be given early in the term and ungraded. Posttests should be after instruction on the topic(s) is complete. For a whole-subject test like the ADT, TOAST, or AMS, this probably means at the very end of the semester. Concept inventories, given that they are topic specific, do not necessarily have to be held to the end of the term but could instead be given after that topical unit is complete. Posttests could be graded (such as a quiz grade) but when used for research typically are not, though again sometimes participation or attendance grades are given. Some instructors provide extra credit for the posttest. An important aspect, though, is that the posttest is not announced in advance, such as an exam would be.

The instruments described here, and others like them (there is a large number in physics as well as other science, mathematics, and engineering topics), have undergone various levels of research in their development, as described above. Arguments made about their reliability and validity are based upon the use of the full and complete instrument, without significant alterations. This means that you should not pull out your favorite five questions for use on your final exam and then compare them with their pretest counterparts and expect a robust understanding of student learning. Likewise, because of the nature of the extensive work behind developing them, the instruments should neither be shared with students in advance nor be allowed to be taken home to become absorbed into the underworld of test sharing and sales.

So how do you get copies of the instruments for your own use? I recommend using PhysPort. Many of the instruments are available there upon free registration and verification for higher education faculty or K–12 teachers. Some of the instruments are published—for example, Bailey et al. (2012) included SPCI v3, but v4 is on PhysPort. Although none of the astronomy instruments are included it in yet, PhysPort also includes a beta version of their Data Explorer that allows an instructor to upload results of certain assessments (such as the FCI) and compare their results with a growing national database. Astronomy instruments are expected to be added in the future (S. McKagan 2018, personal communication). PhysPort also has many useful articles on using assessments, such as one on common concerns around concept inventories (Madsen et al. 2016).

10.5 Conclusions

Diagnostic tests and concept inventories are tools that can help astronomy instructors systematically gauge their students' preinstructional knowledge and changes in that knowledge over time. Used with forethought and reflection, they can provide insights into instructional effectiveness and inform future efforts.

References

Alexander, W. R. 2005, AEdRv, 3, 178
Allen, M. J., & Yen, W. M. 1979, Introduction to Measurement Theory (Prospect Heights, IL: Waveland Press)
American Association for the Advancement of Science (AAAS) 1993, Benchmarks for Science Literacy (New York: Oxford University Press)
Bailey, J. M. 2006, PhD dissertation, Univ. Arizona
Bailey, J. M. 2009, PhTea, 47, 439
Bailey, J. M., Johnson, B., Prather, E. E., & Slater, T. F. 2012, IJSEd, 34, 2257
Bailey, J. M., Lombardi, D., Cordova, J. R., & Sinatra, G. M. 2017, PRPER, 13, 020140
Bardar, E. M. 2006, PhD dissertation, Boston Univ.
Bardar, E. M., Prather, E. E., Brecher, K., & Slater, T. F. 2007, AEdRv, 5, 103
Brogt, E., Dokter, E. F., & Antonellis, J. 2007a, AEdRv, 6, 43
Brogt, E., Dokter, E. F., Antonellis, J., & Buxner, S. 2007b, AEdRv, 6, 99
Brogt, E., Sabers, D., Prather, E. E., et al. 2007c, AEdRv, 6, 25
Brogt, E., Foster, T. M., Dokter, E. F., Buxner, S., & Antonellis, J. 2008, AEdRv, 7, 57
Carlson, J. E., & von Davier, M. 2013, Item Response Theory (Princeton, NJ: Educational Testing Service)
Deming, G. L. 2002, AEdRv, 1, 52
Driver, R., & Easley, J. 1978, SScEd, 5, 61
French, D. A., & Burrows, A. C. 2017, JCSTe, 46, 24
George, D., & Mallery, P. 2009, SPSS for Windows Step by Step: A Simple Guide and Reference, 16.0 Update (9th ed.; Boston, MA: Pearson Education)
Halloun, I. A., & Hestenes, D. 1985, AmJPh, 53, 1043
Hestenes, D., & Wells, M. 1992, PhTea, 30, 159
Hestenes, D., Wells, M., & Swackhamer, G. 1992, PhTea, 30, 141
Heyer, I. 2012, PhD thesis, Univ. Wyoming–Laramie
Hufnagel, B. 2002, AEdRv, 1, 47
Hufnagel, B., Slater, T. F., Deming, G. L., Adams, J. P., Adrien, R. L., Brick, C., & Zeilik, M. 2000, PASA, 17, 152
Kane, M. T. 1992, Psychological Bulletin, 112, 527
Keller, J. M. 2006, PhD thesis, Univ. Arizona
Lindell, R. S. 2001, PhD thesis, Univ. Nebraska–Lincoln
Lindell, R. S. 2004, Lunar Phases Concept Inventory (v2004)
Lindell, R. S., & Olsen, J. P. 2002, in Physics Education Research Conf., Developing the Lunar Phases Concept Inventory, ed. S. V. Franklin, K. Cummings, & J. Marx (College Park, MD: AAPT PERTG)
Lindell, R. S., Peak, E., & Foster, T. M. 2007, in AIP Conf. Proc. 883, Physics Education Research Conf., ed. L. McCullough, L. Hsu, & P. Herron (Melville, NY: AIP), 14–7

Lindell, R. S., & Sommer, S. R. 2003, in AIP Conf. Proc. 720, Physics Education Research Conf., ed. J. Marx, S. V. Franklin, & K. Cummings (Melville, NY: AIP), 73
LoPresto, M. C., & Murrell, S. R. 2009, AEdRv, 8, 010105
LoPresto, M. C., & Murrell, S. R. 2011, JCSTe, 40, 14
Madsen, A., McKagan, S., & Sayre, E. 2016, Addressing Common Concerns about Concept Inventories, https://www.physport.org/recommendations/Entry.cfm?ID=93462
McKagan, S. B. 2018, Research Validation, https://www.physport.org/assessments/tooltips.cfm?Name=ResearchValidation
Miyasaka, J. R., & Ryan, J. M. 1997, Improving Student Assessment Strategies, Big Sky Institute Professional Development Workshop Series
Mulholland, J., & Ginns, I. 2008, RScEd, 38, 385
National Research Council (NRC) 1996, National Science Education Standards (Washington, DC: National Academy Press)
NGSS Lead States 2013, Next Generation Science Standards: For States, by States (Washington, DC: National Academies Press)
Oğuzhan Dinçer, E., & Çobanoğlu Aktan, D. 2017, Journal of Human Sciences, 14, 2021
Partridge, B., & Greenstein, G. 2003, AEdRv, 2, 46
Prather, E. E., Rudolph, A. L., Brissenden, G., & Schlingman, W. M. 2009, AmJPh, 77, 320
Sadler, P. M. 1998, JRScT, 35, 265
Sadler, P. M., Coyle, H., Miller, J. L., Cook-Smith, N., Dussault, M., & Gould, R. R. 2009, AEdRv, 8, 010111
Schlingman, W. M., Prather, E. E., Wallace, C. S., Rudolph, A. L., & Brissenden, G. 2012, AEdRv, 11, 010107
Sherrod, S. E., & Wilhelm, J. 2009, IJSEd, 31, 873
Slater, S. J. 2014, JAESE, 1, 1
Slater, S. J., Schleigh, S. P., & Stork, D. J. 2015, JAESE, 2, 89
Slater, S. J., Slater, T. F., Heyer, I., & Bailey, J. M. 2015, Conducting Astronomy Education Research: An Astronomer's Guide (2nd ed.; Hilo, HI: Pono Publishing)
Slater, T. F., Adams, J. P., Brissenden, G., & Duncan, D. 2001, PhTea, 39, 52
Stork, D. J. 2014, PhD dissertation, Univ. Wyoming–Laramie
Tabachnick, B. G., & Fidell, L. S. 2007, Using Multivariate Statistics (5th ed.; Boston, MA: Pearson Education)
Wallace, C. S., & Bailey, J. M. 2010, AEdRv, 9, 010116
Wallace, C. S., Chambers, T. G., & Prather, E. E. 2018, PRPER, 14, 010149
Wilhelm, J. 2009, School Science and Mathematics, 109, 258
Wilhelm, J., Smith, W., Walters, K., Sherrod, S., & Mulholland, J. 2008, IJSME, 6, 131
Williamson, K. E. 2013, PhD dissertation, Montana State Univ.
Williamson, K. E., Prather, E. E., & Willoughby, S. D. 2016, AmJPh, 84, 458
Williamson, K. E., Willoughby, S. D., & Prather, E. E. 2013, AEdRv, 12, 010107
Zeilik, M. 2003, AEdRv, 1, 46
Zeilik, M., Schau, C., & Mattern, N. 1998, PhTea, 36, 104

Astronomy Education, Volume 1
Evidence-based instruction for introductory courses
Chris Impey and Sanlyn Buxner

Chapter 11

Everyone's Universe: Teaching Astronomy in Community Colleges

Rica Sirbaugh French

Despite the negative stereotypes still overshadowing community colleges, scores of freshmen nationwide are deliberately beginning their college careers at these institutions, and the numbers are increasing more than twice as fast as those of four-year schools. Approximately 300,000 of these students take introductory astronomy each year as the last formal exposure to science most of them will ever have, and at least one-third of these students do so at a community or two-year college. The importance of investing in and devoting resources and training to serve this population—everyone, demographically speaking—cannot be overstated. Yet the overwhelming majority of those who do serve this population are lacking in both areas. The community colleges' heavy emphasis on teaching and student success creates both challenges and opportunities that educators must meet head-on using a variety of methods and innovative strategies, teamwork and faculty support systems, and clever workarounds. Here, we introduce both the student and faculty populations, examine some characteristics of both populations, and offer some advice for those looking to teach introductory astronomy at a community college.

Chapter Objectives

By the end of this chapter, the reader will be able to
- describe the demographics and general characteristics of the population taking introductory astronomy,
- articulate the importance of this population and the implications with respect to science literacy,
- compare and contrast the challenges facing community college students with those of students at four-year institutions,

- assess one's own preparedness to teach astronomy, particularly in the community college setting, and explain why it matters who teaches the introductory courses,
- differentiate teaching at a community college from doing so at a four-year college or university,
- evaluate one's own commitment to teaching as a profession,
- formulate a plan for his/her/their professional development,
- examine and develop strategies and skills for strengthening job applications and interviewing for community college faculty positions, and
- decide whether teaching at a community college might be a good career choice for him/her/them.

11.1 Introduction

Today's society propagates some deeply entrenched and widely varying ideas about what community colleges are and are not. Most folks will readily share their thoughts on everything from the quality of instruction and how two-year schools differ from four-year colleges and universities, to the contrasting student populations and even the qualifications of faculty and administrators. Let's face it: it is hard to argue that there is no longer a lingering stigma attached to teaching, well, almost *any* subject, at a community college. Even seasoned educators are sometimes not immune to this nor do they always have the correct information themselves! It *is* everyone's universe and, unsurprisingly, we all have opinions. Whatever those current opinions are, the data are robust, and there is plenty of evidence to illuminate the true picture. While I have taught both physics and astronomy at larger four-year institutions, I have been at a community college teaching primarily astronomy and the occasional physics or physical science class since 2004. For this chapter, I also asked colleagues at other community colleges about what they thought should be included here. Their insights, whether on hiring practices or teaching the universe to everyone, are simultaneously predictable and revealing. So, let us go straight to the sources, take stock of the situation, and have a look through the lenses of some accomplished practitioners.

11.2 Why It Matters: Get to Know the Players

For those in pursuit of higher education, American community colleges have long been viewed as a "last resort" or even the "land of infinite second chances." And the negative connotations often refer to both students *and* faculty. But why? The very nature and design of the junior college system was, originally, to (1) provide lower-division general education (to everyone), regardless of whether one might want to transfer to a four-year institution for more specialized study, and (2) offer technical and vocational training (to everyone) to support our nation's changing workforce demands (Waggoner et al. 2002). For years, the federal government vigorously championed the public two-year institutions, advocating for the diversification and expansion of these educational opportunities for all Americans. Today, the combined system of community colleges in the United States has evolved into a massive establishment that is now home to the most accessible and arguably most teaching-focused arrangement of postsecondary educational institutions in the nation. Indeed, an ever-increasing fraction of all college-bound students are choosing to take courses at community colleges before transferring to four-year institutions, all while the negative stereotype inexplicably continues to propagate. Their reasons are myriad and not centered simply on lower costs or the misplaced notion that classes at two-year schools are not as rigorous. Rather, these students are deliberately choosing to enjoy smaller class sizes and more personal attention, a stronger sense of community, more tight-knit student support infrastructures, greater availability of general education courses, more flexible schedules, and even geographic convenience.

11.2.1 Enrollments

11.2.1.1 The Bigger Picture

Estimates vary, but it is safe to say that between one-third and one-half of all undergraduates in the U.S. spend at least part of their freshman year enrolled in a community college (Smith et al. 2004; McFarland et al. 2017). The U.S. Department of Education's National Center for Educational Statistics[1] (NCES) projects enrollments in two-year institutions to grow 21% between 2015 and 2026, from 6.5 million to 7.8 million, while those of the four-year institutions increase by only 9% to 11.7 million (McFarland et al. 2017). If that doesn't already have your attention, look at the numbers specific to astronomy.

11.2.1.2 Astronomy

Tucker (1996) speculated that the majority of all college students taking introductory astronomy in the U.S. probably do so at two-year institutions. In the early 2000s, estimates put the number of students taking introductory astronomy in the U.S. at approximately 250,000 each year, with 40%–50% of them doing so at community and other small colleges without astronomy or physics degree programs at the bachelor's level or higher (Fraknoi 2001, 2004). Though there is evidence that slightly more students are now taking introductory astronomy, the fraction that does so in a community college likely remains between one-third and one-half.

The American Institute of Physics[2] (AIP) publishes statistics[3] on introductory astronomy enrollments at institutions granting at least bachelor's degrees. During the 2015–2016 academic year, there were 750 physics departments (Nicholson & Mulvey 2017b) and 81 astronomy departments (Nicholson & Mulvey 2017a), 39 of which are completely separate from their physics counterparts while the other 42 are combined physics and astronomy departments. Departments reported "First Term Introductory Course Enrollments" where they were instructed to include only students taking their first term of a standalone entry-level course (i.e., not a continuation of a sequence).

---

[1] https://nces.ed.gov/.
[2] http://www.aip.org/.
[3] http://www.aip.org/statistics.

Table 11.1. Introductory Astronomy Enrollments for 2015–2016 in Four-year Astronomy (Nicholson & Mulvey 2017b) and Physics (Nicholson & Mulvey 2017a) Degree-granting Institutions Compiled from AIP Statistics

Astronomy and combined departments:	54,056
Physics departments[a]:	143,020
Total:	197,076

[a] While these enrollments include both introductory astronomy and physical science courses, they do not include conceptual physics courses, as introductory physics enrollments are tallied separately in the physics report.

Those in the 750 physics departments included both astronomy and physical science courses because they typically have a significant astronomy component. Table 11.1 shows that year's introductory astronomy enrollments.

The 81 astronomy departments surveyed by AIP are located at institutions also represented in the list of 750 physics departments surveyed. This means that the nearly 200,000 students in the AIP group represent about 25% of the 3011 four-year colleges and universities counted in 2014–2015 by NCES (the latest data available at the time of this writing; Snyder et al. 2018). We do not currently have information on introductory astronomy enrollments in the other 75% of four-year institutions (those without astronomy or physics departments).

Using data from 2011, AIP estimates that 71% of the two-year institutions offering physics courses also offered astronomy courses, resulting in approximately 51,000 students taking introductory astronomy at those institutions (White & Chu 2013b). Because, as AIP points out, this is nearly equivalent to the 52,000 introductory astronomy enrollments in astronomy degree-granting (four-year) institutions in 2010, it is logical to assume a similar parallel for the 2015–2016 data. This adds another 54,000 or so students taking introductory astronomy at the 1616 community colleges and other two-year institutions counted in the NCES data (Snyder et al. 2018). Note, however, that this figure does not include enrollments in two-year institutions that offer astronomy but not physics. Therefore, Fraknoi's (2001, 2004) estimates of 100,000 to 125,000 students per year taking introductory astronomy in two-year schools—which are largely derived from self-reported data from those teaching introductory astronomy at community and other two-year colleges—are likely still reasonable.

Thus, there are *at least* 300,000 students taking introductory astronomy annually in the United States. This is an astounding 10% of incoming freshmen every year (Snyder et al. 2018) and, as near as we can tell, 33%–42% of them are taking that introductory astronomy course (hereafter referred to as Astro 101) at a community college.

11.2.2 Who Takes Astro 101?

Everybody. Seriously. Arguments about how the Astro 101 populations in the two- and four-year institutions are demographically different in significant ways simply do not hold up. Granted, there are some practical considerations that are more prevalent in the populations of two-year schools (addressed later), but those do not impact the general demographics describing who takes Astro 101.

11.2.2.1 The General Education Population: Nonscience Majors
The U.S. turns out less than 500 astronomy majors each year (Nicholson & Mulvey 2017a), so it is pretty obvious that students taking Astro 101 are not astronomy majors. Years ago, it was not a stretch to assume that the overwhelming majority were probably not even science majors. But now, we do not have to assume; we can show that this is definitely the case. Two-thirds or more of students taking Astro 101 report a major or area of interest in a non-STEM field (Deming & Hufnagel 2001; Rudolph et al. 2010). Science majors notwithstanding, these students are the future: they will become journalists, healthcare workers, CEOs, tradespeople, politicians, law enforcement officers, humanitarians, attorneys, parents, and fellow citizens. That introductory astronomy course could be the only college-level science course many of these folks will ever take (Partridge & Greenstein 2003). And—wait for it—they're also the next generation of K–12 teachers!

As many as 40% of those taking any college-level introductory science course indicate that they plan to become licensed teachers (Lawrenz et al. 2005), and in the study by Rudolph et al. (2010), 25% of introductory astronomy students self-identified as education majors. Given the numbers, this represents an almost unprecedented opportunity to help shape our nation's scientific literacy and attitudes about science and its roles in society for literally generations to come (Fraknoi 2001; Prather et al. 2009a; Rudolph et al. 2010). In the words of Rudolph et al. (2010), "we can think of our Astro 101 courses as...professional development courses for future teachers." Indeed, it is perhaps their first professional development experience!

If ever there was an argument for elevating a general education science course to top-tier status with the best-trained faculty and enormous resources, this might well be it. Our experiences with these 300,000 people in the introductory astronomy classroom could be their last formal encounter with science in their entire lives—no matter where you teach it! No pressure, right? Our potential for making lasting positive impacts on the voting public, both now and for the foreseeable future is, frankly, staggering.

11.2.2.2 Student Demographics
One of the most wonderful things about teaching introductory astronomy anywhere is recognizing that your class is truly a representative cross section of humans in America (Deming & Hufnagel 2001; Rudolph et al. 2010). They are of every race and ethnicity, and span the range of socioeconomic classes and academic abilities. Just over 80% come to us through the American public K–12 education system and about one-third have a parent whose education went beyond high school. Roughly 90% have never taken astronomy before, and slightly more women than men take Astro 101. Rudolph et al. (2010) asked 15 different demographic questions of nearly 2000 students enrolled in 69 sections of Astro 101 spread across 31 U.S. institutions. The work of Deming & Hufnagel (2001) derives from 3800 students responding to 12 student background questions in 66 different Astro 101 classes nationwide. Both

included all kinds of educational institutions, illustrating that Astro 101 everywhere is a genuine melting pot in terms of almost every demographic you can think of.

11.2.2.3 Are They Ready for College?
Apparently not. According to ACT (2017), only 37% of 2017's high school graduates meet the college performance benchmark in science, and only 41% do so in math. At the time of this writing, the U.S. Department of Education (2015) reports even more dismal statistics: only 22% and 25% of 12th graders place "at or above 'Proficient'" in science and math, respectively. Perhaps somewhat surprisingly, it is students' preparation in high school *mathematics*—not science (!)—courses that correlates more strongly with success in college science courses (Sadler & Tai 2007). A science course taken in high school will almost always positively impact a college-level science course in that same discipline, but generally speaking, more high school science does not translate to better performance in college-level science across the board. It is the mathematics preparation that matters most. In fact, the more math courses taken and the more advanced those courses are, the higher the rates of overall college persistence and completion (AACC 2016).

ACT (2017) also reports that only 47% of 2017's high school diplomates read at a college level, while not even two-thirds (only 61%) meet the college performance benchmark in English. According to the U.S. Department of Education (2015), only 37% of 12th graders are "at or above 'Proficient'" in reading and only 27% in writing. Complete College America (2016) indicates that of the students enrolling in two-year colleges for the first time, 34% must take remedial courses in English and 52% must do so in math. Combined with the 12% and 24%, respectively, that require remediation in four-year schools, that is an incredible number of students who are not ready for and cannot take college-level English or mathematics courses despite being able to enroll in college. Yet they *can* enroll in your Astro 101 course! Because they are introductory general education courses, virtually none of the introductory astronomy courses at any institution have prerequisites. Remember, too, that most two-year institutions are "open enrollment" institutions, meaning there are no academic entrance requirements. In fact, some students enrolled at community colleges have neither high school diplomas nor GEDs but can still enroll in Astro 101. While this may sound like a horrific rabbit hole to some, there is actually a strangely bright light at the end of this particular tunnel.

Perhaps one of the most surprising—and encouraging—revelations came when Prather et al. (2009b) showed that all of these students, regardless of the institution type, class size, or their backgrounds, are capable of achieving similar learning gains in Astro 101 (note this is part of the same study as the Rudolph et al. 2010 data). For what feels like eons, instructors have argued to the proverbial death—using little to no evidence—that this was not possible, that the four-year institutions have a distinct advantage because their students are "filtered" through academic entrance requirements. Admittedly, it sounded like a plausible contention. The idea that one could actually conduct legitimate education research using his or her own students and that this could provide the data to either refute or support those claims initially flew completely under the radar. But savvy instructors at all kinds of institutions watched, learned, experimented, recorded, tweaked, and reported bits and pieces of what did and did not work in their classrooms over the years as learner-centered teaching strategies (see Chapter 1 of this volume) became more and more prevalent. Discipline-based education research (DBER) gradually gained traction before quickly becoming all the rage. The notion that education research could—and *should*—inform what we do and how we do it in our classrooms, just as our discipline content research informs our science, finally began to take root. Physics education research (PER) led the way for most of us, with astronomy education research (AER) soon to follow, finally garnering some game-changing attention somewhere in the last 10 to 15 years. (See other chapters in this volume, particularly Chapters 1, 3, and 10.)

And now we have the evidence. They may not all be ready for college-level work, but interactive learning methods are capable of helping all students, regardless of academic preparedness or demographics. In fact, Freeman et al. (2014) meta-analyzed over 200 studies of various active-learning strategies used in a variety of undergraduate STEM courses and concluded that the techniques appear generally effective across all STEM disciplines and for all class sizes. Many instructors in the Fraknoi (2004) data even indicated that they developed a strong sense of pride when "students of diverse backgrounds and abilities were able to succeed in their astronomy class." So never fear: a thoughtfully designed and well-implemented learner-centered Astro 101 course (see relevant chapters in this volume, e.g., Chapters 1 and 2) has the potential to bring everyone closer together, both in terms of social constructs and academic performance (Prather et al. 2009b; Rudolph et al. 2010).

11.2.3 Special Considerations

Along with these interesting and refreshingly diverse perspectives comes a set of special considerations that, while certainly not absent from the four-year institutions' populations, are a way of life for the students taking courses at two-year institutions. While all institutions suffer with a contingent of enrollees consistently unprepared for class meetings, those with teaching experience in community colleges know that for their students, these practical considerations, rather than laziness, are most often the culprits. How much do you hold their hands? How much do you hold them responsible for? Is it really our responsibility to "meet them in the middle" as so many administrators keep preaching? An instructor's empathy and sense of compassion wage never-ending battles with the need for structure, rules, and deadlines. So, the culture of the two-year school morphs to adapt. You can read about it, hear about it, and even witness it yourself when you visit another instructor's class. But until you have been in front of those students yourself and interacted with them class after class as their instructor, you do not really know that audience. Until you have experienced it firsthand and dealt with their specific kinds of issues, you don't truly understand it (C. Hirano 2018, personal communication).

11.2.3.1 Time (Not) Spent on Campus
While three-quarters of students at four-year institutions are enrolled full-time, only about one-third of community college students attend full-time (AACC 2018;

Snyder et al. 2018). An estimated 28% of two-year institutions are residential campuses (AACC 2018), but most of us teaching Astro 101 at "traditional" community colleges are not doing so at a residential institution. Numerous community college faculty (myself included) anecdotally cite the combination of an overwhelmingly part-time student population with a nonresidential campus as the primary reason that few students avail themselves of the numerous support systems in place, from individual instructors' office hours and help sessions to the typically robust tutoring, testing, counseling, and other support services offered. These students simply do not spend any more time on campus than they have to, and it is almost certainly a function of the other demands for their time. It is not that they *refuse* to devote more time to their studies; they usually feel they have no choice and are forced to sacrifice school and study time to meet life's other demands.

11.2.3.2 Life, Family, and Culture
A big part of every college student's life is trying to figure out a reasonable school–work–life balance. But the average age of community college students is 28 (AACC 2018), so it is a safe bet that more of these students are already dealing with the responsibilities of raising families of their own. Most of them are holding down either full-time jobs or multiple part-time jobs, and nearly one-fifth of community college students are single parents (AACC 2018). The various forms of "life happens," e.g., childcare snafus, car troubles, sick kids, getting called in to work unexpectedly, etc., are a never-ending struggle among this population. The older "nontraditional" students, who may be working on second careers or coming back for the degree they never finished as a twenty-something, are not immune either, as they are often juggling life's hang-ups while caring for aging parents and helping support their own college-age children.

Do not forget, too, that compared to most four-year institutions, community colleges often have larger fractions of students who are first-generation college students, those for whom English is not their first language, veterans reintegrating into civilian life, and previously incarcerated individuals striving for a fresh start. There are also more two-year schools located in regions with much narrower and very specific demographics, such as tribal colleges or campuses in areas experiencing critical economical distress where most residents are below the local poverty level.

All of these students bring different cultural norms and sets of circumstances with them to school each day. Figuring out how to embrace it all and turn the challenges into strengths and opportunities is one of the hallmarks of teaching both Astro 101 and teaching at a community college.

11.2.3.3 No Filter, No Problem. Wait! Problem…
Students at four-year institutions are "filtered," having jumped through a tedious series of admissions hoops that includes minimum academic achievement standards. In short, they know how to be students. That said, their study habits are not necessarily any better than those of the "unfiltered masses" at the community colleges. Rereading, highlighting or underlining, and "taking notes" (read: "copying") are still the default study tactics despite years of research indicating these

methods are largely ineffective (Roediger 2013). We must guide all of our students, regardless of academic ability or preparedness level, through the kinds of activities that are shown to actually facilitate real learning (see other chapters in this volume).

The fact that many community college students generally do not know how to be students, turns out, is a pretty big deal. The Filtered Ones have amassed and refined a set of skills that many students in the two-year schools have not. They know what it means to set a schedule, organize tasks, acknowledge deadlines, manage their time, and seek out help with respect to their studies—and this is very different from employing those same tasks in other aspects of life. Whether they are good at it or not is an entirely different proposition. The point is they are at least aware that these skills are essential to their academic success. Most students in community colleges either do not yet have this skill set or have not practiced most of it in recent history, so it is long forgotten. Again, they can sometimes manage other aspects of their lives well enough with the analogous skills. But add academic studies into the mix, and things can go sideways pretty quickly.

We end up helping them learn the intricacies of postsecondary education, navigate the bureaucracies that we and our administrations put in place, and reteaching those same life skills as they apply to education, so much so that these curiously named "high-impact practices" now form the basis for many courses, orientations, and entire engagement programs developed and implemented in many community colleges across the nation (CCSE 2013). Now we just have to make these programs and courses integrated, required components of the community college experience. To a college student, "optional" translates to "not gonna happen," so in order to make a difference, engaging community college students must be a deliberate and focused effort. While much of this is out of the hands of most astronomy instructors (such as first-year experience and orientation programs), others such as tutoring, learning communities, supplemental instruction, experiential learning, and early intervention (see other chapters in this volume) can be effectively integrated into our introductory astronomy curriculum.

11.2.4 Who Teaches Astro 101?

11.2.4.1 Not Astronomers!
No kidding. According to Fraknoi (2004), only 23% of introductory astronomy instructors in community colleges have degrees in astronomy and including four-year schools barely raises that figure to 25%. Fraknoi (2004) and Tucker (1996) show that most introductory astronomy instructors have their degrees in physics (you might be one!). But before you hand-wave that away as perfectly acceptable, consider it from this perspective. The enrollment data at the beginning of this chapter show that 48% of students taking Astro 101 do so in a pure physics department and another 40%–50% take the course in a department that does not offer a degree in either physics or astronomy. This means that 88%–98% of these students are taking introductory astronomy with instructors who, themselves, very likely have little to no formal training in astronomy. If your own degree is in physics, ask yourself this, "How much

astronomy-specific content did I get while fulfilling my physics degree requirements?" If you have ever been one of these instructors—you have taught introductory astronomy with only a cursory prior exposure to it—how would you answer this next question (be honest!): "Knowing what you now do, would you say you were truly qualified to teach astronomy?" Answers ranging from a rather unconvincing "sure" and an uneasy "not really" to a resounding "definitely not!" are common from instructors in the professional development workshops I've cofacilitated.[4] Having a degree in physics myself, I can say that my answer to the first question would have been "virtually none" had I not enrolled in an "unnecessary" Astro 101 course simply to maintain full-time enrollment status one term. A subsequent degree in astronomy made all the difference for me personally but had it instead been in physics, I am sure my answer to the second question would have been "definitely not!"

To be clear, no one is questioning whether a physicist is *capable* of teaching astronomy. There is little doubt one most certainly is, obviously having more than adequate academic preparation in the necessary physics. The question is whether those without any experience in the astronomy content should be doing so, given the enormous implications of the introductory astronomy survey course (see *The General Education Population: Nonscience Majors*, Section 11.2.2.1). The state of California thinks so. So does the American Association of Physics Teachers[5] (AAPT)—even while many of those very instructors see it differently.

Those who have taught introductory astronomy know that it is much more than the basic phenomena of Newton's laws, gravity, light, and optics we all learned in "pure" physics courses. But the state of California considers physics and astronomy to be essentially the same thing, a single "discipline" or "area." The discipline is even labeled "Physics/Astronomy," and in order to teach either subject at a community college in California, one must meet the following minimum qualifications: "Master's in physics, astronomy or astrophysics OR Bachelor's in physics or astronomy AND Master's in engineering, mathematics, meteorology or geophysics OR the equivalent" (Woodyard & Levy 2019). The "equivalent" loophole gives individual colleges and districts some leeway in determining what is appropriate for their courses because it allows for things like professional experience commensurate with an earned degree or degree titles that do not *exactly* match (not kidding here) any of those in the list. For example, unless the school or district has local governance policies in place that allow variations in degree titles, an applicant with a bachelor's in astronomy and master's in "engineering physics" does not meet the minimum qualifications and therefore must go through the equivalency process. Typically, an interdisciplinary faculty committee considers equivalency applicants very carefully, examining their academic preparation and professional experience closely before making a recommendation that is passed up the administrative chain,

---

[4] One of the more snarky (and terrifying) analogies sounds something like this. "Oh, by the way, your helicopter pilot has no real training in rotor-wing aircraft. No, no, it's okay. Really. She's more than qualified to fly *fixed*-wing aircraft. You know, *airplanes*? And that's enough. There's no need for special training just because it's a different type of aircraft with a different set of control surfaces."

[5] http://aapt.org/.

subject to further scrutiny and recommendations. Some other states have similar such minimum qualifications or variations on them, making it easy to recognize a qualifying combination of degrees that could exclude astronomy-specific content entirely. A few such examples are specifically called out in the Fraknoi (2004) survey comments, highlighting both this issue and that of a general sense of isolation (discussed in later sections):

> "One instructor with a master's degree in math wrote, 'I actually taught two semesters of astronomy without ever taking an astronomy course myself!' (Whether this is a good or bad thing for the world is left as an exercise to the reader)."
>
> "I wish I had someone to ask questions of. I am a physicist, not an astronomer."
>
> "I am always in need of advice...since I have a PhD in psychology and not the physical sciences."

In the early 2000s, this quandary surfaced enough times both in inquiries from administrators and in the accreditation proceedings of two-year colleges across the nation that the Executive Officer of the AAPT at the time issued a statement (Khoury 2004) citing two main lines of evidence to support their position. Specifically, (1) "The introductory astronomy course is a 'science literacy' course, designed to present a broad background in the subject typically to non-science-oriented students and not for future astronomy 'majors,'" and (2) the basics are "all topics included in a physics teacher's background" because of the "strong overlap ... in the curriculum and skills required in the two areas" and as evidenced by the number of universities with unified departments of physics and astronomy. Some time later, the AAPT Executive Board endorsed and posted a subsequent statement[6] supporting an "emphatic 'Yes'" in response to the question, "Does a degree in physics qualify a person to teach introductory astronomy at the collegiate level?" The Board's position rests on three tenets: "the nature of the curriculum in the two fields of physics and astronomy...on common practice regarding how introductory astronomy is offered across the United States; and...on the role of the introductory astronomy class in the college curriculum." Though this statement largely reconstitutes the article written by the former Executive Officer, the Board does go a bit beyond these superficial arguments by pointedly calling out practical experience (such as working in a planetarium, participating in research, and attending workshops offered by professional societies) as a "sufficient" qualifier. It also includes the AAPT Space Science Committee's recommendation to evaluate potential candidates by examining both one's broad course preparation and relevant work experience.

While all this sounds well and good, the evidence clearly shows that the argument for Astro 101 being an introductory course that serves "non-science-oriented students"

---

[6] AAPT Board of Directors, n.d., AAPT Board Endorsed Position Supporting Physics Teachers as Instructors in Astronomy Courses (College Park, MD: American Association of Physics Teachers), https://www.aapt.org/Resources/policy/Supporting-Physics-Teachers-as-Instructorsin-Astronomy-Courses.cfm.

(see *The General Education Population: Nonscience Majors*, Section 11.2.2.1) supports the position in diametric opposition to the one claimed by AAPT. Indeed, a case could be made that the data argue even more strongly for astronomy instructors to be trained not only in the astronomy-specific content, but also in pedagogy and particularly communicating science to nonscientists! Additionally, the argument about significant overlap in curriculum appears to be, at best, a highly variable function of an institution's program or course design, and at worst, simply false.

Curiously, the AAS seemingly has no official position on the matter. However, in a 2016 report authored by the AAS Education Task Force,[7] the dilemma is specifically called out: "The AAS needs to be mindful of the fact that most Astro 101 instructors are not research scientists in astronomy and may lack the ability to teach—or at least be uncomfortable with teaching—some Astro 101 topics" (Brickhouse et al. 2016).

11.2.4.2 It Matters!
It *does* matter who teaches introductory astronomy. The CCSE (2014) reports that roughly 58% of all courses at community colleges are taught by part-time faculty. Though there are notable exceptions, most part-time faculty have few ties to a given institution and can be less invested in the undertaking. (There is some evidence to suggest this may be more the fault of the institutions themselves rather than the instructors; more on this later.) The connection between Astro 101 and whatever comes next for these students is important—and hinges critically on the experience with that instructor, a point that the Chronicle of Higher Education[8] very recently saw fit to call out (Supiano 2018). Regardless of whether the instructor is full-time or part-time, if the students have a bad experience, it can initiate a butterfly effect. Most notably, (1) community college students taking remedial courses from part-time faculty are less likely to persist to the next course, (2) students taking introductory STEM courses from non-tenure-track faculty in four-year schools are 1.5% more likely to switch to a non-STEM field, and (3) the greater the percentage of non-tenure-track faculty teaching at four-year schools, the less likely students are to graduate (Supiano 2018). Remember how many students take Astro 101? Remember how that course could be their last experience ever with formal science? Remember who they are and what they represent? (See *The General Education Population: Nonscience Majors*, Section 11.2.2.1.) And while it is true that we have few STEM majors in our Astro 101 classes, the power of such a course to draw bright, undecided students into such fields is not at all negligible.

11.2.4.3 Preparation and Training
The Physics versus Astronomy Heavyweight Championship aside, most instructors are generally well educated, with 94% of community college instructors having advanced degrees (Fraknoi 2004): 31% have doctorates and 63% have master's degrees. The 93% of four-year college instructors with advanced degrees includes

---
[7] https://aas.org/education/aas-education-task-force.
[8] https://www.chronicle.com/.

76% doctorates and 17% master's degrees. All this education, and yet a large fraction of STEM graduate students receive no formal training whatsoever in pedagogy or virtually any aspect of teaching or mentoring before stepping into a classroom—which most of us will do at least once during our careers, whether we want to or not. Nearly all AAS members who responded to the Brickhouse et al. (2016) Education Task Force's survey (93%) indicated that they teach or have taught at least one class of some kind and almost three-quarters of respondents teach Astro 101. Approximately one-third of respondents said they received no training whatsoever with regard to teaching and almost 70% indicated no training in mentorship of any kind.

So, what is the aspiring astronomy instructor to do? Professional societies such as the AAS and Astronomical Society of the Pacific[9] (ASP) regularly offer opportunities to learn about both mentoring and teaching practices, often with reduced registration fees for community college and other local educators. The AAPT is exclusively focused on teaching, and the Center for Astronomy Education[10] (CAE) is dedicated specifically to improving the teaching and learning of introductory astronomy, Earth, and space sciences. (More on professional development later.)

11.3 You Matter: The Job of Community College Faculty (in Astronomy)

11.3.1 Environment, Workload, and Resources

In two-year schools (and even many smaller liberal arts and teaching-focused four-year institutions), astronomy is usually one of many disciplines in a multidiscipline department. The most common unit is a variation of a physical sciences department that includes disciplines such as physics, geology, Earth science, oceanography, and physical science. It is not unusual for chemistry to be included, and even things like geography and meteorology are surprisingly common. A full-time astronomy instructor is almost certainly the only astronomer in the department and, more often than one would think, also the only physicist. In fact, it is often the other way around: teaching physics comes first with the astronomy following later, sometimes by choice but sometimes because one was asked to take it on. In some cases, one is hired specifically as a full-time astronomy instructor but either way, it is typical for the faculty member to teach more than just astronomy. Physics and physical science are probably the most common.

The AIP has only recently added astronomy teaching to their survey of physics faculty in two-year colleges so longitudinal comparisons are not yet possible. It is also not possible to disentangle the astronomy data from the physics data, but it is still painfully clear that astronomers and physicists at these institutions are relatively isolated. Sixty percent of surveyed departments had either no or only a single full-time faculty member teaching astronomy and/or physics (White & Chu 2013a), and those lone full-timers are also the folks most likely to be teaching courses in additional disciplines. It is also now clear that a substantial number of those

---
[9] http://astrosociety.org/.
[10] https://astronomy101.jpl.nasa.gov/.

teaching astronomy at two-year colleges are part-time faculty. The part-timers, however, are much more likely to teach only astronomy and physics classes, with only about 20% of them teaching other subjects (White & Chu 2013a).

Full-time instructors can face several challenges that stem from being the lone discipline expert in a multidiscipline department. Duties that are normally within the purview of a department chair often fall to that lone faculty member if the chair lacks the necessary discipline-specific expertise. It is of course reasonable to expect discipline faculty, as part of their regular responsibilities, to handle occasional issues and advocate for their particular programs and students as necessary. But if all of the administrative business for that discipline eventually ends up on the plate of the lone discipline expert who is not the department chair, this is no longer a nonnegligible component of one's workload. Occasionally, the faculty member may receive some compensation in recognition of these additional duties, perhaps along the lines of a "lead instructor" or other similar designation, but most often they do not. When there is not a large number of astronomy classes or students, this may not warrant too much concern. If, on the other hand, the program is larger, has more than a few classes, many students, and several part-time faculty to supervise, the "workload creep" can be substantial.

In contrast to most four-year institutions, many community colleges have little or no instructional support, e.g., lab prep assistants or equipment managers. Though there are exceptions, a lone full-time instructor in the discipline is often responsible for everything, from purchasing equipment and supplies to maintaining that equipment and any associated facilities (e.g., computer lab, observing site, etc.). While it is no longer uncommon to have access to a computer lab, a community college with an actual observatory or planetarium is still an exception. Usually, there are binoculars and/or portable telescopes that must be lugged back and forth between their storage area and a makeshift observing site. More advanced equipment is not all that common and is normally seen only at larger institutions with the even rarer advanced classes and corresponding budgets.

Unless you teach at one of those large institutions with the rare complementary budget, money will be tight. Data from Fraknoi (2004) show the average annual budget for astronomy programs (not including physics) in community colleges to be around $940 and including all of the surveyed institutions raises this figure to only $1127. My own program's budget is right in line with these figures, and colleagues elsewhere report similarly. Keep in mind that this amount is usually meant to encompass everything needed to keep the program running, from replacing equipment to photocopying costs for all classes.

There is little to no money for conference travel, and professional development is frequently limited to in-house workshops and seminars on more universal content like diversity and equity issues, institutional procedures, statewide initiatives, and high-impact practices. Professional development for those teaching astronomy is very specialized, so local opportunities are generally rare. Though professional societies sometimes offer grants or reduced fees to community college instructors, a significant travel distance is almost always involved so it is frequently cost-prohibitive. Note, too, that if you are the only astronomer, finding qualified employees that meet the legal requirements to substitute in the classes you will have to miss is often a sticky subject with department chairs, deans, and other administrators. On a more positive note, more and more external resources have been devoted over the past decade or so to building a robust community of astronomy education professionals, resources, and opportunities, so it is gradually becoming easier to transcend isolation and budget limitations (Waller & Slater 2011).

There are virtually no resources or support for personal research and, frankly, no time to do it anyway. This is okay as almost no two-year institutions have an expectation that you maintain a research program—or ever publish again, for that matter. In practice, the labors of love do still occur. Motivated instructors will maintain ties with collaborators elsewhere and sometimes find the time to squeeze in projects that matter to them.

A full-time faculty member at a two-year institution teaches, on average, the equivalent of five three-credit courses per semester, *every* semester. Of course, exact loads vary across institutions but so do the courses and their credit values. For many though, a full-time teaching load is the equivalent of 15 credits where each one credit is a "package" of one 50-minute classroom hour and one hour of prep work and grading per week. Thus, a full load means 30 hours of instructional time each week: 15 contact hours in class and 15 hours outside of class. Using a 40 hour work week model (I know, don't laugh—more on that later), the remaining 10 hours includes additional student contact time and institutional service duties. At my institution, the expected breakdown is five "student hours" and five hours of "collegial governance" duties. Those five weekly student contact hours must include at least two hours of regularly scheduled drop-in office hours, while the rest of the time is spent on things like responding to students' emails and phone calls, taking additional student meetings, and advising. The remaining five "governance" hours are consumed by various committee meetings (departmental, institutional, and/or district), the work for those committees, and any other duties in service of the institution.

Community colleges in particular are big on the concept of "collegial governance," though that has become somewhat of a buzz phrase in recent years, coming to mean many different things to many different people at many different institutions (go ahead—I dare you to Google it…). Generally speaking, this refers to the practice in which all constituencies participate in a policy of shared governance, each contributing regularly and meaningfully to the functioning and oversight of both the big things (like institution-wide policies and procedures) and the smaller day-to-day operations (like how your department handles prerequisite challenges). As one might expect, the implementations of such a model vary extensively across the nation but as a rule, all full-time faculty at pretty much any institution are expected to participate at some level, and it is even written into the job description. Part-time faculty typically have no such obligation to participate but more and more schools and districts are beginning to offer such opportunities, some with accompanying pay, in order to help foster a sense of community and encourage part-timers to become more involved and invested in their institution.

Most of us are all too aware that the 40 hour work week is basically a unicorn—fantastically elusive and ultimately, a mythical creature. For community college instructors, the killer is almost always the time spent grading. If you end up doing all or even most of the discipline's administrative and support duties, it's even worse. There are, of course, no graduate students, so no teaching assistants, and the nature of the two-year school means that any suitable undergraduates you might try to recruit and train are not likely to stick around long enough for it to be worth the effort. Even if they did, how will you pay them? (You read about your budget a few paragraphs ago, right?) So grading? Yeah, that is probably all you, no matter how many students you have. The trade-off is that you can get to know your students much better and tailor your instruction to address issues you would otherwise miss if you had a grader. That said, it is almost always the bulk of your workload. But there actually may be a couple of possibilities for enlisting the help of qualified undergraduates. Just don't count on mining the astronomy club—there probably isn't one.[11] Nevertheless, if you are willing to put forth the time and effort, there may be some reasonable prospects.

If a student receives federal or state financial aid, he or she might be eligible for work-study funds. If the school does any type of astronomy outreach (like star parties), there is often an argument to be made for hiring a student worker. If there are not enough outreach hours to justify the position, see if combining it with a few hours of teaching assistant duties might work. It does not have to be all about grading either; you might be able to get a lab or observing assistant out of it. Education majors might be interested because they want to be teachers. Psychology and other social science majors might just be interested in observing other humans' behaviors and interactions. STEM majors might prefer grading astronomy homework or being your lab assistant to answering phones or being a receptionist in a front office elsewhere on campus. Others might simply be so proud of their own success in your course that your acknowledgment of it and offer to work as a teaching assistant becomes a life-changing point of encouragement for them. You probably need to go through your school's career center or student employment office for more information on those possibilities. Reach out to the staff in that office. Even if their office cannot help, they might be able to brainstorm other potential solutions. If none of that presents a feasible option, look for more creative workarounds.

Practically all two-year schools have some type of formal course that students can enroll in to earn college credit for internships and/or discipline-related work experience. This can take many forms and is certainly not limited to students wanting to "do astronomy" as a career (see the examples in the previous paragraph). The only real hiccups with this plan are likely to be those caused by the fact that the student has to enroll in and pay for an additional credit course. Depending on the individual student's situation, there may be problems with credit limitations or number of work hours allowed and even financial aid ramifications. Talk with the

---

[11] Only 20% of all respondents in the Fraknoi (2004) study reported having an amateur astronomy group of some kind at their institution. What fraction are in just the two-year schools is unknown, but it must be exceedingly small because the number of available students and the transient nature of the population cause high turnover rates, making it difficult for such a group to persist.

student and if necessary, get appropriate career, academic, and/or financial aid counselors involved in that conversation.

Another possibility might be service learning credit. If the school has a program for students to earn service learning credits, there may be a way for this to qualify. Not everyone understands just how valuable an experience like this can be on a resume or CV, and how it often goes far beyond the astronomy content or the seemingly superficial notion of assigning grades. Gather the facts, think it through, and promote it appropriately.

Whatever the case, do not be shy about advocating for the student and the work itself. Leave no stone unturned. Talk with your department chair and dean, too. Even if it doesn't pan out, you are probably no worse off than when you started—the student(s) will never forget that you tried, and you might have gleaned information that helps you formulate a better plan for making the case next time. Each individual student's situation is different, but who knows? You might end up learning what you need to develop a pilot program that could evolve into a more formal and sustainable solution.

11.3.2 Compensation and Benefits

As one might expect, two-year college instructors are generally paid less than their counterparts at four-year institutions. But like any field, there are exceptions to the rule, and they most often occur in geographic regions with high property taxes and costs of living. Many two-year institutions make use of the "industry standard" academic ranking structure for full-time instructors but a few—like my own—do not. In these cases, the pay structure is frequently based on only two factors: one's level of educational preparation (highest degree and any additional credits) and number of years of classroom teaching experience. Of course, variations exist, particularly if the institution implements an academic rank and reward structure. There are procedures in place for advancing on the salary schedule should you later earn additional credits and/or another degree. Sometimes there are fringe benefits to be had such as tuition reimbursement. But do your homework! You would not want to be denied advancement on the salary schedule because that institution has a policy stating that credits paid for by that institution cannot then be used for advancement on their own salary schedule.

It is also not uncommon for full-time faculty to take on overload teaching assignments. There are various reasons for this, not the least of which is simply to make up for a deficit in income. The pay for teaching overload classes as a salaried employee also varies considerably across institutions. Some calculate an hourly rate based on one's full-time compensation, meaning you get paid nearly the same for an overload class assignment as you do for a regular class assignment. Other institutions default to the part-time salary schedule (see below) for any overload assignments, usually meaning that pay is substantially less. And, as one might imagine, overload assignments can impact one's retirement and leave balances. They even occasionally come with additional responsibilities if that college attaches institutional service or professional development obligations to the number of teaching hours one takes on in a term.

The salary schedule for part-time faculty usually has a similar structure to that of full-timers to account for the same variables (educational preparation and teaching experience). The biggest difference is in the dollar amounts. Part-timers are often paid substantially less than their full-time counterparts (*surprise!*). While full-time positions are almost always fully benefitted positions, the benefits afforded to part-time faculty vary wildly from school to school. Some do offer full benefits packages including insurances, sick leave, paid office hours, and the like, but those are usually the exception and not the rule. Others offer nothing: you are paid an hourly wage for only the time you spend in class or perhaps a stipend per class per term based on the number of credits and that's it. Anything else is up to you.

11.3.3 Other Part-time Challenges

Like many other job markets, full-time faculty positions are greatly outnumbered by part-time ones. Part-time instructors are frequently called "adjunct" professors or instructors, though my own institutional culture maintains that term has a negative connotation in that it implies inferior worth or otherwise devalues the individual in comparison to a full-time instructor. Many part-time faculty have "regular" jobs elsewhere (industry and research positions in particular are prevalent among part-time faculty in STEM fields) and choose to teach one or more courses, often in the evenings after a full work day, because they love teaching. Countless others, however, stitch together the equivalent of a full-time position by teaching several classes spread across multiple institutions each term. In California, these folks are known as the "freeway fliers" because they spend so much time on the road traveling between schools ("freeway faculty" and "roads scholars" are popular monikers in other regions). It is not uncommon for freeway fliers to teach six or seven classes per term (a colleague of mine once taught nine classes in a single semester and still occasionally teaches as many as eight!), all while trying to keep straight the policies, procedures, and deadlines for their different institutions.

While full-time faculty at two-year institutions do have dedicated office space, they often must share it with others and in some cases the "office" is actually a cubicle. Part-timers, unfortunately, do not usually fare even that well. Sometimes the rare unattended office is available for first-come, first-served transient use; sometimes there is a designated workspace with supplies; sometimes there is nothing. If it were only about holding office hours for students, there actually would not be that big of a problem since it is now commonplace for faculty to do so in more inviting spaces, those more conducive to student interaction and collaborative learning. Designated spaces in student services areas, libraries, STEM centers, cafeterias, and other places where students typically hang out—even outdoor spaces—are becoming very popular now for holding office hours and help sessions. But that still leaves most part-timers—the majority of the teaching faculty—without any private or even semiprivate workspace. "My office is the trunk of my car" is a common (not so much a) joke among part-time faculty everywhere.

11.3.4 Rays of Hope

If any of this has left you a bit depressed, let me assure you that despite the challenges, many of us genuinely love teaching in community colleges and would not have it any other way. There are so many reasons! Here are just a few.

11.3.4.1 Autonomy + Academic Freedom

Sure, isolation can sometimes be a problem if you are a single-faculty discipline, but the upside is the number of degrees of freedom you have in virtually all other aspects of the position. The amount of red tape you can cut through is nothing short of a miracle in some cases. For example, you often control the money. How, when, and on what your spend your budget are decisions that *you* make, subject to perhaps a supervisory signature that, depending upon your supervisor's or dean's management style, can sometimes be nearly hassle free. What textbook should you use? Or should you even use one? Again, all you if you are a single-faculty discipline. And though there is not always significant time to devote to research, the lack of "publish or perish" pressure in a two-year college environment means that you are "free" to work on whatever you want, whenever you want!

Did you know you can teach almost whatever you want in an introductory general education course? Yes, you do have to pay attention to certain guidelines and make sure your course outline of record aligns with articulation and transfer agreements. Yet most do not even realize that there is a tremendous amount of academic freedom possible, even within institutional or state guidelines, and introductory astronomy might just be the most flexible course in the universe (pun intended)!

The beauty of the introductory survey course is that it is rarely, if ever, a prerequisite for anything else, except perhaps the first of a two-course introductory sequence (and even then you have two courses with $n-1$ degrees of academic freedom!). Students majoring in a particular discipline do not customarily take the introductory survey, 101-esque version of the course. Astro 101 is that course: generally a single-term "one-off" that majors or minors take only infrequently. So, this version is broad enough that there is a lot of leeway for the instructor to pick and choose what fills in the gaps between the expected larger concepts. Near the beginning of his article on "Teaching at a Community College: Some Personal Observations," Ball (2010) provides an excellent description of this realization and how it manifested in his own adjustment to teaching introductory history courses. Partridge & Greenstein (2003) beautifully describe both the context and what it means specifically for an Astro 101 course. In fact, Section 2.3 of that seminal work became the basis for what many astronomy educators now refer to as "the 'goals' document"[12] distributed by the AAS for many years.

11.3.4.2 Teaching as a Profession

You can now—and without reservation—explicitly acknowledge your commitment to becoming a teaching professional. Communities of excellence in teaching practices exist; seek them out—not only in astronomy and STEM fields in general, but also in other disciplines. There may be one or more groups on campus or even a center for teaching excellence or some other such entity. Commit to and immerse yourself in the culture of teaching as a profession. Know that your colleagues and administrators at two-year schools expect this of you, often unlike the culture at a lot of four-year institutions. You were immersed in the research culture when you were

---

[12] http://tiny.cc/Astro101goals.

in graduate school. Become immersed in the *education research* culture now as a teaching professional.

With the emphasis on DBER in recent years, many colleges are renewing their commitments to teaching excellence and throwing resources behind them. It is no longer just lip service to have a department chair, dean, and/or VP that claims to support educational innovations and new technologies. This means you could have even more freedom in the classroom to try new things and still have support, even if it does not go well the first time. Many institutions are receiving various state and federal funds to support things like additional "basic skills" initiatives, developing more multidisciplinary learning communities, and even supporting STEM resource centers. Periodic conversations with administrators, initially supportive or not, can have them putting their money where their mouths are more often than you might think.

This could also mean more money for professional development opportunities. It is probably obvious by now that lack of time is a significant hindrance to meaningful professional development. But it is also the case that many community colleges require a certain number of professional development hours of their faculty. These obligations are frequently based on the size of one's teaching load and can be met in a variety of ways. Activities ranging from the usual workshops, seminars, and conferences, to simply reading discipline journals and education blogs, and even developing new materials for your courses could satisfy the requirements. Guidelines for what does and does not count as "legitimate" professional development can vary widely among the community colleges, so make sure you connect with your college's professional development coordinator or equivalent before you devote a lot of time that you probably (definitely) do not have to activities that may or may not count. Then adopt the "multiple birds with one stone" mindset: work smarter, not harder.

11.3.4.3 Diversity + Smaller Classes
The magnificent diversity of our students combined with the smaller class sizes (Fraknoi 2004) frequently lends itself to some unbelievably amazing and bizarre (in a good way) class discussions that go virtually unmatched in most other introductory science classes. Remember, you are one of the Filtered Ones, and it is actually worse than that—*you are in a STEM field*—so interacting with this Astro 101 population is good for you. As my colleague Philip Blanco emphasized, "it's different [teaching introductory astronomy] from what you're probably used to …you probably didn't get [this] in grad school…so many different kinds of people. It's so much fun seeing how the different mindsets and personalities interact with the information!" (P. Blanco 2018, personal communication). It is not all that unusual for faculty to ruminate on the irony of having a frustrating day at work only to realize that we actually look forward to the Astro 101 classes precisely because of this invigorating potential.

11.3.5 Some Advice

11.3.5.1 Applying + Interviewing
Before applying for a full-time position at a community college, take the time to do your homework. The two-year schools certainly are not for everyone, so how could

you know? Read through these articles by Rob Jenkins, a frequent and popular author on the topic of teaching in community colleges. One gives a good summary of why you should bother to apply (Jenkins 2014), another is a version of, "community colleges might not be for you if..." (Jenkins 2015), and the latest, Jenkins (2018), discusses why you should not let "prestige bias" prevent you from applying to teach at a community college.

If you decide to take the plunge and apply, research that institution/district and make sure the culture seems inviting to you, like a place you could call home. Nearly all of the advertised positions will be ridiculously oversubscribed so do what it takes to give yourself an edge and rise above the crowd. Justin Zackal (2014) has some advice for those with little teaching experience in his article, "Becoming a Community College Professor." It is a good idea to play up any leadership positions you have previously held, particularly those with a focus on teamwork and community-building. Potential employers want to see that you can motivate folks and nurture a culture of open-mindedness and shared knowledge while still being appropriately authoritative and meeting deadlines. Help potential employers understand that your experience training and leading others has some analogs with facilitating learning in a college classroom. Partnerships and collaborations with other companies and educational institutions and especially outreach experience akin to informal education are also important components. Have you taken any courses in education, even if informal and in a more casual, online environment? Have you read up on developing a personal teaching philosophy? Do you read any newsletters, blogs, or journals on education or teaching? If so, highlight them in ways that help selection committees understand that you are serious about becoming a professional educator.

If you are fortunate enough to get an interview, know what to expect. Given what ought to be seemingly endless variations in the process, it was a little surprising to read in Green and Ciez-Volz (2010) just how similar their description of what it should include is to what actually happens at my own institution. Everyone invited for an interview probably looks like a fantastic teacher and competitive candidate on paper–that is why they got interviews. What makes *you* stand out? Are you connected to teaching communities in your field? Have you done community service or outreach? Hiring a full-time faculty member is a huge investment for that institution. They want the whole package. If you are not truly competitive at all those levels, you might lose out. And, most importantly, recognize that even if you ultimately get the position, it is because the selection committee thought "this person shows great promise," *not* "this person is an awesome finished product" (D. Loranz 2018, personal communication).

If you are interviewing for a part-time position, virtually all of this same stuff still applies. Colleges want faculty who are invested in the profession and the best interests of the students, and who are prepared to make a commitment to their institution. Even if there is less competition for the position(s), the ones for whom the profession is part of their identity will rise to the top.

11.3.5.2 Oh, You're In It Now...
Congratulations, you got the job! If it is a full-time position, remember that you may be the only astronomer. You are probably responsible for all things astronomical at

your institution, from course and program development and management to budgets; from recruiting and supervising part-time faculty to starting or maintaining an outreach program; from advocating for facilities and resources to handling inquiries from community members ("I saw this really strange light in the sky last night and it moved really weird. What was it?" or "I found this cool-looking rock in my backyard and it's got to be a meteorite! Can you verify it for me?"). Juggling all this in combination with your teaching load and institutional responsibilities can be overwhelming at times. It is important to avoid burnout, and especially if you are new at it, to avoid the "teaching trap" (Rockquemore 2015). Have a good support structure in place. Cultivating productive relationships with your colleagues in related disciplines is one way to help combat a sense of isolation. It is also good for your own professional development: visit each other's classes and schedule regular times to meet up and discuss teaching techniques, the latest research, or new learning technologies. Even the occasional discussion about campus politics, the latest administrative decisions, or just a good old-fashioned bout of commiseration is necessary to keep you grounded and sane. In some cases, it might also mean you have "backup"—others who might be willing and able to help you divide and conquer particularly burdensome duties in a pinch.

Know your craft and take it seriously. A stand-out candidate for a full-time position emphasized this importance in an interview, "I can have even more of an impact here. If you're good here, then they [the students] get even more out of it because the ones coming through the...four-year school with the crazy entrance requirements, they'll do well anyway. But here, you really have to have your teaching and learning craft down." (D. Loranz 2018, personal communication). *We spend nearly 100% of our time doing what a lot of faculty at four-year institutions try to get out of: teaching.* Immersion into this culture of teaching as a profession is not something that just happens. You must be deliberate about it. It isn't hard, but you do have to make the effort. Start small, by joining a listserv or reading a blog.

If you are a part-timer, look to the experienced ones. Seek them out at your institution(s) and have the important discussions. Consult with the full-timers, and if gatherings of all the discipline or department faculty are not a regular thing, see if you can change that. There are more opportunities to flex your teaching muscles than you may realize (Shropshire 2017). For example, simply visiting each other's classes and having post-observation discussions can lead to some amazing changes, some small and others transformational.

Whether full- or part-time, there are resources for these types of exchanges already in place at most schools. Seek them out and avail yourself of the opportunities. Seek out the astronomers at other schools in your area. Do not be afraid to reach out; they might be just as keen to connect as you but could not bring themselves to attempt first contact. Resources like CAE's[13] Yahoo group "Astrolrner"[14] or your local chapter of AAPT[5] may be able to help connect you with astronomy and physics educators in your geographic region if you have trouble searching on your own.

---

[13] https://astronomy101.jpl.nasa.gov/.
[14] https://astronomy101.jpl.nasa.gov/community/.

11.3.5.3 Student Evaluations of Teaching
I know, I know; I can practically *hear* your eyeballs rolling. As a rule, students' evaluations of instructors and their teaching methods are inherently flawed, and there are mountains of research on this (Boring et al. 2016; Kelsky 2018; Leef 2014; Stark & Freishtat 2014; and additional references at French 2017). In addition to the "expected" biases, the issue of whether the students are even qualified to judge "good" teaching is a common complaint among instructors. Candid thoughts like the following embody the frustrations of Astro 101 instructors everywhere who are just waiting for the other shoe to drop:

> Aren't these surveys really just sampling students' emotions, weighing their feelings about what they think they need against their internalized expectations of what "learning" science is? Faculty end up frustrated and can waste a lot of time and energy explaining to administrators (and even colleagues in other disciplines!) what astronomy really is and constantly justifying what they do in the classroom. Jobs and careers could be on the line here so faculty can feel real pressure to "dumb down" a course and relax expectations, sacrificing pedagogy and genuine learning just to get better student evaluations (I. Stojimirovic 2018, personal communication).

If this sounds harsh or unreasonable, consider the kinds of questions found on your last round of student surveys and the context—or lack thereof—in which they were answered. Not only is it an almost certainty that every class in every subject surveyed on that campus got *exactly* the same questions, but the students' *interpretations* of those questions is also highly problematic. Students are not trained in pedagogy, classroom management, or evidence-based teaching practices and, frankly, their study "skills" are markedly ineffective (Roediger 2013), particularly because most of them equate memorization and recall with learning. Most students have never heard of Bloom's taxonomy (Heer 2012 and references therein); have you? Let's face it: negative emotions are much more powerful motivators than positive ones, unfortunately. And if we are being honest, most humans consistently resist making objective decisions, particularly in the face of direct evidence showing their preconceived notions are either incorrect or at least strongly biased by their feelings and emotions (Kolbert 2017). Yet the power we give these decisions, feelings, and emotions, in addition to the weight these surveys carry in our tenure reviews and evaluation cycles, is, more often than not, rather disproportionate.

That does not mean that these student surveys are totally useless (you could try data mining the written comments for meaningful morsels). But it does mean you should prepare accordingly. There are things you can do to reduce bias and get meaningful feedback. For example, the Small Group Instructional Diagnosis (SGID)[15] is an evidence-based feedback mechanism conducted as focus groups that, at some institutions, can be utilized in place of—or at least in addition to—

---

[15] Anonymous n.d., Small Group Instructional Diagnosis (SGID), https://www.tacoma.uw.edu/tlt/sgid.

student surveys. My own institution's SGID implementation (MiraCosta College Tenure Review and Evaluation Committee 2019) has been very effective in helping me and my colleagues combat some of the frustration, biases, and futility of generic student surveys, and I cannot recommend the process highly enough. Invest the time and effort. Your job is basically 100% teaching now, so student evaluations and feedback will be a core component of your tenure review or evaluation cycle each time.

11.3.5.4 Discipline Nuts and Bolts
The word "astronomy" is conspicuously scarce in the *AAPT Guidelines for Two-Year College Physics Programs*[16] (Waggoner et al. 2002), mentioned only five times in 35 pages. And though a few parts are now a bit dated, it is still a recommended read for all astronomy, physics, and even physical science instructors, particularly if you are involved in activities like program reviews and advocating for resources, limits on class size, etc. If your department chair and/or dean is not a physicist or astronomer, it is definitely worth asking them to read through it as well. (The appendices include a brief history of two-year colleges in the United States and a summary of the various missions of such institutions, and so are excellent for anyone looking for quick, entry-level exposures to these topics.)

11.3.5.5 Additional Perspectives
Regarding a more general, discipline-independent perspective, there are numerous writings on what it is like to be a faculty member at a community college. One of the classic references is that of Grubb et al. (1999), though based on my own experiences and those of several colleagues over the past 10+ years, I would argue that the situation is not nearly as glum as presented there. To be fair, the perspective that budgets are growing ever tighter and many administrators are still making illogical decisions based on dollars and "butts in seats" has not changed all that much. But there has been a noticeable positive cultural shift over the past decade or so, and I suspect the proliferation of DBER during this time period, particularly in the STEM fields, is largely responsible.

Indeed, many now sing our praises while cheerleading for graduate students and advisors everywhere to not discount job prospects at community colleges (Ball 2010; Jenkins 2014, 2018). So, if you are considering it, or just wondering whether it might be for you, you may want to spend some time reading through the following articles and those cited in "Applying + Interviewing."

Scott (2015) says it like it is, diplomatically calling out the elitist attitudes that contribute to PhD holders ignoring community colleges as potential employers. Though not for everyone, he is right to argue that overlooking them may cause you to "miss out on some of the most gratifying and rewarding work in higher education." Although focused on the humanities, Arteaga (2016) gives some striking examples of why "PhDs (and Advisors) Shouldn't Overlook Community Colleges"

---

[16] http://aapt.org/Resources/tycguidelines.cfm.

while highlighting emerging partner initiatives between two- and four-year schools. Even if there is no formal partnership like any of these in place at your institution, the information in this essay could be helpful for initiating mentorships. In an older piece, Olmstead (2001) describes how teaching at a community college became the best thing that ever happened to her. And finally, a broader, more up-to-date encapsulation of how community colleges have evolved over the years and what the future might hold for us can be found in the excerpt by Gill (2016) posted on the website Tomorrow's Professor.[17]

11.4 Conclusions

Whether you teach part-time or full-time, teaching in a community college is an adventure all its own. In teaching *astronomy* at a community college, your students will be folks of all ages (from high school to post-retirement), with all levels of education and from all backgrounds, with an impressive range of experiences under their belts. You will probably help these students more than you expect to at first, and in ways you might not have anticipated. The challenges and returns are both somewhat surprising and worth it. The experiences in a community college Astro 101 course can be some of the most delightfully bizarre and refreshing of your career, and there are few places like it where you can experience so many facets of humanity simultaneously.

Whether you are completely new to teaching or transitioning from teaching at a different type of institution, come with an open mind and an appetite for professional development. Recognize that your community college colleagues expect you to take your craft very seriously and want to help you succeed in it. Expect to spend nearly all of your time working on your courses, grading, and learning about pedagogy, curriculum development, and institutional service through multiple avenues, such as serving on committees, visiting and engaging with other professors about each others' teaching, and participating in professional development opportunities. If you are coming to a community college via a more typical "academic" pathway (PhD→ postdoctorate→ position at a four-year institution), understand that you will (even if a bit unwittingly at first) trade the "publish or perish" motto for an overwhelming sense of commitment to, and desire to do right by, your students. You will join a cohort of professionals who share this mentality, revere this responsibility, and are eager to help each other—and our students—navigate this journey. It is, after all, everyone's universe.

Acknowledgments

Special thanks go to a cohort of extraordinary professionals at MiraCosta College[18] and countless colleagues everywhere who have helped this community college instructor to better understand her role and develop her craft. Contributing to this work in particular are Philip Blanco, Conrad Hirano, Daniel Loranz, Irena

---

[17] https://tomprof.stanford.edu/welcome.
[18] http://www.miracosta.edu/.

Stojimirovic, the part-time faculty of the MiraCosta College Astronomy Program,[19] and the many generous participants in CAE's[13] Southwest Regional Teaching Exchange, held annually at MiraCosta College[20] since 2010.

References

American Association of Community Colleges (AACC) 2016, Datapoints: More Math, Higher Persistence, Vol. 4 (Washington, DC: American Association of Community Colleges) https://www.aacc.nche.edu/wp-content/uploads/2017/09/DP_Jan.20.pdf

American Association of Community Colleges (AACC) 2018, Fast Facts 2018 (Washington, DC: American Association of Community Colleges) https://www.aacc.nche.edu/wp-content/uploads/2018/04/2018-Fast-Facts.pdf

American College Testing (ACT) 2017, The Condition of College & Career Readiness 2017, Annual Report (Iowa City, IA: ACT), http://www.act.org/condition2017

Arteaga, R. 2016, PhDs (and Advisers) Shouldn't Overlook Community Colleges. Inside Higher Ed, https://www.insidehighered.com/advice/2016/12/20/benefits-phds-considering-teaching-community-colleges-essay

Ball, J. H. 2010, Teaching at a Community College: Some Personal Observations, Perspectives on History 48, https://www.historians.org/publications-and-directories/perspectives-on-history/april-2010/teaching-at-a-community-college-some-personal-observations

Boring, A., Ottoboni, K., & Stark, P. B. 2016, ScienceOpen Research 2016, doi:10.14293/S2199-1006.1.SOR-EDU.AETBZC.v1

Brickhouse, N., Coble, K., Gay, P., et al. 2016, Final Report of the AAS 2016 Task Force on Education (Washington, DC: AAS), https://files.aas.org/EduTaskForce/AAS-Task-Force-on-Education-Report_encrypted.pdf

Center for Community College Student Engagement (CCSE) 2013, A Matter of Degrees: Engaging Practices, Engaging Students (High-Impact Practices for Community College Student Engagement), (Austin, TX: The University of Texas at Austin, Community College Leadership Program), http://www.ccsse.org/docs/Matter_of_Degrees_2.pdf

Center for Community College Student Engagement (CCSE) 2014, Contingent Commitments: Bringing Part-Time Faculty Into Focus (A Special Report from the Center for Community College Student Engagement) (Austin, TX: The University of Texas at Austin, Program in Higher Education Leadership), http://www.ccsse.org/docs/PTF_Special_Report.pdf

Complete College America 2016, Remedial Enrollment and Success, https://completecollege.org/data-dashboard/

Deming, G., & Hufnagel, B. 2001, PhTea, 39, 368

Fraknoi, A. 2001, AEdRv, 1, 121

Fraknoi, A. 2004, AEdRv, 3, 7

Freeman, S., Eddy, S. L., McDonough, M., et al. 2014, PNAS, 111, 8410

French, R. S. 2017, Student Evaluations of Teaching (SET), https://tiny.cc/rfrenchfacultyshareSET

Gill, S. J. 2016, Planning for Higher Education, 45, 1, https://tomprof.stanford.edu/posting/1549

Green, D. W., & Ciez-Volz, K. 2010, New Directions for Community Colleges, 2010, 81

Grubb, W. N., Worthen, H., Byrd, B., et al. 1999, Honored But Invisible: An Inside Look at Teaching in Community Colleges (New York: Routledge)

---

[19] https://tiny.cc/astromcc.
[20] https://www.miracosta.edu/.

Heer, R. 2012, A Model of Learning Objectives Based on a Taxonomy for Learning, Teaching, and Assessing: A Revision of Bloom's Taxonomy of Educational Objectives, http://www.celt.iastate.edu/wp-content/uploads/2015/09/RevisedBloomsHandout-1.pdf

Jenkins, R. 2014, Why You Should Consider Community Colleges, Chronicle of Higher Education, https://www.chronicle.com/article/Why-You-Should-Consider/143851

Jenkins, R. 2015, Community Colleges Might Not Be for You, Chronicle Vitae, https://chroniclevitae.com/news/1183-community-colleges-might-not-be-for-you

Jenkins, R. 2018, Don't Let Prestige Bias Keep You From Applying to Community Colleges, Chronicle of Higher Education, https://www.chronicle.com/article/Don-t-Let-Prestige-Bias-Keep/244745

Kelsky, K. 2018, The Semester's Ending. Time to Worry About Our Flawed Course Evaluations. Chronicle of Higher Education, https://www.chronicle.com/article/The-Semester-s-Ending-Time/243212

Khoury, B. 2004, EO Report – Summer 2004 Announcer, Vol. 34, https://www.aapt.org/aboutaapt/reports/eo-summer04.cfm

Kolbert, E. 2017, Why Facts Don't Change Our Minds, The New Yorker, https://www.newyorker.com/magazine/2017/02/27/why-facts-dont-change-our-minds

Lawrenz, F., Huffman, D., & Appeldoorn, K. 2005, Journal of College Science Teaching, 34, 40

Leef, G. 2014, Student Course Evaluations Aren't Worth Much, and There Are Better Ways, https://www.jamesgmartin.center/2014/11/student-course-evaluations-arent-worth-much-and-there-are-better-ways/

McFarland, J., Hussar, B., & de Brey, C. 2017, The Condition of Education 2017, Annual Report NCES 2017-144 (Washington, DC: U.S. Department of Education), https://nces.ed.gov/pubs2017/2017144.pdf

MiraCosta College Tenure Review and Evaluation Committee 2019, Small Group Iinstructional Diagnosis (SGID) Overview, https://www.miracosta.edu/instruction/trec/downloads/SmallGroupInstructionalDiagnosisOVERVIEW.pdf

Nicholson, S., & Mulvey, P. J. 2017a, Roster of Astronomy Departments with Enrollment and Degree Data, 2016 (College Park, MD: American Institute of Physics), http://www.aip.org/statistics/reports/roster-astronomy-2016

Nicholson, S., & Mulvey, P. J. 2017b, Roster of Physics Departments with Enrollment and Degree Data, 2016 (College Park, MD: American Institute of Physics), https://www.aip.org/statistics/reports/roster-physics-2016

Olmstead, E. 2001, It's the Community-College Life for Me, Chronicle of Higher Education, https://www.chronicle.com/article/Its-the-Community-College/45447

Partridge, B., & Greenstein, G. 2003, AEdRv, 2, 46

Prather, E. E., Rudolph, A. L., & Brissenden, G. 2009a, PhT, 62, 41

Prather, E. E., Rudolph, A. L., Brissenden, G., & Schlingman, W. M. 2009b, AmJPh, 7, 320

Rockquemore, K. A. 2015, The Teaching Trap, https://tomprof.stanford.edu/posting/1418

Roediger, H. L. III 2013, Psychological Science in the Public Interest, 14, 1

Rudolph, A. L., Prather, E. E., Brissenden, G., Consiglio, D., & Gonzaga, V. 2010, AER, 9, 010107

Sadler, P. M., & Tai, R. H. 2007, Sci, 317, 457

Scott, D. 2015, Receiving your doctorate to work at a community college?, Inside Higher Ed: gradhacker, https://www.insidehighered.com/blogs/gradhacker/receiving-your-doctorate-work%E2%80%A6-community-college

Shropshire, V. 2017, in Adjunct Faculty Voices: Cultivating Professional Development and Community at the Front Lines of Higher Education, ed. R. Fuller, et al. (Sterling, VA: Stylus Publishing), chapter 4

Smith, B. L., MacGregor, J., Matthews, R. S., & Gabelnick, F. 2004, Learning Communities and Undergraduate Education Reform (San Francisco, CA: Jossey-Bass)

Snyder, T. D., de Brey, C., & Dillow, S. A. 2018, Digest of Education Statistics 2016, Annual Report, NCES 2017-094 (Washington, DC: U.S. Department of Education), https://nces.ed.gov/pubs2017/2017094.pdf

Stark, P. B., & Freishtat, R. 2014, ScienceOpen Research 2014, doi:10.14293/S2199-1006.1.SOR-EDU.AOFRQA.v1

Supiano, B. 2018, It Matters a Lot Who Teaches Introductory Courses. Here's Why, The Chronicle of Higher Education, https://www.chronicle.com/article/It-Matters-a-Lot-Who-Teaches/243125

Tucker, G. F. 1996, in Astronomy Education: Current Developments, Future Coordination, Vol. 89, ed. J. A. Percy (San Francisco, CA: ASP), 112, http://www.aspbooks.org/publications/89/112.pdf

U.S. Department of Education 2015, The Nation's Report Card, https://www.nationsreportcard.gov/

Waggoner, W., Hogan, W. P., & Keefe, P. 2002, AAPT Guidelines for Two-Year College Physics Programs Professional Guidelines (College Park, MD: American Association of Physics Teachers), http://aapt.org/Resources/tycguidelines.cfm

Waller, W. H., & Slater, T. F. 2011, Journal of Geoscience Education, 59, 179

White, S., & Chu, R. 2013a, Number of Physics Faculty in Two-Year Colleges: Results from the 2012 Survey of Physics in Two-Year Colleges (College Park, MD: AIP), https://www.aip.org/statistics/reports/number-physics-faculty-two-year-colleges

White, S., & Chu, R. 2013b, Physics Enrollments in Two-Year Colleges: Results from the 2012 Survey of Physics in Two-Year Colleges (College Park, MD: AIP), https://www.aip.org/statistics/reports/physics-enrollments-two-year-colleges

Woodyard, L., & Levy, R. 2019, Handbook: Minimum Qualifications for Faculty and Administrators in California Community Colleges Handbook (Sacramento, CA: California Community Colleges Chancellor's Office) https://www.cccco.edu/-/media/CCCCO-Website/About-Us/Reports/Files/CCCCO_Report_Min_Qualifications-ADA-Final.ashx

Zackal, J. 2014, Becoming a Community College Professor, HigherEd Jobs, https://www.higheredjobs.com/articles/articleDisplay.cfm?ID=525

Astronomy Education, Volume 1
Evidence-based instruction for introductory courses
Chris Impey and Sanlyn Buxner

Chapter 12

Making Your Astronomy Class More Inclusive

Bryan Mendez, Angela Speck and Kim Coble

In this chapter, we cover the importance of making our introductory courses inclusive of students from all backgrounds so that all students in astronomy courses specifically, and in STEM generally, feel that they belong. We introduce the reader to a wide variety of axes of diversity that may or may not be familiar. We discuss how to actively engage all of our students and provide strategies to mitigate bias. This includes tangible steps you can take right now to increase inclusion, from setting up your syllabus to daily interactions. We provide the reader with various resources for further reading and for increasing one's own knowledge of these topics.

Chapter Objectives
By the end of the chapter, the reader will be able to
- describe the importance of retaining diverse students and making students feel that they belong in science,
- describe the various axes of diversity that make students unique, and identify opportunities for mitigating bias and improving inclusion, and
- describe concrete ways you can set up your class to be more inclusive.

12.1 Introduction
Astronomy is for everyone. The same sky moves above us; the same Sun, Moon, and stars shine down on us all. Everyone deserves to learn about the discoveries made by our ancestors and know about the big questions that motivate modern researchers.

However, ethnic, racial, and gender diversity is severely lacking in the physical sciences (including astronomy) in the United States, from undergraduate majors through career professionals (AIP Statistical Research Center: www.aip.org/statistics). This is a large departure from the overall undergraduate student body (https://nces.ed.gov/programs/digest/d16/ch_3.asp). There are many factors that contribute to this situation, and the undergraduate educational experience is an important component. Many underrepresented students feel that science is not for them, despite their own strong interests. By making our courses and instruction more inclusive, we can help those students find their place in science (from professional to interested and informed observer).

12.1.1 Making Your Instruction Inclusive

Being inclusive means actively working to engage all of your students. Teaching is not about gatekeeping or weeding out the "unworthy," especially in introductory classes. The three pillars of teaching: content, pedagogy, and equity (sometimes called culturally responsive teaching) are all important and should interact to support good teaching. It is more than simply making the class accessible for a broad diversity of students, though that is a good place to start. This chapter provides practical advice to use in all classroom settings, from large introductory lectures to small graduate seminars. If you are interested in the theoretical motivations for this advice, please see the references provided.

Your students are diverse and probably not like you. Embrace the diversity of your students and recognize the strengths, contributions, and cultural capital that they bring. An important approach to consider is going beyond the old "Golden Rule" of treating others as you would like to be treated. Instead, consider the "Platinum Rule": treat others the way *they* want to be treated. This means you have to do the work to understand those who are different from yourself and what their needs are.

Being inclusive in your teaching can seem daunting. The most important thing you can do is start. It does not have to be complete and perfect from the beginning. Allow yourself the space to learn and grow, the same you would your students. But do start. Start simple and add more levels to your practice as you go.

One helpful consideration is the notion in educational universal design that making accommodations for one group can help all students…sometimes. Be realistic. There are no magic bullets in teaching, no one-size-fits-all solutions. In a diverse classroom, you will likely need to layer different pedagogical techniques in your lectures, discussions, assignments, and exams to reach different kinds of students.

12.2 Dimensions of Diversity

People are diverse, and no two people can ever be expected to think or behave in precisely the same manner. Many of us prize the notion that we are each unique individuals and would like to be dealt with as such. But people are also social by nature. We identify with groups of people who share common characteristics (biological or social). Some groups are larger than others, and some groups have attained more social power than others through the various machinations of history. It is important to be aware of some of the larger group identities that your students will have. In the United States, many of these identities have been underrepresented and marginalized in mainstream culture (e.g., Black/African American, Latinx/Hispanic, Native American/American Indian, Alaskan Native, and Pacific Islander, women, LGBTQIA*, and the differently abled; see Estes et al. 2000). Being inclusive requires knowing about some of the ways these groups have been marginalized and working to counter that in your classroom. In this section, we will examine a few of these group identities.

12.2.1 Gender

First let us attempt to disentangle gender, gender identity, and sexual orientation (Ainsworth 2015). Gender and gender identity are essentially the same thing. One's biological sex is often assumed to be one's gender, but that may not be true. The role we play in life depends on our gender identity—how we experience gender ourselves, and that impacts our interaction with the world. On the other hand, sexual orientation is about attraction/arousal. If one's biological sex matches their gender identity, one is cisgender. If not, one is transgender. If one's sexual attraction is solely toward people of a different gender, one is heterosexual; if it is solely toward the same gender, one is homosexual. However, gender is not a binary system, and neither is sexual orientation. There are multiple genders on a continuum from male to female, as well as agender (Ainsworth 2015). Similarly, there are many different ways in which sexual attraction can occur. Within a nonbinary understanding of gender, we can also be attracted to multiple different genders, and thus one may be bisexual, or queer, which is often used to encompass the many nonheterosexual attractions.

Marginalization of people based on gender comes from structural/societal constructs that make men and women unequal. But gender/gender identity is complex. It is not simply a binary system of male and female. There are multiple dimensions to gender and the level of marginalization and discrimination varies. That said, we can discuss the simple idea that men and women are treated differently (in fact, men are treated differently from any other gender). Much of the discrimination and marginalization of women comes from stereotypes and are born of societal ideas about what women can and cannot do and are generally called sexism. A deep discussion of sexism and its causes are beyond the scope of this work, but can be found in, e.g., Williams & O'Reilly (1998) and Tannen (1990).

For the purposes of this chapter, it is sufficient to say that we behave differently toward people because of their gender because it is ingrained in our society. Women are assumed to be, on average, physically weaker than men, better at household chores, not as good at math, etc. (e.g., Bejerano & Bartosh 2015). Even when we are conscious of these ideas, structural/societal pressure means that we take in these stereotypes and act on them (Leslie et al. 2015; Banchefsky et al. 2016).

Gender discrimination hurts men, too. These stereotypes assume men are stronger both physically and emotionally, and result in encouraging men to not show emotions. They assume that only women are affected by hormones. They do not allow men to be vulnerable. This is bad. This stereotypical view of men is popularly known as "toxic masculinity" and is harmful to men, who can also experience the full range of human emotions.

12.2.2 Ethnicity

Ethnicity and race are both socially constructed concepts that overlap in several respects (see http://www.racismreview.com/blog/2013/02/24/ethnicity-is-a-social-construction-too/). Ethnicity is more closely related to cultural group identity (Helms & Talleyrand 1997). Social scientists recognize its key features to include common ancestry, heritage, geographic origin, and language or dialect. In the United States, ethnicity is often informally used to describe national origin. For the purposes of federal policy, the US Census Bureau currently only recognizes one ethnicity: Hispanic/Latino. The use of this ethnicity is mostly based on movements in the 1960s and 1970s for ethnic groups from Latin America to consolidate political power. It should be noted that most Hispanic/Latino people do not strongly identify with this designation, often identifying more strongly with national origin.

Hispanic and Latino are often used interchangeably but have different meanings to different people. Generally speaking, Hispanic refers to those from Spanish-speaking groups. Latino generally refers to those from Latin America. Brazilians would therefore be Latino, but not Hispanic, and Spaniards would be Hispanic but not Latino. The term Latinx has also come into vogue recently. Spanish, like most Latin-based languages, is a gendered language, with some nouns having specific genders and some adjectives mutable to match the gender of the noun they alter. A man with Mexican heritage would be called a Latino and a woman from Argentina would be called a Latina. The default in the language when gender is not known or when referring to a group of mixed-gendered people is to use the male form. A group of people from Guatemala would be Latinos. This acts to subjugate the female gender, and in an attempt to equalize gender roles via language, many people have taken to using Latinx instead.

As an instructor, you should not presume to know a student's ethnicity based on appearance, name, etc. But you do need to understand that minority ethnic groups in the United States have been historically and are currently marginalized by the majority ethnic group. One of the ways this marginalization takes form generally is to treat the history and values of the majority group as default and view all other traditions as exotic, less important, less valuable, and less right.

One of the ways this marginalization manifests in the astronomy classroom is a tendency to focus on the contributions to astronomical development made in European and American history. Other cultures' contributions are often treated as inconsequential. You can counteract this narrative by including contributions to astronomy from people around the world and incorporating their stories into your instruction (see Section 12.6 for resources).

You may find some discomfort with other traditions. For example, many Native American cultures do not value the separation of spiritual thought from scientific thought the way Western culture does. It is not your place to be the arbiter of these foundational cultural values. Treat other cultures values with respect. It is okay to advocate for your own philosophy, but recognize that cultural arrogance does not create an inclusive environment.

12.2.3 Race

Race is also a socially constructed concept (Smedley & Smedley 2005). It is often treated informally as a biological identifier. It is true that some groups of people are more closely related to each other and will therefore share more inherited traits amongst a particular group. But the variation in the human genome across our species is only about 0.1%, which is relatively small compared to other species. Our closest relatives, the great apes, have greater genetic variety despite more restricted environmental niches and smaller populations. Race, therefore, has very little to do with biology and is again a group identity created by social convention.

Definitions of race vary across geographical region and time. The current racial groups recognized by the US Census are White, Black/African American, American Indian or Alaska Native, Asian, Native Hawaiian or Other Pacific Islander. In the 19th century, the categories were only White, Black, and Mulatto. The US Census Bureau exerts that race is to be self-determined, but one key difference between ethnicity and race is that race is more of an externally determined identity. A black person raised in a white family might find themselves personally identifying with white ethnicity, but society will still see them first as a black person. Race has historically been used as an exclusionary identity marker, a way to quickly decide who is not a member of your group.

The history of race in the United States is important to be aware of. The notion that the white race is superior to all others (intellectually and morally) is called White Supremacy and is widely (and incorrectly) considered to be a fringe, radical attitude in the modern United States. White supremacy has historically been a driving force in social institutions since the invasion of the Americas by Europeans, who violently conquered indigenous societies and pursued genocidal policies to remove them from their land and erase their culture. They did all that while also building an economy on African slave labor. Despite movements toward social justice, racial minorities are still significantly marginalized in many ways, including those that lead to their exclusion in academic settings and in STEM careers (e.g., Nasir & Shah 2011).

12.2.4 LGBTQIA*

The abbreviation LGBTQIA* covers both gender identity (discussed in Section 12.2.1) and sexual orientation. With respect to sexual orientation, societal pressures to conform to heterosexuality have led to marginalization. While it may appear that one's sexual orientation should not impact one's ability to do science, marginalization occurs because of (a) bullying and (b) related socioeconomic pressure. Many youths who come out as nonheterosexual have been ostracized and forced to leave home, which has severe effects on their ability to study, as well as their general well-being. Even students who have had full familial support are likely to have been impacted by people at school who are less understanding. As such, being in the LGBTQIA* community leads to marginalization that affects whether and how well they can pursue studies in STEM fields.

12.2.5 Socioeconomic

People are often marginalized, not by their intrinsic personhood, but by their circumstances, such as socioeconomic status. There are both social and economic barriers to success in academia and elsewhere. One's social class and one's economic status are often intimately linked and can have a devastating impact on one's ability to succeed. For instance, a person from a socioeconomically deprived background may have grown up in a place where the schools are underfunded, and thus had fewer opportunities than those people in more affluent areas. Similarly, people with little means cannot take advantage of summer camps, school trips, etc., that provide educational and personal growth experiences. In addition, people from families with little income often have to work during high school and college, which impacts their ability to spend time on learning. A lifetime of small deprivations related to socioeconomic status may lead to students being underprepared for college as well as extra challenges during college. This is not a small problem; 42% of California State University students reported food insecurity and 11% were homeless at least once in the past year (Crutchfield & Maguire 2018). Standardized testing does not tell us about a student's innate ability or their ability to learn in ideal circumstances, but we judge them accordingly.

12.2.6 Disability

Disability can place people in many kinds of disadvantage in a world designed by and for those of typical ability. Federal and state laws such as the Americans with Disabilities Act (ADA) require educational institutions to allow equal access for those with a variety of impairments. For example, buildings and classrooms at your institution are required to have ramps and/or working elevators and seating for wheelchair access. Most educational institutions also have offices dedicated to providing services for a variety of disabilities.

An interpreter or note-taker may be used for hearing-impaired students. It can be useful to meet with those interpreters before classes to help them learn some of the jargon used in astronomy or for strategies they can use when encountering new vocabulary. If your classroom space is large, you should use a microphone to be sure that you are audible throughout, even if you think you are loud enough. Include as much visual material, including demonstrations, as possible.

Visually impaired students may require special accommodations for exams and homework (such as a person to read the questions and take dictation). You will also find yourself needing to use very descriptive language to help such students mentally interpret many of the highly visual phenomena in astronomy. Use physical manipulatives in demonstrations whenever possible. There are several resources for tactile relief maps of many astronomical phenomena that are great to have on hand (see Section 12.6). A fairly common type of visual disability is color blindness, causing people to not be able to differentiate between certain shades of color pairs (e.g., red–green or blue–yellow). Avoid using color in text and charts to indicate critical information. Instead, use different fonts, points, textures, or labels. Design materials for maximum readability as if they were going to be printed in grayscale.

Use high contrast in colors you do use and provide bright, natural, glare-free ambient lighting to maximize color recognition.

Your disabled students' office on campus will work with you to design appropriate accommodations. They may provide services like audio recordings of your textbook or closed captioning of videos of your lecture. You should also work to make sure that all of your electronic materials for class meet requirements of section 501 of the ADA (things like captioning for videos, metatagging for images, and appropriately structured webpages and PDFs, PPT, Word Docs, etc. for automatic reading software).

Not all disabilities are visible. There are many kinds of physical illness that create conditions that are not visually noticeable. Some conditions may require frequent trips to the restroom (this can be the case for diabetics experiencing high blood glucose). Some chronic pain conditions will cause discomfort after sitting for lengthy periods of time. Offer breaks during longer class sessions to allow people to get up and take care of their physical needs. Do not chastise those who need to either leave the room during class or those who may need to stand in the back of the room during class. Let students know that they should feel free to tend to their needs.

There many types of mental disability that can disadvantage students such as depression, anxiety, and other mood, personality, or psychiatric disorders. These conditions can cause several different kinds of limitations:

- Side effects from psychiatric medications that include drowsiness, fatigue, dry mouth and thirst, blurred vision, hand tremors, slowed response time, and difficulty initiating interpersonal contact
- An inability to block out sounds, sights, or odors that interfere with focusing on tasks
- Limited ability to tolerate noise and crowds
- Restlessness, shortened attention span, distraction, and difficulty understanding or remembering verbal directions
- Difficulty sustaining enough energy to spend a whole day on campus attending classes
- Difficulty managing assignments, prioritizing tasks, and meeting deadlines; inability to participate in multitask work
- Difficulty getting along, fitting in, contributing to group work, and reading social cues
- Anxiety in approaching instructors or TAs
- Difficulty understanding and correctly interpreting criticism or poor grades; may not be able to separate person from task (personalization or defensiveness due to low self-esteem)
- Difficulty coping with unexpected changes in coursework, such as changes in the assignments, due dates or instructors; limited ability to tolerate interruptions
- Severe test anxiety.

Learning disabilities by their very nature disadvantage students in academic settings. There are conditions that impair students' abilities in reading (dyslexia), writing (dysgraphia), and math (dyscalculia). There are also conditions that are characterized by difficulty understanding and using auditory information, or weakness in taking on and using visual information.

Many students may feel uncomfortable revealing their disabilities, fearing the stigmas that might be associated with them. In your syllabus, you can include a statement referring students to the campus disability office (in case they are unaware of its services). But, you can also invite them to contact you individually to discuss their unique needs and what accommodations could be reasonably made. Note that they need not reveal their diagnosis to you to discuss their needs and appropriate accommodations.

12.2.7 Neurodiversity

Another way in which people are diverse is in brain structure and functioning. Many scientists are exploring hypotheses that mental conditions like attention deficit and hyperactivity disorder (ADHD), dyslexia, and autism may have evolutionary advantages that have kept them in the human gene pool for many generations (Brüne et al. 2012). Neurodiversity is a movement to treat these conditions as natural human variations rather than diseases and has been growing for the past 20 years (e.g., Armstrong 2015). Even though this movement does not view neurodiverse people as broken, it does recognize that living within a society developed by and for neurotypical people puts them at a disadvantage, or "disability."

Most colleges and universities have a disabled students' program and policies in place to provide reasonable accommodations to students who have provided documentation of their conditions. Professionals within that program usually contact instructors when one of their students registers for your class and provide a list of necessary accommodations that you can make to help that student succeed. These accommodations are often along the lines of providing extra time and/or distraction-free spaces for quizzes and exams.

The variety and extent of disability that neurodiverse people may experience is quite broad, so individual accommodations are ideal. But there are some general strategies to consider that will make your classroom inclusive of these individuals. Many autistic people have heightened sensitivity to light and sound, and those with ADHD or anxiety disorders find too much activity to be distracting or anxiety inducing.

Work with your department/school to create designated quiet areas where students who feel temporarily overwhelmed can avoid meltdowns. Keep distracting sensory input—such as the buzzing of fluorescent lights—to a minimum. Allow students to customize their personal sensory space by wearing noise-reducing headphones, sunglasses to avoid glare, etc. For longer class sessions, provide breaks so that students can discharge/recharge their activity levels. Provide spaces for those who need to "stimm" (stereotypical behaviors such as hand-flapping, rocking, spinning, or repetition of words and phrases), ideally out of sight of those who would find that activity too distracting.

It is also worth noting that several of the newer classroom techniques promoting social interactions between students can be anxiety inducing in some neurodiverse individuals. Be alert for this and be sure not to pressure anyone into such interactions.

Changing the pace can also be helpful for those with attention deficits. Mix up the amount of lecture, group work, and demonstration during class. Be sure to advertise the planned schedule for each class as many neurodiverse people have anxiety when routines are changed, and they need to be able to anticipate coming changes.

12.2.8 Religion

People's cosmological beliefs and worldviews are often formed by deep cultural identity (Cobern 1989; Wallace et al. 2013). People's beliefs about the fundamental nature of reality shape them in the most profound ways. Basic respect for other worldviews is important in creating an inclusive environment, along with honoring traditions and holidays of religions other than those of the majority group.

In the United States today, Christians are the majority group, and Christian holidays often rule the academic calendar. Christians make up more than 70% of U.S. residents (two-thirds of them being Protestant denominations), and Christian beliefs tend to dominate social spaces, including government. The next largest group of people in the U.S. are the nonreligious (nearly 23%). Jews are nearly 2% of the population, and all other religious groups are each less than 1% of the population (Pew Research: http://www.pewforum.org/religious-landscape-study/).

Marginalization for minority religious groups commonly occurs because of the tendency for the majority group to treat their own traditions as the only ones worth considering. However, groups like Jews and Muslims also face considerable discrimination for historical or current geopolitical reasons.

Because of the tendency to focus on the contributions to astronomy from Europeans and North Americans, there is also a tendency to focus on Christian religious traditions within the history of astronomy. Some ways to counter this would be by discussing the Islamic contributions to astronomy during the middle ages. You can also discuss the lunar nature of the Hebrew and Islamic calendars to demonstrate why Jewish and Islamic holidays do not coincide annually with dates in the solar Gregorian calendar.

An astronomy classroom can be a place where religious views clash with the content matter. Fundamentalist religious beliefs may be challenged by discussions of the formation and evolution of the solar system or Big Bang cosmology. Many students of faith believe that scientists are all atheists and antireligion. This is, of course, not true. Many of the historical figures they may learn about in astronomy: Kepler, Galileo, Newton, Einstein, etc., were deeply religious (see, e.g., Barker & Goldstein 2001; Sobel 1999; Davis 1991; Ursic 2006; Einstein 1930). It can be useful to talk about this aspect of these figures, as their spirituality was often a motivating factor in their curiosity. Again, seek out examples of scientists (historical and modern) from a variety of faiths (including atheists) to highlight in class.

12.2.9 Age

In today's college classrooms, students are coming from a much larger range of ages and life experiences. It is becoming more common for older adults to go to college either as a return for additional education or for the first time. This is especially true in community colleges.

Age discrimination is a common phenomenon in employment but can also be an issue in the classroom. While more common recently, older students are still rare and find themselves a significant minority in most classrooms. Students may express discomfort or lack of interest in socializing across generations. Students in each generation may hold stereotypes about the abilities of each other as well. Younger students may doubt the ability of older students to learn new things. Older students may doubt the wisdom of younger students. Highlight the strengths that each generation brings to the class.

When considering how you assign out of classroom work, you need to consider the limitations on the flexibility of older students. Although it is reasonable to expect a total of 2–3 hours outside the classroom for every credit hour/in-class hour, it is important not to be too prescriptive in how that time is scheduled. Older students may have employment or family obligations constraining their study time. Consider this when scheduling office hours. Making yourself available asynchronously online can be a benefit for many students.

Older students may also have physical limitations different from younger students. Visual acuity and hearing tend to degrade with age. Make sure classrooms are appropriately lit, and your voice is audible to all, with minimal noise.

Older students usually also have a much greater breadth of experience, which can be helpful when relating concepts in physics and astronomy to everyday life.

Another consideration with age is that there may be an age difference between you and your students. This means that the experiences you had in your youth may not always translate to today's youth. Beware of the "back in my day" and "kids today" syndrome.

12.2.10 Family Obligations

Students may have family obligations outside of class. They may have children, parents, spouses, or other family members for whom they provide care. Students may need to work in order to support themselves and their families. It is also important to be aware that many minority ethnic groups prioritize family obligations.

Moderate homework assignments requiring an excessive amount of out-of-class time to complete. Remember that a 3 credit hour course should take a commitment of about 10 hours per week including classroom time, reviews for tests/exams, writing up notes, and homework assignments.

If you hold an after-hours event for the class, like a star party, allow and invite the students to bring along family members.

12.2.11 Intersectionality

People very rarely hold only one group identity. This means that there are multiple ways for a person to become marginalized along more than one dimension of identity. The concept of intersectionality in sociology examines how marginalization interacts and compounds at the intersections of identity (Crenshaw 1989). A black woman faces discrimination in ways that are different from the marginalization of black men or white women (e.g., Carlone & Johnson 2007). A poor, autistic white man will face compounding marginalization in economic and neurodiverse ways, while he might still have social privilege as a white man. As an instructor, it is useful for you to think about how the intersections of identity might disadvantage some of your students more so than a single disadvantage along a single dimension of identity. As a department, it can be helpful to consider challenges faced by students marginalized along more than one dimension of identity, concrete steps faculty can take to support these students, and the characteristics of departments where these students are thriving (Johnson et al. 2017).

12.3 Barriers to Inclusion

There are several ways that marginalization can impede a student's success. Let us briefly examine some of the major barriers that make students feel unwelcome in an academic setting. Retention of underrepresented groups is a problem in STEM. Students are not leaving; they are being pushed out.

12.3.1 Implicit Bias

You have probably been raised surrounded by the dominant Western culture that centers its norms around affluent, White, Christian, heterosexual, cisgendered males, who are physically able and neurotypical. This has likely biased your attitudes toward people not fitting into this particular mold, if only unconsciously. You could think of it as the sociological analog of systematic error in measurement. This implicit bias influences us all, including those from marginalized groups. It is not a moral failing on your part to have these biases. We are all a product of the culture in which we are raised.

There are tools that can help you identify what biases you may hold (https://implicit.harvard.edu/implicit/). These tools are not perfect, but they can still be useful to help you explore your own inherent attitudes. Becoming aware of your own implicit biases can help motivate you to work to counteract them. By shining a light on your implicit bias, you can actually change it and make it less problematic. However, even if the test shows that you are neutral/lack systemic bias, it is still important to counteract the biases endemic to our society through our classroom settings and beyond.

12.3.2 Stereotype Threat

Stereotype threat is the psychological theory that anxiety about reinforcing negative stereotypes about a group identity can be self-fulfilling (Steele & Aronson, 1995; Steele 1997; Spencer et al. 1999; Ben-Zeev et al. 2005). The anxiety is situational and does not require a person to personally believe the stereotype in order for their performance to be impacted. Here is an example of how this could play out:

A young woman is taking a math exam. She is aware of the stereotype that women are not as good at math as men. Her anxiety over doing poorly on exam, and thus confirming the stereotype, negatively impacts her performance on the exam, which she would otherwise do well on.

There are several researched methods shown to be effective in reducing the effects of stereotype threat (see, e.g., Beilock 2010). We discuss those in Section 12.4.

12.3.3 Micro/Macro Aggressions/Affirmations

Humans are aware of social environments, scanning them for clues that affirm belonging or indicate threat. Every human has a need for dignity, i.e., for their life and identity to be respected (Estrada et al. 2018). Macro aggressions are blatant social cues that indicate discrimination, such as blatant racism, hate, and rejection. Micro aggressions are more subtle, often automatic cues (Sue et al. 2007), such as weird facial expressions, insults, and backhanded "compliments" (e.g., you're so "articulate" to a black person or good at math… "for a girl"; see, e.g., Rattan et al. 2012; Barthelemy et al. 2016; Chestnut & Markman 2018). Even software like email clients and word processors that autocorrect non-Anglicized names are adding to the burden of microaggressions. It is important to note that "micro" does not mean there is a small effect; it denotes how common and everyday micro aggressions are (see e.g., Swim et al. 2001). Students from marginalized groups will feel fatigue from experiencing micro aggressions and express being tired of "it" (Estrada et al. 2018).

In addition to reducing macro and micro aggressions, it is also important to increase macro and micro affirmations (Estrada et al. 2018). Macro affirmations are obvious acts of social inclusion in community that affirm human dignity. Examples include facial expressions that convey care, helping, sharing, politeness, and appreciation. Micro affirmations again are more subtle, such as eye contact, tone of voice, showing vulnerability, and kindness. There can also be subtle cues in the environment (e.g., posters) that affirm students' sense of belonging.

12.3.4 Imposter Syndrome

Everybody can be affected by feelings of insecurity and self-doubt from time to time. Imposter syndrome describes the condition where these feelings are frequent and debilitating despite evidence to the contrary (Clance & Imes 1978). Imposter syndrome places you in a state of fear of being revealed as a fraud, that you are not deserving of your achievements. People from all demographic groups can experience this, but it hits those from marginalized groups the hardest. If you are the only woman in an advanced physics class, you may start to wonder if you belong there. If you are the only Latinx graduate student in an astronomy department, you may feel like you were accepted purely to meet the school's diversity quota. This may be compounded by micro- and macroaggressions.

12.4 Strategies to Mitigate Bias and Increase Inclusion

How do we remove barriers and make our classrooms the best learning environment they can be for everybody? We need to create a setting where marginalized students can find validation and a sense of belonging, vent frustrations, and express their full identities. Decreasing negative aspects of the environment does not automatically increase positive aspects; removing barriers does not necessarily lead to a more inclusive experience. Just because your classroom is not overtly biased does not mean that it is welcoming for all. We need to actively do both (Estrada et al. 2018).

Many students and faculty incorrectly believe that intelligence/talent/ability in STEM fields is innate (Dweck 2008). This fixed mindset needs to be overcome by encouraging a "growth mindset," which accepts the brain's ability to become better.

However, the growth mindset does not address external factors that create barriers for some students. A common trap for us is to place too much onus on the students to integrate into our classroom rather than addressing the external structures keeping them from participating. We need to address aspects and barriers beyond the classroom.

Students from marginalized backgrounds bring with them cultural capital (Yosso 2005), i.e., knowledge and ideas that stem from their cultural heritage. We need to accept this cultural capital into our classroom. Combining the "growth mindset" with acknowledgment of cultural capital allows us to not only help students to "play the game" but to "change the game" (Gutierrez 2009). Here we discuss how to achieve such an equitable classroom.

12.4.1 Before the Course

The first step to excellence in teaching, which stands on the three pillars of content, pedagogy, and equity, is to consider how we will approach the course.

12.4.1.1 Professional Development

It is important to engage in some professional development (PD) for equity in teaching. Some of these development activities are self-driven. For instance, engage in self-reflection (Eliason 2019): what are your goals and why? How does your identity affect your teaching (what is/isn't shared with students, how might I be perceived)? Is your teaching style more or less student focused?

There is also more formal PD. For instance, take advantage of workshops, webinars, communities of practice and local mentors to learn inclusive pedagogical and assessment techniques in order to inform your teaching. Use results from education research and existing research-based curricula to diversify your instruction techniques and resources, which can significantly improve inclusion.

Take inventory of your department's competency in equity and inclusion. Consult with or form a diversity and inclusion committee and faculty-learning community/ community of practice in your department.

12.4.1.2 Teaching and Learning Space and Facilities

Beyond PD, we need to consider the space in which we teach. What cues appear in the curriculum or space? Does your classroom highlight only the majority, e.g., via posters and displays? It is important to replace or augment such displays with the scientific contributions of a variety of astronomers, not just those who are white, male, able-bodied, and heteronormative (Cheryan et al. 2009, 2014).

There are several other aspects of course setup we need to consider. Peer mentoring can be a powerful tool, but peer mentors (or tutors) must be actively recruited (more than blanket emails) from across many dimensions of diversity. Meanwhile, technology provides many tools that can help make our classrooms more student centered, but we must recognize that not all students have access to that technology (e.g., their own laptops, calculators, clickers). It is important to eliminate technology barriers.

12.4.1.3 The Syllabus
Your syllabus/course policies and calendar are a place to set the tone and send cues to the students. If your university or department has existing policies in place to accommodate students who have conflicts due to religious practice, medical treatment, and family and/or personal emergencies, state them in the syllabus. If not, generate your own policies.

Beware of organizing off-schedule activities that might exclude some students. For example, review sessions at unscheduled times might be difficult for students who have to work and/or commute via public transportation. Commuting at odd times is particularly challenging for undocumented students, for whom obtaining a driver's license is extremely difficult in some states.

It is important to recognize that students have often developed various coping mechanisms and classroom practices that are alien to you and may even appear disrespectful. For instance, a simple game on a handheld device may actually be a mechanism for focus for a student with ADHD, akin to doodling. We need to recognize that a "no-device" policy may inhibit the learning of some students. Rather than banning electronics, consider best practices such as separate seating areas in class for students who require devices versus students who find devices distracting. Similarly, students who have difficulty sitting may choose to position themselves in a way that might traditionally seem disrespectful. Indeed, even simply being very tall may make the standard classroom environment uncomfortable. It is important to recognize that students need the freedom to situate themselves in a way that works for them to maximize their learning.

Finally, it is good practice to have your syllabus peer-reviewed. Peer-reviewing syllabi with colleagues can help everyone become more equitable. Resources exist to facilitate this sort of peer review (e.g., syllabus checklist in Eliason 2019).

12.4.2 During the Course

Once your course is underway, you need to act on the contract in your syllabus to engage with and teach your students equitably.

12.4.2.1 Affirm Your Students' Identities
Learn your students' names and how to pronounce them correctly. This can be achieved by using name cards/tents. In addition, it is crucial to be aware that a

student's preferred pronoun may not be the one you assume. Students can be invited, if they wish, to indicate a preferred pronoun on a name tag or tent. Some students may prefer to avoid pronouns if possible.

The land on which you are teaching was once the domain of indigenous people. Honor the indigenous heritage of the region where the class is held. This can be done with a simple land acknowledgement at the beginning of the course (https://usdac.us/nativeland).

Ensure that your students are exposed to successful role models from their group who refute negative stereotypes. Beyond refuting negative stereotypes, actively promoting positive stereotypes (e.g., women are good at math) can help lift stereotype threat (Forbes & Schmader 2010).

Consider having students engage in reflective journaling, which has been shown to promote positive learning experiences and aims to affirm students' cultural wealth and intersectional identities. Students journal on prompts designed to affirm their goals, values, and interests, and to relate course content to their everyday lives. Students might also spend time in class sharing their responses, in small or large groups. Examples can be found in Tran et al. (2019), Harackiewicz et al. (2016), and references therein, as well as the popular KQED "Mindshift," https://www.kqed.org/mindshift/50644/using-expressive-writing-to-keep-students-grounded-and-engaged-in-science-courses.

12.4.2.2 Fostering a Growth Mindset and Adopting an Asset Model of Your Students

As discussed above, it is important to foster a growth mindset in yourself and your students. To this end, you must convey that physics is mastered through practice and hard work, not innate, unchangeable talent. Students need to learn that intelligence is like a muscle; it is not fixed but grows with effort. We must promote this conception of intelligence or ability as the norm. It is equally important to teach students that worries about belonging in school (imposter syndrome) are normal, not unique to them or their group, and are transient rather than fixed (e.g., Ben-Zeev et al. 2017).

Rather than approaching your class as people who lack knowledge or skills (a deficit model), approach the classroom with an asset model of your students. As you get to know your students, you will recognize what strengths, weaknesses, needs, and resources your students bring to the classroom, and can adopt appropriate teaching and assessment strategies.

It is also important to recognize and acknowledge your students' cultural capital (Yosso 2005).

12.4.2.3 Ground Rules/Community Agreements and Dynamics in the Classroom

On the first day, you need to set the tone for the course. You should co-create ground rules/community agreement with the students (e.g., Ambrose et al. 2010). What are your expectations? What are theirs? It is also important to communicate explicitly that you value diversity and discuss the idea of micro and macro aggressions. Part of the ground rules should be insisting that micro/macro aggressions are decreased and micro/macro aggressions are increased.

Once the ground rules have been set, it is important to monitor classroom participation and dynamics, starting with yourself. You must work to monitor and counter your own biases. You need to be aware of and refrain from using racist, sexist, ableist, gender-discriminatory, transphobic, or homophobic language in the classroom; if such language is part of the instructional material (which should be rare in an astronomy course), give students content warnings. Be aware of whom you are calling on for questions and answers; avoid choosing one demographic group over another (e.g., only the men) or focusing on one section of the room (e.g., only the front). One way to achieve this is to wait until at least three students have raised their hands. When appropriate and feasible, move away from the front of the room and speak from and to different parts of the class.

Be aware of students who appear visually different from most in class (e.g., people of color, those with visible disabilities) that are sitting in isolated areas. Do not take steps that may make them feel more self-conscious, such as announcing to the whole class that people should move closer to the students in question; rather, take more subtle and universal steps such as calling for students to talk to the person behind, to the right/left of them. Use in-class, cooperative student-centered activities to foster better intergroup relations.

Another way to improve intergroup relations is to emphasize similarities among groups. There are plenty of opportunities for this in astronomy. Note the similarities in calendars from all around the world, or stories regarding certain asterisms or celestial phenomena. For example, the idea of the Sun being pulled across the sky via chariot is common in Greco/Roman and Chinese traditions.

12.4.2.4 Choosing and Designing Assessments
How we assess our students is a crucial piece of achieving equity. There are simple ways to overcome some of the biggest biases. For instance, teach students about stereotype threat so that they attribute anxiety to stereotype threat rather than to the risk of failure; teach students to reappraise arousal as a potential facilitator of strong performance rather than barrier to it. Research on stereotype threat shows that we should not ask people to report a negatively stereotyped group identity before taking a test (Steele & Aronson 1995; Danaher & Crandall 2008).

There are other simple rules that we can follow to make assessment more equitable (e.g., Schinske & Tanner 2014):
- Do not use high-stakes, timed tests; limit use of multiple-choice questions.
- Use gender- and race-fair assessments, communicate their fairness, convey that they are being used to facilitate learning, not to measure innate ability or reify stereotypes.
- Create tests such that the last person naturally finishes in the allotted time; others finish earlier.

Once the assessment assignment has been completed, we must ensure that our grading practices are equitable. There are several ways you can work to reduce possible biases in your grading:
- Use grading rubrics and be sure to share these with students.

- Grade all assignments/tests at once to minimize changes in your mood affecting your assessments.
- When possible, have students submit assignments using student IDs rather than names.
- If available, have more than one grader grade assignments.
- Make use of online services to build and administer assignments, and that grade work automatically.

Post-assessment feedback is also key. Frame critical feedback as reflective of your high standards and your confidence in students' ability to meet those standards. Communicate how you will support students in this effort to meet your standards.

12.4.3 After the Course

As we have previously stated, you should not try to do everything at once. Instead, you should continuously work to improve your teaching to become more inclusive. A key to improving is reflecting on your practice and examining what has worked and what did not work. You can do this personally, but it can be very helpful to also do this collaboratively with colleagues from your department, college/university, or even an online community of practice.

Collect and use classroom/department data to identify achievement/opportunity gaps or issues of classroom climate. Incorporate questions like the dignity survey from Estrada et al. (2018, p. 5), or the CLASS survey (https://www.colorado.edu/sei/class), into your course evaluations to assess how your students are feeling about their sense of inclusion in your class and their attitudes about science.

12.5 Making Astronomy Inclusive

The previous discussion is applicable in most general education college courses regardless of subject area. Here are some ways to specifically become more inclusive in your astronomy teaching.

Much of the content in an astronomy class can be esoteric. In order to help students understand course material, it is important that they are able to relate to the content in some way. In a classroom with a wide diversity of life experiences, you will often need to try a multitude of ways to make the content more relatable, including examples, metaphors, etc.

12.5.1 Examples

The phenomena explored in astronomy are often very far removed from the day-to-day life of students. Capitalize on opportunities to give examples of how a topic operates in our lives. This is often easier at the start of an astronomy course when discussing commonplace phenomena like diurnal and seasonal celestial motions:

- Explore calendars from different cultures and how they use these motions as the basis for different ways of timekeeping.
- Explore the ways in which cultures around the world have expressed their ideas about celestial objects both scientifically and artistically. Use examples

in popular media. This can work even when the example gets a detail wrong. For example, there is a sequence of shots in the film E.T. showing the progression of the Moon. After studying Moon phases, show these scenes to the students and see if they spot a problem. Spoiler alert: the shots show a rising crescent Moon in the evening hours, but of course crescent Moons only rise in morning hours (because the Moon is near the Sun in the sky when it is in a crescent phase). After studying planets and planetary systems, you could have students think about what they could conclude about planets depicted in popular science fiction stories. Why might Mustafar (from Star Wars) be so volcanically active?

- When discussing the electromagnetic spectrum, give examples of sources and detectors of each type of radiation in daily life: microwave ovens and mobile phones, car radios, television remote controls, sunglasses, medical X-ray machines, and potassium-40.
- Describe how athletes use the conservation of angular momentum when doing spinning or tumbling maneuvers: ice skaters, ski jumpers, divers, gymnasts.
- Introduce the concept of Doppler shift by asking students to make the sound of cars zooming by on the street: Neeeyuoooo.

12.5.2 Metaphors

When direct examples are not possible, you can use metaphors to help students relate to a concept:

- Relate photon scattering off particles in the radiative zones of stars to the random walk of a drunk or the game "Plinko" on the game show "The Price is Right."
- Relate the expansion of the universe to the stretching of a rubber sheet or the rising of a bread or cake.

It is important to recognize the cultural context of different metaphors. Many metaphors rely on shared cultural experiences or knowledge. If you describe the habitable zone around a star by calling it the Goldilocks zone, you are making an assumption that your students know the story of "Goldilocks and the Three Bears." Many, especially those raised in other cultures may not know the story and would therefore miss the point. That does not mean that you should not use the term "Goldilocks zone"—it just means that you should tell your class the story so that everyone has the common reference. Likewise, if they have never seen "The Price is Right," you might want to cue up a video showcasing "Plinko."

12.5.3 Connections

The amount of new information in an introductory astronomy class is overwhelming. The universe is really big and filled with lots of neat stuff. It is useful to explicitly make connections between different topics throughout the class. When first introducing orbits in the solar system, you will probably discuss Newton's law of gravity and Kepler's laws of planetary orbits. Each time those concepts return (characterizing exoplanets or binary stars, or discovering dark matter from galactic rotation curves), be sure to make a big point about it. Help students learn new material by building on knowledge they have just acquired.

12.5.4 Demonstrations

Physical demonstrations can help students internalize certain concepts far better than thought experiments or aural descriptions. Tie a tuning fork securely to the end of a string, strike it and then swing it over head to demonstrate the Doppler shift. For hearing-impaired students, you can set up a microphone to record the moving tuning fork and then show the changing waveform it records with simple audio editing software. You can also use a ripple tank to create waves and then move a bath toy around to show the changes in its experience of the frequency of the wave oscillations relative to its motion. Set up a light bulb (or different gas discharge tubes), a diffraction grating, and a webcam to live-project spectra for the classroom. Putting an incandescent light bulb on a dimmer with this setup allows you to show how the spectrum varies with temperature. For visually impaired students, be sure to use very descriptive language. Be sure to prompt students to describe what they are observing with such demonstrations. Have students predict ahead of time what they expect to happen, record their observations, and reconcile their predictions with their observations. Provide structure in helping students analyze demos (and similarly videos) because novice learners will perceive different aspects of the same situation compared to an expert (Eriksson et al. 2014). It is easy for students to see what they want to see (confirmation bias). If possible, do demonstrations or other hands-on activities in small groups, rather than one for the whole class.

12.5.5 Stories

A lot of research has shown that the human brain learns best through narrative; this is one of the reasons that anecdotal evidence can be so persuasive. You can use this to great effect in teaching astronomy. When teaching about observational astronomy and celestial motions, you have thousands of years of human creativity to draw on to help students learn about these concepts. For example, you could tell the Navajo story of dilyéhé (the Pleiades) and the missing boys, which conveys a notion of the period of time when the asterism is not visible and when to plant corn. You can tell the Greek story of Orion and the scorpion to help students remember where these constellations are in the sky and how they move. Apart from those kinds of stories, it is also very helpful to tell the stories of people and how they learned about the cosmos. Telling the personal stories of people like Kepler, Galileo, and Newton is great. However, they only represent a tiny piece of the world. Be sure to point out their nationalities. Failing to do so can send a signal that we do not need to mention their nationalities because they are the default. Be sure to also tell stories about the discoveries of women and of people from all around the world and from all walks of life: Hypatia, Zu Chongzhi, Shen Kuo, Caroline Herschel, Cecilia Payne-Gaposchkin, Annie Jump

Cannon, Henrietta Leavitt, Vera Rubin, Jocelyn Bell Burnell, Muhammad ibn Musa al-Khwarizmi, Subramanyan Chandrasekhar, Chushiro Hayashi, Stephen Hawking, France A. Cordova, and more. It is also worth talking about how modern science is a collaborative endeavor with most research done in teams, and that the largest projects have international participation.

12.6 Resources

Gender
- http://multiverse.ssl.berkeley.edu/women—Unheard Voices, Part 2: Women in Astronomy—a resource guide for teaching astronomy and incorporating contributions from women across history.
- https://justeducationlearning.wordpress.com/2011/12/04/sexism/—A short description/explanation of what is meant by "systemic sexism."
- https://journals.aps.org/prper/collections/gender-in-physics—Special volume of Physical Review Physics Education Research (PRPER) focused on gender issues.

Race and Ethnicity
- https://www.aapt.org/Resources/Race-and-Physics-Teaching.cfm—Special volume of The Physics Teacher that focuses on race.
- https://theconversation.com/decolonise-science-time-to-end-another-imperial-era-89189—"Decolonise Science—Time to End Another Imperial Era" by Rohan Deb Roy—a discussion and description of how colonialism and imperialism have impacted and continue to impact science.
- https://medium.com/@chanda/decolonising-science-reading-list-339fb773d51f—"Decolonising Science Reading List: It's The End of Science As You Know It" is a reading list maintained by Chanda Prescod-Weinstein.
- https://aapt.scitation.org/doi/abs/10.1119/1.4999724—"Teaching About Racial Equity in Introductory Physics Courses" by Abigail R. Daane, Sierra R. Decker, and Vashti Sawtelle (2017).

Sexual Orientation
- https://arxiv.org/abs/1804.08406—LGBT+ Inclusivity in Physics and Astronomy: A Best Practices Guide.
- https://www.aps.org/programs/lgbt/upload/LGBTClimateInPhysicsReport.pdf—LGBT Climate in Physics report from the American Physical Society.

Disability
- https://earthsky.org/space/tactile-astronomy-beyond-sight—"Astronomy Beyond Sight" explains how tactile models of the constellations, Moon, and planets can provide all people with a better appreciation of the universe.

- https://astroedu.iau.org/en/collections/tactileastronomy/—Tactile Astronomy provides hands-on educational activities for sight-impaired students.
- http://depts.washington.edu/astron/outreach/astronomy-for-the-sight-impaired/—Astronomy for the Sight Impaired provides resources for teaching astronomy using various nonvisual techniques.
- https://access.sfsu.edu/ati/content/sf-state-course-accessibility-checklist—SF State Course Accessibility Checklist.
- http://www.astrobetter.com/wiki/tiki-index.php?page=Accessibility—Astrobetter resource page for all things accessibility in astronomy.

Religion
- https://diversity.missouri.edu/guide-to-religions/dates-practices-accomodations/—A good resource for the dates, practices, and potential accommodations of many religious holidays.

Diversity, Equity, and Inclusion
- https://www.astrobetter.com/wiki/Diversity—Equal Opportunity Astronomy: Articles & Resources from AstroBetter.
- http://womeninastronomy.blogspot.com/2018/11/rubrics-and-resources-for-diverse.html—"Rubrics and Resources for a Diverse Faculty and Graduate Student Body" a resource guide from the Women In Astronomy blog.
- http://underrep.com/—The Underrepresentation Curriculum Project.
- https://seachange.aaas.org/—STEM Equity Achievement (SEA) Change is a project of the AAAS aimed at supporting transformational change in diversity and inclusion in higher education.
- http://www.crlt.umich.edu/multicultural-teaching/inclusive-teaching-strategies—Inclusive teaching resources and strategies from the Center for Research on Teaching and Learning at the University of Michigan.

Multicultural Astronomy
- http://multiverse.ssl.berkeley.edu/multicultural—"Unheard Voices, Part 1: The Astronomy of Many Cultures," a resource guide for teaching astronomy and incorporating contributions from across the globe.
- https://astronomerswithoutborders.org/gam2015-news/gam-2015-blog/2701-exploring-the-intersections-of-astronomy-and-culture.html—"Exploring the Intersections of Astronomy and Culture" by Nancy Alima Ali at Astronomers without Borders.
- https://escholarship.org/uc/jac—Journal of Cultural Astronomy.
- http://www.aboriginalastronomy.com.au/—Australian Indigenous Astronomy; a website dedicated to the First Nations of Australia.

Professional Development
- Harvard Implicit Bias Tests: https://implicit.harvard.edu/implicit/.

- PhysPort provides research-based physics education resources, recommendations, curricula, and assessments for the classroom: https://www.physport.org.
  Articles by experts on general classroom practices: https://www.physport.org/recommendations/.
  Recommendations for handling biases in the classroom: https://www.physport.org/recommendations/Entry.cfm?ID=93333.
  How to engage with students more effectively with active learning: https://www.physport.org/recommendations/Entry.cfm?T=productive%20engagement.
- The New Faculty Workshop is organized annually by the American Association of Physics Teachers. Resources and information on the workshop can be found here: http://aapt.org/Conferences/newfaculty/nfw.cfm.
- http://blog.trainerswarehouse.com/diversity-training-games-and-exercises/—A description of group exercises to spark discussions about diversity.
- http://racegenderscience.weebly.com/syllabus.html—Syllabus for a course on race and gender in the scientific community.
- https://drive.google.com/file/d/17a0PCsP7q3wohCpLaJZFJqf_iGKbt-Xq/view—Syllabus for a course on diversity and inclusion in the workplace.
- https://www.aps.org/programs/education/undergrad/bpupp.cfm—Effective Practices for Physics Programs (EP3) Project from the American Physical Society.
- https://instituteonteachingandmentoring.org/—The Institute on Teaching and Mentoring is an annual conference for minority doctoral scholars.
- https://books.google.com/books/about/Scientific_Teaching.html?id=suf0MvxqoLQC&printsec=frontcover&source=kp_read_button#v=onepage&q&f=false—*Scientific Teaching* by Jo Handelsman, Sarah Miller, & Christine Pfund (2007).
- https://extension.usu.edu/diversity/dimensions-of-diversity "Understanding the Dimensions of Diversity"—Resources for learning competencies in diversity.
- https://aapt.scitation.org/doi/10.1119/1.4940167—"Addressing Underrepresentation: Physics Teaching for All" by Moses Rifkin (2016).

References

Ainsworth, C. 2015, Natur, 518, 288

Ambrose, S. A., Bridges, M. W., DiPietro, M., Lovett, M. C., & Norman, M. K. 2010, How Learning Works (New York: Jossey-Bass)

Armstrong, T. 2015, AMA Journal of Ethics, 17, 348

Banchefsky, S., Westfall, J., Park, B., & Judd, C. M. 2016, Sex Roles, 75, 95

Barker, P., & Goldstein, B. R. 2001, in Osiris, Science in Theistic Contexts: Cognitive Dimensions, Vol. 16, ed. J. H. Brooke, M. J. Osler, & J. M. van der Meer (Chicago, IL: Univ. Chicago Press), 88

Barthelemy, R., McCormick, M., & Henderson, C. 2016, PRPER, 12, 020119

Bejerano, A. R., & Bartosh, T. M. 2015, JWMSE, 21, 107

Beilock, S. 2010, Choke: What the Secrets of the Brain Reveal About Getting It Right When You Have To (New York: Free Press)

Ben-Zeev, T., Fein, S., & Inzlicht, M. 2005, Journal of Experimental Social Psychology, 41, 174
Ben-Zeev, A., Paluy, Y., Milless, K. L., et al. 2017, Education Sciences B, 7, 65
Brüne, M., Belsky, J., Fabrega, H., et al. 2012, World Psychiatry, 11, 55
Carlone, H. B., & Johnson, A. 2007, JRScT, 44, 1187
Cheryan, S., Plaut, V. C., Davies, P. G., & Steele, C. M. 2009, Journal of Personality and Social Psychology, 97, 1045
Cheryan, S., Ziegler, S. A., Plaut, V. C., & Meltzoff, A. N. 2014, Policy Insights from the Behavioral and Brain Sciences, 1, 4
Chestnut, E. K., & Markman, E. M. 2018, Cognitive Science, 42, 2229
Clance, P. R., & Imes, S. A. 1978, Psychotherapy: Theory, Research & Practice, 15, 241
Cobern, W. W. 1989, Worldview Theory and Science Education Research: Fundamental Epistemological Structure as a Critical Factor in Science Learning and Attitude Development, http://scholarworks.wmich.edu/science_slcsp/5
Crenshaw, K. 1989, University of Chicago Legal Forum, 140, 139
Crutchfield, R. M., & Maguire, J. 2018, California State University Office of the Chancellor Study of Student Basic Needs, http://www.calstate.edu/basicneeds
Daane, A. R., & Decker, S. R. 2017, PhTea, 55, 328
Danaher, K., Crandall, C. S., & Sawtelle, V. 2008, Journal of Applied Social Psychology, 38, 1639
Davis, E. B. 1991, Science & Christian Belief, 3, 103
Dweck, C. S. 2008, Mindset: The New Psychology of Success (New York: Ballantine Books)
Einstein, A. 1930, Religion and Science, New York Times Magazine, Nov. 9, pp. 1–4
Eliason, M. J., & the Social Justice Pedagogy Plus Working Group, College of Health & Social Sciences, 2019, Social Justice Pedagogy Plus: Transforming Undergraduate Research Methods Courses (Amazon Kindle)
Eriksson, U., Linder, C., Airey, J., & Redfors, A. 2014, EJSME, 2, 167
Estes, Y. Farr, A. L. Smith, P. & Smyth, C. (ed) 2000, Marginal Groups and Mainstream American Culture (Lawrence, KS: Univ. Kansas Press)
Estrada, M., Eroy-Reveles, A., & Matsui, J. 2018, Social Issues and Policy Review, 12, 258
Forbes, C. E., & Schmader, T. 2010, Journal of Personality and Social Psychology, 99, 740
Gutierrez, R. 2009, Teaching for Excellence and Equity in Mathematics, Vol. 1
Handelsman, J., Miller, S., & Pfund, C. 2007, Scientific Teaching (New York: Freeman)
Harackiewicz, J. M., Canning, E. A., Tibbetts, Y., Priniski, S. J., & Hyde, J. S. 2016, Journal of Personality and Social Psychology, 111, 745
Helms, J. E., & Talleyrand, R. M. 1997, American Psychologist, 52, 1246
Johnson, A., Ong, M., Ko, L.T., et al. 2017, PhTea, 55, 356
Leslie, S.-J., Cimpian, A., Meyer, M., & Freeland, E. 2015, Sci, 347, 262
Nasir, N. I. S., & Shah, N. 2011, Journal of African American Males in Education, 2, 24
Rattan, A., Good, C., & Dweck, C. S. 2012, Journal of Experimental Social Psychology, 48, 731
Rifkin, M. 2016, PhTea, 54, 72
Schinske, J., & Tanner, K. 2014, CBE-Life Sciences Education, 13, 159
Sobel, D. 1999, Galileo's Daughter: A Historical Memoir Of Science, Faith, And Love (New York: Walker and Company)
Smedley, A., & Smedley, B. D. 2005, American Psychologist, 60, 16
Spencer, S. J., Steele, C. M., & Quinn, D. M. 1999, Journal of Experimental Social Psychology, 35, 4
Steele, C. M. 1997, American Psychologist, 52, 613

Steele, C. M., & Aronson, J. 1995, Journal of Personality and Social Psychology, 69, 797
Sue, D. W., Capodilupo, C. M., Torino, G. C., et al. 2007, American Psychologist, 62, 271
Swim, J. K., Hyers, L. L., Cohen, L. L., & Ferguson, M. J. 2001, Journal of Social Issues, 57, 31
Tannen, D. 1990, You Just Don't Understand: Women and Men in Conversation (New York: Ballantine Books)
Tran, K., Coble, K., & Eroy-Reveles, A. 2019, in ASP Conf. Ser. 524, Advancing Astronomy for All (San Francisco, CA: ASP), in press
Ursic, M. 2006, Synthesis Philosophica, 42, 267
Wallace, C. S., Prather, E. E., & Mendelsohn, B. M. 2013, AEdRv, 12, 010101
Williams, K. Y., & O'Reilly, C. A., III 1998, Research in Organizational Behavior, 20, 77
Yosso, T. D. 2005, Race Ethnicity and Education, 8, 69

www.ingramcontent.com/pod-product-compliance
Lightning Source LLC
Chambersburg PA
CBHW080546230426
43663CB00015B/2721